T0336198

Driving Transformative Technology Trends With Cloud Computing

Saikat Gochhait
Symbiosis International University (Deemed), India

A volume in the Advances
in Computer and Electrical
Engineering (ACEE) Book Series

Published in the United States of America by
  IGI Global
  Information Science Reference (an imprint of IGI Global)
  701 E. Chocolate Avenue
  Hershey PA, USA 17033
  Tel: 717-533-8845
  Fax: 717-533-8661
  E-mail: cust@igi-global.com
  Web site: http://www.igi-global.com

Library of Congress Cataloging-in-Publication Data

CIP Data Pending
 ISBN: 979-8-3693-2869-9
eISBN: 979-8-3693-2870-5

British Cataloguing in Publication Data
A Cataloguing in Publication record for this book is available from the British Library.

All work contributed to this book is new, previously-unpublished material.
The views expressed in this book are those of the authors, but not necessarily of the publisher.

For electronic access to this publication, please contact: eresources@igi-global.com.

Advances in Computer and Electrical Engineering (ACEE) Book Series

Srikanta Patnaik
SOA University, India

ISSN:2327-039X
EISSN:2327-0403

MISSION

The fields of computer engineering and electrical engineering encompass a broad range of interdisciplinary topics allowing for expansive research developments across multiple fields. Research in these areas continues to develop and become increasingly important as computer and electrical systems have become an integral part of everyday life.

The **Advances in Computer and Electrical Engineering (ACEE) Book Series** aims to publish research on diverse topics pertaining to computer engineering and electrical engineering. **ACEE** encourages scholarly discourse on the latest applications, tools, and methodologies being implemented in the field for the design and development of computer and electrical systems.

Coverage

- Applied Electromagnetics
- Chip Design
- Circuit Analysis
- Computer Architecture
- Electrical Power Conversion
- Optical Electronics
- Qualitative Methods
- VLSI Fabrication

Navigating the Augmented and Virtual Fron-

IGI Global is currently accepting manuscripts for publication within this series. To submit a proposal for a volume in this series, please contact our Acquisition Editors at Acquisitions@igi-global.com or visit: http://www.igi-global.com/publish/.

tiers in Engineering

Titles in this Series

For a list of additional titles in this series, please visit: www.igi-global.com/book-series

R. Siva Subramanian (R.M.K. College of Engineering and Technology, India) M. Nalini (S.A. Engineering College, India) and J. Aswini (Saveetha Engineering College, India)
Engineering Science Reference • copyright 2024 • 315pp • H/C (ISBN: 9798369356135) • US $315.00 (our price)

Harnessing Green and Circular Skills for Digital Transformation
Patricia Ordóñez de Pablos (University of Oviedo, Spain) Muhammad Anshari (Universiti Brunei Darussalam, Brunei) and Mohammad Nabil Almunawar (Universiti Brunei Darussalam, Brunei)
Engineering Science Reference • copyright 2024 • 317pp • H/C (ISBN: 9798369328651) • US $385.00 (our price)

Intelligent Solutions for Sustainable Power Grids
L. Ashok Kumar (PSG College of Technology, India) S. Angalaeswari (Vellore Institute of Technology, India) K. Mohana Sundaram (KPR Institute of Engineering and Technology, India) Ramesh C. Bansal (University of Sharjah, UAE & University of Pretoria, South Africa) and Arunkumar Patil (Central University of Karnataka, India)
Engineering Science Reference • copyright 2024 • 453pp • H/C (ISBN: 9798369337356) • US $465.00 (our price)

Critical Approaches to Data Engineering Systems and Analysis
Abhijit Bora (Assam Don Bosco University, India) Papul Changmai (Assam Don Bosco University, India) and Mrutyunjay Maharana (Xi'an Jiatong University, China)
Engineering Science Reference • copyright 2024 • 326pp • H/C (ISBN: 9798369322604) • US $315.00 (our price)

Applications and Principles of Quantum Computing
Alex Khang (Global Research Institute of Technology and Engineering, USA)
Engineering Science Reference • copyright 2024 • 491pp • H/C (ISBN: 9798369311684) • US $300.00 (our price)

701 East Chocolate Avenue, Hershey, PA 17033, USA
Tel: 717-533-8845 x100 • Fax: 717-533-8661
E-Mail: cust@igi-global.com • www.igi-global.com

Table of Contents

Detailed Table of Contents

Chapter 1

 Michael Onyema Edeh, Coal City University, Nigeria & Saveetha
  School of Engineering, SIMATS, Chennai, India
 Ramesh G., Alva's Institute of Engineering and Technology, India
 Karan Kumar, Alva's Institute of Engineering and Technology, India
 Satyam Pawale, Alva's Institute of Engineering and Technology, India
 Abdullah A., Alva's Institute of Engineering and Technology, India
 Shreyas J., Manipal Institute of Technology Bengaluru/Manipal
  Academy of Higher Education, Manipal, India

This chapter examines the use of ambient intelligence (AmI) technologies to enhance autonomy and quality of life for those with cognitive decline, focusing on advancements in sensors. It proposes a framework to identify gaps and draws insights from applications such as ambient assistive living (AAL), human action recognition, and the industrial internet of things (IIoT). The study highlights technology's role in understanding occupant behavior, supporting services, and maintaining autonomy, addressing decentralized systems, blockchain, adaptive computing, and ethical concerns. The research stresses the need for further studies to ensure safe and effective sensor technology in real-world applications, emphasizing sensors' role in linking computational power with real-world scenarios.

Chapter 2

Naren Kathirvel, Anand Institute of Higher Technology, India
Kathirvel Ayyaswamy, Department of Computer Science and
*   Engineering, Panimalar Engineering College, Chennai, India*
C. Subramanian, Eswari Engineering College, India

Applications that are serverless can be distributed (many services are connected for smooth operation), elastic (resources can be scaled up and down without limit), stateless (interactions and data aren't stored), event-driven (resources are allocated only when triggered by an event), and hostless (apps aren't hosted on a server). Serverless computing is becoming more and more popular as cloud adoption rises. In many respects, serverless computing unleashes the entire potential of cloud computing. We pay only for the resources consumed, and resources are allocated, increased, or decreased dynamically based on user requirements in real-time. It makes sure that when there are no user requests and the application is effectively dormant, resources are immediately scaled to zero. More scalability and significant cost reductions are the outcomes of this. According to research by Global Industry Insights, the serverless industry is expected to reach $30 billion in market value by the end of the forecast period, growing at an above-average rate of 25% between 2021 and 2027.

Chapter 3

Preety Sharma, Maharishi Markandeshwar Institute of Computer Technology and Business Management, India
Ruchi Sharma, Chandigarh School of Business, Jhanjeri, India
Komal Bhardwaj, Maharishi Markandeshwar Institute of Management, India

In recent years, cloud computing has evolved into an indispensable component of modern existence, profoundly reshaping the manner in which we interact with information, services, and applications. Initially, the authors embark on a comprehensive literature survey which elucidates the intricate dimensions of cloud computing. Subsequently, the focus extends to the myriad domains wherein cloud computing has seamlessly embedded itself into our quotidian routines, from the way we manage and share digital files through cloud storage to the facilitation of online learning, telemedicine, and even the optimization of navigation and mapping services, cloud computing is undeniably ubiquitous. The chapter concludes by deliberating on the profound ramifications of cloud computing on contemporary society, emphasizing the significance of this technology in our daily lives. Additionally, it proffers a forward-looking perspective by identifying potential avenues for future research and development; particularly as cloud computing continues its inexorable march towards greater integration and innovation.

Chapter 4

Saikat Gochhait, Symbiosis Institute of Digital and Telecom Management, Symbiosis International University (Deemed), India

Cloud computing is gaining momentum as a subscription-oriented paradigm providing on-demand payable access to virtualized IT services and products across the net. It is a breakthrough technology that is offering on-demand access to various services across the network. Auto-scaling, though quite an attractive proposition to customers and naïve cloud service providers, has its own share of issues and challenges. This work was an attempt to classify and appreciate the auto scaling framework while outlining its challenges. Many effective and efficient auto scaling strategies are being deployed by cloud giants like Amazon AWS, Microsoft Azure, etc.

CDN is constituted of three basic components. A content provider is somebody entrusting the URI namespace of the Web objects to be dispersed. The content provider's server contains all such objects. A CDN provider can be some owner party that enables transportation conveniences to content providers to deliver content in a timely and reliable manner. They may employ geographically distributed caching and/or replica servers (surrogates or edge servers) to duplicate content. Together they may form what we call a web cluster. End users are the customers who use content from the content provider's website.

Organizational memory has a crucial role for businesses, especially in the context of cloud computing. Cloud computing technologies facilitate the storage, management, and access of organizational knowledge and data. By using cloud-based solutions, businesses can enhance the effectiveness of their organizational memory systems. Digitalization, combined with cloud computing, allows for easy access, retrieval, and sharing of knowledge within the organization, regardless of geographical locations or device types. In today's business environment, cloud computing integration is not only convenient but also necessary for organizations to effectively leverage their knowledge and information. It ensures that the organizational memory remains a valuable asset that contributes to informed decision-making, innovation, and sustained success. This study discusses to what extent organizational memory systems, enhanced by cloud computing, will be considered effective in new business conditions.

This chapter focuses on examining how cloud computing can enhance financial management. It aims to make organisations aware of the possibilities of cloud-based solutions for improving financial tasks and help them avoid mistakes when implementing those technologies. The steps entail a systematic literature review that uses guidelines such as preferred reporting items for systematic reviews and meta-analyses (PRISMA). In order to identify an appropriate sample of articles that would answer the research issue, the authors followed the principles of inclusion and exclusion. They compared the abstracts and full texts of the sources in question before considering thirty-seven (37) articles in greater detail. The study also reveals that cloud computing provides a great potential for achieving financial benefits, which include cost reduction, better control and visibility for financial data, improved security and compliance and, last but not least, enabling organisational financial innovation.

Cloud computing has emerged as one of the most disruptive technologies in recent years, changing the way organizations store, process, and manage their data and applications. This chapter aims to provide a comprehensive overview of cloud computing, including its benefits and challenges, the different types of cloud services available, and the security measures that organizations can implement to protect their data in the cloud. The chapter will also examine the various compliance and regulatory requirements that organizations must meet when using cloud services and best practices for secure cloud deployment and management. Additionally, the chapter will also cover the evolution of cloud computing from its beginnings to its current state and future developments, and will also provide real-world examples and case studies of organizations that have successfully implemented cloud computing.

Chapter 9

Pawan Kumar Goel, Raj Kumar Goel Institute of Technology, Ghaziabad, India

In the ever-expanding landscape of cloud computing, concerns over the privacy of sensitive data have become paramount. This chapter delves into the intricate realm of privacy-preserving data storage and processing in the cloud. It addresses the challenges posed by data ownership, control, and the ever-looming threat of data breaches in cloud environments. Focusing on innovative techniques, the chapter explores encryption mechanisms, secure multi-party computation, and trusted execution environments for privacy-preserving data storage. Additionally, it delves into cutting-edge methods such as privacy-preserving machine learning, secure query processing, and tokenization for safeguarding privacy during data processing in the cloud. Real-world case studies exemplify successful implementations, providing insights into practical applications. The chapter concludes by envisioning future trends, including the integration of blockchain and zero-knowledge proofs, and highlights the challenges and opportunities that lie ahead in the pursuit of privacy preservation in cloud computing.

Chapter 10

Sangeetha Ganesan, R.M.K. College of Engineering and Technology, India
Prathusha Laxmi, R.M.K. College of Engineering and Technology, India
Shanmugaraj Ganesan, Velammal Institute of Technology, India

Fog computing has made it possible to extend cloud computing functions to the network edge by assisting the cloud and users in terms of communication, computation, and storage with a widely dispersed deployment of edge devices or fog nodes. Smart grid (SG) networks are recently upgraded networks of interconnected objects that greatly progress the sustainability, dependability, and dependability of the current energy infrastructure. This chapter starts by giving a general overview of the architecture, concept, and key elements of supervisory control and data acquisition (SCADA) systems for the fog-based smart grid. Based on the machine learning techniques employed by the intrusion detection system (IDS), categorise the IDS solutions into nine groups. This chapter also recommends a user privacy-protecting authentication and data aggregation system for the smart grid based on fog. It is possible to offer anonymous authentication using short randomizable signatures and blind signatures, and then use fog nodes to handle billing issues after providing anonymous authentication.

Cryptography, the discipline of disguising information, relies on mathematical principles for encoding and decoding data. This chapter presents an inventive approach to encrypting and decrypting messages, utilizing the R-transformation, an essential integral transform, and the congruence modulo operator. The research illustrates the pragmatic application of these mathematical tools in securing communication through the encoding of sensitive information. By investigating the integration of the R-transformation and modulo operations, this study seeks to highlight their effectiveness in reinforcing the privacy and integrity of data. Through thorough experimentation and analysis, this research introduces a groundbreaking methodology for cryptographic encoding and decoding, shedding light on its potential to fortify the security of confidential information transmission.

This chapter introduces a groundbreaking encryption approach utilizing the Kushare transform and modular arithmetic, departing from conventional cryptographic methods. It delves into the transformative potential of this dynamic duo in rendering sensitive data impenetrable, ensuring secure digital communication. Through meticulous examination of their synergy, this work establishes their remarkable ability to fortify data confidentiality and integrity. Rigorous experimentation and analysis reveal a novel cryptographic technique poised to revolutionize the secure transmission of confidential information in the digital age.

   Sangeetha Ganesan, R.M.K. College of Engineering and Technology, India

   M. Mohamed Ashwak, R.M.K. College of Engineering and Technology, India

   Ahmed J. Shaik Junaidh, R.M.K. College of Engineering and Technology, India

   L. Saran, R.M.K. College of Engineering and Technology, India

   M. Mohan Kumar, R.M.K. College of Engineering and Technology, India

Mobile security dangers have increased as a result of the widespread usage of mobile technology and our growing reliance on it for both personal and professional purposes. The chapter starts off by outlining the numerous mobile security risks, including malware, phishing, data breaches, and unauthorized access, as well as their possible effects on individual and organizational security. The chapter then provides an in-depth discussion of the best practices for mobile security, including the use of strong passwords, encryption, and multi-factor authentication, regular software updates, and the implementation of mobile device management policies. Finally, the chapter concludes by discussing the role of government regulations and industry standards in ensuring mobile security, and the challenges associated with achieving comprehensive mobile security in an ever-evolving threat landscape. Overall, the chapter provides a comprehensive overview of mobile security threats and risks, as well as best practices for mitigating these risks.

Naga Venkata Yaswanth Lankadasu, Lovely Professional University,
    India
Devendra Babu Pesarlanka, Lovely Professional University, India
Ajay Sharma, upGrad Education Private Limited, India
Shamneesh Sharma, upGrad Education Private Limited, India

Recently, there has been a notable increase in the advancement of multimodal emotion analysis systems. These systems try to get a comprehensive knowledge of human emotions by combining data from several sources, including text, voice, video, and images. This complete strategy tackles the constraints of text-only sentiment analysis, which could disregard subtle emotional expressions. This chapter examines the difficulties and approaches related to analyzing emotions utilizing many modes of data, specifically emphasizing combining data, extracting features, and ensuring scalability. This underscores the significance of creating strong fusion techniques and network architectures to integrate various data modalities efficiently. The research also explores the utilization of these systems in domains such as social media sentiment analysis and clinical evaluations, showcasing their capacity to improve decision-making and user experiences.

Tarun Kumar Vashishth, IIMT University, India
Vikas Sharma, IIMT University, India
Kewal Krishan Sharma, IIMT University, India
Prashant Kumar, IIMT University, India
Rakesh Prasad Joshi, IIMT University, India

This chapter offers a thorough examination of the way blockchain generation can make a contribution to the realization of sustainable development goals (SDGs) mounted by the United Nations. Blockchain's inherent functions, inclusive of transparency, and immutability, position it as a powerful tool for addressing international challenges in regions like poverty, healthcare, and renewable strength. By exploring real-world applications in financial inclusion, healthcare, delivery chain management, renewable energy, and governance, the chapter underscores the potential of blockchain to decorate transparency, accountability, and performance. It discusses the present literature, hit implementations, and case studies whilst highlighting the demanding situations, including scalability and regulatory concerns. Emphasizing collaboration, capacity building, and accountable use, the chapter advocates for blockchain's pivotal role in riding sustainable development and fostering a extra equitable and resilient future.

Chapter 16

Gaurav Gupta, Shoolini University, India
Pradeep Chintale, SEI Investment Company, USA
Laxminarayana Korada, Microsoft Corporation, Bellevue, USA
Ankur Harendrasinh Mahida, Barclays PLC, USA
Saigurudatta Pamulaparthyvenkata, VillageMD, USA
Rajiv Avacharmal, University of Connecticut, USA

In the digital age, the fusion of human-computer interaction (HCI) with machine learning and personalization is transforming how individuals engage with technology. This chapter explores this dynamic intersection, envisioning a future of more intuitive, adaptive, and personalized digital experiences. It examines the role of machine learning in HCI, highlighting predictive analytics, natural language processing, and real-time interface adaptation. Personalization is addressed through content recommendation systems, user profiling, and adaptive interfaces. The study also looks at HCI's future in healthcare, e-commerce, and education, and addresses privacy, transparency, bias, and ethics. It underscores the ethical responsibility in deploying these technologies, inviting readers to envision a future where HCI, machine learning, and personalization create responsive, personalized, and ethically sound digital interactions.

Muhammad Hasnain, Abasyn University, Pakistan
Venkataramaiah Gude, GP Technologies LLC, USA
Michael Onyema Edeh, Coal City University, Nigeria & Saveetha
*   School of Engineering, SIMATS, Chennai, India*
Fahad Masood, Abasyn University, Pakistan
Wajid Ullah Khan, Abasyn University, Pakistan
Muhammad Imad, Abasyn University, Peshawar, Pakistan
Nwosu Ogochukwu Fidelia, University of Nigeria, Nigeria

The study addresses the challenge dementia patients face in recognizing handwritten characters by developing a cloud-integrated system that uses a multilayer neural network for character recognition. The system involves four main steps: preprocessing (noise reduction and normalization), segmentation (extracting characters from scanned pages), feature extraction (using a modified zone-based method), and recognition. The extracted features, represented as pixel value vectors, are classified using four machine learning algorithms—support vector machine with RBF, random forest, linear SVM, and logistic regression. The random forest algorithm performs best with an accuracy of 89%. Cloud technology enhances the system's scalability, allowing for real-time processing and remote access, beneficial for dementia care.

Chapter 18

Redouan Ainous, University of Algiers, Algeria

This study delves into the response of higher education institutions around the world to the COVID-19 pandemic, focusing on their capacity to sustain adaptation, resilience, and innovation while upholding their educational mission in a post-COVID-19 environment. The transition from semi-structured setups to more methodological systems, tailored to the post-COVID-19 era, is examined. The analysis assesses the strategies employed by these institutions to safeguard their academic communities from misguided practices. Findings from the study highlight the emergence of novel approaches by educators and the readiness of teachers to adapt to the new normal post-COVID-19. This adaptation is facilitated by cutting-edge technologies, which offer substantial support for flexibility and innovation. The chapter also presents an overview of the applications used by higher education institutions in response to the pandemic, underscoring the vital qualities of resilience and innovation in the transition to the new post-COVID-19 normal.

Preface

Welcome to the second edition of *Driving Transformative Technology Trends With Cloud Computing*. As editor of this volume, I am delighted to present an updated exploration of the intersection between cloud computing and the evolving landscape of digital transformation.

The first edition of this book received acclaim for its comprehensive coverage of key concepts and trends in cloud computing, as evidenced by its inclusion in the esteemed Scopus index. Building upon that success, we have endeavored to deliver a second edition that reflects the latest developments and emerging paradigms in the field.

In this rapidly evolving technological landscape, the integration of cloud computing with other transformative technologies is reshaping industries and driving innovation at an unprecedented pace. The convergence of 5G, artificial intelligence, and cloud computing stands out as a prime example, unlocking new possibilities and catalyzing profound societal impacts.

The chapters in this edition delve into diverse facets of cloud computing, addressing topics such as green computing, edge computing, cloud cryptography, and beyond. From discussions on cloud scalability and service models to explorations of cloud security and deployment strategies, this book offers insights tailored to various stakeholders, from business leaders to developers and data scientists.

Cloud computing, as a model, embodies versatility and adaptability, catering to the unique requirements and perspectives of different individuals and roles within organizations. Whether you are a technology enthusiast, a business strategist, or an IT professional, we believe that this book will provide valuable insights into harnessing the transformative power of cloud computing to drive growth and success in today's digital era.

We extend our gratitude to the contributing authors for their expertise and dedication in shaping this volume. Additionally, we would like to thank the readers for their interest in exploring the dynamic realm of cloud computing and its implications for the future of technology.

Chapter 1: Ambient Intelligence - A Comprehensive Review and Insights into Sensing Technologies

This chapter by Michael Edeh, Ramesh G, Karan Kumar, Satyam Pawale, Abdullah A, and Shreyas J delves into the transformative potential of Ambient Intelligence (AmI) in enhancing autonomy and quality of life, particularly for individuals with cognitive decline. It comprehensively reviews advancements in sensing technologies and presents a framework to identify existing gaps in the field. Key applications such as Ambient Assistive Living (AAL), human action recognition, and the Industrial Internet of Things (IIoT) are explored. The study underscores the crucial role of technology in understanding occupant behavior and maintaining autonomy, while addressing challenges in decentralized systems, blockchain, adaptive computing, and ethical concerns. It calls for further research to ensure the safe and effective application of sensor technology in real-world scenarios.

Chapter 2: Intelligent Serverless Computing Technology and Recent Trends: A Review

Naren Kathirvel, Kathirvel Ayyaswamy, and Subramanian C provide an insightful review of serverless computing, highlighting its growing popularity alongside cloud adoption. They discuss the defining characteristics of serverless applications: distributed, elastic, stateless, event-driven, and hostless. The chapter elaborates on how serverless computing maximizes cloud potential by dynamically allocating resources based on user needs, resulting in significant cost savings and scalability. The market trends predict a substantial growth in the serverless industry, emphasizing its transformative impact on cloud computing.

Chapter 3: Cloud Computing in Everyday Life: Revolutionizing How We Live, Work, and Connect

Preety Sharma, Ruchi Sharma, and Komal Bhardwaj present a comprehensive survey of cloud computing, illustrating its pervasive influence on modern life. From digital file management to online learning and telemedicine, cloud computing has seamlessly integrated into daily routines. The chapter discusses the profound societal impacts of this technology and anticipates future research and development avenues, underscoring its ongoing evolution and increasing integration.

Chapter 4: Auto-Scaling in the Cloud

Saikat Gochhait examines the implications of cloud computing for small and medium-sized enterprises (SMEs), particularly focusing on cybersecurity threats. Through a quantitative survey of SMEs in Australia, this chapter identifies common security challenges and suggests practical measures for improving cloud security. The findings reveal significant variations in security practices among different-sized enterprises and provide actionable insights for enhancing cyber resilience in cloud environments.

Chapter 5: Designing and Implementing a Cloud-Based Content Delivery Network

Saikat Gochhait explores the components and functionalities of cloud-based content delivery networks (CDNs). The chapter details the roles of content providers, CDN providers, and end-users, emphasizing the importance of reliable and timely content delivery. By leveraging geographically distributed caching and replica servers, CDNs enhance the efficiency and performance of web services.

Chapter 6: Digitalization of Organizational Memory

Ozlem Erdas Cicek introduces a novel hybrid cloud and half-tensor compression-aware technology for image security transmission. The chapter begins with an overview of cryptographic fundamentals and compression perception methods before proposing an advanced image encryption and decryption algorithm. The research demonstrates the method's effectiveness in achieving high security and efficiency in network image transmission.

Chapter 7: Transforming Financial Management with Cloud Computing: Strategies, Benefits, and Innovations

Narayanage Dewasiri and Mohit Yadav focus on the transformative potential of cloud computing in financial management. By conducting a systematic literature review, they highlight the benefits of cloud-based solutions, including cost reduction, improved data control, enhanced security, and financial innovation. The chapter also discusses the challenges and strategies for successfully implementing cloud technologies in financial management.

Chapter 8: A Survey on Cloud Security Issues and Challenges

Sangeetha Ganesan, Mohamed Ashwak M, Shaik Junaidh Ahmed J, Saran L, and Mohan Kumar M provide a thorough examination of cloud security issues and challenges. The chapter covers the evolution of cloud computing, its benefits, and the security measures necessary for protecting data. Real-world examples and case studies illustrate successful cloud security implementations, offering best practices for organizations.

Chapter 9: Privacy-Preserving Data Storage and Processing in the Cloud

Pawan Goel addresses the critical concerns of data privacy in cloud environments. This chapter explores advanced techniques for privacy-preserving data storage and processing, including encryption, secure multi-party computation, and trusted execution environments. The study highlights innovative methods such as privacy-preserving machine learning and secure query processing, providing practical insights and future trends in cloud privacy.

Chapter 10: A Survey on Data Security and Privacy for Fog-based Smart Grid Applications

Sangeetha Ganesan, Prathusha Laxmi, and Shanmugaraj Ganesan investigate the intersection of fog computing and smart grid applications. This chapter offers a comprehensive overview of SCADA systems, IDS solutions, and privacy-preserving authentication methods for smart grids. The proposed solutions emphasize the role of fog nodes in enhancing security and efficiency in smart grid networks.

Chapter 11: Applications of the R-Transform for Advancing Cryptographic Security

Tharmalingam Gunasekar and Prabakaran Raghavendran present an innovative approach to cryptographic security using the R-transformation and congruence modulo operator. The chapter illustrates the practical application of these mathematical tools in securing communication, offering a new methodology for encrypting and decrypting sensitive information.

Chapter 12: Advancing Cryptographic Security with Kushare Transform Integration

Raghavendran Prabakaran and Gunasekar T introduce a novel encryption method combining the Kushare transform and modular arithmetic. The chapter explores the transformative potential of this approach in enhancing data security and integrity. Through rigorous experimentation, the study demonstrates the effectiveness of this technique in securing digital communications.

Chapter 13: Survey on Mobile Security - Threats, Risks, and Best Practices

Sangeetha Ganesan, Mohamed Ashwak M, Shaik Junaidh Ahmed J, Saran L, and Mohan Kumar M provide an in-depth analysis of mobile security threats and best practices. The chapter discusses various security risks, including malware, phishing, and data breaches, and offers practical measures for mitigating these risks. It also examines the role of government regulations and industry standards in ensuring comprehensive mobile security.

Chapter 14: Security Aspects of Blockchain Technology

Naga Yaswanth Lankadasu, Devendra Pesarlanka, Ajay Sharma, and Shamneesh Sharma explore the advancements in multimodal emotion analysis systems using blockchain technology. The chapter discusses the integration of text, voice, video, and images to achieve a comprehensive understanding of human emotions. It emphasizes the importance of robust fusion techniques and network architectures in enhancing decision-making and user experiences.

Chapter 15: Leveraging Blockchain Technology for Sustainable Development Goals: A Comprehensive Overview

Tarun Vashishth, Vikas Sharma, Kewal Sharma, Prashant Kumar, and Rakesh Joshi examine how blockchain technology can contribute to achieving the United Nations Sustainable Development Goals (SDGs). The chapter highlights real-world applications of blockchain in financial inclusion, healthcare, supply chain management, renewable energy, and governance. It also discusses the challenges and opportunities in leveraging blockchain for sustainable development.

Chapter 16: The Future of HCI Machine Learning, Personalization, and Beyond

Gaurav Gupta, Pradeep Chintale, Laxminarayana Korada, Ankur Mahida, Saigurudatta Pamulaparthyvenkata, and Rajiv Avacharmal explore the intersection of Human-Computer Interaction (HCI) with machine learning and personalization. The chapter envisions a future of intuitive, adaptive, and personalized digital experiences, addressing privacy, transparency, bias, and ethics. It highlights the ethical responsibility in deploying these technologies and anticipates future developments in HCI.

Chapter 17: Cloud-Enhanced Machine Learning for Handwritten Character Recognition in Dementia Patients

Muhammad Hasnain, Venkataramaiah Gude, Michael Edeh, Fahad Masood, Wajid Ullah Khan, Muhammad Imad, and Nwosu Ogochukwu Fidelia address the challenge of handwritten character recognition for dementia patients. The chapter details the development of a cloud-integrated system using a multilayer neural network. It highlights the system's scalability, real-time processing, and remote access, offering significant benefits for dementia care.

Chapter 18: Sustaining Adaptation to the New Normal: Tenacity and Originality in Higher Education Marketing After the COVID-19 Pandemic

Redouan Ainous examines the response of higher education institutions to the COVID-19 pandemic. The chapter focuses on their adaptation, resilience, and innovation in a post-pandemic environment. It assesses strategies to safeguard academic communities and highlights the role of cutting-edge technologies in supporting flexibility and innovation. The study underscores the importance of resilience and innovation in the transition to the new post-COVID-19 normal.

Each chapter in this volume offers valuable insights into the transformative power of cloud computing and its implications for various aspects of contemporary life and business. We hope that readers will find this collection informative and thought-provoking as they navigate the evolving landscape of technology and innovation.

In concluding this preface, I am profoundly grateful for the opportunity to present the second edition of *Driving Transformative Technology Trends With Cloud Computing*. The journey of curating this volume has been both enlightening and rewarding, as I've had the privilege of collaborating with esteemed authors to explore the intricate nexus between cloud computing and the evolving digital landscape.

From the comprehensive overview of cloud computing's impact on everyday life in Chapter 1 to the innovative encryption techniques discussed in Chapters 9 and 10, each chapter offers a unique perspective on the transformative power of cloud technology. Whether delving into cybersecurity challenges, privacy concerns, or the integration of cloud computing with emerging technologies like fog computing and serverless computing, the chapters collectively highlight the breadth and depth of this dynamic field.

I am particularly excited about the forward-looking insights provided by our contributing authors, who offer glimpses into potential avenues for future research and development. As cloud computing continues to evolve and shape industries across the globe, these perspectives serve as valuable guideposts for navigating the ever-changing technological landscape.

As editor, I extend my heartfelt gratitude to the authors for their expertise, dedication, and scholarly contributions to this volume. I also would like to thank our readers for their interest in exploring the dynamic realm of cloud computing and its implications for the future of technology. It is my sincere hope that this book will serve as a valuable resource for researchers, practitioners, and enthusiasts alike as they endeavor to harness the transformative power of cloud computing in driving growth and innovation.

With warm regards,

Editor:

Saikat Gochhait

Symbiosis International Deemed University, India

Chapter 1
Ambient Intelligence:
A Comprehensive Review and Insights Into Sensing Technologies

Michael Onyema Edeh

https://orcid.org/0000-0002-4067 -3256

Coal City University, Nigeria & Saveetha School of Engineering, SIMATS, Chennai, India

Ramesh G.

Alva's Institute of Engineering and Technology, India

Karan Kumar

Alva's Institute of Engineering and Technology, India

Satyam Pawale

Alva's Institute of Engineering and Technology, India

Abdullah A.

Alva's Institute of Engineering and Technology, India

Shreyas J.

Manipal Institute of Technology Bengaluru/Manipal Academy of Higher Education, Manipal, India

ABSTRACT

This chapter examines the use of ambient intelligence (AmI) technologies to enhance autonomy and quality of life for those with cognitive decline, focusing on advancements in sensors. It proposes a framework to identify gaps and draws insights from applications such as ambient assistive living (AAL), human action recognition, and the industrial internet of things (IIoT). The study highlights technology's role in understanding occupant behavior, supporting services, and maintaining autonomy, addressing decentralized systems, blockchain, adaptive computing, and ethical concerns. The research stresses the need for further studies to ensure safe and effective sensor technology in real-world applications, emphasizing sensors' role in linking computational power with real-world scenarios.

DOI: 10.4018/979-8-3693-2869-9.ch001

INTRODUCTION

Ambient Intelligence (AmI) is a technological breakthrough that uses intelligent technologies to communicate effortlessly with the environment, thus enhancing every aspect of the human experience. The discussion below searches into the vast terrain of ambient intelligence, stressing the incredible developments gained in sensing technologies in an era characterized by rapid improvements in sensing gadgets. Traditional methods of care create significant financial and emotional pressures on caregivers and healthcare professionals while they deal with the challenges posed by cognitive decline. To solve this, Ambient Assistive Living (AAL) technologies with cutting-edge components such as the Internet of Things (IoT) and Artificial Intelligence (AI) have evolved (Jain et al., 2023). These technologies offer not just to complement standard caring but also to enable intelligent learning inside the surrounding area. The assessment goes beyond healthcare, delving into areas as diverse as tourism, industrial operations, and human activity recognition. Sensing technology advancements are critical in a variety of applications, ranging from Multi-Criteria Recommender Systems in tourism destinations to ambient intelligence-assisted computing in Industrial IoT and the use of Bi-Convolutional Recurrent Neural Networks for human action recognition.

However, challenges and research gaps continue in this fast-growing subject, requiring careful evaluations of contributions from other fields. Usability, acceptability, ethical problems, and the necessity for human-in-the-loop interventions are underlined as key themes. A recommended conceptual framework describes future research alternatives in this area, to maximize the potential of sensing technologies in ambient intelligence systems. The review aims to provide valuable insights into the current state-of-the-art in Ambient Intelligence, envisioning a future where intelligent systems seamlessly coexist with human environments, enriching lives and fostering autonomy.

Shifting attention to serious games, a distinct genre that combines interactive technology with education, simulation, and training, has spurred R&D efforts. Recognizing the potential of serious games, international organizations use them as highly effective teaching and training supports in an array of fields. Shifting attention to serious games, a distinct genre that combines interactive technology with education, simulation, and training, has spurred R&D efforts. Recognizing the potential of serious games, international organizations use them as highly effective teaching and training supports in an array of fields. Ambient intelligence (AmI) is the system that makes judgments on the spot and regulates the actions of its environment by interacting with several actuators, sensors, and intelligent gadgets shown in Figure 1 (Teixeira et al., 2019) simplifies the overall structure of the transmission process by providing an overview of AmI Pub/Sub (messaging communication systems).

It shows how the ambient network is divided into multiple subnetworks to accelerate the transmission process. Every communication device possesses a unique trust value, which is determined using an indirect method that can further examine the authenticity of every device. Furthermore, the system may be further divided into two groups, such as malicious and legitimate, by reinforcement learning and indirect computation.

Figure 1. A system overview for ambient communication

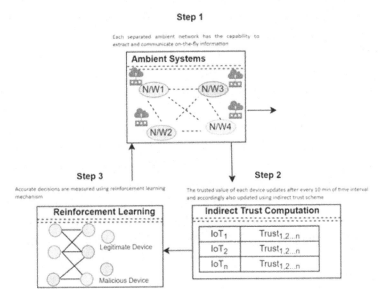

Motivation

The acquisition of environmental and human data via sensor networks is a crucial component in the development of AmI-based systems. Based on AmI, we have created several systems. However, when integrating sensors from various network technologies with agents, services, and applications, these advances have resulted in serious issues (e.g.,hardware incompatibilities, lower performance, etc.). The suitability of current functional architectures for building intelligent environments in line with the AmI paradigm is one of the major issues covered in this section. This section also examines the benefits and drawbacks of the current platforms and assesses if a new one is feasible: the HERA integration with FUSION@. Three fundamental ideas are put forth by ambient intelligence: intelligent user interfaces, ubiquitous computing, and ubiquitous communication. AmI-based systems need to be scalable, easy to use and maintain, dynamic, flexible, robust, and able to respond to changes in context. Furthermore, this type of system aims to achieve resilience and dependability (Teixeira et al., 2019). Complex and adaptable applications must be developed to create AmI-based systems that integrate many subsystems. An application must be separated into modules with distinct functionality as it becomes more complicated. Reusing resources that can be integrated into other systems is becoming more common as a result of the possibility that other applications would need comparable functions. Adopting a shared platform can facilitate the completion of this trend, which is ultimately the best answer. But because those functionalities are implemented in systems that aren't necessarily compatible with other systems, it's challenging to implement.

Reimplementing the necessary features can be an alternative to this strategy. That's usually the simplest and safest method, even though it means extra development time. Reimplementation, on the other hand, may result in redundant functions and a more challenging migration process. Better answers, autonomy, service continuity, and higher levels of flexibility and scalability can be achieved with a distributed architecture than with a centralized one by moving functions more freely to where actions are required. Furthermore, overly centralized systems have limited or overcharged capacities due to unfavourable effects on system functions. Consequently, the system finds it challenging to adjust its behaviour dynamically in response to changes in the infrastructure. Thus, distributed designs seek out resource distribution, programming language independence, and compatibility across many systems.

Methodology

To improve the quality of life for residents with cognitive impairment, this review's methodology methodically examines Cyber-Physical Systems (CPS) in smart buildings. Determining search phrases and defining the study scope are the first steps of the investigation, which is guided by broad research questions. Section 1 provides an explanation of Ambient Intelligence (AmI) and its possible applications in healthcare, while Subsection A delves into issues such as usability and ethical considerations. Foundational insights and important concepts are introduced in Section 2. With a focus on sensing technology, Section 3 examines developments in Ambient Intelligence. To achieve autonomy, hierarchy is emphasized in Section 4, which describes the framework for constructing AmI systems. In the last section, Section 5, an evaluation of FUSION@ and HERA is presented, with a focus on the integration of HERA for ambient intelligence into FUSION@. The study explores the crucial function of Collaborative Filtering (CF) algorithms in Ambient Intelligence (AmI) in Section 6.1, emphasizing the provision of real-time tailored services via User-Based Collaborative Filtering. In Section 6.2, the security protocols for collaborative filtering are examined, with the Paillier cryptosystem being utilized for encryption. Sensor fusion approaches are covered in detail in Section 6.3, including how to integrate data optimally by using the Kalman filter. Applications of AmI are presented in Section 7 and Section 8, final findings highlight AmI's revolutionary influence on user environments and offer future directions.

AMI'S RELATED TERMS

Context

The concept of context is defined as any information characterizing the situation of an entity. Entities, such as people, sensors, places, or objects, relevant to user-application interactions, form the basis of context in intelligent systems. The identification of entities and their relationships within the environment enhances system efficiency, adaptability, and flexibility. Systems utilizing context for these purposes are termed context-aware systems. It's important to note that a system focuses on a subset of entities called the context of interest, representing information vital for the application's purpose (Teixeira et al., 2019; Arif et al., 2023).

Situation Awareness and Decision Making

Situation awareness (SA) is the ability to recognize items in an environment, comprehend what they mean, and project their state shortly. SA prioritizes high-level conceptual knowledge above low-level sensor data in Ambient Intelligence (AmI). SA is necessary for good decision-making, but it is merely acknowledged as an event in the process. Decision-making in AmI includes methods that resemble human thinking, are intrinsically unpredictable, and take into account various objectives. When coping with ambiguous or unclear data, traditional multi-objective decision-making systems confront complications. As a consequence, fuzzy logic, especially L-fuzzy theory, is presented as an appropriate tool for multi-objective decision-making.

L-Fuzzy Theory

The l-fuzzy theory integrates fuzzy logic into multi-objective problems with the environment. It generalizes the fuzzy idea for L-fuzzy sets and relations on any Brouwerian lattice, solving issues with incomparable properties. L-fuzzy theory, unlike fuzzy logic alone, provides a conclusion for every case, making it well-suited for nonlinearity and multi-objectivity. An L-fuzzy controller (LFC) analyses about multi-objective issues as well as generates an easily understood end result for decision-making.

Contextual Model for a Proactive Domain

Machado et al.'s work in AmI unveils a conceptual model for a proactive domain that emphasizes the interaction between context and environment. This model, whose has been expanded in the current study, separates between indicated and current conditions that are influenced by internal or external events. Automated activities generated by particular circumstances aid in decision-making in AmI. The expanded model incorporates aspects critical for multi-objective decision-making in AmI. This bedrock provides a foundation for the future discussion of intrusion detection systems and their use in the Internet of Things (IoT) security landscape.

The study of enabling increased accessibility, usability, and integration of technology such as computers into daily life is known as ubiquitous computing or pervasive computing. As a subset of ubiquitous computing, AmI aims to create environments that are aware of and responsive to human presence. The goal of artificial intelligence (AI), a subfield of computer science, is to develop intelligent agents that can think for themselves, process information, and respond quickly. To improve the intelligence and responsiveness of settings, intelligent automation approaches are applied. Ambient intelligence refers to the intelligence that permeates everything around us. A digital environment that is responsive, flexible, and sensitive to human presence exists. devices that can recognize, anticipate, and maybe adapt to their requirements. a discreet digital space that helps people with day-to-day tasks. It is important to note that AmI encompasses a significant amount of intelligence in addition to elements of pervasive/ubiquitous computing and context-aware computing.Human-computer interaction (HCI) is a field of study that looks into how humans interact with technology. AmI uses a human-cantered design process to build intelligent structures that are easy to use and helpful to people. Sensor networks are a form of distributed system made up of a large number of connected sensors. AmI collects information on the environment and the people that live there via sensor networks.

Enhancing Assisted Living Through Ambient Environment Integration

A new technology that will increase the sensitivity and responsiveness of one's surroundings to their presence. There exists a potential that the surroundings will possess sufficient intelligence to recognize an individual and react appropriately. The term "ambient intelligence" describes the all-pervasive intellect that permeates our environment. An environment that is responsive, flexible, and sensitive to human presence is present in the digital realm. Surrounded by networks of embedded intelligent devices, people in an ambient environment can assess their status, anticipate their needs, and potentially make adjustments. a digital world that helps people in their daily lives without being obtrusive (Jain et al., 2023; Teixeira et al., 2019). The fact that AmI combines a significant component of intelligence in addition to elements of pervasive and ubiquitous computing and context-aware computing is important to note.The best utilization of sensors is essential because AmI is meant to be utilized in real-world settings. Sensors serve as the link between computational power and real-world uses. AmI systems make use of sensor data from the real world. Through sensing and acting, intelligent algorithms are connected to the real environment in which they operate. For such algorithms to be responsive, adaptive, and helpful to users through autonomous systems, a multitude of thinking processes need to occur.A handful of these include decision-making, user modelling, activity recognition and prediction, and spatial-temporal reasoning. AmI systems can perform tasks and influence system users through the application of intelligent, autonomous, and helpful algorithms (Malik and Javed, 2022). AmI can be implemented precisely and effectively with the help of the components shown in Figure 2.

Figure 2. Elements of a smart home's ambient systems

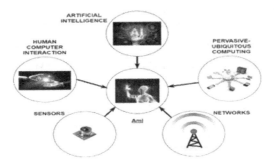

AMI'S INNOVATIONS

We know from Jules Verne's example that guessing the technologies that will change the world of Ambient Intelligence in the future is not a panacea. Nonetheless, it is believed that ambient intelligence technologies will advance gradually. Such rudimentary extrapolations include the risk that they frequently overlook the significant consequences of disruptive forces, however, disruptive forces are by nature is capricious. Technology trends are undoubtedly gaining traction, but rapid direction shifts can be caused by lateral forces. Nonetheless, it is evident that especially in the evolving fields of computers, communication, software, storage, displays, sensors, and digitalization of information (Rathee, Kerrache and Calafate, 2022). All physical modalities' analog signals have opened the door for Ambient Intelligence and will continue to reshape the environment. Data density on integrated circuits is continuing to increase every 18 months under Moore's law. Significant rates of development are seen in other components of distributed computing, such as storage capacity, CPU speed, and (wireless) connection speed. For example, the areal density of HDDs (hard disc drives) has increased annually on average over the past ten years, and this development cycle appears to be continuing smoothly (Rathee, Kerrache and Calafate, 2022). All During that time frame, there was an approximate 400% increase in CPU speed and at least a 200% increase in wireless transmission speed. Above all, the expenses for such goods are decreasing annually, making them accessible for extensive embedded applications.

In this remarkable tale of remarkable and ongoing technological advancement, battery technology is somewhat of a "dark horse." When compared to conventional nickel cadmium (NiCd) types, the capacity (Wh/kg) of Li-ion rechargeable batteries has increased by a factor of 4-5 throughout the past ten years in Figure 3. It has been stated that the energy density of lithium-ion batteries can be up to four times higher when using unusual and (still) costly electrode materials for nickel-metal hydride batteries (such as magnesium-scandium hydride) (Pise, Yoon, and Singh, 2023). However, a lot of effort has to be made to reduce the cost of batteries employing this kind of electrode material as well as their discharge cycle properties.

Figure 3. Performance of present and future battery technologies

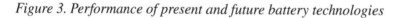
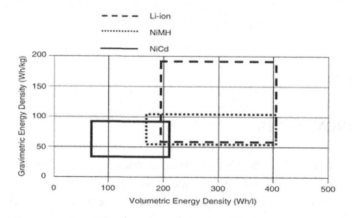

To create the adaptiveness and responsiveness of the Ambient Intelligence environment, significant technological advancements in ultra-low power radio, smart materials, and sensor and micro actuator technology are required, in addition to the "classical" technologies already mentioned. Furthermore, much study and advancement are required in the self-organization components of those Ambient Intelligence devices as well as energy scavenging from the environment to power autonomous, unattended microsystems. Not to mention, every technological component needs to be incorporated into the Ambient Intelligence System's architectural framework so that users may interact with it in several ways at the application level. A "library" of fundamental components for broad ambient intelligence system designs will be formed by these technologies.Current engineering practices indicate that engineers are easily influenced by current trends, which frequently take the form of copying the newest innovations in technology. There are moments when it seems like the industry completely changes course to follow the appeal of the newest technology (Ramana, 2022). Because of this tendency, there has been an unprecedented number of inventions that seem unnecessary compared to any other time in human history. Innovative ideas that are irrelevant or unrealistic can occasionally result from a hasty exploration of what is technologically possible. A common mistake that leads to the failure of technology-driven efforts is the disregard for commercial, social, and economic factors. An even more sustainable perspective holds that people should not be overloaded with new technology; rather, technology should improve people's lives. Rather than overstuffing people with additional devices, technology ought to make their lives easier. Ambient Intelligence environments must prioritize people. Integrating technological building blocks into products and systems that benefit people and make sense within their social and cultural contexts is important.

NETWORKINFO MECHANICAL SYSTEMS (NIMS)

The structure for creating and carrying out ambient intelligence (AmI) systems is called ubiquitous intelligence network info mechanical systems (NIMS). It includes a collection of principles and best practices for creating, putting into use, and assessing AmI systems. The last 10 years have seen breakthroughs in networked embedded detector and actuator technologies, making the aim of intelligence in the atmosphere a reality. This will significantly improve our capacity to view and control the physical world, with applications for consumers, healthcare, business, security, and research and engineering in the natural environment.

Ambient intelligence network info mechanical systems (NIMS) are an architecture for developing and implementing ambient intelligence (AmI) systems. It provides a collection of standards and guidelines for creating, establishing, and evaluating AmI systems. The ultimate goal of ambient intelligence has already become a reality, partly because of advancements in interconnected Embedded sensors that is being tested and actuator technologies during the previous 10 years (Pise, Yoon, and Singh, 2023). With applications for customers, healthcare, company operations, security, and research and construction in the context of nature, this will vastly improve our capacity to observe and control the natural environment.

Significant progress has been achieved with the creation of techniques and entire architectures for scalability, efficient energy networking purposes, sensing, digital signal processing, and embedded computing. Innovative technologies like information technology, electronic components, and sensor systems are being amalgamated and applied in some of the first important monitoring of the environment technologies. However, this change shows a new set of fundamental challenges (Gao, 2023). Heterogeneous sensor networks, in particular, lack the critical aptitude for tracking and reporting their spatiotemporally-dependent detecting uncertainty. Consequently, while sensor networks are capable of gathering data on environmental occurrences, these networks have yet to assess the likelihood that these events will go unnoticed, or how collaboration between measurement error and unidentified transmission of signal characteristics could hinder their capacity to synthesize information collected by many different sensors (Gao, 2023; Tapia et al., 2018).

NIMS is Built on the Following Principles

1. **Sensing**: NIMS systems must be capable of recognizing the surroundings in addition to the people behind them. Many types of sensors, including microphones, video cameras, and sensors that detect movement, are all able to do this, as shown in Figure 4.
2. **Processing**: NIMS systems must be able to process sensor data. This includes identifying between goods, monitoring people, and deciphering events.
3. **Activating**: NIMS equipment must be able to react based on what is going on around them. This may be accomplished by adjusting the illumination, or altering the temperature while singing music.

Figure 4. Basic NIMS's principles

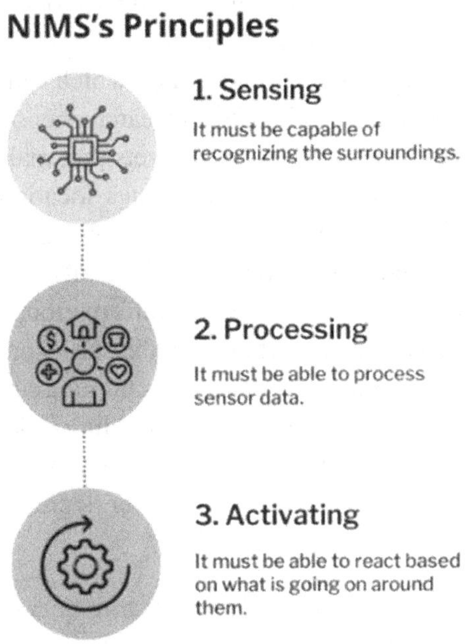

NIMS's Principles

1. Sensing

It must be capable of recognizing the surroundings.

2. Processing

It must be able to process sensor data.

3. Activating

It must be able to react based on what is going on around them.

NIMS System Ecology

The quest for self-awareness has accelerated progress in coordinated movement and sensor diversity. It is clear that a significantly high three-dimensional volume density of installed static sensor nodes, or physical reconfiguration, is required to achieve autonomous measurement and active reduction of sensing uncertainty in complex environments. Infrastructure-enabled mobility is crucial as we strive toward accurate, capable, and sustainable sensing and sampling (Smits et al., 2021). However, achieving scalability for large deployments and flexibility to changing circumstances necessitates an architecture that skilfully combines the advantages of infrastructure and mobile and stationary nodes. In particular, the hierarchy becomes essential for scalability, with the most expensive resources being sparingly dispersed among assets that support a high spatial density of less powerful nodes. Specific applications may favor a larger distribution of elements in a particular tier, and self-aware, self-adapting systems will adjust their own. distribution to optimize application-specific resource costs and benefits. These factors, along with the interaction among tiers, form a System Ecology, as shown in Table 1, where the resources exchanged between tiers along with system architecture define the System Ecology.

Furthermore, this hierarchy of node architecture tiers must include standardized interfaces and methods for cooperation between tiers to exploit hierarchy in favor of scalable, sustainable, robust, and high-performance operations.

The least advanced level of System Ecology consists of stationary nodes that are not connected, such as wireless sensor networks, which can be precisely and independently set up and maintained by NIMS to research phenomena at suitable spatial scales (Jain et al., 2023). The tethered fixed assets that make up the next level are things like storage depots, chemical analysis engines, location beacons, gateways for energy and communications, mobility drive mechanisms, and connected suspension networks. By working together, the three tiers of this info-mechanical network offer a way to produce and move energy as well as information, which can be stored as physical samples or as bits. By assigning suitable tasks and roles autonomously, NIMS operation algorithms improve sensing and sampling capability while overcoming the obstacles of quick spatiotemporal team building (connecting various levels) (Billinghurst and Seichter, 2010). This pertains to prior advancements in robotics and agent systems for homogeneousand, to a lesser degree, heterogeneous teams.

Table 1. NIMS system ecology outlines infrastructure tiers and nodes, highlighting their roles in maximizing energy efficiency, spatiotemporal coverage, and sensor fidelity

	Sensing Fidelity Dimension	Energy Efficiency Dimension	Spatial Coverage Dimension	Temporal Coverage Dimension
Mobile Node Tier	Adaptive Topology and Perspective	Enable Low Energy Transport and Communications	Enable Both Sensing and Sampling in 3-D	Enable Long Term Sustainability
Connected Fixed Node Tier	Optimal, Precise Deployment of Nodes	Enable Energy Production and Delivery Logistics	Enable Optimized Node Location and Sensing Perspective in 3-D	Continuous, In Situ Sensing-Sampling
Untethered Fixed Nodes Tiers	Localized Sensing and Sampling Capability	Event Detection and Guidance for Mobile Assets	Access to Non-Navigable Areas	Continuous Low Energy Vigilance

On the other hand, NIMS deviates from earlier research by incorporating a hierarchically organized System Ecology with a variety of communication channels and sensory resources. Moreover, NIMS operation relied on a multi-objective optimization that was spatially distributed, involved all ecological aspects, and operated across a broad variety of temporal scales (for instance, as determined by the speed of mechanical and data transit).

A complicated design space that may be adjusted to meet application requirements is made possible by the System Ecology. The necessary rate-distortion operating point, for instance, is influenced by the relative requirements of spatial sampling density and physical configuration latency.Thus, the arrangement of stationary and mobile sensors with different operating ranges can be chosen to accommodate changing application and environmental requirements by taking advantage of the System Ecology both during design and during operation (Ramkumar, Catharin and Nivetha, 2019). For instance, a slowly moving mobile sensor node may investigate an area of space with a high sample point density and minimal mobile asset cost, but at the expense of higher measurement latency. Lastly, the System Ecology may comprise unsupported, freely moving surface-bound or airborne robotic systems that enhance monitoring capacity, in addition to the infrastructure-supported nodes of major attention in this technical report.

COMPARISON OF EXISTING APPROACHES THAT INTEGRATE MULTI-AGENT SYSTEMS AND WSNS

The need to more effectively address the issues raised by AmI-based systems led to the creation of both FUSION@ and HERA. The challenge of creating, testing, and debugging distributed applications for devices with constrained resources makes the integration of multi-agent technologies and wireless sensor networks problematic. The maintenance of these distributed programs is made more difficult by the interfaces that were either designed to be overly basic or, in some cases, non-existent (Aarts, Harwig and Schuurmans, 2020). In light of this, studies have developed techniques for the methodical creation of multi-agent systems for WSNs. According to certain studies relating multi-agent technologies to WSNs, the combination of these technologies prolongs the life of wireless sensor nodes by lowering power consumption.

Actor Net focuses on individual sensor nodes, whereas HERA's inclusion with FUSION@ improves the multi-agent system's management of WSN data for efficient solutions. Practical WSN implementations are described in Research, and HERA integration yields encouraging outcomes. For condition monitoring, Baker et al. incorporate Subsense into an already-existing MAS. HERA's lightweight platform, in contrast, has advantages over Subsense because it operates on sensor nodes with 8KB of RAM (Ducatel, 2003). The research employs software agents to oversee transportation, but HERA integration enhances agent capabilities and coordination. The majority of research on WSNs and multi-agent systems talks about Mobile Agents based on WSNs (MAWSN). Routes for mobile agents are planned by me and Wang, while another author is presented by Fok et al. for quick WSN application development. Mobile agents are implemented on wireless sensor nodes by WSageNt. However, HERA is more deeply integrated into FUSION@, resulting in a flexible multi-agent architecture that may be used in a range of contexts.

By using mobile agents to eliminate data redundancy, Chen et al. can save energy and transmit data more quickly. A MAWSN system is proposed by Chen et al. to enhance communication and shorten delivery times. Rajagopalan et al. optimize data communication by using a model of mobile routing agents. By incorporating HERA into FUSION@, a hybrid architecture that capitalizes on the advantages of both models is provided. FUSION@ distributes functionality through intelligent agents and focuses on AmI-based systems (Aarts, Harwig and Schuurmans, n.d.). Hardware agents, which coexist with different devices in a dispersed network, are the specialty of HERA.

Table 2. Comparison of current methods aimed at wireless sensor network integration with multi-agent systems

	Heterogeneous WSNs	Hardware-embedded agents	Context-awareness	AmI-oriented
actorNet	No	Yes	Partly	No
SubSense	No	Yes	Yes	No
Agilla	No	Yes	Partly	No
WSageNt	No	Yes	No	No
FUSION@ + SYLPH	Yes	No	Yes	Yes
HERA (stand-alone)	Yes	Yes	Yes	Yes
FUSION@ + HERA	Yes	Both	Yes	Yes

In a distributed and heterogeneous WSN context, this combination expedites agent-sensor integration, encourages resource reuse and scalability, enhances flexibility, and recovers from errors. A comparison of methods for combining wireless sensor networks and multi-agent systems is shown in Table 2. The ability to connect multi-agent systems with heterogeneous WSNs makes platforms based on SYLPH particularly noteworthy. Examples of these platforms are the integration of SYLPH with FUSION@, the HERA platform, and the recent HERA integration into FUSION@ that is covered in this work. On the other hand, other methods ignore the possibilities of heterogeneous WSNs and concentrate on sensor nodes employing a single radio technology. With a focus on ubiquitous computing and context awareness, FUSION@ and HERA have been developed to meet the demands of ambient intelligence. They stand out from other strategies that don't address these needs because of their focus. The novel part of the HERA integration into FUSION@ is the actual deployment of hardware-embedded agents in heterogeneous wireless sensor networks that are specially designed to satisfy the requirements of ambient intelligence systems. HERA's design, in which agents are directly embedded into sensor nodes, outperforms SYLPH, and its integration into FUSION@ produces an architecture in which software- and hardware-embedded agents interact naturally, an element not taken into account in other techniques.

ALGORITHMS

Collaborative Filtering Algorithm

Algorithms for Collaborative Filtering (CF) are essential in Ambient Intelligence (AmI) environments because they leverage group preferences and behaviors to improve user experience. It helps to personalize services in the context of AmI, where technology is inconspicuously embedded into the environment to anticipate and address consumer demands. These algorithms examine how people interact and what they like to do in the surrounding area, finding trends and connections between users who share the same interests. User-based collaborative filtering (UBCF) is a popular sort of CF algorithm in AmI where recommendations are generated based on the likes and dislikes of other users. The CF algorithm continuously improves its suggestions as people engage with smart systems and devices in an ambient environment, changing to reflect changing user preferences in real time. Moreover, things that are comparable to the ones the user has already selected are recommended through item-based collaborative filtering (Gatica-Perez et al., 2019).

In AmI, efficient data processing and collecting are essential to the success of CF algorithms. A dynamic dataset is created by the collection of user activities and feedback from sensors that are integrated into the surrounding environment. Once this data has been analysed, machine learning techniques are used to find pertinent trends and provide tailored recommendations. In Ambient Intelligence, CF algorithms help make technology more natural and personalized by making it easier for users to interact with it. This allows services and recommendations to be customized to each individual in the ambient ecosystem, based on their specific interests and behaviours.

Firstly, we provide the formulas that underpin collaborative filtering and describe how it operates. We shall provide the most often used methodology and formulas; Van Duijnhoven provides additional methodologies and formulas (Rautaray and Agrawal, 2018; Bordonaro et al., 2020). Determining user similarities and score prediction are the two primary processes in collaborative filtering. User Likenesses. A popular metric for comparing similarities in writing is the so-called Pearson correlation coefficient, which is expressed as:

$$s(u,v) = \frac{\sum_{i \in I_u \cap I_v}\left(r_{ui} - \overline{r}_u\right)\left(r_{vi} - \overline{r}_v\right)}{\sqrt{\sum_{i \in I_u \cap I_v}\left(r_{ui} - \overline{r}_u\right)^2 \sum_{i \in I_u \cap I_v}\left(r_{vi} - \overline{r}_v\right)^2}} \tag{1}$$

Here u and v are users, i stands for an item, I_u and I_v for the sets of things that users u and v have rated respectively, r_{ui} for user u's rating of the item i, and u for user u's average rating (Hong-tan et al., 2021). Every item that receives ratings above average or below average from both users contributes positively to the numerator in this equation. We receive a negative contribution if one user rated an item above average and the other user ranked it below average. The equation's denominator normalizes the similarity by placing it in the interval [-1, 1], where a value of 1 denotes total correspondence and a value of -1 denotes total dissimilarity in preferences.

Estimations, Using the user similarity to interpolate between other users' ratings to get the rating of a new user-item combinations the second phase in the collaborative filtering process. Given the similarities as weights, the following is a widely used prediction formula:

$$\widehat{r_{ui}} = \overline{r_u} + \frac{\sum_{v \in U_i} s(u,v)(r_{vi} - \overline{r_v})}{\sum_{v \in U_i} |s(u,v)|} \tag{2}$$

where item i's rating is represented by the set of users (U_i). Therefore, the prediction consists of the weighted sum of the departuresfrom the averages plus the average rating of the user u.

The Digitization Process

Next, we demonstrate how to encrypt the previously mentioned collaborative filtering formulas using the Paillier cryptosystem (Duric et al. 2023; Quadar et al., 2024). The two huge primes, p, and q, which make up the private key of this encryption, are followed by their product, $n = pq$, and a generator, g, which makes up the public key. Next, $m \in Z_n$, a message is encrypted by

$$\varepsilon(m) = g^m r^n \bmod n^2 \tag{3}$$

where, by simply encrypting all possible values of m and comparing, disables decryption. where r is a random number. This encryption scheme has the excellent feature of

$$\varepsilon(m_1)\varepsilon(m_2) \equiv g^{m_1} r_1^n g^{m_2} r_2^n \equiv g^{(m_1+m_2)}(r_1 r_2)^n (\bmod n^2) \tag{4}$$

It represents the product$m_1 m_2$ encryption. To put it another way, we can add and multiply values on encrypted data thanks to the encryption methodology.The sums of the products in (1) and (2) can be computed using this

Sensor Fusion Algorithm

In Ambient Intelligence (AmI), where the smooth integration of data from several sensors improves the understanding of the environment, sensor fusion techniques are essential. AmI seeks to build intelligent surroundings that are aware of and react to human activity and presence Quadar et al., 2024. In AmI, sensor fusion refers to the process of merging information from many sensors including cameras, microphones, and motion detectors produce a more accurate and complete picture of the environment.The Kalman filter is a popular sensor fusion method used in AmI. To estimate the actual state of the system, this recursive approach merges noisy sensor measurements across time in an optimal manner. In AmI, data from several sensors is combined using Kalman filters to produce a dependable, real-time assessment of the surroundings (Alladi et al., 2023). For instance, by precisely forecasting occupancy patterns, merging data from temperature and motion sensors in a smart home setting via Kalman filters might improve energy efficiency.

In addition, AmI uses Bayesian networks for probabilistic reasoning. By simulating the interactions between many sensors and their uncertainties, these networks enable intelligent systems to make well-informed decisions. When there is a lot of uncertainty and partial information, like in healthcare monitoring systems that combine data from multiple physiological sensors, Bayesian networks are useful. Additionally, sensor fusion for AmI is increasingly using machine learning techniques, such as neural networks (Sabit, Chong and Kilby, 2019). More flexible and context-aware systems are made possible by these algorithms' capacity to recognize intricate patterns and relationships in sensor data. Neural networks, for example, can be trained to identify particular human actions based on inputs from a variety of sensors, which furthers the development of intelligent settings that accommodate personal preferences.

As verbal and nonverbal channels are utilized in human-to-human communication, algorithms for audio tracking and visual tracking can be coupled similarly. This inter-aural delay between two microphone signals can be used by algorithms to estimate the direction of sound, which is useful for tracking human speakers. A visual sense of faces and body movement is also made possible by vision algorithms that employ motion detection and skin tone (Hudec and Smutny, 2022). To identify "noisy face pixels" and follow the speaker's location, data from various sensors can be aggregated at the pixel level.

APPLICATIONS UNDER AmI's

Various applications are there under the AmI's, some of the applications are shown in Figure 5.

1. *Ambient Communication between people* - The ideal settings for terminal-centered interaction situations, in which users either hold as well sit in front of the terminal, are modern telephony and online conferencing systems. Because these are terminal-centric systems, interactions take shape in the manner of on-and-off sessions that begin with a call and finish with a call termination. Socially, a terminal-cantered communications session is comparable to a for-mal meeting that takes place in person. People who have a physical presence in tandem, on the other hand, can utilize a broader variety of interaction modes defined by numerous interpersonal distances that go beyond the traditional face-to-face interaction mode. As a consequence, the model for environmental technology for communication should be based on actual interactions between physically present individuals.

2. *Production-focused locations,* Production-focused sites, such as manufacturing facilities, can self-organize based on the goods being produced' s production/demand ratio. This will involve exact communication between data collection via sensors inside various portions of the manufacturing facilities line and the pool of inquiries via a system for diagnostics that can guide the system's those who make decisions (D' Souza et al., 2019). Hospitals can improve the pro-ductivity of the services they provide by proactively evaluating activity in their rooms to monitor patients' health and progress (Liu et al., 2023). They might additionally improve safety by restricting authorized workers' and patients' access to particular places and machines.

3. *Public transportation*, to make public transport more effective and safer, can benefit from extra technology such as satellite services, GPS-based spatial positioning, then vehicle identification, processing of imagery, and other technologies.

4. *Education-related institutions,* may use technological advances to track students' progress at work, frequency of attendance at certain places, and related to their health such as nutrition advice based on their habits and the type of intake they choose.

5. *Emergency services* and fire organizations, along with feed examples, can improve the response to a hazard by more efficiently discovering the place and also by planning the route to the area in collaboration with street services Chen et al., 2022). The prison service additionally can locate a spot where a hazard is

occurring or is predicted to occur and better prepare security workers for access to it (Huang et al., 2023).

Figure 5. Various applications of AmI's

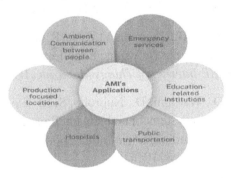

CONCLUSION AND FUTURE ENHANCEMENTS

This study, delves into the realm of Ambient Intelligence (AmI) and its recent advancements in computer science, emphasizing the strategic use of technology to enhance user environments. Smart homes emerge as a pivotal aspect of AmI, experiencing growing interest under various labels like "intelligent ubiquitous systems." The field is marked by a surge in scientific events, publications, commercial initiatives, and government-led projects, reflecting the increasing recognition of AmI's potential. AmI centers on the integration of computation to benefit individuals, representing a significant paradigm shift in computer science. The autonomy and proactive nature of AmI systems, while empowering, also pose challenges, demanding careful consideration of predictability and reliability. Addressing these concerns is crucial for ensuring the safety and utility of the environments in which we live and work. Looking ahead, the evolution of AmI will focus on refining natural language processing, developing context-aware systems, incorporating advanced sensors for precision, and implementing robust security measures. Ongoing research will explore self-learning algorithms, energy-efficient optimizations, and new applications in areas such as urban environments, smart homes, and healthcare. The trajectory of Ambient Intelligence will also be influenced by advancements in edge computing and AI-driven decision-making, leading to more intelligent, adaptive environments that enhance user experiences and overall quality of life.

REFERENCES

Aarts, E. (2020). Ambient Intelligence. J. Denning (ed.) *The Invisible Future*. McGraw Hill, New York.

Aarts, E., Harwig, H., & Schuurmans, M. Ambient Intelligence. In Denning, J. (Ed.), *The Invisible Future* (pp. 235–250). McGraw Hill.

Alladi, T., Agrawal, A., Gera, B., Chamola, V., & Yu, R. (2023). Ambient Intelligence for Securing Intelligent Vehicular Networks: Edge-Enabled Intrusion and Anomaly Detection Strategies. *IEEE Internet of Things Magazine*. IEEE.

Arif, Y. M., Putra, D. D., Wardani, D., Nugroho, S. M. S., & Hariadi, M. (2023). Decentralized recommender system for ambient intelligence of tourism destinations serious game using known and unknown rating approach. *Heliyon*, 9(3), e14267. 10.1016/j.heliyon.2023.e1426737101510

Billinghurst, M. (2010). *Hartmut Seichter*. Human-Centric Interfaces for Ambient Intelligence.

Bordonaro, A., De Paola, A., Lo Re, G., & Morana, M. (2020). Smart Auctions for Autonomic Ambient Intelligence Systems. *2020 IEEE International Conference on Smart Computing (SMARTCOMP)*. IEEE. 10.1109/SMARTCOMP50058.2020.00043

Chen, J., Yu, H., Guan, Q., Yang, G., & Liang, Y.-C. (2022). Spatial Modulation Based Multiple Access for Ambient Backscatter Networks. *IEEE Communications Letters*, 26(1), 197–201. 10.1109/LCOMM.2021.3124277

Ducatel, K., Bogdanowicz, M., Scapolo, F., Leijten, J., & Burgelman, J. (2003). *Ambient Intelligence: From Vision to Reality*. IST Advisory Group Draft Rep., Eur. Comm.

Gao, X., Alimoradi, S., Chen, J., Hu, Y., & Tang, S. (2023). Assistance from the Ambient Intelligence: Cyber-physical system applications in smart buildings for cognitively declined occupants. *Engineering Applications of Artificial Intelligence*, 123, 106431. 10.1016/j.engappai.2023.106431

Gatica-Perez, D., Lathoud, G., McCowan, I., Odobez, J.-M., & Moore, D. (2019). Audio-visual speaker tracking with importance particle filters. *Proceedings IEEE ICIP*. IEEE.

Huang, Y., & Li, M.. (2023, September). Performance Optimization for Energy-Efficient Industrial Internet of Things Based on Ambient Backscatter Communication: An A3C-FL Approach. *IEEE Transactions on Green Communications and Networking*, 7(3), 1121–1134. 10.1109/TGCN.2023.3260199

Jain, V., Gupta, G., Gupta, M., Sharma, D. K., & Ghosh, U. (2023). Ambient intelligence-based multimodal human action recognition for autonomous systems. *ISA Transactions*, 132, 94–108. 10.1016/j.isatra.2022.10.03436404154

Jain, V., Gupta, G., Gupta, M., Sharma, D. K., & Ghosh, U. (2023). Ambient intelligence-based multimodal human action recognition for autonomous systems. *ISA Transactions*, 132, 94–108. 10.1016/j.isatra.2022.10.03436404154

Li, H. (2021). Big data and ambient intelligence in IoT-based wireless student health monitoring system. *Aggression and Violent Behavior*. Elsevier Ltd.

Liu, P., Zhu, G., Wang, S., & Jiang, W. (2023, January). Toward Ambient Intelligence: Federated Edge Learning With Task-Oriented Sensing, Computation, and Communication Integration. *IEEE Journal of Selected Topics in Signal Processing*, 17(1), 158–172. 10.1109/JSTSP.2022.3226836

Malik, U. M., & Javed, M. A. (2022). Ambient Intelligence assisted fog computing for industrial IoT applications. [Elsevier Ltd.]. *Computer Communications*, 196, 117–128. 10.1016/j.comcom.2022.09.024

Pise, A., Yoon, B., & Singh, S. (2023). Enabling Ambient Intelligence of Things (AIoT) healthcare system architectures. [Elsevier Ltd.]. *Computer Communications*, 198, 186–194. 10.1016/j.comcom.2022.10.029

Quadar, N., Chehri, A., Jeon, G., Hassan, M., & Fortino, G. (2022). Cybersecurity Issues of IoT in Ambient Intelligence (AmI) Environment. *IEEE Internet of Things Magazine*. IEEE.

Ramana, T. V., Thirunavukkarasan, M., Mohammed, A. S., Devarajan, G. G., & Nagarajan, S. M. (2022). Ambient intelligence approach: Internet of Things based decision performance analysis for intrusion detection. *Computer Communications*, 195, 315–322. 10.1016/j.comcom.2022.09.007

Ramkumar, M. O., Sarah Catharin, S., & Nivetha, D. (2019). Survey of Cognitive Assisted Living Ambient System Using Ambient Intelligence as a Companion. *IEEE Proceeding of International Conference on Systems Computation Automation and Networking*. IEEE. 10.1109/ICSCAN.2019.8878707

Rathee, G., Kerrache, C. A., & Calafate, C. T. (2022). Ambient Intelligence for Secure and Trusted Pub/Sub Messaging in IoT Environments. [Elsevier Ltd.]. *Computer Networks*, 218, 109401. 10.1016/j.comnet.2022.109401

Rautaray, S. S., & Agrawal, A. (2018). Vision based hand gesture recognition for human computer interaction: A survey. Artificial Intelligence. *RE:view*, 43.

Sabit, H., Peter, H. J. C., & Kilby, J. (2019). Ambient Intelligence for Smart Home using The Internet of Things. *2019 29th International Telecommunication Networks and Applications Conference (ITNAC)*. IEEE. 10.1109/ITNAC46935.2019.9078001

Smits, M., Nacar, M., Ludden, G. D. S., & van Goor, H. (2021). *Stepwise Design and Evaluation of a Values-Oriented Ambient Intelligence Healthcare Monitoring Platform. Remote patient monitoring.* Elsevier Ltd.

Tapia, D. I., Fraile, J. A., Rodríguez, S., Alonso, R. S., & Corchado, J. M. (2018). Integrating hardware agents into an enhanced multi-agent architecture for Ambient Intelligence systems. *Information Sciences*, 222, 47–65. 10.1016/j.ins.2011.05.002

Teixeira, M. S., Maran, V., Oliveira, J. P. M., Winter, M., & Machado, A. (2019). *Situation-aware model for multi-objective decision making in ambient intelligence.* Applied Soft Computing. Elsevier Ltd. 10.1016/j.asoc.2019.105532

Teixeira, M. S., Maran, V., Oliveira, J. P. M., Winter, M., & Machado, A. (2019). Situation-aware model for multi-objective decision making in ambient intelligence. *Applied Soft Computing*, 81, 105532. 10.1016/j.asoc.2019.105532

William, J. (2014). *Networked Infomechanical Systems (NIMS) for Ambient Intelligence.* UCLA Center for Embedded Networked Sensing.

Chapter 2
Intelligent Serverless Computing Technology and Recent Trends:
A Review

Naren Kathirvel

Anand Institute of Higher Technology, India

Kathirvel Ayyaswamy

https://orcid.org/0000-0002-5347-9110

Department of Computer Science and Engineering, Panimalar Engineering College, Chennai, India

C. Subramanian

https://orcid.org/0000-0003-2629-3182

Eswari Engineering College, India

ABSTRACT

Applications that are serverless can be distributed (many services are connected for smooth operation), elastic (resources can be scaled up and down without limit), stateless (interactions and data aren't stored), event-driven (resources are allocated only when triggered by an event), and hostless (apps aren't hosted on a server). Serverless computing is becoming more and more popular as cloud adoption rises. In many respects, serverless computing unleashes the entire potential of cloud computing. We pay only for the resources consumed, and resources are allocated, increased, or decreased dynamically based on user requirements in real-time. It makes sure that when there are no user requests and the application is effectively dormant, resources are immediately scaled to zero. More scalability and significant cost reductions are the outcomes of this. According to research by Global Industry

DOI: 10.4018/979-8-3693-2869-9.ch002

Insights, the serverless industry is expected to reach $30 billion in market value by the end of the forecast period, growing at an above-average rate of 25% between 2021 and 2027.

INTRODUCTION

Serverless computing (SC) is a method of providing backend services on a need-based basis. Through serverless providers, users can create and execute applications without having to consider the underlying infrastructure. When a business uses a serverless vendor for backend services, the cost is determined by the vendor's computation; no set bandwidth or server count needs to be reserved or paid for because the service is auto-scaling. Even though it has a different name, the physical server is still used; Developers don't necessarily know this (Sudha & Kathirvel, 2023).

When the Web was born, anyone who wanted to build a Web application had to buy the expensive and time-consuming physical hardware needed to run a server.

In cloud computing, where one could rent a set number of servers or a set amount of server space remotely (Naveneethan, 2022). In order to make sure that a surge in activity or traffic won't surpass their monthly allotment and disrupt their applications, developers and businesses that rent these fixed units of servers typically overbuy. It can therefore be the case that a large portion of the paid server space is wasted. To alleviate this problem, cloud manufacturers have come up with auto-scaling models. However, even with auto-scaling, unintended increases in activity, such as DDoS attacks, can impose significant costs. Developers use pre-packaged functions such as Google Cloud Functions and Microsoft Azure Functions to operate so-called serverless applications that either work Function as a service (FaaS) or computation as a service (CaaS).

Fundamentals of SC

Developers can purchase back-end services using serverless computing on a flexible "pay-as-you-go" basis, meaning they only pay for the services they need. This is like switching from your cell phone data plan that has a set monthly limit to a plan that only charges for the actual amount of data used (Kathirvel et al., 2022).

Although these backend services are still provided by the server, the term "serverless" is a bit confusing because the provider manages all aspects of the infrastructure and server space. Developers don't have to worry about servers at all when their work is serverless.

Techniques in Serverless Computing

The two domains of application development are often separated into 1. frontend and 2. backend. The portion of the program, people can view and interact with SC, (i.e) the layout visually, is called the frontend. Portion of the program that is hidden from the user's view is called the backend, and it consists of the database and server that store user information and business logic as shown in the Figure 1.

Figure 1. Front end and back end server request

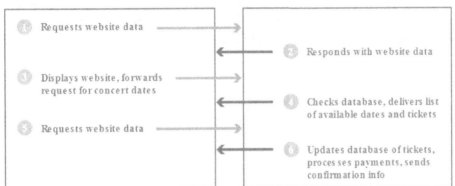

Consider, for illustration, a website that offers concert tickets. The browser sends a request to the back-end server, which returns website information in response when the user types the website address in the browser window (Sudha & Kathirvel, 2022c). The user then sees the website and the user interface, which may include form fields that the user can fill in as well as text and graphic content. After that, the user can use one of the frontend form fields to look up their preferred musical act. The user will send another request to the backend when they click "submit." The background function queries its database to see if the performer with that name is present and if, what their upcoming performance date and quantity of ticket is available.

In addition to providing database and storage capabilities, the majority of serverless providers also offer FaaS platforms, such as Cloudflare Workers (Kathirvel et al., 2021). A developer can run brief code segments on the network server edge with Function as a Service. By creating a sectional architecture using FaaS, developers may create a more scalable codebase without having to invest resources in maintaining the underlying backend.

FaaS

Function-as-a-Service is a serverless approach for running modular programs at the boundary. With FaaS, developers can quickly build and modify code that will be performed when a certain event occurs, such the user clicks on an element in the web application. This mechanism is a low-cost approach to implementing microservices and facilitates code scalability (Subramaniam et al., 2021).

Microservices

Using microservice architecture in a web application would be like creating a work of visual art out of a mosaic tile collection as shown in the Figure 2. An artist can easily add, change and fix one record at a time. It is like to painting the entire composition on a single canvas if architecture were monolithic.

Figure 2. Microservice architecture

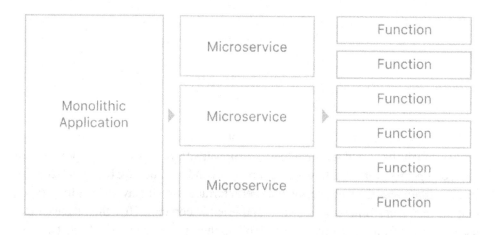

Microservices architecture is the process of building an application from a collection of modular parts. Developers find it attractive when an application is divided into microservices because it allows them to easily generate and alter small code parts that can be integrated into their codebases (Leitner et al., 2019). As opposed to this, uniform architecture integrates totally of the code into a single, massive system. Uniform minor application modifications in large monolithic systems necessitate a laborious deploy procedure. This deployment difficulty is removed with FaaS (Kathirvel & Naren, 2024a).

Web developers can concentrate on creating application code by using serverless code, such as FaaS, which handles server allocation and backend services.

Figure 3. Cost benefits of serverless computing

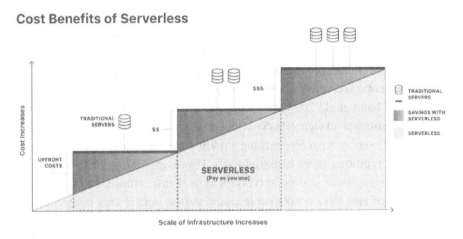

Advantages of Serverless Computing

Reduced costs: Serverless computing is usually relatively cheap, as traditional back-end cloud providers (server allocation) often charge users for unused CPU time or free space (see Figure 3).

Scalability made simple: When utilizing serverless architecture, developers don't need to worry about regulations when expanding their code (Gobinath, Ayyaswamy, & Kathirvel, 2024; Kathirvel, 2023). A serverless service provider takes care of every on-demand scale (Aluvalu et al., 2024a).

Serverless services provided by cloud providers include Microsoft Azure Functions, Amazon Web Services Lambda, Google Cloud Functions, and IBM Open-Whisk, which are good examples.

Serverless Compare to Other Cloud Backend Models

Two terms that are frequently used interchangeably with SC are Platform-as-a-Service (PaaS) and Back-end-as-a-Service (BaaS). These models don't always fit the serverless requirements, despite their shared commonalities (Kathirvel & Shobitha, 2023).

With the help of the BaaS service model, front-end developers may focus on writing front-end code while the cloud service provider takes care of backend tasks like data storage. BaaS applications, on the other hand, might not meet either of these requirements, whereas serverless applications function on the edge and are event-driven (Bhatia et al., 2024).

The platform-as-a-service (PaaS) concept allows architects to construct and launch applications by basically renting middleware and operating systems from a cloud provider, among other essential tools. However, scaling PaaS applications is more challenging than scaling serverless apps. Furthermore, PaaS often function off-the-edge and have a noticeable initialization period that is missing from server-based applications (Kathirvel & Pavani, 2023).

Cloud suppliers that host infrastructure on behalf of their clients are collectively referred to as infrastructure-as-a-service (IaaS) providers (Sudha & Kathirvel, 2022b). Although serverless functionality may be offered by IaaS providers, the phrases are not interchangeable.

What Is Next for Serverless?

As serverless providers find ways to get around some of the problems with serverless computing, the technology continues to advance. Cold beginnings are one of these disadvantages.

The provider typically deactivates a serverless service that hasn't been used for a while in order to save energy and avoid over-provisioning. When a user launches an application that calls it later, the serverless provider will have to start it up again and host that function. Term "cold start" refers to the substantial lag that this initial period contributes (Bhupathi, 2023).

Once the function is operational, following requests will be delivered significantly more quickly (warm begins); but, if the function is not used again for some time, it will eventually go for dormant (Satishkumar et al., 2024b).

In order to solve this issue, Cloudflare Workers has spun up serverless tasks ahead of time, during the TLS handshake. The outcome is a FaaS platform with no cold starts since Workers functions spin up at the edge in much less time—even less time than it takes to finish the handshake. Check out our Developer guide to learn how to use Cloudflare Workers.

We should anticipate a greater use of serverless architecture when the disadvantages of doing so are resolved and edge computing gains traction.

Simplified backend code: With FaaS, programmers can create basic applications that each perform a specific function, such initiating a request to an API, independently.

Faster turnaround: Serverless architecture has an opportunity to significantly shorten the time to market. to release corrections for bugs and fresh functionality, developers don't need to go through a laborious deploy procedure; instead, they may add and edit code as needed.

SERVERLESS MODEL WORKS

The programmer creates an application with a function that controls the program's reaction to a specific user activity (Sudha & Kathirvel, 2023). Pre-packaged FaaS products are typically offered by cloud providers to ease developers' coding and incorporate pre-built backend components (Khang et al., 2024b; Kathirvel, Rithik, & Naren, 2024).

The method and time at which the function will be activated are defined in an event. For instance, the program might wish to retrieve and send specific data when the user makes an HTTP request. An event is the term for this "if-then" sequence.

A user action triggers the event after the program is deployed and available to the user.

After receiving the event from the application, the cloud provider dynamically allots the resources required to react to the action in accordance with the predetermined function (Kathirvel & Gobinath, 2024).

The client receives the information or any additional outcome that the function's parameters specifies. Crucially, no resources will be allotted and no data will be kept in an intermediate stage if there is no user request (Sudha & Kathirvel, 2022a). This minimizes storage costs and guarantees that the user receives just the most recent and updated data, making your apps real-time.

Key Components of Architecture

FaaS, the core element of serverless technology, is responsible for executing the computation that determines how services are allocated in a given scenario (Gobinath, Kathirvel, Rajesh Kanna et al, 2024). Whichever is the kind of cloud infrastructure that is being utilized, you can select from purpose-built FaaS offerings like AWS Lambda for Amazon Web Services (AWS), Microsoft Azure Functions for Azure, Google Cloud Functions for the Google Cloud Platform (GCP), and IBM Cloud

Functions for private or hybrid environments. These steps will read the backbone database, retrieve the reply, and deliver it when the user starts an event.

A significant component of serverless functioning is the client interface. Serverless architecture cannot be forced into any application. Short bursts of queries, stateless interactions, and adaptable integrations must all be supported by the interface (Kathirvel & Maheswaran, 2023). Additionally, the interface needs to be built to work with both very high and low volume data transmissions as shown in the Figure 4.

A stateless interaction will begin on the web server, following the user's inception and ending before the FaaS service does. The backend database, which houses the data that is sent to users, is separate from the web server. Let's say you are a provider of internet video content. The internet server is therefore at which customer inquiries, applications, FaaS answers, and additional data are hosted until they are stopped due to serverless computing is transient. Conversely, video material will be retained in the backend storage, ready to be retrieved in response to user queries.

Figure 4. Key components

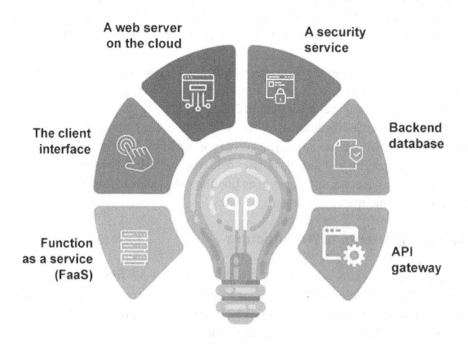

One of the main reasons serverless operations need security is:

Thousands of queries are handled concurrently by the application. Before responding to a request, it must first undergo authentication (Kathirvel et al., 2023).

Its stateless architecture prevents the storage of previous interaction histories. Future interactions cannot be validated by the application based on past ones.

The serverless paradigm complicates matters of openness and oversight. Security intelligence must be gathered from the millions of occurrences that are daily logged.

There are several services and providers engaged since serverless architecture is spread. The entire terrain needs to be safeguarded.

The data that has to be shared with the user is kept in the backend database. Static content repositories, SQL databases, media storage, and live broadcasting modes are a few examples of this. Designers usually employ Backend as a service (BaaS) services to further minimize managerial and upkeep work. Most cloud providers also have BaaS alternatives that integrate with their FaaS packages.

FaaS and the client interface, or components 1 and 2, are connected by the API gateway. The FaaS service uses an action that the user takes to initiate an event, which is relayed via the API portal. The client interface's functionality can be increased by connecting it through the intermediary to a variety of FaaS services.

SERVERLESS COMPUTING

Overview of Architecture

Typically, hosting a software program online entails overseeing a server architecture. This usually refers to a physical or virtual server that requires management in addition to the OS and additional internet hosting functions required for the app to run correctly as shown in the Fig. 5. While using a server that's virtual from an internet-based service like Amazon eliminates real problems with hardware or Microsoft, some level of operating system and web server software maintenance is still necessary.

"Serverless technology computing" is an execution model for cloud-based services that enables the cloud service to operate servers on behalf of the customers it serves by providing resources such as machines as needed. Because cloud service providers still utilize server to run client code, the term "serverless" is deceptive. For architects of serverless applications, however, challenges related to capacity planning, virtualization or physically server installation and management, resilience to faults, and scalability do not arise (Kathirvel, Naren, Nithyanand et al, 2024). Serverless computing uses short bursts of computing, storing the result, rather than storing assets within volatile memory. An application does not have any computer resources assigned to it when it is not in use. The real amount of resources used by an application determines pricing (Kounev et al., 2023). Code deployment into production can be made easier with serverless computing. Code distributed in conventional ways, like microservices or monoliths, can be combined with serverless code. As an alternative, programs can be developed to run entirely without provided servers (Aske & Zhao, 2018). This is not to be confused with networking or computer methods like peer-to-peer (P2P) that operate without a physical server (Kathirvel, Gopinath, Naren et al, 2024).

Figure 5. Working of serverless computing

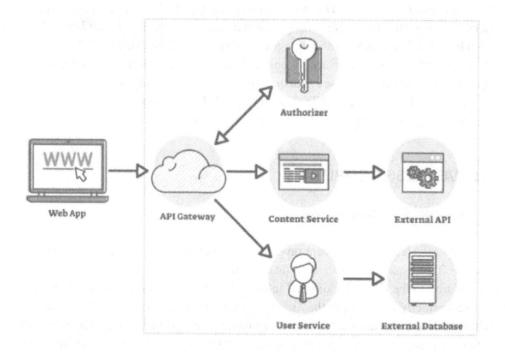

EXAMPLE OF SERVERLESS COMPUTING

Global leaders in business have been using serverless computing to provide their clients with high-availability (Gobinath, Ayyaswamy, & Kathirvel, 2024), high-performance online services. Among the noteworthy instances are:

Major League Baseball Advanced Media (MLBAM)

The Major League Baseball Association is one of the larger and most established athletic associations in the USA. The company runs a program called Statcast that gives customers access to precise and up-to-date sports analytics. You may perform intricate searches on the Statcast website using information such as pitch velocity, pitch type, season type, and individual player names. It can provide accurate data and help users make decisions about baseball games by utilizing serverless computing.

Autodesk

For the bandwidth-intensive and mission-critical construction, architecture, and engineering sectors, Autodesk provides robust software. It released a new tool named Tailor that could swiftly generate unique Autodesk accounts for businesses with all the required setups. With just two FTES handling the solution, Autodesk was able to launch Tailor in just two weeks by utilizing a serverless architecture.

Netflix

Netflix, one of the biggest over-the-top (OTT) video companies in the world, has long supported serverless computing. Since 2017 and before, it has been utilizing serverless to create a platform that can manage thousands of modifications every day. The only thing that Netflix developers have to do is define the adapter code, which controls how the platform reacts to user requests and system requirements. At the core of Netflix's exclusive Dynamic Scripting Platform is serverless architecture, which manages platform modifications, provisioning, and end-user delivery.

RAPID TECHNOLOGICAL ADVANCEMENT AND INDUSTRY

IR 5.0 is characterized by cutting-edge technologies such as quantum computing, advanced artificial intelligence, and nanotechnology. The rapid pace of innovation can be challenging for industries and governments to keep up with. With this dimension we can further explore the multifaceted challenges posed by rapid technological advancement and their implications in the context of IR 5.0. The technological advancement can be divided into two main dimensions:

Disruption and Adaptation

Rapid technological advancement drives disruptive changes in industries. Traditional business models and operations are upended as emerging technologies offer new opportunities and efficiencies. This challenges industries to constantly adapt to remain competitive. Failure to do so can result in obsolescence, as witnessed in sectors that couldn't keep pace with digitization. Apart of that deciding where to allocate resources for technological innovation is a complex task. Industries must identify which technologies are most relevant to their operations and invest strategically. Poor resource allocation may lead to missed opportunities or wasted investments. Besides that, the rapid technological advancement can exacerbate economic inequality. While some sectors flourish, others decline, leading to job displacement and wage disparities. Addressing these social and economic disparities becomes an imperative for industries to ensure inclusive growth and societal cohesion.(George & Hovan George, 2023; Taj & Jhanjhi, 2022)

Regulatory and Ethical Hurdles

Rapid technological change often outpaces the development of regulatory and ethical frameworks. This regulatory lag poses legal and ethical challenges for industries. They must navigate issues such as data privacy, intellectual property rights, safety, and ethical technology use. The absence of clear guidelines can lead to misuse, privacy breaches, or ethical dilemmas. In other words, this has also created a demand for skilled professionals in emerging technologies frequently outstrips supply. Industries struggle to attract, retain, and upskill a workforce capable of harnessing these technologies. The scarcity of talent in fields like AI, quantum computing, and cybersecurity can hinder innovation and competitiveness.(Tavares et al., 2022a)

RAPID TECHNOLOGICAL ADVANCEMENT AND GOVERNMENT

Regulation and Legislation

Governments must develop and adapt regulatory frameworks to address the rapid advancement of technology. This includes rules regarding data privacy, intellectual property rights, and the ethical use of technologies. Striking the right balance between enabling innovation and protecting public interests is a challenge. This gap raises legal and ethical challenges. Government and industry must navigate issues like data privacy, intellectual property, safety, and ethical use of technologies. The absence of clear guidelines can lead to misuse, privacy breaches, or even ethical dilemmas. The global nature of IR 5.0 necessitates international collaboration. Governments must work together to address cross-border issues, such as data flows and technology standards, while safeguarding their national interests and security. Nevertheless, as technological advancements increase the vulnerability of digital infrastructure, governments must focus on enhancing cybersecurity measures. Cyberattacks can have national security implications. Collaborating with industries to safeguard critical infrastructure is crucial.(Mourtzis, 2021a; Saniuk et al., 2022a)

Workforce Development

Government plays a role in promoting workforce development and reskilling initiatives. Ensuring that the labour force is equipped with the skills required in the rapidly evolving job market is essential for societal stability and economic growth. IR 5.0 brings with it a demand for new and advanced skills, such as data analytics, AI, quantum computing, and cybersecurity. The existing workforce may not possess these skills, leading to a significant skill mismatch. Governance needs to facilitate the rapid acquisition of these skills through education and training programs. Automation and AI can displace traditional jobs. Governance has the responsibility to manage the societal impact of job loss. This may involve designing policies for reskilling and upskilling the workforce to transition into new, tech-related roles. Ensuring that all segments of the population, including disadvantaged groups, have access to the opportunities created by IR 5.0 is a governance challenge. This requires addressing the digital divide, making education and training accessible to everyone, and creating policies that promote inclusivity. Governance needs to adapt labour market policies to align with the changing nature of work. Policies related to contract work, benefits, and worker protections may need to be reevaluated and updated to suit the needs of a more technology-driven workforce. Encouraging and facilitating public-private partnerships can be essential in addressing workforce development challenges. This collaboration can help in the creation of specialized training programs and research initiatives that bridge the gap between the workforce and industry requirements.

In the transition to Industrial Revolution 5.0 (IR 5.0), we confront an array of intricate technological challenges that will shape the course of our future. The rapid pace of technological obsolescence necessitates constant adaptation and upskilling for individuals and organizations, with the risk of lagging behind ever-present. Bridging the digital skills gap and ensuring that all members of society can harness the potential of advanced technologies is not only a challenge but also a moral imperative. Moreover, the ethical and regulatory complexities of IR 5.0 are paramount. As we grapple with the ethical dilemmas posed by artificial intelligence, data privacy, and the responsible use of technology, the development of robust frameworks and regulations becomes crucial. Simultaneously, the expanding threat landscape of cybersecurity looms large. Protecting our digital infrastructure and safeguarding sensitive information require continuous vigilance and innovation. Balancing the demands of a transforming workforce with evolving skills and preparing for jobs that are yet to emerge is a formidable task. The global scale of these challenges necessitates international collaboration in technology and governance. In addressing these hurdles, we must find a delicate equilibrium between technological innovation and responsible use, ensuring that the benefits of IR 5.0 are accessible and beneficial to all. Meeting these technological challenges head-on will define our ability to navigate the complexities of this new industrial era and harness its potential for the greater good of society.

INCORPORATING SOFT SKILLS

Incorporating soft skills in education is a crucial challenge in the context of Industrial Revolution 5.0 (IR 5.0) due to the transformation of the job market and the evolving needs of the modern workforce. IR 5.0 places a significant emphasis on holistic development, recognizing that success in the modern world goes beyond technical skills. Soft skills like communication, collaboration, adaptability, and emotional intelligence are considered essential for personal and professional success. The challenges of IR 5.0 often require cross-disciplinary solutions. Incorporating soft skills into the curriculum prepares students to work effectively in multidisciplinary teams, fostering creativity and innovative problem-solving. IR 5.0 introduces adaptive and personalized learning environments, which allow students to progress at their own pace. This personalized learning approach provides opportunities to assess and develop individual soft skills. In IR 5.0, collaboration is key, not only among students but also between educators. The educational approach is more collaborative, mirroring the soft skills being taught. Educators and students work together to create a learning ecosystem that nurtures these skills.

Soft skills encompass digital citizenship, which includes digital etiquette, online collaboration, and responsible use of technology. Students need to develop these skills to navigate the digital landscape of IR 5.0 effectively. IR 5.0 raises ethical issues related to technology and data use. Soft skills like ethical reasoning and decision-making become crucial in navigating these complex ethical considerations in education and beyond. Educators must be competent in teaching soft skills. This requires their own professional development to effectively foster these skills in students. Strategies for experiential learning, feedback, and reflection are essential components of this development. Assessing soft skills can be challenging. Educators must develop valid and reliable methods to assess communication, collaboration, adaptability, and other soft skills. Traditional assessment methods may need to evolve to capture these skills effectively. Soft skills like cross-cultural understanding, empathy, and effective communication across diverse backgrounds are increasingly important in a globalized world. Preparing students for global competence is a challenge that requires an international perspective in education.

Lifelong Learning

The challenge of lifelong learning in education is significantly impacted by Industrial Revolution 5.0 (IR 5.0) due to the changing nature of work, the rapid evolution of technology, and the need for individuals to continuously adapt and acquire new skills throughout their lives. In IR 5.0, technological advancements are occurring at an unprecedented rate. This requires individuals to continuously update their skills and knowledge to remain relevant in the job market. Lifelong learning becomes imperative for staying employable. IR 5.0 emphasizes skill-based education over traditional degree-based education. Lifelong learners need access to target. The use of technology in education facilitates personalized learning paths, enabling individuals to learn at their own pace and tailor their educational journeys to their specific needs and career goals. ed, just-in-time learning opportunities to acquire specific skills required for their chosen careers.

Lifelong learning often involves online education platforms. Individuals must be digitally literate to navigate these platforms effectively. This presents challenges for those who are less familiar with technology. Lifelong learning resources, including online courses and educational materials, need to be accessible to a diverse population, regardless of socio-economic background. Overcoming barriers to access and affordability is a challenge in promoting lifelong learning. As the nature of work evolves, traditional degrees may become less important. Individuals need a system of flexible credentials and certifications that reflect their ongoing skill development. Education institutions must adapt to provide these. Lifelong learning often involves the integration of knowledge and skills from multiple disciplines. Education systems need to promote interdisciplinary learning to enable individuals to solve complex, multifaceted problems. Assessing the effectiveness of lifelong learning is challenging. Traditional metrics like degrees may not reflect the breadth and depth of skills and knowledge acquired through lifelong learning. Developing new assessment methods is essential.

In conclusion, Industrial Revolution 5.0 (IR 5.0) has ushered in a transformative era for education, replete with intricate challenges. The rapid evolution of technology requires constant adaptation of curricula and teaching methods, underscoring the importance of lifelong learning for educators and students alike. Bridging the digital divide and ensuring equitable access to advanced technologies remains a pressing concern. Moreover, the paradigm shifts toward soft skills, ethical technology use, and interdisciplinary learning necessitates a profound overhaul of educational models. Assessment methods must evolve to accurately measure the dynamic skills demanded in this new era. The development of global perspectives and international collaboration is pivotal in an interconnected world. As we navigate these challenges, we must invest in resources, professional development, and educational policies that enable a seamless transition into IR 5.0. Educators play a central role in cultivating adaptive, ethically aware, and digitally proficient learners who possess not only technical skills but also the soft skills and ethical grounding to thrive in this rapidly changing landscape. By addressing these challenges, education can remain a vital force in individual empowerment and societal progress amidst the dawn of IR 5.0.

CONCLUSION

A new cloud computing paradigm called serverless computing is being used to create a variety of software applications. It releases developers from laborious and prone to error infrastructure administration, allowing them to concentrate on the application logic at the granularity of function. Its distinct feature, however, presents fresh difficulties for the creation and implementation of serverless-based systems. There have been significant scientific efforts made to address these issues. An extensive survey of the literature is presented in this article to describe the current state of serverless computing research. Additionally, it determines research priorities, trends, and widely-used serverless computing platforms.

REFERENCES

Aske, A., & Zhao, X. (2018). Supporting Multi-Provider Serverless Computing on the Edge. *Proceedings of the 47th International Conference on Parallel Processing Companion*. ACM. 10.1145/3229710.3229742

Ayyaswamy, K. (2024). Enhancing Digital Technology Planning, Leadership, and Management to Transform Education. In Bhatia, M., & Mushtaq, M. T. (Eds.), *Navigating Innovative Technologies and Intelligent Systems in Modern Education* (pp. 1–9). IGI Global. 10.4018/979-8-3693-5370-7.ch001

Baarzi, A. F., Kesidis, G., Joe-Wong, C., & Shahrad, M. (2021). On Merits and Viability of Multi-Cloud Serverless. *Proceedings of the ACM Symposium on Cloud Computing. SoCC '21*. Association for Computing Machinery. 10.1145/3472883.3487002

Bhupathi, J. (2023). MMF Clustering: A On-demand One-hop Cluster Management in MANET Services Executing Perspective. *International Journal of Novel Research and Development*, 8(4), 127-132.

Gobinath, V., Ayyaswamy, K., & Kathirvel, N. (2024). Information Communication Technology and Intelligent Manufacturing Industries Perspective: An Insight. *Asian Science Bulletin*, 2(1), 36–45. 10.3923/asb.2024.36.45

Gobinath, V. M., Kathirvel, A., Rajesh Kanna, S. K., & Annamalai, K. (2024). Smart Technology in Management Industries: A Useful Perspective. *Artificial Intelligence Applied to Industry 4.0*. Wiley. 10.1002/9781394216147.ch5

Hellerstein, J., Faleiro, J., Gonzalez, J., Schleier-Smith, J., Screekanti, V., Tumanov, A., & Wu, C. (2019). Serverless Computing: One Step Forward, Two Steps Back. arXiv:1812.03651.

Kathirvel, A. (2023). *Systematic Number Plate detection using improved YOLOv5 detector*. Institute of Electrical and Electronics Engineers. .10.1109/ViTE-CoN58111.2023.10157727

Kathirvel, A. (2024a). Applications of Serverless Computing: Systematic Overview. In Aluvalu, R., & Maheswari, U. (Eds.), *Serverless Computing Concepts, Technology and Architecture* (Vol. 221-233). IGI Global. 10.4018/979-8-3693-1682-5.ch014

Kathirvel, A. (2024b). Innovation and Industry Application: IoT-Based Robotics Frontier of Automation in Industry Application. In Satishkumar, D., & Sivaraja, M. (Eds.), *Internet of Things and AI for Natural Disaster Management and Prediction* (pp. 83–105). IGI Global. 10.4018/979-8-3693-4284-8.ch004

Kathirvel, A., & Gobinath, V. M. (2024). A Review on Additive Manufactuing in Industrial. *Modern Hybird Machince and Super Finishing Process: Technology and Application.* CRC Publiser/Chapman and Hall.

Kathirvel, A., Gopinath, V. M., Naren, K., Nithyanand, D., & Nirmaladevi, K. (2024). Manufacturing Smart Industry Perspective an Overview. *American Journal of Engineering and Applied Sciences,* 17(1), 33–39. 10.3844/ajeassp.2024.33.39

Kathirvel, A., & Maheswaran, C. P. (2023). Chapter 8: Enhanced AI-Based Intrusion Detection and Response System for WSN. *Artificial Intelligence for Intrusion Detection Systems.* CRC Publiser/Chapman and Hall. https://www.taylorfrancis.com/chapters/edit/10.1201/9781003346340-8/enhanced-ai-based-intrusion-detection-response-system-wsn-kathirvel-maheswaran10.1201/9781003346340-8

Kathirvel, A., Maheswaran, C. P., Subramaniam, M., & Naren, A. K. (2023). Quantum Computers Based on Distributed Computing Systems for the Next Generation: Overview and Applications. *Handbook of Research on Quantum Computing for Smart Environments.* IGI Global.10.4018/978-1-6684-6697-1.ch025

Kathirvel, A., & Naren, A. K. (2024a). Critical Approaches to Data Engineering Systems Innovation and Industry Application Using IoT. In *Critical Approaches to Data Engineering Systems and Analysis.* IGI Global. 10.4018/979-8-3693-2260-4.ch005

Kathirvel, A., & Naren, A. K. (2024b). Diabetes and Pre-Diabetes Prediction by AI Using Tuned XGB Classifier. In Khang, A. (Ed.), *Medical Robotics and AI-Assisted Diagnostics for a High-Tech Healthcare Industry* (pp. 52–64). IGI Global. 10.4018/979-8-3693-2105-8.ch004

Kathirvel, A., Naren, K., Nithyanand, D., & Santhoshi, B. (2024). Overview of 5G Technology: Streamlined Virtual Event Experiences. *Advances of Robotic Technology,* 2(1), 1–8. 10.23880/art-16000109

Kathirvel, A., & Pavani, A. (2023). *Machine Learning and Deep Learning Algorithms for Network Data Analytics Function in 5G Cellular Networks.* Institute of Electrical and Electronics Engineers Inc publisher. .10.1109/ICICT57646.2023.10134247

Kathirvel, A., Rithik, G., & Naren, A. K. (2024). Automation of IOT Robotics. In *Predicting Natural Disasters With AI and Machine Learning.* IGI Global. 10.4018/979-8-3693-2280-2.ch011

Kathirvel, A., & Shobitha, M. (2023). *Digital Assets Fair Estimation Using Artificial Intelligence.* Institute of Electrical and Electronics Engineers. .10.1109/ViTECoN58111.2023.10157310

Kathirvel, A., Subramaniam, M., Navaneethan, S., & Sabarinath, C. (2021). Improved IDR Response System for Sensor Network. *Journal of Web Engineering, 20*(1). 10.13052/jwe1540-9589.2013

Kathirvel, A., Sudha, D., Naveneethan, S., Subramaniam, M., Das, D. & Kirubakaran, S. (2022). AI Based Mobile Bill Payment System using Biometric Fingerprint. *American Journal of Engineering and Applied Sciences, 15*(1), 23-31. 10.3844/ajeassp.2022.23.31

Kounev, S., Herbst, N., Abad, C., Iosup, A., Foster, I., Shenoy, P., Rana, O., & Chien, A. (2023). Serverless Computing: What It Is, and What It Is Not? *Communications of the ACM.*

Leitner, P., Wittern, E., Spillner, J., & Hummer, W. (2019). A mixed-method empirical study of Function-as-a-Service software development in industrial practice. *Journal of Systems and Software*, 149, 340–359. 10.1016/j.jss.2018.12.013

Naveneethan, S. (2022). Identifying and Eliminating the Misbehavior Nodes in the Wireless Sensor Network. In *Soft Computing and Signal Processing.* Springer International Publishing. 10.1007/978-981-16-7088-6_36

Subramaniam, M., Kathirvel, A., Sabitha, E., & Anwar Basha, H. (2021). Modified Firefly Algorithm and Fuzzy C-Mean Clustering Based Semantic Information Retrieval. *Journal of Web Engineering, 20.* 10.13052/jwe1540-9589.2012

Sudha, D., & Kathirvel, A. (2022a). The effect of ETUS in various generic attacks in mobile ad hoc networks to improve the performance of Aodv protocol. *International Journal of humanities, law, and social sciences, Kanpur philosophers, 9*(1), 467-476.

Sudha, D., & Kathirvel, A. (2022b). An Intrusion Detection System to Detect and Mitigating Attacks Using Hidden Markov Model (HMM) Energy Monitoring Technique. *Stochastic Modeling an Applications, 26*(3), 467-476.

Sudha, D., & Kathirvel, A. (2023). The performance enhancement of Aodv protocol using GETUS. *International Journal of Early Childhood Special Education (INT-JECSE), 15*(2). 10.48047/INTJECSE/V15I2.11

Tozzi, C. (2021). What Is Serverless Computing? *ITPro Today.*

Van Eyk, E., Iosup, A., Abad, C. L., Grohmann, J., & Eismann, S. (2018). A SPEC RG Cloud Group's Vision on the Performance Challenges of FaaS Cloud Architectures. *Companion of the 2018 ACM/SPEC International Conference on Performance Engineering.* ACM. 10.1145/3185768.3186308

Zhao, H., Benomar, Z., Pfandzelter, T., & Georgantas, N. (2022). Supporting Multi-Cloud in Serverless Computing. *2022 IEEE/ACM 15th International Conference on Utility and Cloud Computing (UCC)*, (pp. 285–290). IEEE. 10.1109/UCC56403.2022.00051

Chapter 3
Cloud Computing in Everyday Life:
Revolutionizing How We Live, Work, and Connect

Preety Sharma
https://orcid.org/0009-0005-9918-8449

Maharishi Markandeshwar Institute of Computer Technology and Business Management, India

Ruchi Sharma
Chandigarh School of Business, Jhanjeri, India

Komal Bhardwaj
https://orcid.org/0000-0002-9378-5542

Maharishi Markandeshwar Institute of Management, India

ABSTRACT

In recent years, cloud computing has evolved into an indispensable component of modern existence, profoundly reshaping the manner in which we interact with information, services, and applications. Initially, the authors embark on a comprehensive literature survey which elucidates the intricate dimensions of cloud computing. Subsequently, the focus extends to the myriad domains wherein cloud computing has seamlessly embedded itself into our quotidian routines, from the way we manage and share digital files through cloud storage to the facilitation of online learning, telemedicine, and even the optimization of navigation and mapping services, cloud computing is undeniably ubiquitous. The chapter concludes by deliberating on the profound ramifications of cloud computing on contemporary society, emphasizing the significance of this technology in our daily lives. Additionally, it proffers a

DOI: 10.4018/979-8-3693-2869-9.ch003

forward-looking perspective by identifying potential avenues for future research and development; particularly as cloud computing continues its inexorable march towards greater integration and innovation.

INTRODUCTION

Cloud computing has emerged as a transformative technology that has redefined the way we interact with information, services, and applications. It has become deeply ingrained in our daily lives, whether we are aware of it or not. Cloud computing, in its essence, refers to the delivery of computing services such as storage, processing, and networking over the internet This is a paradigm for information technology services where users can get hardware and software across a network on demand without requiring a device or specific location (Mell & Grance, 2011). This practice of storing and accessing data and applications on remote servers hosted over the internet, as opposed to local servers or the computer's hard drive.

According to the National Institute of Standards and Technology, cloud computing is a model that enables services that can be quickly supplied and implemented with the least amount of administrative labour or service contact, and it is ubiquitous, easy, and shared with a pool of customised computing resources (Marston, 2011). Cloud computing, often known as Internet-based computing, in which the user receives a resource as a service via the Internet. Files, photos, documents, and other storable documents can all be considered types of data that are stored. An alternative to the on-premises datacenter is offered by cloud computing. In an on-premises datacenter, we are responsible for handling all aspect of the setup process, including networking configuration, firewall configuration, operating system installation, virtualization, hardware acquisition and installation, and data storage setup. We take on the responsibility of maintaining it for the duration of its existence after completing all the setup. However, if we go with cloud computing, then purchasing and maintaining the hardware is the responsibility of the cloud company. A vast array of software and platform as a service are also offered by them. The cost of the cloud computing services would vary depending on consumption. Moreover, Investigating better IT services with less money out of pocket is made feasible by cloud computing. The rise in popularity of software as a service can be attributed to cloud computing's influence on the development and procurement of IT hardware.

Cloud computing is a computer paradigm that provides many clients with highly scalable IT-enabled capabilities as a service (Uzoma, & Okhuoya, 2022). It is the application of computer technology based on the internet for a range of services such as storage capacity, processing power, business applications, or component (Haynie, 2009). It is a collection of network-enabled services that provide easily navigable, scalable, assured, and reasonably priced services that are usually customized (Wang et al., 2008). Cloud computing is a computing approach where several external users receive highly scalable IT-related services via the internet (Plummer et al., 2008).

A lot of businesses are using the cloud to supply their services. Here are a few noteworthy instances:

- Google – The company provides Google Docs to its users along with a plethora of other services like email access, document apps, text translations, maps, online analytics, and much more through a private cloud.
- Microsoft — The company presently offers its office applications in the cloud and offers Microsoft® Office 365® online service, which enables the migration of content and business intelligence tools into the cloud.
- Salesforce.com – This company runs its application suite on the cloud for its clients, and its Force.com and Vmforce.com products give developers tools to create personalized cloud services.

In this paper, we aim to explore the extensive role that cloud computing plays in our daily lives. We will begin by providing a brief historical overview of cloud computing and its evolution. Following that, we will conduct a comprehensive literature survey to highlight key research papers, authors, and sources that have contributed significantly to the field. Subsequently, we will delve into the various areas where cloud computing is seamlessly integrated into our daily routines. Finally, we will conclude by discussing the implications of cloud computing in our society and suggest potential avenues for future research and development.

LITERATURE REVIEW

Mell and Grace (2011) provides a foundational definition of cloud computing, outlining the essential characteristics, service models, and deployment models. It has become a reference point for understanding cloud computing concepts. The Berkeley View paper by Armnrust et al. (2009) offers a comprehensive analysis of cloud computing's impact on various industries and its potential to reshape the IT landscape. They introduces key cloud computing challenges and opportunities which then became a standard to use cloud computing in day to day life. Manzoor (2019) provides an in-depth exploration of cloud computing concepts, technologies, and practical applications. It serves as a valuable resource for understanding the breadth of cloud computing. A survey paper by Ghorbel et al. (2017) discusses the security challenges associated with cloud computing and presents potential solutions to address these issues, offering valuable insights into securing cloud-based services.

Senyo et al. (2018) review paper presents a comprehensive bibliography of cloud computing research, providing researchers with a valuable resource for further exploration. A survey paper by Tang et al. (2015) discusses the various security management aspects of cloud computing, shedding light on the importance of securing cloud-based services and data. Kumar & Lu (2010) in their paper explores the energy-saving potential of offloading computational tasks to the cloud, particularly in the context of mobile devices, highlighting its relevance to mobile app users. Martínez, et al. (2015) focusing on the education sector, in their paper presents a state-of-the-art survey of cloud computing applications and benefits in educational settings, including e-learning platforms and student collaboration tools. Kumar & Buyya (2012) examine the environmental impact of cloud computing and discuss strategies for achieving greener cloud solutions, making it relevant in the context of sustainability and environmental awareness. Eskrootchi et al. (2020) in their paper provides insights into the use of cloud computing in healthcare data sharing systems, highlighting the potential to improve patient care through efficient data management. Muda et al. (2020) discuss the role of cloud computing in enhancing government services, promoting transparency, and facilitating citizen engagement in the context of e-government initiatives. Sobhy et al (2018) exploring the intersection of cloud computing and robotics, this paper provides insights into the potential of cloud robotics in enabling advanced automation and remote control of robots. Kalyani & Collier (2021) in their paper surveys the use of cloud computing in agriculture, discussing applications such as precision farming, crop monitoring, and data-driven decision-making for farmers. Rajasekaran et al. (2020) focusing on disaster management, in this paper explores the role of cloud computing in improving disaster response, data collection, and coordination among relief agencies.

USAGE OF CLOUD COMPUTING IN DAILY LIFE

Cloud computing gives users access to cloud-based email and calendaring services. Apps for calling and messaging, like Skype and WhatsApp, are also developed on cloud infrastructure. Not just on your smartphone, but also in the cloud service, are the files and communications you send and receive. There are many different applications for cloud computing in many different fields and sectors. The following are a few of the most popular uses:

Cloud Storage and File Sharing

Cloud storage and file sharing have transformed the way we manage digital content. By utilizing remote servers accessible via the internet, these services, exemplified by platforms like Dropbox, Google Drive, and iCloud, enable users to store, synchronize, and share files seamlessly across devices. This convenience has not only revolutionized personal data management but also streamlined collaborative work in professional settings. Users can effortlessly access their documents, photos, and videos from anywhere, fostering productivity and ensuring data availability while reducing the need for physical storage devices. Cloud storage and file sharing are now integral components of our daily digital routines Armbrust et al. (2009) and Senyo et al. (2018).

Figure 1. Usage of cloud computing in daily life

Email and Communication

Email and communication services have been revolutionized by cloud computing. Cloud-based email platforms such as Gmail and Outlook store messages, attachments, and contacts on remote servers, ensuring accessibility from anywhere with an internet connection. This enables efficient, real-time communication for both personal and professional use. Moreover, cloud-powered communication tools like Zoom and Microsoft Teams have become essential for remote work, virtual meetings, and collaboration among global teams. Cloud computing enhances the reliability, scalability, and security of these services, making email and communication more flexible, accessible, and indispensable in our daily lives Kumar & Lu (2010).

Social Media and Entertainment

Social media and entertainment have undergone a profound transformation due to the pervasive influence of cloud computing. Popular platforms like Facebook, Instagram, and Twitter harness cloud infrastructure to support their vast user bases and deliver real-time updates, multimedia content, and interactive features. This scalability ensures seamless user experiences, even during traffic spikes or when sharing media-rich content.

Moreover, streaming services like Netflix and Spotify heavily rely on cloud computing to provide on-demand access to movies, TV shows, and music. The cloud enables content storage, management, and global distribution, making it possible for users to enjoy a rich library of entertainment content from any device with an internet connection.

The integration of cloud computing in social media and entertainment not only enhances accessibility but also encourages user engagement and collaboration. It has ushered in an era of interactive and personalized entertainment experiences, redefining how we connect, share, and consume content in our daily lives Muda et al. (2020).

E-Commerce and Online Shopping

Cloud computing has revolutionized the landscape of e-commerce and online shopping, fundamentally altering how businesses operate and consumers shop. Leading e-commerce giants like Amazon, Alibaba, and eBay leverage cloud infrastructure to manage massive product catalogs, process transactions, and offer personalized shopping experiences.

Cloud-based services enable e-commerce websites to scale dynamically during peak shopping seasons, ensuring uninterrupted service and faster load times. This scalability also facilitates the use of advanced analytics and machine learning algorithms for product recommendations and targeted marketing, enhancing the overall shopping experience.

Moreover, cloud computing empowers smaller e-commerce businesses to compete effectively by providing access to cost-effective and scalable resources, such as serverless computing and cloud-based databases.

In essence, cloud computing has enabled e-commerce platforms to offer seamless, secure, and efficient online shopping experiences to consumers worldwide. It has transformed how we discover, purchase, and receive goods, making online shopping an integral part of our daily lives Kalyani & Collier (2021).

Online Learning and Education

The integration of cloud technology has enabled the widespread adoption of online educational platforms and tools. Cloud-based Learning Management Systems (LMS) like Moodle, Canvas, and Blackboard provide educators and students with easy access to course materials, assignments, and collaborative tools, fostering a more flexible and interactive learning environment.

Cloud computing ensures that educational resources, such as video lectures, textbooks, and assignments, can be stored, managed, and accessed securely from anywhere, at any time. This flexibility has made online learning accessible to a global audience, breaking down geographical barriers.

Furthermore, cloud-based collaboration tools and video conferencing platforms, such as Zoom and Google Meet, have become integral for remote learning and virtual classrooms. Cloud technology enables real-time interactions, facilitating student-teacher engagement and peer collaboration.

In summary, cloud computing has democratized education, making it possible for learners of all ages to access quality educational content and collaborate remotely. It has reshaped how we acquire knowledge and skills, making online learning an essential part of our daily educational experiences González (2015).

Healthcare and Telemedicine

Cloud computing has significantly impacted healthcare and telemedicine, enhancing patient care and medical services. Cloud-based Electronic Health Records (EHR) systems securely store and share patient data among healthcare providers, ensuring comprehensive and coordinated care. Telemedicine platforms utilize the cloud to facilitate remote consultations, enabling patients to connect with healthcare professionals from their homes. Cloud technology enhances the scalability and accessibility of healthcare services, reducing geographical barriers and improving healthcare access, especially in underserved areas. It also supports data analytics and machine learning applications for medical research, diagnosis, and treatment planning. Cloud computing has become vital in modern healthcare, offering efficient and patient-centered solutions that are integrated into our daily healthcare experiences Eskrootchi (2020).

Navigation and Maps

Cloud computing plays a pivotal role in navigation and mapping services, transforming how we navigate our daily lives. GPS and mapping applications like Google Maps, Waze, and Apple Maps rely on cloud-based data storage and processing to provide real-time traffic updates, accurate directions, and location-based services. The cloud enables seamless integration of data from various sources, including user-generated information and live traffic feeds, ensuring up-to-date and reliable navigation assistance. These services have become an integral part of our daily routines, guiding us through unfamiliar places, optimizing routes, and even recommending nearby businesses and services. Cloud-powered navigation and maps enhance convenience and efficiency in our everyday travels.

Internet of Things (IoT)

Cloud computing is the backbone of the Internet of Things (IoT), transforming our daily lives through smart devices. IoT devices collect and transmit data to cloud platforms, where it is processed, analyzed, and made accessible in real-time. From smart thermostats and wearable fitness trackers to industrial sensors and connected appliances, IoT relies on the cloud to enable remote monitoring, automation, and control. This technology enhances convenience, efficiency, and productivity in various aspects of our daily routines, including home automation, healthcare, transportation, and manufacturing. Cloud-powered IoT is instrumental in creating a connected world where devices seamlessly interact to improve our lives.

Finance and Banking

In the realm of finance and banking, cloud computing has ushered in a wave of innovation and efficiency. Financial institutions employ cloud technology for secure transaction processing, customer account management, and data analytics. The cloud enables banks to scale their operations, ensuring uninterrupted services and robust security measures. Additionally, it facilitates the development of fintech solutions, including mobile banking apps and digital wallets, enhancing customer experiences. Cloud-based analytics and machine learning assist in fraud detection and risk assessment. Overall, cloud computing has transformed how we conduct financial transactions and access banking services, making them more convenient, accessible, and secure in our daily financial interactions Muda (2020).

Gaming

Cloud computing has revolutionized the gaming industry, allowing for innovative approaches to gaming experiences. Cloud gaming platforms like Google Stadia, NVIDIA GeForce NOW, and Xbox Cloud Gaming (formerly known as Project xCloud) stream games directly from the cloud to users' devices. This eliminates the need for high-end gaming hardware, making gaming more accessible and convenient. Gamers can play high-quality, resource-intensive games on various devices with lower latency. The cloud also enables cross-platform play and seamless game updates. This transformation has made cloud gaming an integral part of our daily gaming experiences, offering flexibility and expanding the gaming community across different platforms and devices.

CONCLUSION AND FUTURE SCOPE

Cloud computing has profoundly impacted our daily lives, offering convenience, scalability, and accessibility across various domains. Its role is only expected to grow as technology continues to evolve. However, as cloud adoption increases, concerns about security, privacy, and data governance persist. Future research should focus on addressing these challenges while exploring innovative applications of cloud computing in emerging fields such as edge computing, quantum computing, and AI-driven cloud services.

In conclusion, cloud computing is no longer a mere technology trend but an integral part of our modern existence. It empowers individuals, businesses, and organizations to thrive in an increasingly digital and interconnected world. Understanding its significance and potential is essential as we continue to navigate the evolving landscape of technology and society.

REFERENCES

Armbrust, M., Fox, A., Griffith, R., Joseph, A. D., Katz, R. H., Konwinski, A., & Zaharia, M. (2009). *Above the clouds: A berkeley view of cloud computing (Vol. 17)*. Technical Report UCB/EECS-2009-28, EECS Department, University of California, Berkeley.

. Eskrootchi, R., Arjmandi, M. K., Langarizadeh, M., & Yuvaraj, M. (2020). Key factors influencing the adoption of Cloud Computing Technology in the Medical Sciences University libraries. *Library Philosophy and Practice*, 1-27.

Ghorbel, A., Ghorbel, M., & Jmaiel, M. (2017). Privacy in cloud computing environments: A survey and research challenges. *The Journal of Supercomputing*, 73(6), 2763–2800. 10.1007/s11227-016-1953-y

González-Martínez, J. A., Bote-Lorenzo, M. L., Gómez-Sánchez, E., & Cano-Parra, R. (2015). Cloud computing and education: A state-of-the-art survey. *Computers & Education*, 80, 132–151. 10.1016/j.compedu.2014.08.017

Haynie, M. (2009). Enterprise cloud services: Deriving business value from Cloud Computing. *Micro Focus*, 56-61.

Kalyani, Y., & Collier, R. (2021). A systematic survey on the role of cloud, fog, and edge computing combination in smart agriculture. *Sensors (Basel)*, 21(17), 5922. 10.3390/s2117592234502813

Kumar, K., & Lu, Y. H. (2010). Cloud computing for mobile users: Can offloading computation save energy? *Computer*, 43(4), 51–56. 10.1109/MC.2010.98

Kumar, S., & Buyya, R. (2012). Green cloud computing and environmental sustainability. *Harnessing green IT: principles and practices*, 315-339.

Manzoor, A. (2019). Cloud Computing Applications in the Public Sector. In *Cloud Security: Concepts, Methodologies, Tools, and Applications* (pp. 1241-1272). IGI Global. 10.4018/978-1-5225-8176-5.ch063

Marston, S., Li, Z., Bandyopadhyay, S., Zhang, J., & Ghalsasi, A. (2011). Cloud computing—The business perspective. *Decision Support Systems*, 51(1), 176–189. 10.1016/j.dss.2010.12.006

Mell, P., & Grance, T. (2011). *The NIST Definition of Cloud Computing. National Institute of Standards and Technology*. NIST.

Muda, J., Tumsa, S., Tuni, A., & Sharma, D. P. (2020). Cloud-enabled E-governance framework for citizen centric services. *Journal of Computer and Communications*, 8(7), 63–78. 10.4236/jcc.2020.87006

. Plummer, D. C., Bittman, T. J., Austin, T., Cearley, D. W., & Smith, D. M. (2008). Cloud computing: Defining and describing an emerging phenomenon. *Gartner, 17*, 1-9.

Rajasekaran, R., Govinda, K., Masih, J., & Sruthi, M. (2020). Health Monitoring System for Individuals Using Internet of Things. In *Incorporating the Internet of Things in Healthcare Applications and Wearable Devices* (pp. 150–164). IGI Global. 10.4018/978-1-7998-1090-2.ch009

Senyo, P. K., Addae, E., & Boateng, R. (2018). Cloud computing research: A review of research themes, frameworks, methods and future research directions. *International Journal of Information Management*, 38(1), 128–139. 10.1016/j.ijinfomgt.2017.07.007

Sobhy, A. R., Khalil, A. T., Elfaham, M. M., & Hashad, A. (2018). Cloud Robotics: A Survey. *International Journal of Latest Research in Engineering and Technology*, 4(05), 46–52.

Tang, S., Li, X., Huang, X., Xiang, Y., & Xu, L. (2015). Achieving simple, secure and efficient hierarchical access control in cloud computing. *IEEE Transactions on Computers*, 65(7), 2325–2331. 10.1109/TC.2015.2479609

. Uzoma, B. C., & Okhuoya, I. B.(2022) A research on cloud computing.

Wang, L., Tao, J., Kunze, M., Castellanos, A. C., Kramer, D., & Karl, W. (2008). Scientific cloud computing: Early definition and experience. In *2008 10th IEEE international conference on high performance computing and communications* (pp. 825-830). IEEE.

Chapter 4
Auto–Scaling in the Cloud

Saikat Gochhait

https://orcid.org/0000-0003-4583-9208

Symbiosis Institute of Digital and Telecom Management, Symbiosis International University (Deemed), India

ABSTRACT

Cloud computing is gaining momentum as a subscription-oriented paradigm providing on-demand payable access to virtualized IT services and products across the net. It is a breakthrough technology that is offering on-demand access to various services across the network. Auto-scaling, though quite an attractive proposition to customers and naïve cloud service providers, has its own share of issues and challenges. This work was an attempt to classify and appreciate the auto scaling framework while outlining its challenges. Many effective and efficient auto scaling strategies are being deployed by cloud giants like Amazon AWS, Microsoft Azure, etc.

INTRODUCTION

Cloud Computing is gaining momentum as a subscription-oriented paradigm providing on-demand payable access to virtualized IT services and products across the net (Ai et al., 2016). It is a breakthrough technology that is offering on-demand access to various services across the network (Bhatia et al., 2018). Currently, Amazon, Dell, Google, HP, IBM, Salesforce, Rackspace etc are few of the popular service providers (Agrawal & Bhatt, 2015; Sagar, 2016). Cloud computing being an on-demand payable service enables reduction in power and resource consumption. However, consumer demand and application usage can be varied across different times of a day, week, month and year. Hence, capacity planners need to develop a resilient infrastructure elastic, flexible and robust enough to handle peak demands on an immediate basis. In technical terms cloud service providers need to have efficient

DOI: 10.4018/979-8-3693-2869-9.ch004

combat mechanisms to guard their customers especially new start-ups from what is called Slashdot effect (Fazli & Shulman, 2017). The Slashdot effect is characterised by a sudden, significant increase in a firms load resulting in slowing down or crashing of their servers. To effectively handle such fluctuating demands cloud computing has adopted auto scaling as one of its features. Auto scaling or cloud elasticity enabler dynamically distributes (acquires and releases) required computational resources (virtual machine instances) to applications to match their current demands appropriately (Dougherty et al., 2012). The technique is advantageous as it reduces idle time while increasing server utilization and reducing harmful emissions like CO_2 (Dougherty et al., 2012). Auto scaling enables the cloud service provider to maintain their QoS (Quality of Service) agreement with the client while scaling up resources when demand increases and releasing free resources when demand decreases in a dynamic fashion (Evangelidis et al., 2017; Gopal Dhaker, 2014). It further provides a consistent mechanism to efficiently scale out or scale in instances as demand increases or decreases (Xiao et al., 2014). This chapter analyzes the auto scaling feature of cloud computing in detail.

TYPES OF SCALING

Cloud auto scaling is the key feature that allows service providers to dynamically provision their resources as on client demand (Agrawal & Bhatt, 2015). To handle this distribution cloud service providers are now officially maintaining a guaranteed SLA (Service-Level Agreement) with their clients. This ensures that a cloud automatically allocates more resources through either scale-up or scale-out in cases of high demand (Banker & Jain, 2014; Hwang et al., 2016; Netto et al., 2015). At its most basic level, a cloud can either be scaled up/down or in/out (Hirashima et al., 2016). These types of cloud auto scaling are elaborated below:

i.   Horizontal Scaling: Ability to connect multiple hardware or software entities like servers etc so that they work in cohesion as a single logical unit (Kriushanth et al., 2013). It implies increasing the number of entities doing the same job. Most of the existing cloud service providers are good at this. Also referred to as scaling out. Though the mechanism provides larger scale resources but may also waste resources sometimes (Yang et al., 2013). Further the new added virtual machines cannot be immediately put into operation and may require several minutes to boot. It is also a costly approach as compared to auto scaling (Yang et al., 2013). Very useful in dealing with traffic (Beaumont, 2014).

ii. Vertical Cloud Scaling: Increase the ability or capacity of existing infrastructure i.e. adding more resources or replacing an existing server with a more specialized one. Also referred to as scaling up. It is generally implemented through altering partition of resources in a VM (Yang et al., 2013). As compared to horizontal scaling it can scale virtual resources in a few milliseconds without shutting down the machine. The only limiting factor can be amount of physical resources available to a VM. On the brighter side it can resize your server with zero code change (Beaumont, 2014).

iii. Hybrid Scaling: An intelligent amalgamation of vertical as well as horizontal scaling is being effectively applied in real world to achieve an optimal scaling strategy. SmartScale (Dutta et al., 2012) is based on this technique to optimize resource handling as well as reconfiguration costs.

As per another classification, scaling can also be classified as manual and auto, where auto scaling further can be either reactive or proactive. Table I below gives a preliminary comparison of reactive and proactive scaling technique.

Table 1. Cloud scaling types

S. No	Technique	Users	Pros	Cons
1	Manual Scaling (Kaur et al., 2018; Lorido-Botrán et al., 2013)	Amazon EC2 (AWS Auto Scaling)	Involves manual forecasting and manual addition of resources.	Time Consuming requires constant supervision as well as advance forecasting of altering demands.
2	Auto Scaling	AWS, Google Cloud, Windows Azure, Facebook	Pre-configuration to automatically create new instances upto a maximum specified threshold.	Response time may not be necessarily fast, efficient capacity planning still required, Slashdot may strike (Reese, 2008)
i	Reactive Scaling (Hirashima et al., 2016; Liu et al., 2015; Lorido-Botrán et al., 2013)	Amazon EC2	Simple to set up. Easy to implement.	Difficult to tune and set correct thresholds, thus unable to cope with sudden load bursts. Longer Virtual Machine boot up time (Nikravesh et al., 2015).
ii	Proactive Scaling (Lorido-Botrán et al., 2013)	(Tran et al., 2017)	Considers VM boot up time	Suitable in situations with predictable load characteristics. Also called cyclic or event-based as one knows beforehand when there is going to be increase in traffic.

Auto-Scaling Frameworks

Auto Scaling being a novel key component of cloud frameworks has been effectively implemented in a number of public as well as private cloud instances to effectively handle consumer load. This section describes certain significant auto-scaling frameworks implemented for the cloud. Table I below enlists the same:

Table 2. Significant cloud auto-scaling frameworks

S. No	Ref.	Framework	Description	Remarks
1	(Gandhi et al., 2014; Gandhi et al., 2017)	Dependable Compute Cloud (DC2)	Automatically scales cloud infrastructure to meet user-specified performance requirements. Proactively learns system parameters for each application through Kalman filtering.	Integration with vertical and predictive scaling models can further enhance its genericity.
2	(Gandhi et al., 2017; Tseng et al., 2018)	Fuzzy-based Real-time Auto-Scaling (FARS) mechanism	Dynamic, real-time automatic scaling of internet applications in cloud environment through container-based virtualization technology.	FRAS enables faster reaction to rapidly-changing service Demand pressures.
3	(Shen et al., 2011)	CloudScale	Elastic resource Scaling automated for multi-tenant cloud computing infrastructures.	Lightweight, non-intrusive, low-resource and cost incurring alternative.
4	(Biswas et al., 2017)	Hybrid Resource Auto Scaling	Combines a machine learning proactive approach with a reactive approach for scaling resources to adapt to changes in workload demands.	Profit generator for intermediary cloud provider and cost reducer for the user while elimination need for capacity planning.
5	(AWS, n.d.-g)	Amazon Web Services	A cloud web-hosting platform offering reliable, scalable, easy to use and cost-effective solutions for varied services through an Elastic Compute Cloud (EC2) service.	It incorporates Elastic Load balancing (ELB) facility to automatically auto-scale incoming request traffic across multiple Amazon EC2 instances.
6	(Bhatia et al., 2018)	Dynamic Auto Scaling	Adaptive threshold tuning strategy that can quicken the conception of virtual machines as per traffic pattern. Utilizes a dynamic auto scaling module by means of Infrastructure as a Code.	Results in the reduction of response latency of the web application under a stress workload.

Table II above highlights some of the significant auto-scaling techniques for cloud. To take complete advantage of the cloud environment, it is important to efficiently choose an appropriate auto scaling strategy that can adjust resources in accordance to the incoming load in a cost as well as service- optimized manner (Lorido-Botrán et al., 2013).

Advantages of Auto-Scaling

Like all technology auto-scaling also has its own set of advantages as well as disadvantages. If not implemented properly it can cause disastrous effects. To better appreciate the same, we first try to understand the advantages of this scheme:

a. Minimizes response time during high load and reduces cost during low load (Dougherty et al., 2012): Auto Scaling can result in better cost management as it is capable of dynamically increasing and decreasing capacity as and when required. Studies have found that cost savings upto 57% can be achieved where there is a linear correlation between expenditure and IT resource requirements (Selvon-Bruce, 2016).

b. Better Fault Tolerance: Auto Scaling can automatically detect an unhealthy instance and replace it with another one while terminating the unhealthy one. It can also help in configuring and creating multiple availability zones.

c. Better Availability: Auto Scaling helps ensuring that a particular application always has the right capacity to handle incoming traffic.

d. Almost Zero Capital Expenditures: Due to auto scaling in the cloud one does not need to plan or expend money on buying, installing, configuring and maintaining multiple servers, operating systems, databases etc. With Auto Scaling one can directly start running their application in the AWS cloud or any other Cloud Service Provider (CSP) and continue growing resources as required. Example: Blue Spurs (Selvon-Bruce, 2016).

Issues Due to Auto-Scaling

Auto-Scaling is not just a policy or inherent characteristic. Further achieving auto scaling in a cloud environment is not an easy task (Bhushan, 2012; Nilabja Roy, 2011). For it to be completely successful it needs to successfully address a number of issues, some of which are outlined below:

a. **Virtual Machines be provisioned and booted quickly to meet response time demands effectively as load fluctuates** (Dougherty et al., 2012): A Virtual Machine may take upto 10 min to boot up and be ready to handle incoming user traffic. Reducing this boot up time is important in the cloud as delay of even a few minutes may result in application failure. (Mahfuzur, 2016) achieves provisioning elasticity through a hybrid approach that combines static and dynamic provisioning to provide a better infrastructure to the cloud.

b. **Concurrent Resource Scaling conflict for multiple co-located applications** (Shen et al., 2011): Scaling conflicts may arise when available resources are insufficient to accommodate all scale-up requirements on specific hosts. For predicting such conflicts either some application scale-up requirements are discarded or VM migration is employed to moderate the conflict. To resolve such a case local conflict handling and migration-based conflict handling schemes are employed to resolve conflicts (Gupta et al., 2011).

c. **Absence of Universal, reliable auto-scaling policies** (Evangelidis et al., 2017): Heterogeneity of the cloud resources combined with large configuration space for parameters to be taken into account challenge defining reliable, generic auto-scaling policies for public cloud providers.

d. **MAPE Loop** (Maurer et al., 2011; Qu et al., 2016): To guarantee Quality of Service in the cloud, different goals have to be dynamically achieved between the customer and the Cloud Service Provider (CSP). To manage such infrastructural demands, autonomic computing has been proposed as a solution (Maurer et al., 2011). Basic design of autonomic system is represented through the Monitoring, Analysis, Planning, Execution (MAPE) loops. This loop has been extended further as the MAPE-K loop where K stands for Knowledge. However, choosing a suitable MAPE or MAPE-K system for a cloud remains an invincible research endeavour.

e. **Differentiation between valid and malicious traffic** (Goseva-Popstojanova et al., 2014; Kriushanth et al., 2013): Web systems are continuously under security vulnerability and threat due to their constant exposure to varied clients through browsers. Hence, characterization and classification of malicious cyber activity is important. The same is a challenge in auto scaling as scaling an application resource to handle malicious traffic can prove to be suicidal.

f. **State-transition overhead** (Nilabja Roy, 2011):When the number of resources available to a VM are altered it results in state-transition overhead. In auto scaling strategies both acquiring and releasing resources with altering workload causes overhead. Numerous factors like calling the cloud API to start the resource allocation, booting up both the machine and application at specific states generates overhead. Reducing this overhead to the minimal possible is desirable option generally achieved through implementation of effective workload forecasting strategies.

g. **Bad Configuration** (Kriushanth et al., 2013): Badly configured auto scaling shall increase the cost rather than reducing the same.

h. **Yo-Yo Attack** (Efi Arazi School of Computer Science, 2016): Oscillates the auto scaling mechanism between scale up and scale down phases by attacking the cloud periodic overload bursts. Results in performance deteoriation along with cost dwindling. Specifically this attack is hard to detect. It is also known as reduction of quality attack. It reveals the vulnerability of the auto scaling mechanism.

Auto Scaling Through Amazon AWS: A Case

To maintain applications on the cloud and adjust them to user request traffic at the least possible cost, Amazon AWS is a popular alternative among many CSPs (AWS, 2014a; AWS, 2014b; AWS, 2016; AWS, 2018; AWS, n.d.-a; AWS, n.d.-b; AWS, n.d.-c; AWS, n.d.-d; AWS, n.d.-e; AWS, n.d.-h). AWS a popular short form for Amazon Web Services is an Amazon subsidiary providing on-demand cloud computing platforms to individuals, organizations and government on a paid use basis. The AWS cloud is one of the leading cloud service providers to many varied client applications. Table III below lists some actual clients of the AWS cloud:

Table 3. Some noteworthy clients of AWS cloud

S. No	Client	Description	Scaling Strategy
1	Expedia (AWS, n.d.-h)	An online travel-booking service provider (www .expedia.co.in) that globally supports all websites under the expedia brand through Expedia Worldwide Engineering (EWE). In 2010, expedia started using Amazon AWS to launch Expedia Suggest Services (ESS). The company further plans to enhance its agility and resiliency by migrating 80 percent of its mission-critical apps to the AWS cloud in the next 2-3 years span.	As per records expedia processes approximately 240 requests per second. AWS considerable advantage is the fact that it relies on AWS auto scaling to meet capacity demands at all times.
2	Pinterest (AWS, 2018)	One of the world's largest visual bookmarking tools provider with over 70 million monthly active user's base and 50 billion pins. Company relies on AWS to maintain developer velocity, site scalability, and multiple petabytes of data across its massive search index.	To handle its large customer base expedia also relies on AWS auto scaling to robustly handle all demands 24X7.
3	ABP News (AWS, n.d.-d)	ABP News Network (ANN) one of the leading TV news network in the country operates in five Indian languages with a user base of over 150 million audiences per week. To meet the consumer demand for immediate ubiquitous access to content it has adopted a server less architecture using AWS.	With an estimated growth of 150-500 million page views along with traffic spikes of up to 6 times during peak periods ANN has robustly managed its scaling through the AWS auto scaling.

continued on following page

Table 3. Continued

S. No	Client	Description	Scaling Strategy
4	Abof (AWS, n.d.-c)	The Aditya Birla online fashion store (www.abof .com) is an e-commerce venture spanning across over 500 Indian cities. With an attractive GUI for desktop as well as mobile clients the stores also provide a 3D trial room facility. To manage this huge conglomerate in a server less, maintenance free framework the group switched from the IBM e-commerce application stack to the AWS.	The motivation behind choice of AWS cloud was the ease of use. Hence, the online store launched in 2015 created on IBM technology stack all-in on AWS. Auto Scaling is used to handle peak time customer traffic.
5	ACTi (AWS, n.d.-e)	Founded in 2003, ACTi is a leading end-to-end IP video surveillance solution provider. To overcome the customer cost involved in deploying large scale physical infrastructures, ACTi has adopted the AWS cloud to provide cloud-based solutions to all clients big or small alike.	The company leveraged multiple AWS products like the Amazon Elastic Compute Cloud (EC2) for computing power etc. It deploys Amazon Route 53 and Elastic load balancing to effectively distribute incoming traffic across multiple EC2 instances.
6	Adobe (AWS, n.d.-f)	Adobe is a renowned provider of varied enterprise software to Fortune-100 companies and many multinational giants. It has also adopted the AWS cloud to enable multi-terabyte customer operating environments.	To manage peta, tera and gigabytes of customer data with ease Adobe relies on the AWS auto scaling.

Table III above is only a glimpse of the AWS cloud success story and tip of its long-list of customers. The AWS auto scaling feature allows simple and fast application scaling options for applications demanding multiple resources across multiple services in minutes. It enables a simple yet powerful user interface to allow users build their scaling plans for different resources like Amazon EC2 instances, Amazon ECS tasks, Amazon Dynamo tables and Amazon Amora replicas. AWS allows performance optimization with balanced cost expenditure to ensure that an application always has the correct resources at the appropriate time.

Though many professionals are against the AWS auto scaling(Reese, 2008), however fact remains that many real-life organizations have effectively tapped their client traffic through it. Getting started with AWS Auto Scaling is also not difficult and can be done easily either through AWS Management Console, Command Line Interface (CLI) or SDK. Further this service is absolutely free for the client as they have to only pay for the resources being used and Amazon CloudWatch monitoring fees. Instead this facility is one among the building blocks if you wish to use an Amazon EC2 instance. Briefly described the set up involves four major tasks as listed below:

i.   Generate a Launch template
ii. Generate an Auto Scaling Group
iii. Verify your Auto Scaling Group

iv. Delete your Scaling Infrastructure (Optional)

The step-by-step detailed guidelines for the same can be accessed from https://docs.aws.amazon.com/autoscaling/ec2/userguide/GettingStartedTutorial.html (AWS, n.d.-g).

FUTURE DIRECTIONS AND CONCLUSION

Auto Scaling though quite an attractive proposition to customers and naïve cloud service providers, has its own share of issues and challenges. This work was an attempt to classify and appreciate the auto scaling framework while outlining its challenges. Many effective and efficient auto scaling strategies are being deployed by cloud giants like Amazon AWS, Microsoft Azure etc. However, this is not the end of the road. Many other extensions to the auto scaling framework are also being researched. Certain significant ones are outlined below:

i.   **Enabler to Elastic Computing through Elastic Scaling** (Ai et al., 2016; Benz & Bohnert, 2015; Saini & Pandey, 2017): Elastic Scaling is an extension of auto scaling that improves performance further by detecting and elevating issues during program runtime. It implements statistical process monitoring and control along with Western Elastic rules to scale cloud application performance (Benz & Bohnert, 2015; Lorido-Botran et al., 2014).

ii. **Inter-Cloud Auto Scaling** (Kamiya, & Shimokawa, 2020): A natural extension to auto scaling for implementing meta-cloud computing systems. It extends auto scaling by spanning it across multiple cloud computing systems. Hence, it originates new virtual machines outside original cloud computing system. A major advantage of this framework is the fact that instead of user selecting the appropriate cloud computing system, the meta-cloud system automatically allocates a suitable cloud computing system for a new virtual machine on basis of pre-defined cloud selection policies. As a result inter-cloud auto-scaling also results in higher external bandwidth and reduces the round trip time lag between the clients and servers. "Soarin" a prototype system for the meta-cloud model is already implemented.

iii. **Auto Scaling through Workload Classification** (Ali-eldin et al., 2013): Workload Analysis and Classification (WAC) tools are being proposed to analyze workloads and propose them to the most suitable elasticity controllers based on workloads characteristics and business level objectives.

Case Study

Shopify is a global commerce platform powering more than 500,000 entrepreneurs and businesses, and in 2016 they served over 100 million shoppers. They are based in Ottawa, Canada, but have a global presence with over 900 engineers.

Having outgrown their previous hosted CI provider, Shopify needed to reduce their build times from 40 minutes to less than 10 minutes. At the same time, they were scaling their engineering team from 300 to 900 and expanding across multiple time zones.

Buildkite enabled Shopify to auto-scale their build servers to match their engineering teams' peak demand, and they now run almost 10,000 concurrent build agents. Buildkite's agent architecture allowed them to take full advantage of cloud cost reduction features, providing a much larger compute capacity for the same cost, and allowed them to smoothly transition from AWS to Google Cloud.

In the face of 300% team growth, Shopify has maintained their targets of keeping build times under 10 minutes, and have been able to apply the same scaling techniques to their key Android and iOS projects.

REFERENCES

Agrawal, K., & Bhatt, N. (2015). *Survey On Scalability In Cloud Environment*, 2(3), 18–22.

Ai, W., Li, K., Lan, S., Zhang, F., Mei, J., Li, K., & Buyya, R. (2016). *On Elasticity Measurement in Cloud Computing* (Vol. 2016). Sci. Program.

Ali-eldin, A., Tordsson, J., Elmroth, E., & Kihl, M. (2013). *Workload Classification for Efficient Auto-Scaling of Cloud Resources.*

AWS. (2014a). *2U Case Study.* Amazon Web Services (AWS). https://aws.amazon.com/solutions/case-studies/2u/.

AWS. (2014b). *6waves Case Study.* Amazon Web Services (AWS). https://aws.amazon.com/solutions/case-studies/6waves/

AWS. (2016). *91App Case Study.* Amazon Web Services (AWS). https://aws.amazon.com/solutions/case-studies/91app/

AWS, . (2018). Pinterest Case Study. https://aws.amazon.com/solutions/case-studies/pinterest/

AWS. (n.d.-a). 9Splay Case Study. Amazon Web Services (AWS). https://aws.amazon.com/solutions/case-studies/9splay/.

AWS. (n.d.-b). *Abema TV Case Study.* Amazon Web Services (AWS). https://aws.amazon.com/solutions/case-studies/abema-tv/..

AWS. (n.d.-c). *abof Case Study.* Amazon Web Services (AWS). https://aws.amazon.com/solutions/case-studies/abof/.

AWS. (n.d.-d). *ABP News Case Study.* Amazon Web Services (AWS). https://aws.amazon.com/solutions/case-studies/abp_news/.

AWS. (n.d.-e). *ACTi Case Study.* Amazon Web Services. https://aws.amazon.com/solutions/case-studies/acti-case-study/.

AWS. (n.d.-f). *Adobe Systems Case Study.* Amazon Web Services (AWS). https://aws.amazon.com/solutions/case-studies/adobe/.

AWS. (n.d.-g). *Cloud Computing Services.* Amazon Web Services (AWS). https://aws.amazon.com/

AWS. (n.d.-h). Expedia Case Study. AWS. https://aws.amazon.com/solutions/case-studies/expedia/

Banker, G., & Jain, G. (2014). *A Literature Survey on Cloud AutoScaling Mechanisms. International Journal of Engineering Development and Research,* 2(4).

Beaumont, D. (2014). *How to explain vertical and horizontal scaling in the cloud - Cloud computing news.* IBM. https://www.ibm.com/blogs/cloud-computing/2014/04/09/explain-vertical-horizontal-scaling-cloud/

Benz, K., & Bohnert, T. M. (2015). Elastic Scaling of Cloud Application Performance Based on Western Electric Rules by Injection of Aspect-oriented Code. *Procedia Computer Science,* 61, 198–205. 10.1016/j.procs.2015.09.193

Bhatia, J., Patni, S., Trivedi, H., & Bhavsar, M. (2018). *Infrastructure as a Code in Cloud Environment for Dynamic Auto Scaling,* 16(1), 159–164.

Bhushan, S. (2012). *A Comprehensive Study on Cloud Computing.* Research Gate.

Biswas, A., Majumdar, S., Nandy, B., & El-Haraki, A. (2017). A hybrid auto-scaling technique for clouds processing applications with service level agreements. *Journal of Cloud Computing (Heidelberg, Germany),* 6(1), 29. 10.1186/s13677-017-0100-5

Dougherty, B., White, J., & Schmidt, D. C. (2012). Model-driven auto-scaling of green cloud computing infrastructure. *Future Generation Computer Systems,* 28(2), 371–378. 10.1016/j.future.2011.05.009

Dutta, S., Gera, S., Verma, A., & Viswanathan, B. (2012). SmartScale: Automatic Application Scaling in Enterprise Clouds. *2012 IEEE Fifth International Conference on Cloud Computing,* , pp. 221–228. 10.1109/CLOUD.2012.12

Efi Arazi School of Computer Science. (2016). *DDoS and Cloud Auto-Scaling Mechanism.* Efi Arazi School of Computer Science.

Evangelidis, A., Parker, D., & Bahsoon, R. (2017). Performance Modelling and Verification of Cloud-Based Auto-Scaling Policies. *Proc. - 2017 17th IEEE/ACM Int. Symp. Clust. Cloud Grid Comput. CCGRID 2017,* (pp. 355–364). IEEE. 10.1109/CCGRID.2017.39

Fazli, A. & Shulman, J. (2017). *The Effects of Autoscaling in Cloud Computing on Product Launch.*

Gandhi, A., Dube, P., & Karve, A. (2014). Adaptive, Model-driven Autoscaling for Cloud Applications. *11 th USENIX Conf. Auton. Comput.* Research Gate.

Gandhi, A., Dube, P., Karve, A., Kochut, A. P., & Zhang, L. (2017). Providing Performance Guarantees for Cloud-deployed Applications. *IEEE Transactions on Cloud Computing,* 7161(c), 1–14.

Gopal Dhaker, D. S. S. (2014). #1, Auto-Scaling, Load Balancing and Monitoring As service in public cloud\n,. *IOSR Journal of Computer Engineering*, 16(4), 39–46. 10.9790/0661-16413946

Goseva-Popstojanova, K., Anastasovski, G., Dimitrijevikj, A., Pantev, R., & Miller, B. (2014). Characterization and classification of malicious Web traffic. *Computers & Security*, 42, 92–115. 10.1016/j.cose.2014.01.006

Gupta, M., Boyd, L., & Kuzmits, F. (2011). The evaporating cloud: A tool for resolving workplace conflict. *International Journal of Conflict Management*, 22(4), 394–412. 10.1108/10444061111171387

Hirashima, Y., Yamasaki, K., & Nagura, M. (2016). Proactive-reactive auto-scaling mechanism for unpredictable load change. *Proc. - 2016 5th IIAI Int. Congr. Adv. Appl. Informatics, IIAI-AAI 2016*, pp. 861–866. IEEE. 10.1109/IIAI-AAI.2016.180

Hwang, K., Bai, X., Shi, Y., Li, M., Chen, W. G., & Wu, Y. (2016). Cloud Performance Modeling with Benchmark Evaluation of Elastic Scaling Strategies. *IEEE Transactions on Parallel and Distributed Systems*, 27(1), 130–143. 10.1109/TPDS.2015.2398438

Kamiya, Y. & Shimokawa, T. (2020). *A Study about Web Application Inter-Cloud.*

Kaur, I., Narula, G. S., Wason, R., Jain, V., & Baliyan, A. (2018). Neuro fuzzy—COCOMO II model for software cost estimation. *International Journal of Information Technology : an Official Journal of Bharati Vidyapeeth's Institute of Computer Applications and Management*, 10(2), 181–187. 10.1007/s41870-018-0083-6

Kriushanth, M., Arockiam, L., & Mirobi, G. J. (2013). Auto Scaling in Cloud Computing : An Overview. *International Journal of Advanced Research in Computer and Communication Engineering*, 2(7), 2870–2875.

Liu, Y., Rameshan, N., Monte, E., Vlassov, V., & Navarro, L. (2015). ProRenaTa: Proactive and reactive tuning to scale a distributed storage system. *Proc. - 2015 IEEE/ACM 15th Int. Symp. Clust. Cloud, Grid Comput.* (pp. 453–464). IEEE. 10.1109/CCGrid.2015.26

Lorido-Botrán, T., Miguel-Alonso, J., & Lozano, J. (2013). Comparison of Auto-scaling Techniques for Cloud Environments. *Actas las XXIV Jornadas Paralelismo.*

Lorido-Botran, T., Miguel-Alonso, J., & Lozano, J. A. (2014). A Review of Auto-scaling Techniques for Elastic Applications in Cloud Environments. *Journal of Grid Computing*, 12(4), 559–592. 10.1007/s10723-014-9314-7

Mahfuzur, R. (2016). *Improved Virtual Machine (VM) based Resource Provisioning in Cloud Computing.*

Maurer, M., Breskovic, I., Emeakaroha, V. C., & Brandic, I. (2011). *Revealing the MAPE Loop for the Autonomic Management of Cloud Infrastructures.* IEEE. 10.1109/ISCC.2011.5984008

Netto, M. A. S., Cardonha, C., Cunha, R. L. F., & Assuncao, M. D. (2015). Evaluating auto-scaling strategies for cloud computing environments. *Proc. - IEEE Comput. Soc. Annu. Int. Symp. Model. Anal. Simul. Comput. Telecommun. Syst. MASCOTS*, (pp. 187–196). IEEE.

Nikravesh, A. Y., Ajila, S. A., & Lung, C. H. (2015). Towards an Autonomic Auto-scaling Prediction System for Cloud Resource Provisioning, *Proc. - 10th Int. Symp. Softw. Eng. Adapt. Self-Managing Syst. SEAMS 2015*, (pp. 35–45). IEEE. 10.1109/SEAMS.2015.22

Nilabja Roy, A. (2011). Efficient Autoscaling in the Cloud using Predictive Models for Workload Forecasting. *IEEE 4th Int.Conf. Cloud Comput.* IEEE.

Qu, C., Calheiros, R. N., & Buyya, R. (2016). *Auto-scaling Web Applications in Clouds: A Taxonomy and Survey* (Vol. V).

Reese, G. (2008). *On Why I Don't Like Auto-Scaling in the Cloud.* O'Reilly Broadcast. http://broadcast.oreilly.com/2008/12/why-i-dont-like-cloud-auto-scaling.html

Sagar, S. (2016). *Auto Scaling Load Balancing Features in Cloud Richa Thakur*, 3(1), 21–25.

Saini, D., & Pandey, A. (2017). *Analysis of Scalability Factor in Cloud Computing*, 2(6), 675–678.

Selvon-Bruce, A. (2016). How Auto-Scaling Techniques Make Public Cloud Deployments. *Cogniz. 20-20 insights.* .

Shen, Z., Subbiah, S., Gu, X., & Wilkes, J. (2011). CloudScale: elastic resource scaling for multi-tenant cloud systems. *Proc. 2nd Symp. Cloud Comput.*, (pp. 1-14). 10.1145/2038916.2038921

Tran, D., Tran, N., Nguyen, G., & Nguyen, B. M. (2017). A Proactive Cloud Scaling Model Based on Fuzzy Time Series and SLA Awareness. *Procedia Computer Science*, 108, 365–374. 10.1016/j.procs.2017.05.121

Tseng, C., Tsai, M., Yang, Y., & Chou, L. (2018). A Rapid Auto-Scaling Mechanism in Cloud Computing Environment.

Xiao, Z., Member, S., Chen, Q., & Luo, H. (2014). *Automatic Scaling of Internet Applications for Cloud Computing Services*, 63(5), 1111–1123.

Yang, J., Liu, C., Shang, Y., Mao, Z., & Chen, J. (2013). Workload Predicting-Based Automatic Scaling in Service Clouds, *2013 IEEE Sixth Int. Conf. Cloud Comput.*, (pp. 810–815). IEEE. 10.1109/CLOUD.2013.146

Chapter 5
Designing and Implementing a Cloud–Based Content Delivery Network

Saikat Gochhait
https://orcid.org/0000-0003-4583-9208
Symbiosis Institute of Digital and Telecom Management, Symbiosis International University (Deemed), India

ABSTRACT

CDN is constituted of three basic components. A content provider is somebody entrusting the URI namespace of the Web objects to be dispersed. The content provider's server contains all such objects. A CDN provider can be some owner party that enables transportation conveniences to content providers to deliver content in a timely and reliable manner. They may employ geographically distributed caching and/or replica servers (surrogates or edge servers) to duplicate content. Together they may form what we call a web cluster. End users are the customers who use content from the content provider's website.

INTRODUCTION

The last few decades have witnessed tremendous growth as well maturity of Internet as well as Internet-driven services (Pathan and Buyya, 2006; Anjum et al., 2017). Consumption of multimedia content available on the Internet has witnessed changing trends (Fan et al., 2018). Particularly consumption of video content has transformed from offline viewing to online streaming (eg: Netflix). Real-time vid-

DOI: 10.4018/979-8-3693-2869-9.ch005

eo conferencing through solutions like Skype is now possible through all internet enabled devices. Continuous sharing of video content through online services like Youtube, Facebook etc has further augmented the ubiquitous consumption of video content through the Internet. With this brisk proliferation of internet ecosystem (internet enabled web services as well as applications), popular Web services often witness high demand resulting into overcrowding and bottleneck issues leading to hotspot generation (Androutsellis-Theotokis and Spinellis, 2004). Unmanageable user demands on such services affect their performance and availability. Reproducing identical data or services over numerous mirrored Web servers located at geographically varied positions is a general mechanism implemented by service providers to gain on performance, bandwidth and scalability. In such a scenario a user request can be easily directed to the closest server thus reducing user reaction time as well as network impact.

Technically, called content delivery network (CDN) or content distribution network (CDN) is actually an umbrella of geographically scattered networks comprising of proxy servers as well as their data centres (Pathan and Buyya, 2006). It is an important component of the present Internet architecture (Wang et al., 2017). The purpose of such networks is to dispense services spatially comparative to end-users resulting in high accessibility as well as performance. In the current context, CDNs forms a level in the internet environment serving a large as well as varied section of Internet data together with web objects like transcripts, graphics and scripts, downloadable objects (media files, software, documents), applications (e-commerce, portals), social networks, video streaming and live streaming media (Elkotob and Andersson, 2012). Content Delivery Networks (CDNs) are handing a crucial responsibility in content hosting, orchestration, mashup, transmission, and edge contact (Fan et al., 2018). Present, Content owners compensate CDN operators to send their content to the customers. CDN operators further sustain ISPs, carriers and network operators for hosting its servers in their data centres. These networks have found success as they have been able to surmount the fundamental restrictions of the Internet in terms of user supposed Quality of Service (QoS) when using web content (Pathan and Buyya, 2006).

In actuality a CDN duplicates data from the original server to cache servers deployed across the globe to robustly distribute the same to end users in a opportune fashion from close by best possible surrogates (Balachandran et al., 2013). CDN apparatus can be spread over nodes in either consistent or diverse environments in varied forms as well as structures. Further these systems may be wholly centralised or decentralised as need be. Control sharing and internetworking in such systems may also assume varied forms as per requirement. A CDN framework may be deployed to deliver one or many of the several functionalities listed below (Ma et al., 2016; Stamos et al., 2009).

- **Request Redirection:** redirecting an incoming request to the nearest available surrogate server through techniques like bypass congestion to overcome SlashDot effect or flash crowds.

- **Content Outsourcing and Distribution:** replicates data to dispersed proxy servers on behalf of the original server.

- **Content Negotiation Services:** to answer definite needs of individual/ group users.

- **Management Services:** managing network parts for efficient handling, monitoring usage as well as reporting.

CDN content implies digital data assets constituting of encoded media as well as metadata. Encoded media may be constituted by static, dynamic or continuous data including web pages, images, audio, video as well as documents. Metadata is the content narrative providing for recognition, detection, classification and organization of multimedia data over the web. To deliver its expected functionalities any content delivery network is constituted of three chief components, namely: a content provider, a CDN provider and end users (Pallis and Vakali, 2006). Figure 1 below depicts the same.

CDN is constituted of three basic components. A **content provider** is somebody entrusting the URI namespace of the Web objects to be dispersed. The content provider's server contains all such objects. A **CDN provider** can be some owner party that enables transportation conveniences to content providers to deliver content in a timely and reliable manner. They may employ geographically distributed caching and/or replica servers (surrogates or edge servers) to duplicate content. Together they may form what we call a web cluster. **End users** are the customers who use content from the content provider's website. By distributing data to the surrogates in a mechanism that all of them utilize the same URL as well as CDNs achieve transparency for the end user.

CDN content providers scrutinize the web as an instrument to deliver affluent multimedia data to the end user (Hofmann and Beaumont, 2005). Almost all key content providers like CNN, Reuters, Yahoo, Youtube, Google etc employ CDNs to attain quick and speedy content contact (Wang et al., 2017). Any decline in service quality shall result in unsatisfied user and reduction in organization's financial incentives. Hence, organizations are always on the lookout for technologies to improve service quality to users accessing their site. In the past few years CDNs have received extensive recognition as a resolution to provision on-demand competence as well as quick content accessibility (Wang et al., 2017). A number of technologies have evolved in this regard to improve service provisioning and content delivery over the web. When deployed, the network sustaining these technologies forms a content delivery network.

This chapter provides a comprehensive taxonomy for CDN in terms of its content networking techniques, the different ongoing trends in content distribution, notable content delivery service providers, further extensions to CDN, different research issues in CDN etc. We also discuss the Amazon Cloud Force Ecommerce CDN to clarify the implementation specifics of a CDN.

CONTENT NETWORKING TECHNIQUES

A CDN may be deployed in multiple locations over multiple backbones, in order to reduce bandwidth costs, improve page load time and increase content availability. Hence, the number of nodes/ servers constituting a CDN may vary as per the architecture.

User requests to a CDN are routed through a request routing system. This request routing system is basically constituted of two main modules, namely the request routing algorithm and the request routing mechanism (Anjum et al., 2017. Together both these modules guarantee that the user request is directed to the most appropriate edge server.

i.   Request Routing Algorithm (Hofmann and Beaumont, 2005; *Content request routing and load balancing for content distribution networks*, 2001). Request for data is algorithmically focussed to nodes most favourable in some mechanism. When working on performance optimization, nearest as well as highest available locations for delivering data to the customer may be selected. However, in cost optimization, least expensive location may be chosen instead. Cost optimization may result in selection of least expensive locations instead. For an optimal setting these aspirations may align as edge servers close to the end-user or at the border of the network have an upper hand in terms of cost as well as performance.

ii. Request Routing Mechanism: Content Delivery Networks enhance the end-to-end network through dispensing it on a number of intellectual applications utilizing varied procedures to optimize content delivery. The consequential stiffly knitted overlay utilizes web caching, server-load balancing, request routing as well as content services. We briefly describe these technologies below:

   a) Web Cache (*Global load balancing across mirrored data centers,* 2001; Mathew, Sitaraman and Shenoy, 2012): They are used to store popular content on the server with the highest demand. As a result these shared network machinery reduces bandwidth, server load and perks up client response time for the stored content. Web cache is inhabited either based on user requests (pull caching) or through preloaded content dispersed from content servers (push caching) (Mathew, Sitaraman and Shenoy, 2012).

b) Server-Load Balancing(*Global load balancing across mirrored data centers,* 2001): It utilizes techniques like service-based (global load balancing) (*Global load balancing across mirrored data centers,* 2001) or hardware-based web-switch, content switch or multilayer switch to split traffic among numerous servers or web caches. In this scenario the switch is allocated an IP address. The traffic reaching the switch is then transferred to one of the authentic web servers linked to the switch. The advantage shall be load balancing, improved capability, better scalability as well as reliability by load redistribution.

c) Request Routing (*Content request routing and load balancing for content distribution networks,* 2001; Vakali and Pallis, 2003).: It forwards client requests to the best available content supply to serve the request. Varied algorithms are used for this purpose like global server load balancing, DNS-based request routing, HTML rewriting, and any casting.

An actual CDN is actually realised through a number of algorithms, protocols and techniques. Like, proximity for choosing the nearest node is done through a diversity of techniques like proactive probing, reactive probing, and connection monitoring. Content Delivery is performed through a variety of mechanisms like manual feature duplication, active web caches and global hardware load balancers. There are many available content service protocol suites Stamos et al., 2009; Hofmann and Beaumont, 2005) designed to provide access to varied content services distributed through a content network like the Internet Content Adaptation Protocol (ICAP) (Pallis and Vakali, 2006), Open Pluggable Edge Services (OPES) Protocol etc (Penno et al., 2004).

CDN TRENDS

CDNs can be described as a novel virtual overlay to the basic Open Systems Interconnection (OSI) model (Pathan and Buyya, 2006). This layer enables network services for varied types of applications. In this section we discuss certain significant CDN trends or applications:

i. **Telco CDNs** (Li and Simon, 2013): rapid growth of streaming video traffic on the Internet has increased capital expenditure of broadband providers. To overcome this, telecommunication service providers are launching their own CDNs to reduce the demand on the backbone network as well as reduce the infrastructure reserves. Telco CDNs are better as compared to traditional CDNs as they the network used for video content transmission. As a result the video data can be delivered more quickly and reliably as compared to general internet.

ii. **Federated CDNs** (Famaey et al., 2013; Pimental et al., 2015) :HTTP Adaptive Streaming Services are a collection of novel streaming services that permit end users to become accustomed to video quality as per present network conditions. As they utilize the HTTP infrastructure they are suitable for deployment on any existing CDN. However, they also suffer from challenges like content distribution through servers and latency due to request redirection. The association/interconnection of CDNs further propagate these inconveniences as it increases the number of redirects.

iii. **Edns-client-subnet EDNS0 option** (Streibelt et al., 2013): August 2011, a worldwide conglomerate of principal Internet service providers led by Google pronounced their official operation of the edns-client-subnet IETF Internet-Draft, which is projected to precisely concentrate DNS resolution rejoinders. Through the edns-client-subnet EDNS0 alternative, the recursive DNS servers of CDNs will exploit the IP address of the appealing client subnet when solving DNS requests. If a CDN depends on the IP address of the DNS resolver in place of the client when determining DNS requests, it can inaccurately geo-locate a client if the client is using Google any cast addresses for their DNS resolver, leading to latency issues.

NOTEWORTHY CONTENT DELIVERY SERVICE PROVIDERS

It needs to be noted that, every Internet Service provider can also make available a content delivery network. Many significant content delivery service providers are available today. Table I below attempts to classify them.

Table 1. Some significant content delivery service providers

S.No	CDN Type	CDN Provider	Description	Service Type
Traditional Commercial CDNs				
1	Akamai (Wang et al., 2017; Nygren, Sitaraman and Sun, 2010).	Akamai Technologies	Deploy web server clusters in numerous geographical locations to have better responsiveness for customers.	Provides CDN services like streaming.

continued on following page

Table 1. Continued

S.No	CDN Type	CDN Provider	Description	Service Type
2	Amazon CloudFront (Wang et al., 2017)	Amazon	Global CDN service delivering accelerated delivery of websites, APIs, video content as well as other web objects.	Integrates with Amazon Web Services (AWS) and other products to provide a simple mechanism to accelerate content to end users.
3	Azure CDN (Resemi and Chezian, 2016).	Microsoft	Again a cloud –based global solution for delivering high-bandwidth content.	Can serve as a cache for serving dynamic content.
4	Google Cloud CDN (Wang, Huang and Rose, 2018).	Google	Leverages Google's globally distributed edge points of presence to accelerate content delivery for websites and applications served from Google Cloud Storage and Compute Engine	Lowers network latency, offloads origins, and reduces serving cost.
5	Cachefly (*Content Delivery Network - All About CDNs in One Place* – GlobalDots, 2018)	Cachefly Inc.	World's first TCP-anycast based CDN for throughput. Provides infinite scalability, global PoP distribution alongwith 24/7 domestic support and instant purging.	Delivers client highest-quality videos and IPTV files at speeds better than any other CDNs.
6	EdgeCastNetworks (Gupta and Kumar, 2014)	Verizon Digital Media Services	Media-optimized CDN to handle modern internet demands. Best performing and most reliable CDN service. Quora, Lenovo, Novica and CafePress are its clients.	Provides PCI-Complaint dynamic acceleration, Application delivery, HTTP/HTTPs caching, Streaming, Storage, DNS as well as DDoS mitigation.
7	KeyCDN (*Content Delivery Network - All About CDNs in One Place* – GlobalDots, 2018)	KeyCDN Inc.	Powerful and simple-to-use CDN to ensure high performance in an affordable manner.	Speeds up games, software delivery, advertisements, CMS, websites etc.
8	Incapsula (*Content Delivery Network - All About CDNs in One Place* – GlobalDots, 2018)	Incapsula Inc.	A cloud based application delivery platform that is integrated with popular websites like Mox, SIEMENS etc.	Employing CDN for security, DDoS protection, load balancing and failover services to clients.

continued on following page

Table 1. Continued

S.No	CDN Type	CDN Provider	Description	Service Type
9	CDNlion (Gupta and Kumar, 2014)	CDNlion Inc	Global CDN provider that enables customers speed up websites, images as well as video streaming.	Offers content caching, security, transparent pricing, CMS integration, load balancing etc through an easy to use dashboard.
10	Limelight (*Content Delivery Network - All About CDNs in One Place* – GlobalDots, 2018)	Limelight Networks	Private CDN service enabling users to deliver their digital content across the globe on any specific device.	Enables publishers to deliver content like videos, operating systems updates, online games etc to any smart device.
11	MetaCDN (Wang et al., 2017; Broberg, Buyya and Tari, 2009)	MetaCDN Inc.	Exploits storage cloud assets to build up an integrated overlay network.	It eliminates the intricacies of handling manifold storage providers by wisely mapping content before placing it on storage providers based on QoS, coverage or budget preferences.
12	Rackspace cloud Files (*Content Delivery Network - All About CDNs in One Place* – GlobalDots, 2018)	Rackspace Inc.	Cloud-based CDN to host large files and static websites.	Cloud computing based cloud file storage and pay as you go business model.
13	Swarmify (*Content Delivery Network - All About CDNs in One Place* – GlobalDots, 2018)	Swarmify Inc.	Video delivery CDN compatible with almost all browsers without any extra installations/plugins.	Offers 100% up-time as well as delivery SLA with less cost. Is notably resilient, reliable and easy.
14	Softlayer CDN (*Content Delivery Network - All About CDNs in One Place* – GlobalDots, 2018)	SoftLayer CDN Inc.	Distributes content as required. Ensures efficient content delivery without any overhead storage costs.	Offers complete traffic control, unique networks through cloud security.
15	Cloudflare(*Content Delivery Network - All About CDNs in One Place* – GlobalDots, 2018)	Cloudflare Inc.	Next Generation Content Delivery Network to enable security, performance and reliability through efficient, emerging technologies.	Online services to protect and speed up online websites.

continued on following page

Table 1. Continued

S.No	CDN Type	CDN Provider	Description	Service Type
16	MaxCDN (*Content Delivery Network - All About CDNs in One Place* – GlobalDots, 2018)	MaxCDN Inc.	Large, secure CDN with built-in WAF, DDoS.	Boasts of an intelligent best-path routing along with on-the-fly analysis to monitor packet loss and latency.
17	Coral CDN (*The Coral Content Distribution Network*, 2018)	CoralCDN Inc.	A decentralized, self-organizing, peer-to-peer web-content allocation network. Coral CDN leverages the cumulative bandwidth of volunteers managing the software to take up and disperse traffic for web sites using the system. CoralCDN duplicates content in fraction to the content's recognition, irrespective of the publisher's resources---thus democratizing content publication.	Free and open content distribution network based on peer to peer technology.

CDN EXTENSIONS

Conventional CDN approaches suffer from a number of technical as well as commercial challenges. To overcome them many extensions to the traditional CDNs have been suggested. Some notable ones are highlighted in Table I below:

Table 2. Significant content delivery network extensions

S.No	CDN Extension	Description	Advantage	Limitation	Commercial Examples
1	Peer-Assisted Content Delivery Networks Anjum et al., 2017;	To overcome demands of video users during peak hours an alternative CDN scheme to mitigate CDN stress with loss of QoS. PACDN employs P2P networks with traditional server-based CDN to self-scale P2P swarm capacity when load increases while maintaining QoS.	Economically viable alternative ; remarkably reduces burden of user request on content delivery servers;	Unreliability of peer-to-peer networks; lack of encouragement for peer involvement; copyright issues; maintaining Quality of service (QoS);	Kankan; LiveSky; Akamai NetSession; Spotify

continued on following page

Table 2. Continued

S.No	CDN Extension	Description	Advantage	Limitation	Commercial Examples
2	Self-Adaptive Mobile Content Delivery Network (SAMCDN) (Ho et al., 2017).	To overcome vehicular network (VANET) challenges like self-motivated topology and large-scale scenarios, an alternative CDN scheme that relies on content replication in deliberately selected vehicles and its distribution to receivers in an locales of interest.	Scalable Algorithm for information distribution in VANETs, confirmed improved performance as compared to statistical mechanisms.	The near optimal solution requires more simulation for generalisations.	Not Available
3	Java Application Delivery Framework for use in a Content Delivery Network (Davis et al., 2003)	The patent details a CDN Java application deployment model offering Java enabled edge servers.	Especially for Java based Web applications and Web services.	It is a CDN Java application framework, their extensions to other Java comparable language based applications is further desirable.	Not Available
4	Mobile Content Delivery Network (Silva et al., 2017)	Is a network of servers cooperating to optimize delivery of content to users on any type of mobile or wireless network.	Reduced Bandwidth requirement; global content availability over a network.	High latency; huge variation in download capacity	Neumob; Instart Logic
5	Energy Efficient Content Delivery Networks (Mathew, Sitaraman and Shenoy, 2015)	To reduce the energy costs of operating a CDN a novel technique named cluster shutdown is proposed to turn off a complete cluster of servers in a CDN that are deployed within a data center.	Provides efficient power savings through realistic power-saver equipments without compromising bandwidth or end user performance.	Integrating cluster shutdown into both global load balancer as well as local load balancer may result in enhanced efficiencies for future.	Akamai
6	Multi-Source Content Delivery Networks Liu and Yu, 2016; Hashemi and Bohlooli, 2018)	Collaborating multiple CDN providers through real-time load balancing gives rise to what is popularly known as MultiCDN	Superior solution as compared to mono CDN as leaves no chance for ones CDN to crash and thus no outages or downtimes.	Effective load balancing techniques shall be desirable to maintain efficacy of the different CDNs.	MultiCDN .
7	CODIS Content Delivery Network (Hlavacs et al., 2005)	Content Delivery Improvement over Satellite (CODIS) is an EU Project aimed at setting up and implementing a satellite-based CDN as a continental CDN.	CODIS QoS was remarkably better than many wired CDNs	Effective mechanisms of determining content popularity still require better solutions.	Alcatel
8	Hybrid CDN-P2P system for Video-on-Demand (Kang and Yin, 2010; Huang et al., 2008)	A hybrid CDN-P2P system for Video-on-Demand system.	Being a hybrid system it combines the reliability as well as quality control of a CDN with the scalability of a CDN.	Further improvements in P2P technologies for live streaming as well as VoD applications is desirable.	LiveSky

continued on following page

Table 2. Continued

S.No	CDN Extension	Description	Advantage	Limitation	Commercial Examples
9	Relay-based multipoint content delivery for wireless users in an information-centric network (Frangoudis, Polyzos and Rubino, 2016)	In a CDN varied content demands varied performance requirement. A multi-objective optimization can thus ensure that appropriate subsets of users are activated as relays on item-to-item basis.	Better Quality-of-Experience for especially video content; significant reliability, delivery time as well energy-cost tradeoffs.	Integrating the scheme with typical wireless equipment within the existing PSI prototype.	Not Available
10	Extension of Intrusion Prevention, Detection and Response System for Secure Content Delivery Networks (Resmi and Chezian, 2016)	To overcome the security and resource allocation issues of CDN due to its flexible nature, an optimal hybrid algorithm using game theory and honeypot techniques for securing CDN against intrusion is proposed.	Proposed algorithm named E-IPDRS prevents CDN from intrusion and unauthenticated behaviours with reduced control and communication overhead.	The system though tested on a decentralized environment, can also be significantly tested in a centralised environment.	Not Available

Table 2 above enlists certain significant content delivery network extensions. It can be noted here that different extensions of content delivery networks focus on improving the performance of the network through some particular aspect. Once these extensions are developed and stable they can further be amalgamated to realize a more efficient Content Delivery Network.

ISSUES OF CONCERN IN CDN

i.   **Security Mechanism:** As a CDN deals with multimedia content across the Web, the prime concern is that the security policies and framework must be properly defined. Issues like copyright management, performance or quality of service management for enormous data transmission, bandwidth efficiency etc also needs to be dealt with. Further security is an important issue of any CDN to prevent misuse of its resources. Protocols like Overlay Communication Protocol (OCP) have been proposed to secure signalling communication in CDN (Pimentel et al., 2015). Considering all elements of a content delivery framework this protocol masks the network structure from potential attackers.

ii. **Covert Channels:** Due to their open nature, they are at risk of being abused by the attacker. A malicious content provider (MCP)/visitor (MCV) may exploit a CDN to build a covert channel. In this scenario a MCV may utilize the MCPs content through varied edge servers. Using varied edge servers may generate varied access patterns, to encode undisclosed/covert messages. This can lead to what is termed as the CDN covert channel attack (Wang et al., 2017). Wang et al. (2017) have simulated such an attack on a commercial CDN namely Amazon CloudFront. These attacks are used to transmit covert information while bypassing internet censorship protocol. For Example: Botnet Command & Control. Work on such attacks is still limited. However, to mitigate such attacks special routing servers can be established to forward user requests to edge servers. However, this solution may compromise the complete CDN service in case of a DoS attack. To overcome these limitations of routing server's use of a certificate token generating routing server is advocated.

iii. **High Scalability:** The Internet is witnessing an explosion of multimedia especially video data over it. As of 2015, it has been estimated that more than 400 hours of video are uploaded on Youtube each minute (Fan et al., 2018). As per cisco, IP video traffic shall constitute 82% of complete consumer Internet traffic by 2020(Fan et al., 2018; Cisco, 2014). Enhanced by this amplification of videos and other data on Internet, demand for storage, bitrates as well as network bandwidth has become a serious challenge for CDN providers. They continuously need to deal with these issues effectively to maintain performance and undisrupted service.

iv. **High Quality of Service** (Fan et al., 2018): Users today are expecting high definition (HD) video service. As a result QoS standards for CDN providers have heightened. To meet this demand CDN providers continuously need to keep getting better on server side as well as network-level performance.

v. **High Flexibility** (Fan et al., 2018): Internet content consumption trends have witnessed a shift from a moderately analytical, controlled mode to a exceedingly dynamic mode. Streaming large live videos as well as on-demand ones can significantly boost network traffic as well as network congestion. This may eventually result in degraded customer experience. Traditional CDNs are generally statically deployed, using a centralized redirection mechanism. However, this framework is not suited for dynamic adjustment resulting in performance penalties. The enhanced flexible service demand has created a void for novel CDNs that are vertically customizable as per user requirement and varied content.

MetaCDN Broberg, Buyya and Tari (2009) is offering a solution to issue iii, iv and v by blurring the boundaries between stakeholders and promoting cooperation. Hybrid CDN-P2P (Kang and Yin, 2010; Garmehi and Analoui, 2016). architectures are also providing scalable solutions to the above issues. Federated CDNs Famaey et al. (2013) have also been deployed successfully by Cisco to establish a multi-footprint logical CDN to help overcome storage and bandwidth issues.

Information-centric networking (ICN) is also rising as a potential paradigm for proficient information/content distribution (Kim et al., 2016). It allows information distribution through lesser bandwidths in wired testbed networks. Integrating content distribution as a native network feature ICNs have been found to be particularly useful in mobile ad-hoc network environments for competent content sharing (Carofiglio et al., 2013). To implement ICN, Content Centric Networking (CCN) architecture has attracted attention as through content naming it caches content in intermediate routers to reduce bandwidth and energy usage through multiple delivery of the same content.

AMAZON CLOUDFRONT: ECOMMERCE CDN

Many notable CDN are already deployed and successfully operating in the web space. Amazon a popular and successful E-Commerce company launched their storage cloud Amazon S3 in US in 2006 and in Europe in 2008 (Wang et al., 2017). In November, 2008 they launched CloudFront, a global CDN with 14 edge locations namely 8 in the US, 4 in Europe and 2 in Asia (Wang et al., 2017; Broberg, Buyya and Tari, 2009). CloudFront is a CDN that ensures secure, high speed delivery of data, videos, applications and APIs to viewers. CloudFront is further integrated with the AWS global infrastructure as well as software to work effortlessly with services like AWS Shield (for DDoS mitigation), Amazon S3 (elastic load balancing) etc.

CloudFront distributes web content through a global network of data centres called edge servers (*API Version 2016-08-01 Amazon CloudFront : DeveloperGuide*, 2016; *API Version 2016-03-10*, 2016). Every user content request is directed to the nearest possible edge location with the lowest latency (time delay). Notably CloudFront is not a continual storage provider, instead it is comparable to a proxy cache, with files positioned to the varied CloudFront locations on requirement and deleted automatically when not required. It offers a straightforward, pay-as-you-go pricing model integrated into one's current AWS support subscription. The benefits of CloudFront over other commercial CDNs are as follows:

i. Globally available expanding Content Delivery Network: This CDN is assembled upon the constantly intensifying global AWS infrastructure that presently includes 54 accessibility zones over 18 geographic locations. Currently CloudFront has 117 PoP (points of presence) including 106 edge locations with 11 regional edge caches spread in 56 cities across 25 nations. This spread ensures that each application delivers high scalability, availability and performance for all customers all over the globe.

ii. Content Security at the Edges: CloudFront is a highly-secure CDN that delivers both application as well as network level protection. Further CloudFront customers are also benefitted through the automatic protections of AWS Shield at no extra cost. CloudFront is furthermore impeccably incorporated with AWS WAF and AWS Shield Advanced to help guard your applications from more complicated threats and DDoS attacks. CloudFront's infrastructure is also amenable with PCI, DSS, HIPAA, and ISO to guarantee protected delivery of your most susceptible data. One can further convey safe APIs or applications using SSL/TLS, and advanced SSL features that are enabled automatically. AWS Certificate Manager (ACM) can be used to simply craft as many custom SSL certificates as required and instantly install them to your CloudFront distributions at no extra cost. ACM automatically handles certificate renewal.

iii. Programmable CDN: Lambda@Edge allows easy code execution across global AWS locations, enabling quick end-user response with the lowest latency. Code can further be activated through Amazon CloudFront events, like content requests from or responses to origin servers and viewers. One pays only for the compute time that one uses with no charges for code execution. Further, Amazon CloudFront characteristics can be programmatically configured through APIs or the AWS Management Console.

iv. High Performance: The Amazon CloudFront content delivery network is optimized for low latency and high data transfer speeds. CloudFront's intellectual routing is based on real-world latency dimensions constantly assembled from well-liked Internet sites, including Amazon.com. CloudFront is unswervingly linked with hundreds of end-user ISPs and utilizes the AWS backbone network to hasten the deliverance of your content end-to-end.

v. Cost Effective: CloudFront follows a simple pricing formula-pay only for the data transmit and requests used to convey content to your customers. There are no direct payments or fixed platform fees, no long-term commitments, no premiums for dynamic content, and no requirements for professional services to get started. Users of AWS origins such as Amazon S3 or Elastic Load Balancing, pay only for storage costs, not for any data shared between these services and CloudFront.

vi. Deep Integration with Key AWS Services: Amazon CloudFront is totally included with and optimized to work with popular AWS services including Amazon Simple Storage Service (Amazon S3), Amazon Elastic Compute Cloud (Amazon EC2), Elastic Load Balancing, and Amazon Route 53 to help hustle up DNS resolution of applications delivered by CloudFront. Amalgamation with AWS Lambda allows you to accomplish routine logic across the AWS global network without overseeing servers.

Remarkably with a simple initial setup, CloudFront works intangibly to pace up content delivery. We give a brief overview of the CloudFront configuration steps involved:

i.   Configure the original servers from which CloudFront retrieves the files for distribution globally. This server is actually storing the actual objects and may be either Amazon S3 or some HTTP server either running on Amazon EC2 or independently.

ii.   Objects on the original web servers may include web pages, images, video, or any other data that can be served on a HTTP server.

iii. From the original server details one creates a CloudFront distribution detailing CloudFront where to fetch objects from when they are requested through one's website or application.

iv.   CloudFront shares the distribution details across all its edge servers where cache copies of objects need to be maintained.

v.   One's this is done, the website / application now uses the domain name provided by CloudFront for your domain name.

vi.   Additionally one may also configure the original servers to add headers to the object files; deciding how long they stay in the cache.

Once the above configuration is complete, this is how CloudFront deals with users requesting your content:

i.   A customer accesses the website and requests for some object like an image, media file or data file.

ii.   DNS routes the request to the nearest CloudFront edge server with lowest latency.

iii. At the edge server, CloudFront checks its cache for the requested files. If available, CloudFront immediately returns the files to the user. If the files are not available, then:

   a. CloudFront compares user request with the distribution specification and forwards the request to the actual corresponding server for the original file type.

   b. The origin server transfers the file to the edge server.

   c. As soon as the first byte arrives from the origin, CloudFront transfers the file to the user.and adds the file to cache for some other future user request.

iv.   After an object has been in the edge server for almost 24 hours, CloudFront shall

   a. Forward the next request to the original server to ensure that the edge location has the latest version of the same.

   b. If the version is latest, CloudFront delivers it to the end user. If not, the original server sends the latest version to CloudFront which is then delivered to CloudFront as well as updated in the cache for future use.

REFERENCES

Androutsellis-Theotokis, S., & Spinellis, D. (2004, December). A survey of peer-to-peer content distribution technologies. *ACM Computing Surveys*, 36(4), 335–371. 10.1145/1041680.1041681

Anjum, N., Karamshuk, D., Shikh-Bahaei, M., & Sastry, N. (2017). Survey on peer-assisted content delivery networks. *Computer Networks*, 116, 1339–1351. 10.1016/j.comnet.2017.02.008

Balachandran, A., Sekar, V., Akella, A., & Seshan, S. (2013). Analyzing the potential benefits of CDN augmentation strategies for internet video workloads. *Proceedings of the 2013 conference on Internet measurement conference - IMC '13*, (pp. 43–56). ACM. 10.1145/2504730.2504743

Broberg, J., Buyya, R., & Tari, Z. (2009). MetaCDN: Harnessing 'Storage Clouds' for high performance content delivery. *Journal of Network and Computer Applications*, 32(5), 1012–1022. 10.1016/j.jnca.2009.03.004

Carofiglio, G., Morabito, G., Muscariello, L., Solis, I., & Varvello, M. (2013). From content delivery today to information centric networking. *Computer Networks*, 57(16), 3116–3127. 10.1016/j.comnet.2013.07.002

Cisco, "Cisco Global Cloud Index : Forecast and Methodology, 2014–2019. (2014). (pp. 1–41). White Pap.

Davis, A., Thomas, J. Parikh, S. Pichai, E. Ruvinsky, D. Stodolsky, M. Tsimelzon, W., & Weihl, E. (2003). Java application framework for use in a content delivery network (CDN). *Provisional Appl. Ser. No. 60/347,481*.

Elkotob, M., & Andersson, K. (2012). Challenges and opportunities in content distribution networks: A case study. In *GC'12 Work. 4th IEEE Int* (pp. 1021–1026). Work. Mobil. Manag. Networks Futur. World Challenges. 10.1109/GLOCOMW.2012.6477717

Famaey, J., Latré, S., van Brandenburg, R., van Deventer, M. O., & De Turck, F. (2013). *On the Impact of Redirection on HTTP Adaptive Streaming Services in Federated CDNs*. Springer. 10.1007/978-3-642-38998-6_2

Fan, Q., Yin, H., Min, G., Yang, P., Luo, Y., Lyu, Y., Huang, H., & Jiao, L. (2018). Video delivery networks: Challenges, solutions and future directions. *Computers & Electrical Engineering*, 66, 332–341. 10.1016/j.compeleceng.2017.04.011

Frangoudis, P. A., Polyzos, G. C., & Rubino, G. (2016). Relay-based multipoint content delivery for wireless users in an information-centric network. *Computer Networks*, 105, 207–223. 10.1016/j.comnet.2016.06.004

Garmehi, M., & Analoui, M. (2016, October). Envy-Free Resource Allocation and Request Routing in Hybrid CDN–P2P Networks. *Journal of Network and Systems Management*, 24(4), 884–915. 10.1007/s10922-015-9359-3

Gupta, M., & Kumar, D. (2014). State-of-the-art of Content Delivery Network. *International Journal of Computer Science and Information Technologies*, 5(4), 5441–5446.

Hlavacs, H., Haddad, M., Lafouge, C., Kaplan, D., & Ribeiro, J. (2005, May). The CODIS Content Delivery Network. *Computer Networks*, 48(1), 75–89. 10.1016/j.comnet.2004.10.004

Ho, P.-H., Li, M., Yu, H.-F., Jiang, X., & Dán, G. (2017, February). Special Section on Mobile Content Delivery Networks. *Computer Communications*, 99, 62. 10.1016/j.comcom.2017.01.008

Hofmann, M., & Beaumont, L. R. (2005). *Content networking : architecture, protocols, and practice*. Morgan Kaufmann.

Huang, C., Wang, A., Li, J., & Ross, K. W. (2008). Understanding hybrid CDN-P2P. *Proceedings of the 18th International Workshop on Network and Operating Systems Support for Digital Audio and Video - NOSSDAV '08*, (pp. 75). IEEE.

Hyunjoong, S. (2011). PcubeCast: A novel peer-assisted live streaming system. *2011 IEEE International Conference on Peer-to-Peer Computing*, (pp. 212–215). IEEE. 10.1109/P2P.2011.6038738

Kang, S., & Yin, H. (2010). A Hybrid CDN-P2P System for Video-on-Demand. *2010 Second International Conference on Future Networks*, (pp. 309–313). IEEE. 10.1109/ICFN.2010.83

Kim, D., Kim, J. H., Moon, C., Choi, J., & Yeom, I. (2016). Efficient content delivery in mobile ad-hoc networks using CCN. *Ad Hoc Networks*, 36, 81–99. 10.1016/j.adhoc.2015.06.007

Li, Z., & Simon, G. (2013, September). In a Telco-CDN, Pushing Content Makes Sense. *IEEE Transactions on Network and Service Management*, 10(3), 300–311. 10.1109/TNSM.2013.043013.130474

Liu, Y., & Yu, S.-Z. (2016, April). Network coding-based multisource content delivery in Content Centric Networking. *Journal of Network and Computer Applications*, 64, 167–175. 10.1016/j.jnca.2016.02.007

Ma, M., Wang, Z., Su, K., & Sun, L. (2016). *Understanding Content Placement Strategies in Smartrouter-based Peer CDN for Video Streaming.*

Mathew, V., Sitaraman, R. K., & Shenoy, P. (2012). *Energy-aware load balancing in content delivery networks. 2012 Proceedings IEEE INFOCOM.* IEEE.

Mathew, V., Sitaraman, R. K., & Shenoy, P. (2015, June). Energy-efficient content delivery networks using cluster shutdown. *Sustainable Computing : Informatics and Systems*, 6, 58–68. 10.1016/j.suscom.2014.05.004

Nygren, E., Sitaraman, R. K., & Sun, J. (2010, August). The Akamai network. *Operating Systems Review*, 44(3), 2–19. 10.1145/1842733.1842736

Pallis, G., & Vakali, A. (2006, January). Insight and perspectives for content delivery networks. *Communications of the ACM*, 49(1), 101–106. 10.1145/1107458.1107462

Pathan, A. K., & Buyya, R. (2006). A Taxonomy and Survey of Content Delivery Networks. *Grid Comput. Distrib. Syst. GRIDS Lab. Univ. Melb. Park. Aust.*, 148, 1–44.

Penno, R., Chen, R., Labs, B., & Technologies, L. (2004). An Architecture for Open Pluggable Edge Services (OPES). *Status; Riksorgan för Sveriges Lungsjuka*, 1–17.

Pimentel, H. M., Kopp, S., Simplicio, M. A.Jr, Silveira, R. M., & Bressan, G. (2015). OCP: A protocol for secure communication in federated content networks. *Computer Communications*, 68, 47–60. 10.1016/j.comcom.2015.07.026

Resmi, A. M., & Chezian, R. M. (2016). An extension of intrusion prevention, detection and response system for secure content delivery networks. *2016 IEEE Int. Conf. Adv. Comput. Appl.*, (pp. 144–149). IEEE. 10.1109/ICACA.2016.7887940

Seyyed Hashemi, S. N., & Bohlooli, A. (2018, July). Analytical modeling of multi-source content delivery in information-centric networks. *Computer Networks*, 140, 152–162. 10.1016/j.comnet.2018.05.007

Silva, C. M., Silva, F. A., Sarubbi, J. F. M., Oliveira, T. R., Meira, W.Jr, & Nogueira, J. M. S. (2017, April). Designing mobile content delivery networks for the internet of vehicles. *Vehicular Communications*, 8, 45–55. 10.1016/j.vehcom.2016.11.003

Stamos, K., Pallis, G., Vakali, A., & Dikaiakos, M. D. (2009). Evaluating the utility of content delivery networks. *Proceedings of the 4th edition of the UPGRADE-CN workshop on Use of P2P, GRID and agents for the development of content networks - UPGRADE-CN '09*, (pp. 11). ACM. 10.1145/1552486.1552509

Streibelt, F., Böttger, J., Chatzis, N., Smaragdakis, G., & Feldmann, A. (2013). Exploring EDNS-client-subnet adopters in your free time. *Proceedings of the 2013 conference on Internet measurement conference - IMC '13*, (pp. 305–312). ACM. 10.1145/2504730.2504767

Vakali, A., & Pallis, G. (2003, November). Content delivery networks: Status and trends. *IEEE Internet Computing*, 7(6), 68–74. 10.1109/MIC.2003.1250586

Wang, Y., Shen, Y., Jiao, X., Zhang, T., Si, X., Salem, A., & Liu, J. (2017). Exploiting Content Delivery Networks for covert channel communications. *Computer Communications*, 99, 84–92. 10.1016/j.comcom.2016.07.011

Wang, Z., Huang, J., & Rose, S. (2018). Evolution and challenges of DNS-Based CDNs. *Digital Communications and Networks*, 4(4), 235–243. 10.1016/j.dcan.2017.07.00534124418

Chapter 6
Digitalization of Organizational Memory

Ozlem Erdas Cicek
Necmettin Erbakan University, Turkey

ABSTRACT

Organizational memory has a crucial role for businesses, especially in the context of cloud computing. Cloud computing technologies facilitate the storage, management, and access of organizational knowledge and data. By using cloud-based solutions, businesses can enhance the effectiveness of their organizational memory systems. Digitalization, combined with cloud computing, allows for easy access, retrieval, and sharing of knowledge within the organization, regardless of geographical locations or device types. In today's business environment, cloud computing integration is not only convenient but also necessary for organizations to effectively leverage their knowledge and information. It ensures that the organizational memory remains a valuable asset that contributes to informed decision-making, innovation, and sustained success. This study discusses to what extent organizational memory systems, enhanced by cloud computing, will be considered effective in new business conditions.

INTRODUCTION

Organizational memory address to the cumulative knowledge, information, and experiences that an organization gains and keeps over time. It presents as the organizational corresponding of human memory, facilitating firms to attain from past actions, make knowledgeable decisions, and accustomed to varying situations. Nevertheless, it cannot be stocked in a sole depository like human memory. Cloud computing technologies have a remarkable role in enabling the storage, administer, and reach of organizational memory. By ascending cloud-based solutions, institutions

DOI: 10.4018/979-8-3693-2869-9.ch006

can improve the efficiency of their organizational memory systems, which smooth approachability, recovery, and sharing of knowledge across the organization.

Organizational memory has a significant effect for institutions in several means. Initially, it grants for the detainment of lessons learned from past achievements and deficiencies, which cultivates endless advancements. Second, it helps informed decision-making by equipping archival data, benchmarks, and understandings. Third, a well-administered organizational memory can trigger innovation by supplying a infrastructure for new notions and problem-solving. Finally, it supports to decorating and boosting the culture and values of the organization.

Even though organizational memory is significant for firms, it gets inconvenient if not it is administered correctly. Efficiently overseeing this collective knowledge is crucial for maintaining competitiveness and attaining enduring success. The key to achievement in managing the organizational memory is digitalizing the knowledge which involves the process of converting, storing, and managing an organization's knowledge and information in digital formats, often facilitated by cloud computing solutions. This digitalization simplifies the accessibility, retrieval, and sharing of organizational knowledge.

In the contemporary fast-paced and data-driven business landscape, digitalization, combined with cloud computing, is not merely a convenience but a necessity for organizations aiming to harness their knowledge and information efficiently. It guarantees that the organizational memory stays a valuable asset, fostering informed decision-making, innovation, and enduring achievements. To what extent has the digitalization process accelerated by Industry 4.0 technological evolution changed the effectiveness of organizational memory systems, particularly those integrated with cloud computing capabilities? Besides, during the Covid-19 pandemic period, the level of use of technology in business processes has increased, and job execution techniques have changed significantly. To what extent will the adoption of new work procedures and changes in work groups necessitate the re-establishment of corporate memory systems capable of preserving the living knowledge of past successes and failures, perhaps through enhanced cloud-based platforms? This study delves into the effectiveness of organizational memory systems in adapting to new business conditions, highlighting the importance of incorporating cloud computing technologies in the design of modern organizational memory systems.

DIGITALIZATION

Digitalization and subsequent transformation are catalysts for changes in the corporate landscape, ushering in new technologies rooted in the internet, thereby influencing society at large. It's crucial to distinguish between "digitalization" and "digitization." Digitization involves converting analog and noisy information into digital data. On the other hand, digitalization refers to organizational changes and shifts in business models due to the increased adoption of digital technologies, enhancing both performance and business scope (Rachinger et al., 2018). This transformation involves converting analog data into a digital language, ultimately fostering improved business relationships, adding value to the economy, and benefiting society as a whole (Reis et al., 2020). In its report, Capgemini (2011) evaluated it as an important step for businesses in many industries to establish digital connections with consumers and stakeholders during the digital transformation process and to design products and services using smart technologies (Tutkunca, 2020).

The Digital Transformation signifies the shift from mechanical and analog electronic expertise of the 19th and 20th centuries to digital electronics. According to Kane et al. (2015), the incorporation of digital technologies such as social media, mobile programming, data analysis, and cloud services has a profound impact on how information is processed. Organizations that haven't matured enough in utilizing digital technology may encounter limited advantages, while those that have gained sufficient experience are undergoing transformation. Tutkunca (2020) states that digital-based strategies supports innovation.

Only digital objects with intrinsic value can conceivably function as digital resources. Due to the distinct features of digital objects, as opposed to conventional physical properties, valuable digital objects are susceptible to easy replication and, without adequate protection, may swiftly diminish in value. Modularity offers protection to digital resources by concealing the specific aspects of the module, making only interfaces available for utilization. Therefore, digital properties can be described as "a specific class of digital objects that (a) are modular, (b) encapsulate objects of value, assets, and/or capabilities, (c) are accessible by way of a programmatic bitstring interface". For instance, a programming package is recognized as a digital property, whereas an arbitrary character on a hard drive is not; the valuation of a digital resource is contingent on the background (Grover et. al., 2022).

The rapid rise of digital technologies profoundly affects every aspect of our lives, especially in how employees are administered. The integration of technology in the establishment enhances efficiency through data, applications, and cooperation tools, helping people work seamlessly from distinct locations by using any device. The digital workplace, a virtual reinterpretation of traditional employment, reflects the profound influence of digitalization on the organization (Dabic et al., 2023). This transformation is not merely a buzzword but an immediate and substantial force shaping the future of work.

In the digital innovation and transformation process, companies have come to realize the importance of using digital tools to interact with their key collaborator (Tutkunca, 2020).

With the rise in internet usage through social media, the proliferation of internet-connected devices worldwide, and the development of interconnected systems, also known as the internet of things, have arose. Businesses have begun developing strategies to transfer their actual business processes to digital world.

Without the digital transformation of existing businesses, addressing future economic and environmental challenges sustainably is impossible (Bican and Brem, 2020). Key digital technologies as shown in Figure 1, including cloud computing, has a significant place in supporting innovation and sustainable development in organizations.

Figure 1. Key technologies of digitalization

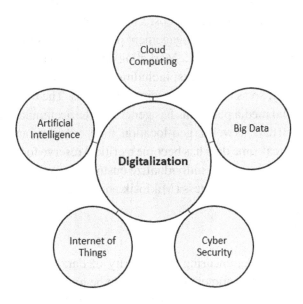

Internet of Things (IoT)

The Internet of Things (IoT) includes enabling physical devices to gather and transact data by connecting them to the Internet. IoT applications have revolutionized our lives, providing value to individuals and companies alike. The estimating for the quantity of tools linked by IoT universally is 43 billion by 2023, displaying a tendency to means with calculation and communicative skills. IoT means supply beneficial understandings for marketing and innovation by allowing the realm of consumer behaviour. In addition, IoT furnishs continuous data exchange among physical tools, helping in the apprehending ding and estimation of consumer behaviour. (Sestino et al., 2020).

Artificial Intelligence (AI) and Machine Learning (ML)

Artificial Intelligence (AI) and Machine Learning (ML) technologies are altering the approaches organizations execute and make decisions. They could investigate enormous datasets, ascertain intricate patterns, and make forecasting with unparalleled truthfulness. In the realm of producing, the continuous process of digitalization has sparked off remarkable progress, namely in the synthesis of machine learning and optimization methods. This combination focuses on enhancing manufacturing processes, streamline operations, and gives resource inefficiencies, ultimately causing to improved productivity and cost savings (Weichert et al., 2019). In addition, the marketing and consumer engagement prospect is presently experiencing a powerful influence from AI and ML. Marketing analysts are utilizing these tools to attain viewpoint about various forms, including customer behaviour, inclinations, and market tendency, so as to make conscious decisions. The utilization of mobile marketing and social media platforms has generated the accumulation of enormous quantity of personal data, as well as geo-location, time, concerns, and demographics. This on-going and real-time data has become a critical reserve for marketers, which enable them to direct strategies, individualize customer experiences, and optimize attempts for maximum effectiveness (Miklosik and Evans, 2020).

Cyber Security

As businesses digitize, ensuring the security of data and systems is crucial. Business operations and customer confidence can be protected from data breaches and cyber threats with prosperous cybersecurity solutions. The complexity of the digitalized cyber environment increases the frequency of cyber-attacks, emphasizing the growing importance of cyber resilience. Cybersecurity management becomes vital for organizations, balancing the advantages of digitalization and cybersecurity investments with economic sustainability, particularly for enterprises which are not large-scaled (Annarelli and Palombi, 2021).

Big Data

With vast amounts of data available, companies are leveraging big data for competitive advantage. Traditional data-processing systems are inadequate, leading to the development of technologies like Hadoop and Hbase. Big data technologies support a variety of tasks, including data engineering and processing, which contribute to methods and activities belonging to data mining and data science. (Provost and Fawcett, 2013).

Cloud Computing

Cloud computing has emerged as the leading domain for online business, offering services that greatly benefit customers, including large-scale organizations, IT professionals, and beyond. Its influence extends to various fields such as health care, electronic businesses, remote education systems, and professional communication. In software development, cloud computing plays a significant role, thanks to its distinctive features that enhance efficiency. These properties encompass data storage, server utilization, network infrastructure, data security, pay-as-you-go pricing, and the utilization of computing methods (Gochhait et al., 2022). Moreover, cloud-based solutions enable remote access to digital tools, applications, and data from anywhere with an internet connection, leveraging the scalability and flexibility offered by cloud platforms. This accessibility promotes collaboration among distributed teams, helps remote work, and improves information sharing across the organization (Rosenthal et al., 2010).

Nevertheless, it is remarkable to recognize that cloud-based systems present significant security risks that can impact data integrity, availability, and virtualization. Despite these concerns, cloud providers are making significant investments in prosperous security measures and compliance certifications to protect data and ensure agreement with regulatory requirements. Organizations can enhance their cybersecurity stance, mitigate risks, and preserve the integrity and confidentiality of their digital assets by utilizing cloud-based security solutions (Basu et al., 2018).

The utilization of the above digital technologies can also help businesses to innovate, operate sustainably, and achieve broader societal and environmental goals. It is important to acknowledge that digitalisation goes beyond advanced technology and involves a change in mindset, as well as the implementation of digital solutions in fundamental aspects of the economy. In the online realm, creating a profile is crucial, and it is equally important for industrial policies and governments to adopt the digital economy, which can create numerous job opportunities (Veljković et al., 2020).

ORGANIZATIONAL MEMORY

In psychology, 'memory' is introduced as the complex processes used to store, carry, and remind information and experiences. This cognitive function is crucial to various aspects of human cognition and behaviour, and involves three distinct phases: "encoding, storage, and retrieval". In the encoding phase, sensed information is transformed into a format suitable for memory storage. Once encoded, information is stored in various memory systems. Retrieval is the subsequent stage that involves bringing stored information back into conscious awareness. Retrieval cues, such as contextual clues or associations, play a crucial role in triggering the recall of specific memories (Melton, 1963).

In the computational arena, "memory" takes on a defined role as the system enabling perceptions or experiences to be stored beyond real-time, accessible later, and forming a permanent record independent of the sender-receiver connection (Özhan, 2017).

Organizational memory constitutes the amassed knowledge derived from past experiences within an organization, serving as a valuable resource for decision-making. This reservoir of knowledge is constructed through processes facilitating information acquisition, integration, retention, and retrieval. The temporal processes inherent in organizational memory extend beyond mere information collection, requiring internalization as organizational knowledge. Notably, not all information is retained; selection is guided by the perceived importance of information and the availability of organizational capabilities necessary for retention (Bhandary and Maslach, 2018).

The complexity of organizational memory lies in its dynamic processes of information acquisition, interpretation, and retention, transcending mere collection and storage. Specialized storage and retrieval processes are essential for organizations to acquire and represent information as valuable knowledge during decision-making. The definition of organizational memory encompasses both its content and the associated processes. Organizations are urged to curate and preserve information related to information systems, management, economy, systems, decision-making, communication, corporate strategy, and production. These elements, if preserved as a legacy to the future, can yield significant benefits. Therefore, the establishment and meticulous operation of protection strategies and infrastructures are imperative (Stein, 1995).

Organizational memory is the knowledge that has been accumulated from past experiences, which resides in the organization and can be used towards making decisions. It is built through processes that facilitate information acquisition, integration, retention and retrieval. This cache of retained knowledge can prove valuable to organizational decision makers when drawing on past experience.

Organizational memory is the knowledge that has been accumulated from past experiences, which resides in the organization and can be used towards making decisions. It is built through processes that facilitate information acquisition, integration, retention and retrieval. This cache of retained knowledge can prove valuable to organizational decision makers when drawing on past experience.

Organizational memory is the knowledge that has been accumulated from past experiences, which resides in the organization and can be used towards making decisions. It is built through processes that facilitate information acquisition, integration, retention and retrieval. This cache of retained knowledge can prove valuable to organizational decision makers when drawing on past experience.

Information management is one of the crucial elements in this context. The goals of knowledge management are to ensure the growth, transmission and preservation of knowledge in the organization. Today, an important part of the organizational memory consists of digital documents whose number will gradually increase. Digital information within institutions is stored in the form of files (text, images, video, audio and program codes) and databases. Some of these data are digital versions of printed documents. Others may likewise be physical printed versions of digital information. In any way, information is valuable and must be protected (Özhan, 2017).

DIGITALIZATION OF ORGANIZATIONAL MEMORY

Preserving organizational memory is crucial for maintaining a competitive edge, as it encompasses the practices learned over time that contribute to a company's unique strengths. Memory loss occurs when knowledge held by experienced employees is not adequately preserved, often due to factors such as retirement, transfer, or promotion to roles where specific accumulated knowledge is less relevant or unnecessary in its current form. While companies may implement mentoring programs to pass on expertise, these initiatives typically target new hires and focus on facilitating their transition to becoming effective workers. To address the broader issue of knowledge preservation, it becomes imperative to digitalize the organization's knowledge and memory (Chosnek, 2010).

The evolution of advanced information technologies and associated processes has given rise to the improvement and utilization of databases and expert systems as integral elements of organizational memory. In the context of fostering a thinking organization, the information infrastructure required to support such cognitive processes is increasingly distributed to optimize support for solving problems at individual-level. An Organizational Memory System (OMS) as seen in Figure 2 is conceptualized as a system designed to facilitate the application of knowledge from the past to current activities, thereby enhancing the organization's effectiveness. This establishes an effectiveness-based framework for understanding and implementing an OMS. Essentially, an Organizational Memory System is a system that either (1) realizes segments of the organizational knowledge base through information and communications technologies or (2) facilitates tasks, functions, and procedures linked to the utilization of the organizational knowledge base (Ji and Salvendy, 2002).

Figure 2. Organizational memory system

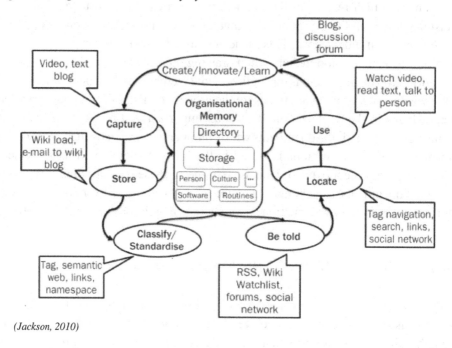

(Jackson, 2010)

Digitalizing organizational memory involves the process of converting, storing, and managing an organization's knowledge and information in digital formats. This digitalization facilitates easy access, retrieval, and sharing of knowledge within the organization. Digitalization of organizational memory starts with identifying and documenting the knowledge. One should firstly identify the key knowledge areas and information that are critical to your organization's operations and goals. After the identification of the knowledge, both explicit knowledge (documents, procedures, manuals) and tacit knowledge (expertise, experiences, insights) should be documented in a structured manner.

Appropriate digital tools and platforms that align with the organization's needs and objectives should be selected. Common options include:

1. **Document Management Systems (DMS)** play a crucial role in capturing, organizing, and preserving the vast array of documents generated within an enterprise. These systems provide a detailed framework for classifying documents, reflecting the diverse range of events and processes within an organization. Internal documents cover a wide range of materials, such as meeting memos, operational records (e.g., job plans, progress reports, and delivery notes), sales statistics, forecasts, training materials, and managerial documents. On the other

hand, the comprehensive storage of varied documents such as presentations, publicity materials, financial information, technical aspects of components, company policies etc. is instrumental in forming a substantial part of the organizational memory, as it encapsulates critical information related to the enterprise's functioning and history (Zantaout and Marir, 1999).

2. **Knowledge Management Systems (KMS)** constitute a category of information systems designed to facilitate the management of corporal knowledge. These systems based on digital technologies are crafted to develop various facets of knowledge processes within the organization which includes creating, storing, retrieving and transferring knowledge. Some Knowledge Management (KM) initiatives do not exclusively involve the implementation of information technologies, while many rely on IT as a crucial enabler, recognizing its role in supporting KM in diverse ways. IT applications within KM initiatives encompass finding experts or recorded sources of knowledge through online directories and database searches, fostering collaboration and knowledge sharing in virtual teams, accessing information from past projects, and analyzing transaction data to understand customer needs and behaviour, among other functionalities (Alavi and Leidner, 2001).

   The role for IT in knowledge management is not unique because there is no uniform technology constituting KMS. Three most used applications of KMS include:

   - Coding and Sharing of Best Practices: KMS facilitates the identification, codification, and dissemination of best practices within the organization.
   - Creation of Organizational Knowledge Directories: KMS supports the development and maintenance of directories that house the collective knowledge and expertise of individuals within the organization.
   - Creation of Knowledge Networks: KMS contributes to the establishment and nurturing of networks that help the transaction and flow of knowledge among organizational members (Alavi and Leidner, 2001).

3. **Intranet portals** are applications designed to facilitate access to both internal and external information within a company. These portals serve as a singular gateway through which users can unlock a wealth of stored information, both within and outside the organization. A user can access a personalized homepage after logging in to the intranet portal through a web browser. This homepage

offers an integrated view of diverse information, presenting users with summaries of informational objects such as reports and organizational documents. The intranet portal acts as a centralized hub, streamlining access to critical data and supporting users in making informed business decisions (Ji and Salvendy, 2002).

4. **A Content Management System (CMS)** helps users to work on digital content on the Internet by software applications. The process of creating and modifying content is made easier by CMSs that allows individuals or teams to work with digital content without extensive technical expertise. CMSs typically include document storage, version control, collaboration, and workflow management capabilities. In terms of organizational memory, CMSs have a strategic role in centralizing, organizing, and preserving knowledge and information. They also support ongoing business activities and decision-making processes and ensure accessibility easily. (Addey et al., 2003).

5. **Enterprise Resource Planning (ERP) systems** are a collection of software tools created to organize various business processes and functions into a unified and centralized platform. The main goal of such system is to improve operational efficiency, consolidate processes, and provide real-time visibility into critical business activities. ERP systems includes a variety of modules for managing financial assets, human resources, supply chain, manufacturing processes, customer relationships etc. Serving as a central hub, an ERP system consolidates organizational data, simplifies business processes, promotes collaboration, and maintains a historical record of activities. ERP systems further help organizational memory by constructing a complete and unified information storage which facilitates an intelligent decision-making and progressive development (Scott and Vessey, 2000).

After constructing an OMS with selected digital tools, the main concern is to keeping the OMS safe. Documents in the OMS may contain delicate information related to online meetings as well as decisions that impact individuals. Recent developments in knowledge management emphasize the importance of enhancing access control to personal information associated with corporal data which is mainly crucial for network institutions. Failure to safeguard sensitive information in the OMS can lead to negative outcomes. This may cause users to refrain from collaborating by withholding their opinions or not being honest which can affect the quality of discussions and decision-making process negatively. Furthermore, the absence of privacy protection could have unintended consequences for users who anticipate a private system but discover that their activities are being tracked. Hence, it is the OMS should essentially develop a policy to assure all users' privacy for active collaboration (Ochoa et al., 2009).

As a result, institutions have to digitalize in an era when data is so important and technology is developing rapidly. Digitalization ensures the effective use of information and ensures that corporate memory remains a valuable asset which helps organizations make smart decisions, innovate faster and achieve long-term success. A digital corporate memory system can help make accurate and intelligent predictions for the future by inferring the organization's past successes and failures.

Historical Aspects of Digitalization of Organizational Memory

The digital systems used for managing organizational knowledge (OMS) have evolved significantly since the 1990s by advances in technology, changes in business practices, and shifts in organizational needs. In the early 1990s, creating document repositories was the primary focus of OMS which aimed to digitize and centralize information in order to make them easier to access. Intranets and knowledge bases emerged as platforms for organizing and sharing information within organizations. However, these systems often lacked sophisticated search capabilities, collaboration features were limited, and knowledge sharing was mainly document-centric since email was the primary way of communication. During the late 1990s, search engines and retrieval algorithms which makes it easier to find information within OMS have improved (Hackbarth and Grover, 1999; Olivera, 2000).

From 2000 to 2010, collaboration became a central focus, leading to the rise of collaborative tools and platforms. OMS facilitated knowledge sharing among employees by incorporating wikis, forums, and social networking features. The significance of creating a knowledge sharing culture has been understood by organizations which needs a higher level of user engagement and participation. For this reason, Content Management Systems (CMS) and content sharing tools have become popular for creating and managing knowledge repositories (Addey et al., 2003).

After the mid-2010s, a major turning point in the development of OMS was reached, thanks to the advanced search capabilities of AI and machine learning that provide more accurate and personalized search results. Additionally, OMS has helped organizations make data-driven decisions and reveal hidden information by extracting features from big data. Features of cloud-based systems such as greater scalability, accessibility and cost-effectiveness were causing many OMS to move to the cloud. In summary, cloud-based solutions have gained importance in preserving organizational memory by promoting remote access and collaboration in organizations (Sefidanoski, 2018).

As a result, OMS have evolved from basic document repositories to complex platforms powered by artificial intelligence, with features that support collaboration, enable data-driven decision-making, and foster a culture of knowledge sharing. The evolution of OMS reflects the dynamic nature of technology and the growing recognition of the strategic importance of managing and promoting organizational knowledge.

The Efficiency of Organizational Memory System in Digital Context

Digitalization policies, integral components of overarching information strategies, has a remarkable role in forming the contours of organizational memory frameworks, especially with the integration of cloud computing. This influence permeates all echelons of organizational memory, spanning individual, group, and corporate levels. The transformation wrought by digitalization imparts distinctive manifestations to explicit and tacit knowledge as fundamental constituents of organizational Memory (Çakmak and Yılmaz, 2012)

The significance of these systems is paramount in upholding the institutional memory of an organization. The synergy between information systems and the overarching system, as crucial elements of organizational memory, stands directly influenced by the prevailing culture of knowledge sharing in the digitalization milieu. (Çakmak and Yılmaz, 2012; Özhan, 2017).

The proliferation of digital projects underscores the need for a recalibration of digital protection and security systems, encompassing firewalls, security policies, and operating systems, alongside cloud-based security measures. These adjustments become imperative to counteract elements that pose threats to organizational memory. The pivotal role of organizational memory manifests in various dimensions such as learning and improvement, decision-making processes, fostering innovation, and shaping organizational culture. Knowledge management, encapsulating documentation, training and development, and information technology, forms a cornerstone in travelling the evolving seas of the digital world (Özhan, 2017).

In the digital age, there are significant challenges for organizations such as information loss, information overload, and resistance to knowledge sharing caused by the proliferation of data. To handle these challenges, contemporary organizational memory systems powered by cloud-based solutions integrate Enterprise Resource Planning (ERP) systems, document management systems, and intranet portals. This integration not only supports a more dynamic knowledge repository but also adapts to the evolving needs of the organization. Furthermore, the strategic application of metadata such as keywords, authors, creation dates, and document types enhances information discoverability and facilitates efficient knowledge retrieval (Çakmak and Yılmaz, 2012; Özhan, 2017; Foroughi et al., 2020).

A continuous cycle of updates and maintenance is needed to ensure access control and security and to encourage information sharing and collaboration. This can be facilitated with cloud-based monitoring and analysis tools. Monitoring and analytics, as well as data management and analysis, must be redesigned in a digital context. The rise of digital systems allows organizations to collect, store and analyze big data, leading to data-driven insights that support improved decision-making and discovery of new opportunities (Özhan, 2017).

The entire process of digitalizing an organization's memory includes the steps such as converting, storing and managing information and knowledge into digital formats. Thanks to this migration, corporal memory could be accessed, retrieved and shared easily within the organization. The rise in remote working and virtual collaboration with the utilization of advanced search capabilities powered by AI, ML, and cloud-based solutions and with the help of knowledge graphs, personalization, mobile accessibility, cybersecurity measures, content management systems (CMS) are reshaping the digital landscape (Özhan, 2017; Foroughi et al., 2020).

In summary, digitalization has serious consequences for organizational memory because it has changed the way knowledge and information are stored, accessed and shared within an organization. Although digitalization provides many benefits in terms of accessibility, efficiency, collaboration and security, it also brings challenges such as information overload, cyber security vulnerabilities and the need to develop a solid culture of information sharing. The practice of digitizing knowledge management highlights the importance of digitally designing corporate memory systems. Accurate prediction of new situations becomes more possible thanks to digitally enhanced corporate memory systems that will contribute to the sustainable development of institutions by taking advantage of past successes and failures.

Organizational Memory Systems in the Era of Cloud Computing

As for the cloud computing, it can support the digitalization process for organizational memory systems.

Cloud computing is an innovative information technology model which has become a popular business strategy for providing IT resources. It allows for easy and quick access to a shared pool of configurable computing resources, including networks, servers, storage, and applications, from any location via the Internet or a network (Benlian et al., 2018). Cloud services can be quickly deployed with minimal management effort and tailored to meet customer needs, requiring limited communication with the cloud provider. Key properties of cloud-based systems contain "service-based provision of IT resources, on-demand self-service, ubiquitous access, multitenancy, location independence, rapid elasticity, and pay-as-you-go billing". Therefore, they can be used to design effective organizational memory systems (Sunyaev, 2020).

Cloud services are commonly categorized into three models as shown in Figure 3, which are "hierarchically organized according to the abstraction level of the capability provided and the provider's service model". These models include Infrastructure as a Service (IaaS), Platform as a Service (PaaS), and Software as a Service (SaaS) (Mell and Grance, 2011). Providers in the market have developed competencies specifically about these distinct layers, namely "software, platform, and infrastructure" (Marston et al., 2011). Organizational memory systems mostly use the SaaS model of cloud computing. This involves providing services such as enterprise resource planning (ERP) services, digital signature, customer relations management (CRM) applications, and other applications that manage financials, sales, and billing (Gochhait et al., 2022).

Figure 3. Three models of cloud services

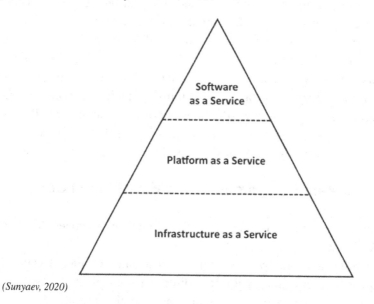

(Sunyaev, 2020)

Of the transformative mechanisms of cloud computing, platformization is the most relevant to organizational memory systems. Decoupling and recombination are also transformative mechanisms of cloud computing. Platformization involves creating cloud-based platforms that are specifically designed to store, manage, and retrieve organizational knowledge and information. Organizations can develop scalable, reliable, and cost-effective memory systems that support collaboration, search and retrieval, security, and integration with other organizational processes by leveraging cloud platforms. Platformization enables organizations to take advantage of cloud-based services to enhance the functionality and capabilities of their memory systems, facilitating efficient knowledge management and decision-making processes (Sunyaev, 2020).

While customers rely on cloud providers consistently, they often have minimal personal interaction with them and possess only limited insight into the providers' attributes, intentions, and potential future actions. Some risks include "multitenancy, loss of control, location intransparency, lack of availability, compromised ease of use, vendor lock-in, limited-service continuity" (Sunyaev, 2020). Organizational memory systems may be subject to certain risks. Firstly, these systems often contain sensitive and critical data. Hosting this data on cloud systems may raise concerns about losing control over its management, security, and privacy, as the organization relies on the cloud provider for these aspects. Secondly, uninterrupted access to information and knowledge is vital since the availability of organizational memory systems is essential. Downtime or disruptions to the cloud service can impede productivity and decision-making within the organization. Additionally, organizations may encounter challenges if they become overly reliant on a single cloud provider for their memory systems. Switching providers or transitioning to on-premises solutions can be complicated and expensive which results in vendor lock-in and reduced flexibility. Finally, ensuring the continuous operation of organizational memory systems is crucial for maintaining productivity and preventing data loss. However, disruptions or discontinuations in cloud services can interrupt service continuity and potentially result in data loss or corruption.

The contribution of cloud computing to organizational memory can be summarized as follows:

- Organizational memory is prone to the risk of data loss caused by hardware failures, natural disasters, or cyber-attacks. Cloud services have robust back-up and recovery mechanisms which ensure the integrity of organizational memory by providing reliable data protection measures.
- Cloud-based storage solutions enable easy and secure access to organizational memory from any location with an Internet connection. This accessibility feature promotes teamwork, even though team members are placed in different physical locations. Moreover, employees are allowed to access critical information in real-time.
- Scalable storage is a requirement for organizations to keep large amounts of data without the obligation for extensive on-premises infrastructure. Cloud computing provides virtually unlimited storage capacity which ensures growth of organizational memory without limitations in order to meet the needs of the business.
- The centralized data management is another concern for corporations which need to organize, categorize, and manage their information assets effectively.

Cloud platforms centralize data to improve the overall coherence and accessibility of organizational memory.

- Cloud computing provides powerful data analysis tools that allow organizations to unlock hidden gems within their data. Raw information is transformed into clear insights by the data analytics tools to make smarter decisions and achieve better results for businesses.
- Cloud services create integrated systems to work seamlessly with other business tools with free data flow which makes all organizational information accessible and usable by different software programs.
- Cloud storage is often cheaper than traditional methods, particularly for small and medium-sized businesses. Unlike traditional storage, organizations only pay for what they use, and there's no need for expensive upfront hardware costs. By this way, cloud storage becomes a practical way for businesses to store their information.
- Cloud providers emphasize security measures and compliance certifications to ensure that organizational memory is protected against unauthorized access, data breaches, and regulatory violations. An enhanced security posture helps maintain the confidentiality, integrity, and availability of sensitive information.

Cloud Computing as a Tool for Organizational Memory Systems: Case Studies

With today's technological improvements, organizations who embrace cloud computing to improve their organizational memory have a chance for enhancing collaboration and driving innovation in their respective fields. This section provides some real-life examples of companies as well as a fictional company adopting cloud computing to their organizational memory systems.

1. Netflix could be a primary case study that has heavily relied on cloud computing to manage its huge amount of content and user data. The company is known as a leading streaming platform known for its vast library of movies, TV shows, and original content. Netflix was confronted with the challenge of efficiently managing vast amounts of data related to viewer preferences, content performance, and global streaming operations. They needed a scalable and agile solution for knowledge management to drive content personalization, decision-making, and operational excellence. The company transitioned from traditional data centers to Amazon Web Services (AWS) in 2009, allowing it to scale its infrastructure according to demand. By leveraging AWS's storage services, such as Amazon S3, Netflix can efficiently store and access its extensive library of movies and

TV shows. This cloud adaptation has not only improved organizational memory by centralizing data storage but has also enabled Netflix to deliver seamless streaming experiences to millions of users worldwide (Hasimi and Penzel, 2023).

2. Another case study, GE Healthcare, which is a leading provider of medical imaging and information technologies, adopted cloud computing to enhance its organizational memory in the healthcare sector. The company needed a scalable, secure, and collaborative knowledge management system to centralize expertise, streamline information sharing, and facilitate data-driven decision-making across its global operations. GE Healthcare developed a SaaS platform by partnering Microsoft Azure to enable healthcare providers to securely store, analyze, and share medical imaging data and patient information. This cloud-enabled platform has significantly improved collaboration among healthcare professionals, streamlined data management processes, and facilitated better decision-making based on comprehensive patient records (Sultan, 2014).

3. In the tourism sector, Airbnb is a global hospitality marketplace has challenged to manage its extensive database of property listings, guest information, and transactional data. The company transitioned to AWS for its cloud infrastructure needs, leveraging services like Amazon DynamoDB for scalable and high-performance database storage. This cloud adaptation has allowed Airbnb to maintain a centralized repository of organizational memory, enabling hosts and guests to access information, manage bookings, and facilitate seamless communication through the platform's cloud-based architecture.

4. The last case study is NASA Jet Propulsion Laboratory (JPL) which aimed to enhance its Mars education and outreach program by leveraging technology to engage the public and foster interest in planetary exploration, specifically Mars. JPL faced the challenge of creating an interactive and engaging platform that allows individuals to explore Mars virtually, interact with the Mars community, and contribute meaningfully to the mission of Mars exploration. The goal was to leverage cloud computing technology to facilitate this interactive experience without overwhelming JPL's internal resources or infrastructure. By leveraging Microsoft Azure's cloud services, JPL can store and analyze vast amounts of scientific data collected from missions like the Mars Rover and the user community. The cloud-based platform has facilitated community engagement, knowledge sharing, and scientific contributions while inspiring public interest and excitement about Mars exploration. This initiative not only benefits the public by providing a fun and educational experience but also allows NASA to enhance its organizational memory by centralizing information related to space exploration, research findings, and mission operations (Kundra, 2010).

5. Companies such as Mercer conduct market wage research and design a pool where companies in a certain region or line of business will provide data entry with the subscriptions they will obtain. In order to carry out an effective wage management function in terms of retaining employees, it will be useful to know the salaries at the level of titles in a company's competitors or in other companies in nearby locations. Thus, an appropriate human resources management strategy can be developed. When a member enters the title information, job descriptions and wage information for each business title, a pool that can benefit from cloud computing will emerge. While these data management systems may enable filtering, it may be possible to create an organizational memory system at a sectoral or geographical level for the same location.

6. Sari and Kurniawan (2015) developed a case study to illustrate the role of cloud computing with the perspective of technology infrastructure and knowledge management process. This case can be extended to organizational memory context.

This company aims to savvy to manage internal data and external data by store it in the cloud with the aim of structuring organizational memory system. Using technology infrastructure will affect the firm via: (a) Reach refers to the ability to connect and access something efficiently of this gain; (b) Depth pertains to the level of detail and the quantity of information that can be effectively communicated through a particular medium. (c) Richness enhances the capacity to facilitate comprehensive and meaningful communication and (d) Aggregation improves the capability to efficiently store and process information rapidly. There are 2 main view points in the model: Customer view and technology view. The infrastructure model was constructed with 4 components (Figure 4): A private cloud is created for internal organizational use and focuses on internal generic applications. A public cloud is set up for a particular group of consumers within the company who share common interests. A hybrid cloud is designed to provide core business applications internally and is connected to applications in other cloud infrastructures, such as private and public clouds. A VPC (Virtual Personal Computer) is designed for specific applications developed internally to support core business applications. They are the types of tools that can be considered as attributes in the design of organizational memory systems.

The core business application is deployed in a hybrid cloud environment, seamlessly linking both private and public clouds. which can be recorded and kept in organizational memory systems. This setup is specifically designed to facilitate swift updates for new users by leveraging the connectivity to the public cloud via their portal. The rationale behind hosting the generic application in the private cloud and connecting it through the hybrid cloud is to ensure convenient access to emails and streamlined data backup processes for organizational memory system members. Therefore, the company's application is not only hosted in the private cloud but also integrated into the hybrid cloud, with the generic application being linked to the hybrid cloud infrastructure.

Figure 4. Technology infrastructure model

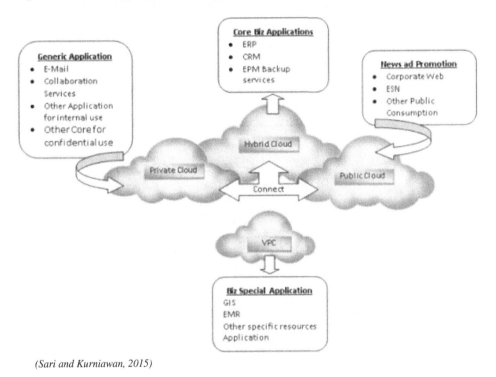

(Sari and Kurniawan, 2015)

The knowledge management starts by accessing external data from the public cloud via a portal, connecting with users of organizational memory system in the Build Knowledge phase. During this step, the data gets categorized and stored in a shared memory system. Subsequently, the data is converted into actionable information and published using document management to enhance understanding in the Hold Knowledge phase. The company can then leverage this external data that can be transferred to organizational memory system for fresh insights and innovation through the Pool Knowledge phase. Lastly, in the Apply Knowledge phase, the company gains easier access to the continuously expanding data, facilitating informed decision-making and adaptation to rapid changes. (Figure 5).

From this perspective, the company can forego constructing its infrastructure and instead concentrate on ensuring that services and operations run smoothly. This approach enables easy modular upgrades and the addition of users in organizational memory system. Leveraging cloud technology as an infrastructure simplifies data filtering for the company, particularly in handling the swiftly growing data volumes. Cloud computing, as a data repository, offers efficiency by eliminating the need to purchase a physical server for a design of organizational memory system.

Figure 5. Knowledge management process

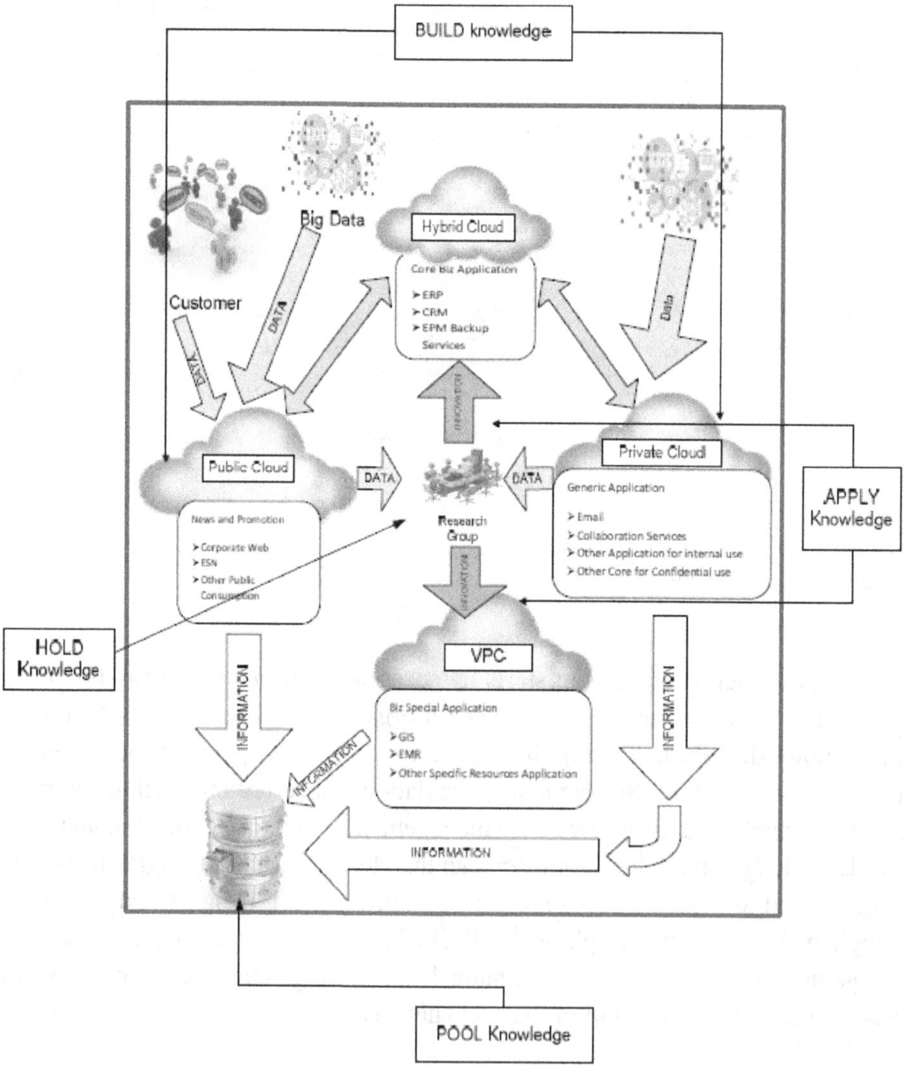

(Sari and Kurniawan, 2015)

As can be seen from the case studies, cloud computing contributes to organizational memory by its key features such as scalable storage, accessibility, security, cost efficiency, and integration. Ongoing evolution of cloud technologies have a potential to further enhance organizational memory through advanced analytics, AI-driven insights, and emerging cloud capabilities. Cloud computing has a strategic importance in shaping the future of organizational memory management and driving innovation within businesses.

IMPLICATIONS

Agile methodologies make it possible for organizations to quickly respond to changing customer needs (Khalid et al., 2022). Real-time data and analytics facilitate data-driven decision-making at all levels of the organization. Digital tools and remote work options can enhance work-life balance and job satisfaction. Collaborative platforms promote better communication and teamwork among employees.

Organizations can digitize their organizational memory, making knowledge and information easily accessible, searchable, and secure. This can ultimately improve decision-making and organizational efficiency. Digitalization has significant implications for organizational memory, affecting how knowledge and information are stored, accessed, and utilized within an organization. Organizational memory is a critical asset that enables organizations to learn, adapt, and thrive. Effective management of this collective knowledge is essential for staying competitive and achieving long-term success. Organizations must carefully plan, manage, and adapt their digital memory systems to maximize the benefits while addressing potential drawbacks.

In essence, cloud computing allows individuals and organizations to access IT resources as needed, from any device, at any time, and on a pay-per-use basis. With its key features like on-demand self-service, resource pooling, elasticity, and scalability, cloud computing opens up a wide range of advantages and favors for individuals and organizations alike (Sunyaev, 2020).

ORIGINALITY

Technological advancements have significantly changed the way organizations execute their operations, largely through Industry 4.0 and Industry 5.0. Elements of organizational memory systems will be reconsidered on a corporal scale depending on the digitalization process. The study has original value in terms of indicating how to consider the elements of corporate memory systems in the context of digitalization. Digitalization emphasizes the importance of contextual variables in the design of organizational memory systems. It is an original finding to reveal that culture of knowledge sharing is an important variable on the digital platform for developing organizational memory systems. Developing organizational memory system strategies for all business function systems within the organization is valuable in practice. Effective use of resources to develop organizational memory systems can contribute to ensuring sustainability, which is of great interest to businesses.

CONTRIBUTION

This paper offers the following contributions to current research in organizational memory systems:

It offers the digitalization effect for the memory systems in the organizations. The theoretical connections suggested represent a significant contribution to enhancing our understanding of organizational memory systems in the digital era. The introduction of a new research perspective and the conceptualization of digitalization for organizational memory contribute to the continuously evolving literature on digital transformation and organizational memory systems research. This is particularly relevant for the elements of corporate memory systems and some contextual variables. It explains the dimensions that system developers should consider when developing a corporate memory system with a high level of digital intensity.

While cloud computing has historically been perceived as a way of creating a value for information technologies, such as economic benefits through IT deployment and utilization (Schneider and Sunyaev, 2016), it also has the potential to transform and enable the creation of novel services and business models. This transformative potential can lead to elemental and massive innovations, helping individuals and organizations as a whole (Benlian et al., 2018).

REFERENCES

Addey, D., Ellis, J., Suh, P., & Thiemecke, D. (2003). *Content management systems (tools of the trade)*. Glasshaus.

Alavi, M., & Leidner, D. E. (2001). Knowledge management and knowledge management systems: Conceptual foundations and research issues. *Management Information Systems Quarterly*, 25(1), 107–136. 10.2307/3250961

Annarelli, A., & Palombi, G. (2021). Digitalization capabilities for sustainable cyber resilience: A conceptual framework. *Sustainability (Basel)*, 13(23), 13065. 10.3390/su132313065

Basu, S., Bardhan, A., Gupta, K., Saha, P., Pal, M., Bose, M., & Sarkar, P. (2018, January). Cloud computing security challenges & solutions-A survey. In *2018 IEEE 8th Annual Computing and Communication Workshop and Conference (CCWC)* (pp. 347-356). IEEE. 10.1109/CCWC.2018.8301700

Benlian, A., Kettinger, W. J., Sunyaev, A., & Winkler, T. J. (2018). Special section: The transformative value of cloud computing: a decoupling, platformization, and recombination theoretical framework. *Journal of Management Information Systems*, 35(3), 719–739. 10.1080/07421222.2018.1481634

Bhandary, A., & Maslach, D. (2018). *Organizational memory. The Palgrave Encyclopedia of Strategic Management*. Palgrave Macmillan.

Bican, P. M., & Brem, A. (2020). Digital business model, digital transformation, digital entrepreneurship: Is there a sustainable "digital"? *Sustainability (Basel)*, 12(13), 5239. Advance online publication. 10.3390/su12135239

Çakmak, T., & Yılmaz, B. (2012). Overview of the Digitalization Policies in Cultural Memory Instutions, *International Symposium on Information Management in Changing World*. Research Gate.

Capgemini. (2011). *Digital Transformation: A Roadmap for Billion-Dollar Organization (Report)*.

Capgemini Consulting Chosnek, J. (2010). Maintaining the corporate memory. *Journal of Loss Prevention in the Process Industries*, 23(6), 796–798. 10.1016/j.jlp.2010.08.004

Dabić, M., Maley, J. F., Švarc, J., & Poček, J. (2023). Future of digital work: Challenges for sustainable human resources management. *Journal of Innovation & Knowledge*, 8(2), 100353. 10.1016/j.jik.2023.100353

Foroughi, H., Corailo, D., Foster, W. M. (2020). Organizational Memory Studies. *Organization Studies, 41*(12), htps://10.1177/0170840620974338

Gochhait, S., Butt, S. A., Jamal, T., & Ali, A. (2022). Cloud Enhances Agile Software Development. In I. Management Association (Ed.), *Research Anthology on Agile Software, Software Development, and Testing* (pp. 491-507). IGI Global. 10.4018/978-1-6684-3702-5.ch025

Grover, V., Tseng, S.-L., & Pu, W. (2022). A theoretical perspective on organizational culture and digitalization. *Information & Management*, 59(4), 103639. 10.1016/j.im.2022.103639

Hackbarth, G., & Grover, V. (1999). The knowledge repository: Organizational memory information systems. *Information Systems Management*, 16(3), 21–30. 10.1201/1078/43197.16.3.19990601/31312.4

Hasimi, L., & Penzel, D. (2023). A Case Study on Cloud Computing: Challenges, Opportunities, and Potentials. In *Developments in Information and Knowledge Management Systems for Business Applications* (Vol. 6, pp. 1–25). Springer Nature Switzerland. 10.1007/978-3-031-27506-7_1

Jackson, P. (2010). *Web 2.0 Knowledge Technologies and the Enterprise, Smarter, Lighter and Cheaper*. Chandos Information Professional Series. Chandos.

Ji, Y. G., & Salvendy, G. (2002). Development and validation of user-adaptive navigation and information retrieval tools for an intranet portal organizational memory information system. *Behaviour & Information Technology*, 21(2), 145–154. 10.1080/01449290210136756

Kane, G. C., Palmer, D., Phillips, A. N., & Kiron, D. ve Buckley, N. (2015). *Strategy, not technology, drives digital transformation*. MIT Sloan Management Review and Deloitte University Press.

Khalid, A., Butt, S. A., Jamal, T., & Gochhait, S. (2022). Agile Scrum Issues at Large-Scale Distributed Projects: Scrum Project Development At Large. In *Research Anthology on Agile Software, Software Development, and Testing, edited by Information Resources Management Association* (pp. 388–398). IGI Global. 10.4018/978-1-6684-3702-5.ch019

Kobsa, A., & Schreck, J. (2003). Privacy through pseudonymity in user-adaptive systems. *ACM Transactions on Internet Technology*, 3(2), 149–183. 10.1145/767193.767196

Kundra, V. (2010). *State of public sector cloud computing*. Federal Chief Information.

Marston, S., Li, Z., Bandyopadhyay, S., Zhang, J., & Ghalsasi, A. (2011). Cloud computing — The business perspective. *Decision Support Systems*, 51(1), 176–189. 10.1016/j.dss.2010.12.006

Mell, P., & Grance, T. (2011). *The NIST definition of cloud computing*. NIST. https:// nvlpubs.nist.gov/nistpubs/Legacy/SP/nistspecialpublication800-145.pdf

Melton, A. W. (1963). Implications of short-term memory for a general theory of memory. *Journal of Verbal Learning and Verbal Behavior*, 2(1), 1–21. 10.1016/ S0022-5371(63)80063-8

Miklosik, A., & Evans, N. (2020). Impact of big data and machine learning on digital transformation in marketing: A literature review. *IEEE Access : Practical Innovations, Open Solutions*, 8, 101284–101292. 10.1109/ACCESS.2020.2998754

Ochoa, S. F., Herskovic, V., Pineda, E., & Pino, J. A. (2009). A transformational model for Organizational Memory Systems management with privacy concerns. *Information Sciences*, 179(15), 2643–2655. 10.1016/j.ins.2009.01.041

Olivera, F. (2000). Memory systems in organizations: An empirical investigation of mechanisms for knowledge collection, storage and access. *Journal of Management Studies*, 37(6), 811–832. 10.1111/1467-6486.00205

Özhan, E. (2017). Kurumsal hafızanın korunmasında sistemin önemi. *Arşiv dünyası*, (18-19), 1-10.

Provost, F., & Fawcett, T. (2013). Data science and its relationship to big data and data-driven decision making. *Big Data*, 1(1), 51–59. 10.1089/big.2013.150827447038

Rachinger, M., Rauter, R., Müller, C., Vorraber, W., & Schirgi, E. (2019). Digitalization and its influence on business model innovation. *Journal of Manufacturing Technology Management*, 30(8), 1143–1160. 10.1108/JMTM-01-2018-0020

Reis, J., Amorim, M., Melão, N., Cohen, Y., & Rodrigues, M. (2020). Digitalization: A Literature Review and Research Agenda. In: Anisic, Z., Lalic, B., Gracanin, D. (eds) *Proceedings on 25th International Joint Conference on Industrial Engineering and Operations Management – IJCIEOM. IJCIEOM 2019*. Lecture Notes on Multidisciplinary Industrial Engineering. Springer, Cham. 10.1007/978-3-030-43616-2_47

Rosenthal, A., Mork, P., Li, M. H., Stanford, J., Koester, D., & Reynolds, P. (2010). Cloud computing: A new business paradigm for biomedical information sharing. *Journal of Biomedical Informatics*, 43(2), 342–353. 10.1016/j.jbi.2009.08.01419715773

Sari, R. A. T. N. A., & Kurniawan, Y. (2015). Cloud computing technology infrastructure to support the knowledge management process (a case study approach). *Journal of Theoretical and Applied Information Technology*, 73(3), 377–382.

Schneider, S., & Sunyaev, A. (2016). Determinant factors of cloud-sourcing decisions: Reflecting on the IT outsourcing literature in the era of cloud computing. *Journal of Information Technology*, 31(1), 1–31. 10.1057/jit.2014.25

Scott, J. E., & Vessey, I. (2000). Implementing enterprise resource planning systems: The role of learning from failure. *Information Systems Frontiers*, 2(2), 213–232. 10.1023/A:1026504325010

Sefidanoski, A. (2018). Deep learning and optimization of organizational memory. *SAR Journal-Science and Research*, 1(3), 115–118.

Sestino, A., Prete, M. I., Piper, L., & Guido, G. (2020). Internet of Things and Big Data as enablers for business digitalization strategies. *Technovation*, 98, 102173. Advance online publication. 10.1016/j.technovation.2020.102173

Stein, E. W. (1995). Organization memory: Review of concepts and recommendations for management. *International Journal of Information Management*, 15(1), 17–32. 10.1016/0268-4012(94)00003-C

Sultan, N. (2014). Making use of cloud computing for healthcare provision: Opportunities and challenges. *International Journal of Information Management*, 34(2), 177–184. 10.1016/j.ijinfomgt.2013.12.011

Sunyaev, A. (2020). *Cloud Computing, (in Internet Computing).* Springer.

Tutkunca, T. (2020). İşletmelerde Dijital Dönüşüm ve İlgili Bileşenlerinin Analiz Edilmesi Üzerine Kavramsal Bir Araştırma. Çağ Üniversitesi. *Sosyal Bilimler Dergisi*, 17(1), 65–75.

Veljković, S. M., Raut, J., Melović, B., & Ćelić, Đ. (2020). Development of Digital Entrepreneurship and New Business Models as a Result of the Expansion of Information Systems. In: Anisic, Z., Lalic, B., Gracanin, D. (eds) *Proceedings on 25th International Joint Conference on Industrial Engineering and Operations Management.* Springer, Cham. 10.1007/978-3-030-43616-2_42

Weichert, D., Link, P., Stoll, A., Rüping, S., Ihlenfeldt, S., & Wrobel, S. (2019). A review of machine learning for the optimization of production processes. *International Journal of Advanced Manufacturing Technology*, 104(5-8), 1889–1902. 10.1007/s00170-019-03988-5

Zantout, H., & Marir, F. (1999). Document management systems from current capabilities towards intelligent information retrieval: An overview. *International Journal of Information Management*, 19(6), 471–484. 10.1016/S0268-4012(99)00043-2

Chapter 7
Transforming Financial Management With Cloud Computing:
Strategies, Benefits, and Innovations

Narayanage Jayantha Dewasiri
https://orcid.org/0000-0002-5908-8890
Sabaragamuwa University of Sri Lanka, Sri Lanka

Mohit Yadav
https://orcid.org/0000-0002-9341-2527
O.P. Jindal Global University, India

ABSTRACT

This chapter focuses on examining how cloud computing can enhance financial management. It aims to make organisations aware of the possibilities of cloud-based solutions for improving financial tasks and help them avoid mistakes when implementing those technologies. The steps entail a systematic literature review that uses guidelines such as preferred reporting items for systematic reviews and meta-analyses (PRISMA). In order to identify an appropriate sample of articles that would answer the research issue, the authors followed the principles of inclusion and exclusion. They compared the abstracts and full texts of the sources in question before considering thirty-seven (37) articles in greater detail. The study also reveals that cloud computing provides a great potential for achieving financial benefits, which include cost reduction, better control and visibility for financial data, improved security and compliance and, last but not least, enabling organisational financial innovation.

DOI: 10.4018/979-8-3693-2869-9.ch007

INTRODUCTION

Overview of Cloud Computing

Cloud computing has revolutionised business operations, allowing users instant access to a pool of reconfigurable hardware, software, storage space, applications, services, and hardware. This forms flexibility and cost-effectiveness that different organisations can achieve with this technology regarding their information technology (IT) requirements, as defined by Yuniarto in 2023. Indeed, from its early stages as a relatively unestablished technology platform, cloud computing has morphed into a contemporary organisational support system, delivering solutions from elementary file-storing providers to intricate, all-encompassing enterprise systems. The emergence of cloud computing has positively impacted by offering flexible and fast deployment of new applications and services (Rehan, 2024). Nowadays, cloud computing is a crucial enabler of transition on a virtual plane by increasing productivity levels and providing new opportune niches in several sectors.

Overview of Financial Management

Financial management is the process that entails planning, directing, controlling, and coordinating the flow of financial resources in an organisation or institution (Petty et al., 2015). Financial management is defined as the management of the financial assets of an organisation using principles such as managerial principles, which are essential in financial management. Financial management can ensure an organisation is poised for efficient resource mobilisation, realisation of fulfilling its financial goals, and sustainability. The primary duties of financial management involve developing a budget, forecasting, investing, record keeping, and controlling cash flows, which are essential for sound business decisions and financial stability (Shroff et al., 2024). In the contemporary business world, financial management is also comprised of picking and minimising risk and legal requirements and using numerical information to foster innovation and sustainable business development. The two studies discovered that proper financial management and the appropriate application of financial assets are crucial to organisational success as they impact the functioning and decision-making process, from staff appointments to developing critical strategies.

Intersection of Cloud Computing and Financial Management

Cloud computing and finance management have brought colossal advancements in how business organisations manage their financial affairs. It is also important to note that cloud-based Subsidiary ledgers and Financial applications have numerous advantages, including security, real-time data availability, and enormous cost savings (Chen & Metawa, 2020). These solutions facilitate financial management and processing, enabling organisations to swiftly leverage data and adopt evidence-based strategies (Jhurani, 2022). Cloud technology solutions applied to finance can help minimise the risks of data entry errors and automate most of the mundane processes involved in financial management while offering better tools for financial modelling, forecasting, and analysis. One, cloud-based solutions are usually more adaptable than operational on-premise ones. At the same time, the latter enables organisations to quickly adapt to changing market conditions and new or modified regulations. With the rise of cloud implementation in corporate entities, integrating the cloud computing concept in performing financial management alters conventional business practices toward a more flexible, accessible, and innovative approach. This transformation has its risks. For instance, there is a risk regarding data security and compliance with the set legal standards; nevertheless, the gains are always higher than the costs. From the result above, it can be observed that organisations can supplement many benefits in terms of financial performance and operation efficiency by engaging the cloud. This chapter deals with how cloud financial management systems can be implemented, considers the advantages of the use of these systems, learns significant issues that may occur during the implementation of cloud financial management, and finally, brings into focus the future trends relating to the use of cloud financial management systems. The article discusses how cloud computing alters the financial scenario in a single package. This pertains to detailing the benefits and possibilities of cloud-based financial management solutions with examples and case histories.

METHODOLOGY

This chapter aims to identify and describe the types of information sources and the subsequent methodological approach applied in the present work is a Systematic Literature Review (SLR) coherent with the PRISMA flow diagram used in the studies conducted by Dewasiri et al. (2022), Jayawardena and Dewasiri (2023), Karunarathne et al. (2024), Rathnasiri et al. (2024) and It also stabilises the evaluation of prior literature, industry analysis, and case studies to follow a systematic and standard approach. This review is based on the following research questions: What opportunities does cloud computing bring to financial management? What are possible best practices for cloud implementation? How can organisations mitigate the risks when using cloud computing to handle their financial data? How do the new technologies affect the advancement of cloud financial management? The articles subjected to an initial search generated 537 records from the databases searched such as Google Scholar and IEEE explore using technical terms such as "cloud computing," "financial management," "data security," "compliance," "cloud computing in finance," "blockchain in financial management". While considering articles for inclusion, emphasis was on articles that discussed the use and effect of cloud computing on financial management and or contained implementation reports, research papers, and industry articles. Studies on the brink or unrelated to the topic, including non-empirical data, were excluded. Such exclusion was omitted, and articles that were out-of-topic were excluded. Information retrieved from the selected articles was structured and categorised into essential issues, improvements and disadvantages, approaches to implementation and likely developments in the future. Specifically, a review of titles and abstracts followed by a review of the full text led to the exclusion of 543 irrelevant and duplicate articles and finally identified 37 entirely suitable for detailed analysis. The study conducted a PRISMA flow diagram, highlighting the study selection process to reduce bias in the results. Based on the synthesised data derived from examining the selected literature, analysis and interpretation of the fines provide essential insight and recommendations for organisations seeking to harness the power of cloud technologies for their financial processes.

THE ROLE OF CLOUD COMPUTING IN FINANCIAL MANAGEMENT

Cloud-Based Financial Applications

Technology has taken the upper hand in most financial management tasks through cloud applications that offer different software packages. These diverse applications include accounting applications, budgeting, payroll, financial reporting, and enterprise resource planning (ERP) hosted on cloud facilities. Due to the cloud's capability, these applications can be easily accessed at any time and location, making it significantly convenient and practical. The essential aspects of cloud financial applications include features such as real-time and automatic data reception entry and analysis, online financial reports and statements, audio and video conferencing integration, and sharing (Ionescu & Diaconita, 2023). These features improve accuracy and save time to reduce dependency on manual work and free up the finance teams for value addition work. By going to the cloud, organisations would be very effective in ensuring that their financial systems are in harmony with the current changes in their regulations, which are added to the present improvement in the industry, which makes it comply with the set standards and regulations.

Advantages of Cloud Computing for Financial Management

Integrating cloud computing in managing finances has numerous benefits, among the more important ones. Cost: Cloud computing spearheads financial mechanisms since it is cheaper than the other conventional models of a system (Gharpure, 2021). This way, organisations can decrease reliance on large capital expenditures and continuous maintenance costs associated with Traditional IT solutions. Instead, through a concept of 'logical subscriptions', they have the resources that align with their operations and financial capacity. Also, people could state that thanks to cloud solutions, organisations can quickly adapt the number of employees and related financial management resources according to their current business needs and be neither oversupplied nor undersupplied (Nandgaonkar & Raut, 2014). Security and compliance are other imperative and valuable uses of cloud computing in financial management (Yalamati, 2024). Some leading cloud service providers use standard security measures, including data encryption, user account authorisation to multiple factors, security checks of the cloud at least once every three months, and others. Furthermore, these providers ensure they are in touch with the regulatory measures to enable firms to adhere to different financial novelties and measures.

In addition, access to real-time data also forms another revolution in the cloud computing environment, where users can analyse the data in real-time (Yang et al., 2017). Decision-makers in financial organisations can receive timely financial information and make decisions using data analysis tools that improve the quality of financial decisions and strategies. This real-time capability makes it possible for businesses to quickly adapt to either financial shenanigans or rewarding discrepancies while at the same time flexibly competing within the market.

Case Studies

There are many benefits, to name the most compelling ones: Cloud accounting gives substantial financial savings and increases productivity (Gharpure, 2021). When organisations adopt cloud solutions, they should spend less on initial investments in IT systems and recurrent maintenance costs. As for them, it is possible to use a somewhat practical and flexible system of subscription tariffs corresponding to their work requirements and financial indications. Furthermore, it is pertinent to note that cloud solutions provide the elasticity and adaptability needed for organisations to match changes in their business requirements to the available financial management resources without being over or under-prepared (Nandgaonkar & Raut, 2014).

Financial management has other crucial advantages for focusing on cloud computing, including increased security and compliance (Yalamati, 2024). Large cloud service providers use strict security measures like encrypting data, passwords that require a second form of authentication or biometric verification, and regular testing of the firms' security measures to prevent any compromise of confidential financial details. Furthermore, these providers keep themselves updated with the latest regulations so companies can adequately follow legal and financial regulations.

Real-time data access and analysis are other revolutionary benefits of cloud computing technology, Yang et al., 2017. Administrators and financial managers of these institutions can obtain current and accurate financial data and develop revised forecasts and analyses from advanced analytics tools, leading to improved decisions and planning. This makes its operation real-time, enabling it to respond quickly to any financial irregularities or impending opportunities to prevent or exploit in a competitive market.

Case Study 1: Netflix

The world's streaming giant, Netflix, uses cloud computing for several business processes across its organisations, including finance (Naseer, 2023). For instance, Netflix has considered Amazon Web Services (AWS), which increased the company's ability to conduct financial reporting and analysis (Singh & Agarwal, 2014). The strategic cloud-based platform allows Netflix to store and process large datasets, showing subscriber acquisition pace, revenue, and cost at the exact moment. This makes it possible for the finance team to react appropriately in analysis and make the right decisions for the company, which helps the firm stay relevant in the entertainment industry.

Case Study 2: Capital One

Capital One is perhaps one of the world's most reputed credit card companies, and it has come under the spotlight consistently over a short period. This is a particular case of the global financial services organisation Capital One, which successfully adopted the concept of cloud computing to improve its financial processes. Thus, transferring its central financial systems to AWS has helped Capital One improve its approach to data protection, meeting the regulations, and provision of disaster recovery. The cloud environment ably supports multi-tenancy, real-time financial information processing, risk management, and reporting capabilities. This transition has helped Capital One to contain operational expenses while boosting flexibility, thus delivering services to clients by developing new and innovative financial solutions.

Case Study 3: General Electric

One global company that has followed this trend of posting consistent profits for several years and across different fiscal years is General Electric (GE). For example, General Electric (GE) commonly integrated a cloud-based ERP system to address numerous deficiencies with centralised and integrated financial systems. After speaking with GE about its experience implementing Oracle Cloud ERP, we have some key takeaways: These include getting real-time financial reporting and analysis, which offers possibilities to enhance business decisions and strategies. Furthermore, via applications such as ERP, the IT infrastructural cost was minimised, and flexibility in meeting changing market and business requirements was increased.

Case Study 4: Unilever

Microsoft Azure has been adopted by numerous organisations in the modern world to support their ambitions in the marketing space. Unilever, a global consumer goods manufacturer, also leveraged it for efficient financial management (Anitah, 2019). Such financial processes are generalized across the company through the cloud platform; hence, there is standardisation and precision. As financial transactions generate real-time data, Unilever's finance team has tools that can help it track performance, mitigate risks associated with inefficiency, and find new ways for cost optimization and productivity increase. It has also helped improve the efficacies of cloud-based shared service across geographies and overall financial operations.

Case Study 5: Airbnb

Airbnb, a leading online platform for short-term accommodations and other travelling experiences has adopted cloud-based financial management arrangements to foster further growth and sustain its worldwide expansion (Buhalis et al., 2019). For instance, through contracts and actualisations, it has incorporated NetSuite and other cloud-based accounting tools to simplify its financial management process, starting with generating invoices, processing expenditures, and reporting its financial performance. The cloud platform gets them real-time financial data, which can be utilised effectively and efficiently for decision-making purposes as well as for distributing and employing the resources most effectively and avail the opportunities as per the regulations of different countries.

Case Study 6: Kellogg's

The global food company Kellogg's decided to utilise the SAP S/4HANA for Cloud in the financial management field. Briefly, it could be concluded that the cloud-based ERP system at Kellogg's has helped to increase the effectiveness and productivity of the company, as well as reduce the number of possible mistakes. This real-time information facilitates improved internal budgeting, planning, and decision-making about future trends in financial options for Kellogg's. In addition, it addresses compliance with financial regulations, strengthens the security of the company's assets and provides adequate support for financial activity.

Hence, these case studies highlight the multifaceted use and the potential value of embracing cloud computing technology in handling financial management tasks. They capture a direction of when and where problems might emerge but stress the need to approach these issues correctly and select proper cloud solutions to turn challenges into opportunities that can bolster the success of a business venture with cloud-based financial management systems. Cloud-Based Solutions for Administrative Services Conclusion: The implementation of cloud-based solutions has led to the enhancement of efficiency, accuracy, scalability, and compliance, thereby making it possible for these companies to achieve better business results.

STRATEGIES FOR IMPLEMENTING CLOUD FINANCIAL MANAGEMENT

Planning and Assessment

The first step of managing finance in the cloud environment is planning and analysis (Mahalle et al., 2020). Managers must understand their businesses' requirements and objectives when choosing the cloud solution to fit their strategic plan. This entails evaluating the existing financial structures and procedures to identify strengths, weaknesses, opportunities and threats. Awareness of these aspects also enables the definition of goals for the cloud shift, such as increasing reporting reliability, protecting information, or cutting down costs.

Choosing the Right Cloud Solutions

According to Ramachandran et al. (2014), choosing the right cloud financial software or model is very delicate for an implementation. Organisations must have ways of selecting the solutions they use: functionality, scalability, security, ease of use and cost. Convenient vendor analysis and comparison are needed to identify which one can be suitable for the organisation. The following should be part of this process: evaluating the vendor's reputation, the vendor, the financial position of the vendor, and their customer support and compliance to standards. Lastly, the chosen solution should be able to accommodate the growing need as well as future technological developments.

Implementation and Integration

Cloud-based financial systems' implementation and, more so, the integration has to be done more carefully and watchfully. The first phase is to present a concrete overall schedule for implementation to indicate the activities, time frame and actors of the change. This plan should also contain procedures for migrating the older financial data to the new system without any hitches. This is helpful, especially when integrating into another system in the organisation, to ensure the continuity of business processes across organisational departments. This may include interacting with internal and contracted IT departments to implement the new system and coding new components that can be integrated into the new system to solve technical issues.

Training and Change Management

A particular emphasis should be placed on ensuring that users follow the new environment and are ready to adopt it since implementing cloud financial management is among the most challenging tasks for modern organisations (Okai et al., 2014). Additional extensive awareness enhancement training should be provided to all personnel concerning the novel features, aspects, and advantages of the additional functions. This training should reflect the needs and roles of the particular users in the organisation – from the financial experts to the IT personnel. The transitional processes also require effective change management strategies to address the problem of organisational resistance. It entails informing the change's rationale, the advantages of the new system, and how the change will affect operations. By continuing to support the new system and explaining solutions for the mentioned concerns, such as creating help desks or user forums, it is possible to amass the problem and maintain the subjects' confidence within the new system.

Therefore, introducing cloud financial management systems encompasses various steps, including strategic planning, choosing correct applications, integration, and teaching change management. Therefore, by implementing these overall strategies, organisations will be in a vantage position to implement a working model of cloud financial management, enhancing efficiency, accuracy and flexibility in the financial processes.

BENEFITS OF CLOUD COMPUTING FOR FINANCIAL MANAGEMENT

Cost Efficiency

Another appealing advantage of shifting towards cloud-based solutions is cost-effectiveness within the financial management sphere, as Youssef (2012) described. SaaS solutions, for example, adopt a usage-based pricing strategy to increase the organisation's flexibility and minimise the capital investment in IT architectures. With this model, firms can transact enterprise only for the services they consume, helping manage expenses and effectively distributing the budget. Another advantage of combining computing with cloud providers is that they manage system maintenance, updates, and security, thus minimising the operational costs of hiring internal IT people. This, in turn, enhances the central resources since an organisation would not be spending much on daily IT management issues.

Improved Financial Visibility and Reporting

It is known that cloud computing even improves financial visibility and reporting (Hsu & Lin, 2016). Ubiquity features for financial data are available with the help of cloud-based financial management systems, mainly because organisations can disseminate real-time updated reports for various financial analyses. The use of sophisticated analysis of data in such systems allows the finance teams to categorise trends, track performance, and draw proper conclusions. Acquiring the most accurate financial information as soon as possible increases transparency and accountability since all the interested parties are promptly informed of the state of the organisational financials. Improved reporting options also assist in ensuring compliance with the legal standards in an organisation since the information disclosed is reliable and timely.

Enhanced Security and Compliance

A secure environment is crucial for any organisation's financial framework, and cloud computing offers basic security features to protect essential financial data (Padhy et al., 2011). The major players within the cloud have strict security measures, including encoding, authorisation, and security audits. They prevent financial information from being accessed or manipulated by other people and from cyber-attacks. Besides, cloud providers often conform to sectorial laws and regulations, such as GDPR and SOX, that help organisations meet regulatory requirements. The important thing is that by using cloud providers' experience in security, businesses protect their financial data against various risks.

Agility and Innovation

Cloud computing increases flexibility and creativity in financial management because of its weak time-to-market of financial applications and services (Liu et al., 2018, Vihari et al., 2022). It becomes easier for organisations to put into practice new financial management instruments and systems and can keep improving or inventing them without interruption. Another advantage of cloud solutions is attained scalability, which allows a company to readily adapt its management capacity as needed with finances and in response to any alterations on the market. Flexible operation is precious in the present world and business environment, characterised by constant changes and high volatility that require firms to adapt fast. Autonomous platforms often use AI and machine learning since they provide accurate financial analysis, forecasting, and decision-making capabilities.

Consequently, cloud computing encompasses several benefits in financial management: Cost-effectiveness, financial visibility and reporting, secure compliance, velocity and innovation. These advantages assist organisations in managing their finances effectively and making sound decisions that improve business performance. Hence, by incorporating cloud-based solutions to manage their financials, a business is well placed to compete within such an environment and achieve sustainable growth.

CHALLENGES AND CONSIDERATIONS

Data Security and Privacy Concerns

Confidentiality and data protection are prime concerns in cloud-based financial management systems (Amponsah et al., 2022). Hazards and susceptibilities are other critical elements of organisations that need to be managed, including unauthorised access, data loss, and cyber-attacks (Dolezel & McLeod, 2019). Regarding data protection, it is critical to employ measures to safeguard the data from various dangers, including ciphering to secure the data, using passcodes and other proofs of identity, and ordinary surveillance to check on the security levels present. Besides, organisations need to implement best data protection practices like applying secure data access measures, frequently updating security standards and training the organisational workforce on security measures. Additional measures include selecting reliable cloud service providers that meet high safety requirements; in this way, the risks and data confidentiality regarding important financial data are minimised.

Compliance and Regulatory Issues

One of the major issues is that any organisation applies complicated financial regulation standards in the context of cloud computing. Organisations must guarantee compliance of their financial management systems that Cloud service with various standards and legal expectations, the General Data Protection Regulation (GDPR), Sarbanes-Oxley Act (SOX), and Payment Card Industry Data Security Standards (Williams & Adamson, 2022). Consequently, compliance entails gaining a well-understood appreciation of these regulations and then aspiring to take the proper steps to fulfil those regulations' expectations. To conclude, compliance helps the organisation avoid penalties by law; also, by maintaining a compliance culture within the organisation, the organisational reputation and the confidence stakeholders place in the institution are well protected.

Technical and Organizational Challenges

The technical and organisational aspects are the primary considerations for addressing technical and organisational changes when using cloud-based financial information systems. When implementing SaaS, cloud systems must be linked with other current on-premises or other older systems, thus causing integration problems (Diaz et al., 2016). These require a coherent integration strategy with the backing of IT professionals who can set up interfaces with other applications, fix compatibility problems and ensure data synchronisation across the various systems. Thirdly and most importantly, of course, is the ability to effectively manage change within organisations, which is a crucial factor in successful adoption. Some employees may resist change because they are new systems that must be learned, or they might feel that change will affect their workflow badly. Various strategies for managing change include communications, training and development programs, and support to minimise opposition during the change process. It can also complement these by encouraging stakeholders to participate in the change process and resolve their misconceptions that can reduce the new system's acceptance and efficiency.

Cost Management

While shifting towards cloud-based solutions was cost-effective, managing these costs can still be complicated. In dealing with cost management, organisations need to be cautious of hidden costs, which include fees for data transfer, storage beyond a limit or if an organisation uses a specific add-on service that is a premium service. The primary emphasis on optimising cloud expenditure is employing measures that lower costs and boost efficiency. Some of these best practices are: Cloud utilisation should always be observed, cloud management tools offered by the vendors should be used, and over-cost alerts should be set up for expenditure tracking. Further, organisations must occasionally examine their cloud service plans to apply the best and most efficient practices corresponding to their usage parameters and organisational requirements. It is essential for organisations not to fall victim to the financial risks of cloud computing since, considering the approach mentioned by Avram in 2014, it is possible to emphasise the existence of significant financial benefits which will give organisations a competitive edge; however, a unique cost management strategy has to be used to ensure that no potential for financial risks will be realised.

Performance and Reliability Concerns

The last crucial issue that has to be addressed when implementing cloud-based financial management systems is the consistently high rates of service delivery and availability (Cleary & Quinn, 2016). The financing operations directly depend on the data access and the fast and efficient performance of the transactions. One disadvantage of software is that if it incurs downtime or slow performance, vital financial processes are affected, resulting in a slow report turnaround, problems with cash flow and general inefficiencies. Organisations must acquire services from providers with proven reliability and performance to avoid such issues. High availability cannot be achieved without elaborating reliable disaster management and business scenarios, which will help reduce the impact of possible outages. Furthermore, organisations must stay vigilant about cloud systems' performance and collaborate with providers and vendors to assess and manage infrastructure and problems (Malallah et al., 2023). Control over highly reliable and high-quality cloud services provides continuity and efficiency of financial operations and the organisation's business stability.

As a result, we can reap significant benefits in implementing cloud-based financial management systems. However, we must also carefully manage data security, compliance, technical integration, organisational change, and cost implications. Solving these challenges and issues involves having a good strategy with sound and robust security measures, compliance programs and controls, integration and change management plans, and setting active cost control procedures. This means that organisations can consider the above factors effectively and enhance the use of cloud financial management systems, thereby improving financial operations' efficiency, accuracy, and flexibility.

FUTURE TRENDS IN CLOUD FINANCIAL MANAGEMENT

Emerging Technologies

Cloud financial management specialisation is rapidly evolving as a direct result of the development of such innovative solutions as artificial intelligence (AI) and machine learning (ML). Hence, technologies like artificial intelligence (AI) and machine learning (ML) transform the CFO's work by automating rote tasks, enhancing data analysis capacity, and delivering forecasts. AI enables several functions of managing invoices, detecting fraudulent activities, and offering personalised recommendations for the financial domain (Ionescu & Diaconita, 2023). Machine learning algorithms can examine large datasets in the financial market to identify trends in operations and forecast future trends for better planning. These advanced technologies assist in the enhancement and enable organisations to understand the workings of their financial aspects, thus boosting innovation and competition.

Another technological development likely to have broad implications is blockchain systems and technologies. Blockchain provides an efficient means of documenting transactions due to its decentralised, transparent and secure mechanisms; financial records credibility can be thus boosted (Dewasiri et al., 2024). It also applies to the auditing and compliance systems and contract management and helps eliminate risks from improper reporting. Blockchain implementation in the financial organisation can bring fundamental changes in standard financial management practices, increasing the speed and reliability of transactions and providing ways for verification.

Evolving Cloud Services

New advancements in cloud financial applications are constantly contributing towards the future development of financial operations. Real-time computing is increasingly being incorporated, automated compliance verification is constantly improving, and easy-to-use graphical user interfaces for financial management are improving. Such novelties improve organisational finance and offer detailed and immediate management of fiscal processes.

The advances in cloud deployment, such as the Public, Private, and Hybrid clouds, also impact financial management tactics (Sangroya et al., 2020; Senyo et al., 2018). The public cloud delivers value for money with high levels of flexibility for organisations, while the private cloud provides an organisation's financial department with the required security on the data. Hybrid cloud solutions benefit organisations by efficiently meeting cost and capacity needs and security, depending on the organisation's needs. The choice of the deployment model depends on several factors, including the legal requirements, the fiscal restraints and the properties of financial operations. Therefore, as cloud services continue to improve the customer's experience and change in the future, businesses should prepare to receive more specialised and flexible services to fulfil their particular needs regarding financial management.

The Future of Financial Management

As to the outlook, it is pretty perfectible to prognosticate that the succeeding financial managements shall be dominated by digitalisation and technologies. Available forecasts and estimations suggest that embedding AI, blockchain, and other novel technologies into the systems used for managing and controlling finances will become mainstream by Soundararajan and Shenbagaraman (2024). The following technologies will enhance better forecasting of financial needs, managing risks, and decision-making. However, the advancement of new technology in cloud services ensures better and improved solutions for managing finances in established business environments.

In the long run, the prospects that stem from such changes are significant, such as precision, speed, and, thus, strategy. However, the following challenges must be considered: data security, regulatory requirements, and continuous investments in technology and talent. Organisations overcoming these issues will have better chances to utilise cloud financial management's opportunities, bring innovations, and continually improve their performance.

Hence, cloud financial management is also expected to change significantly based on the advancing technology and newer types of cloud services. Such trends must be followed, and the organisation has to pursue the course of action to harness the positive aspects and avoid the negatives. In this way, each person can successfully deal with financial management and gain an advantage amidst the shifts in the business world.

CONCLUSION OF THE STUDY

Cloud integration in financial management is a revolutionary change in how organisations deal with their operations. This chapter has investigated the numerous advantages of implementing cloud-based financial management solutions, such as financial returns, a better understanding of the organisation's financial status, compliance with security standards, flexibility and innovation. These advantages increase the efficiency of the financial processes, making the correct decisions and getting better results for a business. These areas included the issues of planning and evaluation, choice of cloud solutions, integration, and training and change management, which the author connected with the concept of decision-making for successful implementation. Managing these factors makes the transition easier and leads to the optimal use of the solutions offered by cloud financial management systems.

However, going through this cloud adoption process is not without its challenges. Organisations must make vital decisions, such as data protection and privacy, legal matters, technology and administrative costs, etc. Organisations can avoid these risks and be sure that their cloud-based financial systems are implemented and work efficiently by choosing the best strategies and relying on experience. In the future, management at the financial level may be impacted significantly by existing high technologies such as AI, machine learning, and blockchain. These technologies and the progress in cloud services and deploying strategies are persistently shaping the environment for new opportunities in terms of efficiency, accuracy, and strategic comprehension. Organisations that can predict and adapt to these changes will be in an excellent position to harness all the possibilities of cloud financial management. This will help them continue to encourage creativity and establish growth in an ever-growing, saturated market.

Finally, incorporating cloud computing solutions in the management of financial aspects is not a mere trend but a significant advancement that presents significant opportunities and benefits for organisations. Thus, the goals of implementing cloud-based financial management systems can be achieved if businesses focus on understanding the strategies and the challenges arising from their implementation. This transformation ensures that performance increases and sustainability is achieved in the long run.

REFERENCES

Amponsah, A. A., Adekoya, A. F., & Weyori, B. A. (2022). Improving the financial security of national health insurance using cloud-based blockchain technology application. *International Journal of Information Management Data Insights*, 2(1), e100081. 10.1016/j.jjimei.2022.100081

Anitah, J. N. (2019). *Industry 4.0 Technologies and Operational Performance of Fast Moving Consumer Goods Manufacturers in Kenya: A Case Study of Unilever Kenya and L'oreal East Africa* [Doctoral dissertation, University of Nairobi].

Avram, M. G. (2014). *Advantages and challenges of adopting cloud computing from an enterprise perspective*. Procedia Technology. 10.1016/j.protcy.2013.12.525

Buhalis, D., Harwood, T., Bogicevic, V., Viglia, G., Beldona, S., & Hofacker, C. (2019). Technological disruptions in services: Lessons from tourism and hospitality. *Journal of Service Management*, 30(4), 484–506. 10.1108/JOSM-12-2018-0398

Chen, X., & Metawa, N. (2020). Enterprise Financial Management Information System based on cloud computing in a big data environment. *Journal of Intelligent & Fuzzy Systems*, 39(4), 5223–5232. 10.3233/JIFS-189007

Cleary, P., & Quinn, M. (2016). Intellectual capital and business performance: An exploratory study of the impact of cloud-based accounting and finance infrastructure. *Journal of Intellectual Capital*, 17(2), 255–278. 10.1108/JIC-06-2015-0058

Dewasiri, N. J., Baker, H. K., Banda, Y. W., & Rathnasiri, M. S. H. (2022). The Dividend Decision Model: A Possible Solution for the Dividend Puzzle. In *Exploring the Latest Trends in Management Literature*. Emerald Publishing Limited. 10.1108/S2754-586520220000001013

Dewasiri, N. J., Dharmarathna, D. G., & Choudhary, M. (2024). Leveraging Artificial Intelligence for Enhanced Risk Management in Banking: A Systematic Literature Review. Singh, R., Khan, S., Kumar, A., & Kumar, V. (Ed.) *Artificial Intelligence Enabled Management: An Emerging Economy Perspective*. De Gruyter. 10.1515/9783111172408-013

Díaz, M., Martín, C., & Rubio, B. (2016). State-of-the-art, challenges, and open issues in the integration of the Internet of things and cloud computing. *Journal of Network and Computer Applications*, 67, 99–117. 10.1016/j.jnca.2016.01.010

Dolezel, D., & McLeod, A. (2019). Managing security risk: Modelling the root causes of data breaches. *The Health Care Manager*, 38(4), 322–330. 10.1097/HCM.0000000000000028231663871

Gharpure, R. (2021). Effect of Cloud computing technology adoption on Reduction in Costs: A critical review from the business perspective. [TURCOMAT]. *Turkish Journal of Computer and Mathematics Education*, 12(10), 4391–4399.

Hsu, C. L., & Lin, J. C. C. (2016). Factors affecting the adoption of cloud services in enterprises. *Information Systems and e-Business Management*, 14(4), 791–822. 10.1007/s10257-015-0300-9

Ionescu, S. A., & Diaconita, V. (2023). Transforming Financial Decision-Making: The Interplay of AI, Cloud Computing and Advanced Data Management Technologies. *International Journal of Computers Communications & Control, 18*(6), e5735, 1-19.

Jayawardena, N. S., & Dewasiri, N. J. (2023). *Food Acquisition and Consumption Issues of South Asian Countries: A Systematic Literature Review and Future Research Agenda*. FIIB Business Review. 10.1177/23197145231194113

Jhurani, J. (2022). *Driving Economic Efficiency and Innovation: The Impact of Workday Financials in Cloud-Based ERP Adoption. International Journal of Computer Engineering and Technology*. IJCET.

Karunarathna, K. S. S. N., Dewasiri, N. J., Singh, R., & Rathnasiri, M. S. H. (2024). What Does Artificial Intelligence–Powered ChatGPT Bring to Academia? A Review. Singh, R., Khan, S., Kumar, A., & Kumar, V. (Ed.) *Artificial Intelligence Enabled Management: An Emerging Economy Perspective*. De Gruyter. 10.1515/9783111172408

Liu, S., Chan, F. T., Yang, J., & Niu, B. (2018). Understanding the effect of cloud computing on organisational agility: An empirical examination. *International Journal of Information Management*, 43, 98–111. 10.1016/j.ijinfomgt.2018.07.010

Mahalle, A., Yong, J., & Tao, X. (2020). ITIL process management to mitigate operations risk in cloud architecture infrastructure for the banking and financial services industry. *Web Intelligence*, 18(3), 229–238. 10.3233/WEB-200444

Malallah, H. S., Qashi, R., Abdulrahman, L. M., Omer, M. A., & Yazdeen, A. A. (2023). Performance analysis of enterprise cloud computing: A review. *Journal of Applied Science and Technology Trends*, 4(1), 1–12. 10.38094/jastt401139

Nandgaonkar, S. V., & Raut, A. B. (2014). A comprehensive study on cloud computing. *International Journal of Computer Science and Mobile Computing*, 3(4), 733–738.

Naseer, I. (2023). AWS Cloud Computing Solutions: Optimizing Implementation for Businesses. Statistics. *Computing and Interdisciplinary Research*, 5(2), 121–132. 10.52700/scir.v5i2.138

Nicho, M., Fakhry, H., & Haiber, C. (2011). An integrated security governance framework for effective PCI DSS implementation. [IJISP]. *International Journal of Information Security and Privacy*, 5(3), 50–67. 10.4018/jisp.2011070104

Okai, S., Uddin, M., Arshad, A., Alsaqour, R., & Shah, A. (2014). Cloud computing adoption model for universities to increase ICT proficiency. *SAGE Open*, 4(3), 1–10. 10.1177/2158244014546461

Padhy, R. P., Patra, M. R., & Satapathy, S. C. (2011). Cloud computing: Security issues and research challenges. [IJCSITS]. *International Journal of Computer Science and Information Technology & Security*, 1(2), 136–146.

Petty, J. W., Titman, S., Keown, A. J., Martin, P., Martin, J. D., & Burrow, M. (2015). *Financial Management: Principles and Applications*. Pearson Higher Education.

Ramachandran, N., Sivaprakasam, P., Thangamani, G., & Anand, G. (2014). Selecting a suitable cloud computing technology deployment model for an academic institute: A case study. *Campus-Wide Information Systems*, 31(5), 319–345. 10.1108/CWIS-09-2014-0018

Rathnasiri, M. S. H., Dewasiri, N. J., & Kumar, A. A. (2024). Policy Framework and Implementation Strategies for Sri Lanka's Transition to a Net-Zero Economy. In *Net Zero Economy, Corporate Social Responsibility and Sustainable Value Creation: Exploring Strategies, Drivers, and Challenges* (pp. 43–60). Springer Nature Switzerland. 10.1007/978-3-031-55779-8_3

Rehan, H. (2024). Revolutionizing America's Cloud Computing: The Pivotal Role of AI in Driving Innovation and Security. *Journal of Artificial Intelligence General Science,* 2(1), 239–240.

Sangroya, D., Kabra, G., Joshi, Y., & Yadav, M. (2020). Green energy management in India for environmental benchmarking: From concept to practice. *Management of Environmental Quality*, 31(5), 1329–1349. 10.1108/MEQ-11-2019-0237

Senyo, P. K., Addae, E., & Boateng, R. (2018). Cloud computing research: A review of research themes, frameworks, methods and future research directions. *International Journal of Information Management*, 38(1), 128–139. 10.1016/j.ijinfomgt.2017.07.007

Shroff, S. J., Paliwal, U. L., & Dewasiri, N. J. (2024). Unravelling the impact of financial literacy on investment decisions in an emerging market. *Business Strategy & Development*, 7(1), e337. 10.1002/bsd2.337

Singh, H. P., & Agarwal, A. (2014). Leveraging the Revolutionary Paradigm of Cloud Computing: The Case of Netflix. *MuMukshuJournal of HuManities Referred Journal*, 6(1), 177–185.

Soundararajan, R., & Shenbagaraman, V. M. (2024). Enhancing financial decision-making through explainable AI and Blockchain integration: Improving transparency and trust in predictive models. *Educational Administration: Theory and Practice*, 30(4), 9341–9351.

Vihari, N. S., Yadav, M., & Panda, T. K. (2022). Impact of soft TQM practices on employee work role performance: Role of innovative work behaviour and initiative climate. *The TQM Journal*, 34(1), 160–177. 10.1108/TQM-03-2021-0092

Williams, B., & Adamson, J. (2022). *PCI Compliance: Understand and implement adequate compliance with PCI data security standards*. CRC Press. 10.1201/9781003100300

Yalamati, S. (2024). Data Privacy, Compliance, and Security in Cloud Computing for Finance. In Whig, W., Sharma, S., Sharma, S., Jain, A., & Yathiraju, N. *Practical Applications of Data Processing, Algorithms, and Modeling* (pp. 127–144). IGI Global.

Yang, C., Huang, Q., Li, Z., Liu, K., & Hu, F. (2017). Big Data and cloud computing: Innovation opportunities and challenges. *International Journal of Digital Earth*, 10(1), 13–53. 10.1080/17538947.2016.1239771

Youssef, A. E. (2012). Exploring cloud computing services and applications. *Journal of Emerging Trends in Computing and Information Sciences*, 3(6), 838–847.

Yuniarto, D. (2023). Implementing cloud computing in companies to increase business efficiency. *Jurnal Info Sains: Informatika Dan Sains*, 13(02), 633–639.

Chapter 8
A Survey on Cloud Security Issues and Challenges

Sangeetha Ganesan
ⓘ https://orcid.org/0000-0001-7347-2162
R.M.K. College of Engineering and Technology, India

Mohamed Ashwak M.
R.M.K. College of Engineering and Technology, India

Shaik Junaidh Ahmed J.
R.M.K. College of Engineering and Technology, India

L. Saran
R.M.K. College of Engineering and Technology, India

Mohan Kumar M.
R.M.K. College of Engineering and Technology, India

ABSTRACT

Cloud computing has emerged as one of the most disruptive technologies in recent years, changing the way organizations store, process, and manage their data and applications. This chapter aims to provide a comprehensive overview of cloud computing, including its benefits and challenges, the different types of cloud services available, and the security measures that organizations can implement to protect their data in the cloud. The chapter will also examine the various compliance and regulatory requirements that organizations must meet when using cloud services and best practices for secure cloud deployment and management. Additionally, the

DOI: 10.4018/979-8-3693-2869-9.ch008

chapter will also cover the evolution of cloud computing from its beginnings to its current state and future developments, and will also provide real-world examples and case studies of organizations that have successfully implemented cloud computing.

INTRODUCTION

Cloud computing has emerged as one of the most disruptive technologies in recent years, changing the way organizations store, process, and manage their data and applications. The technology allows companies to access a wide range of computing resources, including servers, storage, and applications, over the internet. This eliminates the need for organizations to invest in and maintain their own IT infrastructure, which can be expensive, time-consuming, and complex.

The use of cloud services has grown rapidly in recent years, driven by the benefits of scalability, cost-effectiveness, and flexibility. With the cloud, organizations can easily scale their IT resources up or down as needed, which can be especially beneficial for businesses that experience fluctuations in demand. Additionally, cloud services are typically offered on a pay-as-you-go basis, which allows organizations to reduce their IT costs by only paying for the resources they use. And lastly, the cloud provides organizations with the flexibility to access their data and applications from anywhere, at any time, which can be especially beneficial for companies with remote workers or multiple locations.

However, as more sensitive information is stored in the cloud, the risk of data breaches and other security incidents increases. Cloud services can be a target for cyber-attacks, and organizations must take the necessary steps to protect their data in the cloud. Additionally, organizations must meet compliance and regulatory requirements when using cloud services, such as data protection laws and industry-specific regulations.

This paper aims to help organizations understand the benefits and risks associated with cloud computing and make informed decisions about their use of cloud services. By clearly understanding the technology and its potential implications, organizations can effectively leverage the power of cloud computing to improve their operations, reduce costs, and increase their competitiveness.

BACKGROUND

Cloud computing is an on-demand feature on the internet, for computing applications, resources, applications, data storage, networking capability, and development tools at a remote server data centre which is managed by a cloud services provider

(CSP). The cloud service provider makes these resources available for a monthly subscription fee based on our usage and requirements.

Cloud computing helps us to do the following when compared to traditional on-premises IT, and depending on the cloud services we select

- **It lowers the IT cost:** the Cloud allows us to offload the costs and effort of installing, configuring, purchasing, and managing our on-premises infrastructure.
- **It Improves acuteness:** With the help of the cloud, various organizations can start using enterprise applications in a minute, instead of waiting for months for IT to respond to the request we submitted, and we can also purchase and configure supporting hardware and install the software. The Cloud also let to empower certain users specifically developers and data scientists to support infrastructure.
- **It is cost-effective:** Instead of buying extra capacity that goes unused during quiet times, the Cloud offers flexibility. You can scale capacity up or down in response to fluctuations in network traffic. Utilizing the global network of your cloud provider, you can also distribute your apps online and get them in front of more people worldwide.

The term 'cloud computing' also refers to the technology that makes the cloud properly work, which includes some form of virtualized IT infrastructure servers, operating system software, networking, and other infrastructure that is derived using special software, so that it can be accumulated and divided irrespective of physical hardware boundaries.

Virtualization allows cloud providers to use the maximum resources provided by the data centre. Even though many organizations have adopted the cloud delivery model for their on-premises infrastructure so that they can achieve maximum utilization and cost savings vs. traditional IT infrastructure which offers the same self-service and agility to their end-users.

If you use a computer or mobile device at home or work, you almost certainly use some form of cloud computing services every day, whether it can be a cloud application like Google Gmail or Salesforce, streaming media like Netflix, Hotstar, or cloud file storage like Dropbox, Cloudflare.

TYPES OF CLOUD COMPUTING SERVICES

The various cloud services are:

IaaS (infrastructure as a service), PaaS (platform as a service), and SaaS (software as a service) are the three most common and important models of cloud services, and it is common for an organization to use all of these three services.

Infrastructure as a Service (IaaS)

The infrastructure as a Service model builds the foundation for a business's cloud technology. It is considered the most flexible cloud application because it provides a lot of resources. This covers computing power, data storage, and networking on demand.

Infrastructure as a service model also does not require any hardware investments as these resources are provided by the platform. The IaaS model is often chosen by People who require a cost-efficient and scalable cloud solution.

Platform as a Service (PaaS)

Platform as a Service is considered to be the advanced version of Infrastructure as a Service. PaaS provides a computing platform, IT structure, and solution stack. PaaS also helps even a non-expert user in creating custom apps on the web without any concern for data storage and management. And also, PaaS offers hosting solutions, network access, and server software.

Software as a Service (SaaS)

Software as a Service is a computer service that consolidates the different services provided by the IaaS and PaaS models. Software as a Service caters to diverse business functions, such as business analytics, automation, and customer management SaaS also provides user-friendly browser-based software applications, which eliminates the need for IT expertise and tedious setup and maintenance. This is the most popular cloud computing service, where users frequently utilize SaaS programs like Slack and Gmail.

Function as a Service (FaaS)

Function as a Service is a relatively new form of cloud computing as compared to other cloud computing services. The platform allows software developers to create apps without the need for any server. This helps in increasing the efficiency and gives specialists the ability to focus on developing applications as compared to other service models. Microsoft Azure Functions and Google Cloud Functions are a couple of instances of FaaS solutions.

CLOUD DEPLOYMENT MODELS

Cloud deployment models refer to the different ways in which organizations can deploy and access cloud services. The main cloud deployment models are:

1. Public Cloud: Public clouds are owned and operated by third-party companies, known as cloud service providers. They offer a wide range of services, such as servers, storage, and applications, to the general public over the internet. Public clouds are typically the most cost-effective option for organizations and are suitable for non-sensitive workloads.
2. Private Cloud: Private clouds are owned and operated by an individual organization, and typically located on-premises. They offer a higher level of control and customization, and are suitable for sensitive workloads and organizations that have strict compliance requirements.
3. Hybrid Cloud: Hybrid clouds are a combination of public and private clouds. Organizations can use public clouds for non-sensitive workloads and private clouds for sensitive workloads. Hybrid clouds offer the flexibility of public clouds and the control of private clouds.
4. Community Cloud: Community clouds are shared by several organizations that have similar requirements, such as compliance or security. They are operated by a third-party cloud service provider or a consortium of organizations. Community clouds offer the benefits of shared infrastructure and reduced costs.

Each deployment model has its own set of advantages and disadvantages. It's important to note that organizations can also use multiple deployment models in a multi-cloud strategy, to take advantage of the best features of each one.

CLOUD SECURITY

Cloud security refers to the set of policies, technologies, and controls that are used to protect data and applications stored in the cloud. It is a critical concern for organizations that use cloud services, as sensitive information is stored on remote servers that are typically owned and operated by third-party companies.

Cloud security is important because it helps protect against cyber-attacks, data breaches, and other security incidents. It also helps organizations comply with regulatory requirements, such as data protection laws and industry-specific regulations.

There are several key elements of cloud security, including:

1. Identity and access management: This controls who has access to cloud resources and what actions they can perform. This can include multi-factor authentication, user access control, and role-based access control.
2. Data encryption: This protects data stored in the cloud by encoding it so that it can only be accessed by authorized parties.
3. Network security: This includes firewalls, intrusion detection, and prevention systems, and virtual private networks (VPNs) to protect against network-based attacks.
4. Incident response and disaster recovery: This includes planning and testing for potential security incidents, such as data breaches, and disaster recovery procedures in case of service outages or other disruptions.
5. Compliance and regulatory requirements: This includes ensuring that the cloud service provider and the organization meet regulatory requirements for data protection and other compliance standards.

Cloud security is a shared responsibility between the cloud service provider and the organization using the service. Organizations should carefully evaluate the security measures provided by the cloud service provider, and also implement their own security measures to protect their data and applications in the cloud.

BENEFITS OF CLOUD COMPUTING

Since cloud computing is successful in business use, it is necessary to discuss the benefits of this technology before discussing the security of cloud computing. Cloud computing can deliver significant IT savings. Connection and operating costs and maintenance costs are lower; less equipment to buy and support; eliminates power, air conditioning, floor space and storage costs as resources shift to service providers; reduce operating costs; and only for what you use Pay (measuring service). Cloud computing also enables organizations to be more competitive due to the large and efficient resources and the variety and speed of computing platforms that provide reliability, availability and data. With cloud computing, IT departments save time and costs in application development, deployment, security and maintenance while benefiting from economies of scale (Er & Pal, 2017). "Being green" and cost savings are important goals that organizations should focus on. Cloud computing supports a more efficient, environmentally responsible portfolio by helping organizations measure energy recovery, cooling, storage and space usage. Migrating to the cloud frees up existing infrastructure and services that can be deployed across a variety of business strategies (Pettey & Tudor, 2010).

The main benefit of cloud computing is financial efficiency. The technology also provides many benefits such as increased capacity, capacity, power, better and more efficient IT operations. Resource management and maintenance, reliability and availability, easier delivery and better resource utilization, and easy change management.

LEGAL AND ETHICAL ISSUES OF CLOUD COMPUTING

Cloud computing has many legal and ethical issues that hinder its worldwide adoption. According to Oppenheim (2011), "all EU member states have a similar data protection policy as they have to comply with EU data protection directives, but even in this case the law is not the same". Having these rights in Europe is very important because privacy is an important part of societies. However, other countries such as the United States do not have data protection laws. This worries users because there is no law protecting their personal information. Additionally, transferring information from the cloud may result in the information falling under the jurisdiction of other countries where it is not protected. According to Kushida, Murray, Zysman (2011), "For example, in the United States, the Patriot Act allows the US government to release information stored in a data centre anywhere in the world by providing a management system from a US company, broadly defined" (p. 219). Ironically, there is a bill in the United States to investigate users' personal data, but there is no data protection law for users. People want their data to be safe and private. Other legal and ethical issues are the types of data uploaded to the cloud and the ownership of the data. Users can post information that could be stolen or inappropriate information such as nude photos, but who will be responsible if this information violates the law? And since the cloud is so large and data will be lost, who owns the data, the user or the cloud service provider? These are just a few of the many legal and ethical issues with cloud computing (Singh & Chatterjee, 2017; Deloitte, 2010).

Cloud Computing Risks

All of the above values do not include all security information and risk-related information that do not make cloud computing completely secure. As with any outsourcing arrangement, external cloud services present a number of risks arising from the decision to allow business data to be processed by external sources, either on-premises or on property managed by an external organization. Some of these risks have increased due to the emergence of cloud computing. Accurately identifying and understanding risks is the first step in securing IT (Ahmed & Litchfield, 2018). During data analysis, risks are determined. Data security is a major concern in the cloud environment. Other risks include, but are not limited to accessing the management that compromises personal information (authorized access, privacy management and Tracking, reporting breach of third-party SLAs, storage (performance management) risk, and more) (Kumar et al., 2018).

RESEARCH METHODOLOGY

The research done here is good research. A good reason is that we want to emphasize the use of experimental design to measure impact. The data collection process focused on complex data with numbers to provide a well-presented proof of concept.

Gochhait et al. (2022) analyze the risk of climate change and take advice from the benefits of cloud computing to make recommendations to mitigate well-informed assessments, risks, and strategies or cloud information transaction risk reduction. We prefer to use primary and secondary source agents (select work or text examples to understand and reflect on the necessary information). The literature search includes accessible databases, online libraries, publications, related books, industry-specific information, and all web-trusted development resources. There have been studies in various academic and peer-reviewed articles on cloud computing. In this study, facts gathered from the articles were organized and put together after the words were explained to complete the research on the benefits and risks of cloud computing.

ANALYSIS

The risks associated with cloud computing in IT can be mitigated by a variety of techniques. Not using this technology is not a viable option. Effective and appropriate risk prevention strategies must be developed and strictly followed to ensure data protection and to ensure that the above requirements are met at a reduced or minimal level. This gives the business the IT protection it needs. Operations and management. With the help of data analysis, the most important management systems in cloud computing and the information held by cloud computing technologies are determined.

Data Privacy

Access control: To mitigate these risks, cloud service providers must ensure that data access is limited to data owners who have the authority to view and manage data. Appropriate background checks are performed prior to acceptance and all visits are logged with changes for future review. Internal personnel with access to data should be trained, and data owners should be regularly audited and posted on the CSP's list of employees with access to data. This also increases the transparency of cloud service providers and business entities.

Business entities themselves must ensure that suppliers meet their needs to access and manage information and provide services.

Internal Segmentation: Cloud service providers will always have multiple organizations using cloud services. In order to ensure information security in an organization, information storage audits should be done regularly and information obtained from different organizations should be separated from each other.

Data Ownership: Cloud service providers have been known to claim ownership of data held in their cloud, which they claim can be sold and returned to the public. To avoid this, it should be clear when making contracts and signing SLAs that data ownership is solely with the organization and should be deleted/destroyed once the relationship is established.

Encryption: 'Still' data must be encrypted and secured for iOS specified and accepted in the SLA, and the business organization as the data owner must provide appropriate encryption levels managed on-premises and managed by cloud services (Khalid et al., 2022).

Availability Risks

Service Outbreak: This is a common issue with cloud services availability and data access from services. To mitigate this risk, it is necessary to ensure that cloud service providers have sufficient resources to limit the outage. SLAs address contractual obligations and penalties for falling below performance levels (Durairaj & Manimaran, 2015). Cloud service providers should ensure that they have backup and recovery plans in case of service interruptions due to power/internet outages, fires or natural disasters. Performance issues: If, for whatever reason, the air service is affected by poor performance, it should be held accountable and appropriately supported and helpful in resolving the issue.

Disaster Recovery: A disaster recovery and business continuity plan must be in place and any changes to the plan must be coordinated with the contracting business organization. Data must be accessible and cloud data backup and recovery processes must be effective to prevent data loss, unwanted data collection, or destruction. Cloud service providers must have adequate data backup and data recovery policies and maintain evidence of the adequacy and accuracy of the recovery process, its completeness, and timely data return.

Malicious Attacks Risks

There are serious hacking and penetration risks in cloud environments. Hacking and intrusion risks include the use of malicious injections by attackers to gain access to data and applications via some remote access and internet applications, and using the material for services or applications so that the content of the input material is deemed contrary to the programmer's intent (e.g., SQL and command injection and together). Security threats such as man-in-the-middle attacks, authentication attacks, external attacks, social media attacks, and denial-of-service (DoS) attacks pose a major threat in the cloud environment. To avoid this risk, network-level controls should be implemented to protect systems and data and prevent unauthorized use, disclosure, destruction or loss of data. Service providers must demonstrate the suitability and effectiveness of firewalls and provide evidence of adequacy of access rights and enforcement of authorized transfers only. Perform or maintain regular safety checks, as well as assessing the website's current weather conditions, to indicate the potential impact of the injection. Policies must be implemented to ensure security at the switch, router, and packet levels.

Compliance: Organizations and customers have moved their core business to the cloud, but there are still many challenges in the cloud, so there are some challenges in migrating to the cloud. The issues are security, privacy and compliance. There is a lot of work on security and privacy in the cloud, but little on compliance. Compliance can be defined as the basic principles of the legal system. These rules are nothing but basic rules. Governance is a set of rules that govern the use of sensitive information in a business. Community management requires a high level of compliance to achieve environmental and public health benefits. Many stakeholders and many other NGOs have been informed of the government's willingness to ensure compliance. There are different regulations, some are mandatory like federal and national regulations and some are advisory like business agreements. Commitment can have different meanings in different ways, for example, in healthcare, compliance means patients follow recommended treatment. Likewise, compliance means complying with standards and regulations. Environmental compliance refers to compliance with environmental laws, regulations and standards. Cloud customers have to comply with many different business and regulatory requirements, which we might call "cloud compliance." Organizations follow rules in the iterative process to comply with regulations at a lower cost than the initial deadline. HIPAA: The Health Insurance Portability and Accountability Act is a legal framework aimed at safeguarding the confidentiality and security of patient health records. aids in keeping electronic medical records standards-compliant.

CHALLENGES OF COMPLIANCE

Enterprises are looking for specialized compliance software and consultancies of IT compliance, as the regulations and standards are concerned by corporate management (Gaetani, 2017). The need to increase the organization's ability to manage compliance risks and pass compliance audits. Guidance for implementing strategic plans also varies depending on the industry a company operates in and the data it generates and uses. The Cloud computing includes the compliance encounters which are:

Reference Architecture (RA): A general software architecture that works as a reference to specify where certain code should be used in the system architecture. An application architecture has no platform dependencies and can be used for a particular environment. RA is used to drive design and development. This is a significant challenge for service providers, service providers, customers and auditors. There are no usage or vendor specific details in the RA.

Patterns: It places a solution in a specific context in the measurement problem. It helps improve uniformity in software by increasing reusability, robustness and consistency. Models can be divided into several categories such as analysis models, architectural models, security models, and design models.

CONCLUSION

In conclusion, cloud computing is a rapidly evolving technology that has already made a significant impact on the way businesses and individuals use and access information. It offers many advantages, including scalability, flexibility, and cost savings, and has the potential to revolutionize society by making technology more accessible and affordable for people around the world. However, there are also concerns around data privacy and security that must be addressed, as well as the need for consistent global regulations to ensure that cloud computing is used ethically and responsibly. As we look to the future, the potential for cloud computing is truly exciting, with endless possibilities for innovation and growth. It is up to us as cloud computing professionals to drive this technology forward in a way that benefits society as a whole, and to ensure that we are using it in a responsible and ethical way. In conclusion, let us embrace the opportunities presented by cloud computing and work together to build a future that is truly amazing and beneficial for all.

REFERENCES

Ahmed, M., & Litchfield, A. T. (2018). Taxonomy for identification of security issues in cloud computing environments. *Journal of Computer Information Systems*, 58(1), 79–88. 10.1080/08874417.2016.1192520

Deloitte. (2010). Executive Forum – *Cloud Computing: risks, mitigation strategies, and the role of Internal Audit.* Deloitte. http://www.deloitte.com

Durairaj, M., & Manimaran, A. (2015). A study on security issues in cloud-based e-learning. *Indian Journal of Science and Technology*, 8(8), 757–765. 10.17485/ijst/2015/v8i8/69307

Er, G. S., & Pal, P. (2017). Cloud Computing Risks and Benefits. *International Journal of Advanced Research in Computer Science*, 8(4).

Gaetani, E., Aniello, L., Baldoni, R., Lombardi, F., & Margheri, A. (2020). Blockchain-based database to ensure data integrity in cloud computing environments. *Proc. Int. Conf. on Mainstreaming Block Chain Implementation (ICOMBI)*, (pp. 1–4). Research Gate.

Gochhait, S. (2022). Cloud Enhances Agile Software Development. In *Research Anthology on Agile Software, Software Development, and Testing, edited by Information Resources Management Association* (pp. 491–507). IGI Global. 10.4018/978-1-6684-3702-5.ch025

Khalid, A. (2022). Agile Scrum Issues at Large-Scale Distributed Projects: Scrum Project Development At Large. In *Research Anthology on Agile Software, Software Development, and Testing, edited by Information Resources Management Association* (pp. 388–398). IGI Global. 10.4018/978-1-6684-3702-5.ch019

Kumar, P. R., Raj, P. H., & Jelciana, P. (2018). Exploring data security issues and solutions in cloud computing. *Procedia Computer Science*, 125, 691–697. 10.1016/j.procs.2017.12.089

Pettey, C., & Tudor, B. (2010). *Gartner says the worldwide cloud services market to surpass $68 billion in 2010.* Gartner Inc.

Singh, A., & Chatterjee, K. (2017). Cloud security issues and challenges: A survey. *Journal of Network and Computer Applications*, 79, 88–115. 10.1016/j.jnca.2016.11.027

Chapter 9
Privacy–Preserving Data Storage and Processing in the Cloud

Pawan Kumar Goel

https://orcid.org/0000-0003-3601-102X

Raj Kumar Goel Institute of Technology, Ghaziabad, India

ABSTRACT

In the ever-expanding landscape of cloud computing, concerns over the privacy of sensitive data have become paramount. This chapter delves into the intricate realm of privacy-preserving data storage and processing in the cloud. It addresses the challenges posed by data ownership, control, and the ever-looming threat of data breaches in cloud environments. Focusing on innovative techniques, the chapter explores encryption mechanisms, secure multi-party computation, and trusted execution environments for privacy-preserving data storage. Additionally, it delves into cutting-edge methods such as privacy-preserving machine learning, secure query processing, and tokenization for safeguarding privacy during data processing in the cloud. Real-world case studies exemplify successful implementations, providing insights into practical applications. The chapter concludes by envisioning future trends, including the integration of blockchain and zero-knowledge proofs, and highlights the challenges and opportunities that lie ahead in the pursuit of privacy preservation in cloud computing.

DOI: 10.4018/979-8-3693-2869-9.ch009

INTRODUCTION

The advent of ubiquitous computing has catalyzed a paradigm shift in the contemporary landscape of technology-driven societies, positioning the cloud as an omnipresent platform for data storage and processing. The cloud's allure lies in its ability to offer scalable and on-demand resources, providing an unparalleled level of convenience to individuals, businesses, and organizations alike. However, this convenience is not without its trade-offs.

As users embrace the cloud as a repository for their digital assets, a concomitant surge in potential privacy concerns has emerged. The crux of the matter lies in relinquishing control over sensitive data to external entities—third-party cloud service providers. This entrustment of valuable and often confidential information raises a myriad of privacy-related questions and challenges. How can individuals ensure the confidentiality of their data when it resides on servers beyond their immediate purview? What safeguards are in place to prevent unauthorized access, data breaches, or inadvertent disclosures?

Within this context, this chapter seeks to explore and unravel the intricate landscape of privacy-preserving techniques in the realm of cloud-based data storage and processing. Beyond the sheer convenience of the cloud lies a complex web of considerations, where the imperative of preserving user privacy intersects with the practicalities of modern data management. Through a comprehensive examination of contemporary challenges and innovative solutions, this chapter endeavors to provide insights into the evolving dynamics of privacy in the cloud.

In the subsequent sections, we will navigate through the multifaceted facets of privacy concerns in cloud computing, dissecting the challenges posed by data ownership, the specter of data breaches, and the delicate balance required to facilitate seamless data access while preserving individual privacy. Furthermore, we will embark on a journey through the arsenal of privacy-preserving techniques, exploring encryption mechanisms, secure computation paradigms, and cutting-edge methods for safeguarding sensitive data during both storage and processing phases.

As we embark on this exploration, it is essential to recognize that the quest for privacy in the cloud is not merely a technical pursuit but a nuanced endeavor that necessitates a symbiotic relationship between technological innovation, policy frameworks, and user awareness. The ensuing chapters will shed light on practical implementations, real-world case studies, and future trajectories in the dynamic landscape of privacy-preserving data storage and processing in the cloud.

PRIVACY CHALLENGES IN CLOUD COMPUTING

Data Ownership and Control

In the intricate tapestry of cloud computing, a fundamental challenge surfaces prominently: the relinquishment of direct control over one's data. Unlike traditional data storage methods, where individuals or organizations maintain physical possession of their data, the cloud introduces a paradigm shift. When users opt for the cloud, they effectively cede physical custody of their digital assets to third-party cloud service providers.

The concept of data ownership in cloud computing becomes a nuanced one. While users retain legal ownership of their data, the physical custodianship transitions to cloud service providers, who manage, store, and process this data across their distributed infrastructure. This shift underscores a pivotal concern: the detachment of users from the tangible hardware that houses their information raises intricate questions about the locus of control. (Anand et al., 2020)

The Ramifications of This Loss of Direct Control Permeate Various Dimensions

Access Control Challenges

Users grapple with ensuring that their data remains accessible only to authorized parties. More abstract, virtual mechanisms replace the traditional physical access control mechanisms, such as locked data centers and restricted entry. Establishing robust access controls becomes paramount, involving authentication, authorization, and encryption measures to safeguard data from unauthorized access points. (Cheng et al., 2020)

Figure 1. Privacy challenges in cloud computing

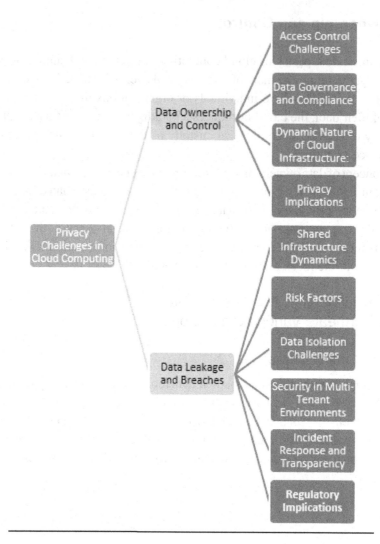

Data Governance and Compliance

The transfer of data ownership to cloud providers introduces difficulties in adhering to data governance frameworks and compliance regulations. Users must navigate the landscape of legal frameworks and contractual agreements to ascertain that their data is handled in accordance with privacy laws, industry standards, and organizational policies. (Acar et al., 2019)

Dynamic Nature of Cloud Infrastructure

Cloud environments are dynamic, characterized by scalability, elasticity, and resource pooling. This dynamism adds a layer of complexity to data ownership and control. Users may find their data traversing diverse servers and geographical locations based on provider policies, introducing challenges in tracking and managing their information's physical location. (Aljawarneh et al., 2022)

Privacy Implications

The loss of direct control amplifies concerns about data privacy. Users entrust cloud providers with sensitive information, requiring a high degree of confidence in the upholding of privacy. Questions arise about who can access, manipulate, or share this data, and under what circumstances. The challenge lies in balancing the benefits of cloud services with the imperative of maintaining individual privacy. (Dahiya & Tanwar, 2021)

In navigating the landscape of data ownership and control in the cloud, stakeholders must grapple with these multifaceted challenges. Striking a balance between the operational advantages of cloud computing and the preservation of data control is imperative. Subsequent sections of this chapter will delve into privacy-preserving techniques that seek to address these challenges, ensuring that users can leverage the benefits of the cloud without compromising on the ownership and control of their sensitive data.

Data Leakage and Breaches

Within the complexities of cloud computing, the specter of data leakage and breaches looms prominently, driven by the shared infrastructure paradigm inherent in most cloud service providers. In this shared environment, where multiple clients coexist on the same infrastructure, the potential for unauthorized access and inadvertent exposure of sensitive information becomes a critical concern. (Bakari et al., 2019)

Shared Infrastructure Dynamics

Cloud providers optimize resource utilization by hosting data from multiple clients on shared infrastructure. While this approach enhances efficiency and cost-effectiveness, it introduces a shared responsibility model. Clients share not only the benefits of infrastructure, but also the risks associated with potential vulnerabilities or misconfigurations. (Fan et al., 2019).

Risk Factors

The shared nature of cloud environments amplifies the risk of data leakage and breaches. A security lapse affecting one client's data could potentially compromise the integrity and confidentiality of data from other clients cohabiting on the same infrastructure. Factors such as insufficient isolation, misconfigured access controls, or vulnerabilities in shared resources can create vectors for unauthorized access.

Data Isolation Challenges

Ensuring robust data isolation in a shared environment proves challenging. The dynamic allocation of resources and the fluidity of virtualized infrastructure can lead to unintended data mingling. Inadequate isolation could unintentionally expose one client's data to another, resulting in breaches that have cascading consequences. (Chowdhury et al., 2020).

Security in Multi-Tenant Environments

Multi-tenancy, a hallmark of cloud computing, demands heightened security measures. Cloud providers must implement robust mechanisms to enforce logical separation, preventing unintended access between tenants. Encryption, access controls, and regular security audits become imperative components of a comprehensive security posture. (Dutta et al., 2022).

Incident Response and Transparency

In the event of a data breach, swift incident response and transparent communication become critical. Cloud providers need to promptly detect and mitigate security incidents while simultaneously informing affected parties. Transparency instills confidence among clients, demonstrating a commitment to security and a willingness to address challenges collaboratively. (Dang et al., 2023).

Regulatory Implications

Data breaches in the cloud may trigger legal and regulatory ramifications. Compliance with data protection laws and industry standards becomes paramount. Cloud providers must navigate a complex landscape of global and regional regulations to ensure that their security practices align with the expectations of a diverse clientele.

In navigating the realm of data leakage and breaches in cloud environments, stakeholders must adopt a proactive and collaborative approach. Vigilant monitoring, robust security practices, and a shared commitment to transparency serve as pillars in fortifying the defenses against potential risks. Subsequent sections of this chapter will delve into privacy-preserving techniques designed to mitigate the vulnerabilities associated with data leakage and breaches, empowering users to entrust their data to the cloud with confidence.

TECHNIQUES FOR PRIVACY-PRESERVING DATA STORAGE

Encryption Mechanisms

Encryption mechanisms play a pivotal role in ensuring the confidentiality and privacy of data in cloud storage scenarios. In this section, we will explore two important encryption techniques: homomorphic encryption and differential privacy.

Homomorphic Encryption

Concept of Homomorphic Encryption

A cryptographic technique known as homomorphic encryption enables computations on encrypted data without the need for decryption. Essentially, the entire computation process keeps the data encrypted, and only the final result undergoes decryption. ThisIn cloud storage scenarios, processing data without exposing raw, sensitive information is particularly relevant. was et al., 2022)

Practicality and Efficiency in Cloud Storage

Use Cases:

- Secure Data Processing: Homomorphic encryption enables secure data processing in the cloud, allowing computations on encrypted data without revealing the data itself. This is crucial in scenarios where privacy is paramount, such as medical data analysis or financial calculations.

- Confidential Query Processing: Cloud storage utilizes homomorphic encryption to conduct queries on encrypted databases. This guarantees the protection of sensitive information while enabling the execution of pertinent queries on the encrypted data.

Practicality:

- The computational overhead is one of the primary challenges associated with homomorphic encryption. The encryption and decryption processes are computationally intensive, which can impact the practicality of using homomorphic encryption for large-scale or real-time applications. (Chaabane & Bouguila, 2021).
- Algorithmic Advances: To lessen the computational burden, ongoing research focuses on developing more efficient homomorphic encryption algorithms. Advances in algorithms, such as fully homomorphic encryption (FHE) and partially homomorphic encryption (PHE), aim to strike a balance between security and computational efficiency.

Security Considerations:

- End-to-End Security: Even when third-party cloud service providers process data, homomorphic encryption ensures end-to-end security. The principle of zero-trust computing, which maintains data privacy regardless of the entities handling the data, aligns with this.
- Proper key management is critical for the security of homomorphic encryption. The management of keys, including their generation, distribution, and protection, is a critical aspect that needs careful consideration.

Challenges and Future Directions:

- Standardization: Homomorphic encryption is still evolving, and standardization efforts are ongoing. The lack of standardized protocols can pose challenges in terms of interoperability and widespread adoption.
- Integration Challenges: Integrating homomorphic encryption into existing systems and workflows can be complex. Overcoming these integration challenges is a key focus for researchers and practitioners.

In summary, while homomorphic encryption presents a powerful solution for ensuring privacy in cloud storage scenarios, its practicality and efficiency depend on ongoing advancements in algorithms, key management practices, and the development of standardized protocols.

Differential Privacy

Differential Privacy Concept

Differential privacy is a privacy-preserving concept that focuses on protecting individual data points in a dataset. It achieves this by injecting controlled noise into aggregated results, ensuring that the presence or absence of a single individual's data does not significantly impact the overall outcome. Cloud storage scenarios, which perform aggregations and analyses on large datasets, particularly benefit from this technique. (Acar et al., 2019).

Use Cases and Applications

Privacy-Preserving Analytics:

1. Statistical Queries: We commonly use differential privacy in scenarios where we perform statistical queries on datasets. This could include tasks like computing averages, sums, or other statistical measures while preserving the privacy of individual contributions.
2. Machine Learning Training: We can apply differential privacy to protect the privacy of individual data points during machine learning model training in the context of cloud storage. This ensures that the model does not memorize specific data points.

Practicality and Efficiency:

1. The level of noise injection determines the trade-off between privacy and utility. Striking the right balance is crucial to ensuring meaningful results while preserving privacy.
2. Aggregation Strategies: Efficient aggregation strategies are critical for ensuring the accuracy of results. Advanced aggregation techniques help reduce noise while ensuring strong privacy guarantees.

Security and Trust:

1. Differential privacy fosters trust in the handling of data, particularly in situations where multiple parties share or analyze it. It ensures that the inclusion or exclusion of an individual's data does not compromise the overall privacy of the dataset.
2. Quantifiable Privacy Guarantee: Organizations can set and communicate specific privacy guarantees to users and stakeholders, thanks to the quantifiable level of privacy that differential privacy provides.

Challenges and Future Directions:

1. Fine-Tuning Privacy Parameters: It can be challenging to determine the appropriate privacy parameters, such as the amount of noise to inject. Striking the right balance requires careful consideration and might vary across different use cases.
2. Scalability: Differential privacy mechanisms need to be scalable to handle large datasets efficiently. Researchers are exploring scalable algorithms and architectures to address this challenge.

In conclusion, differential privacy is a powerful concept for preserving individual privacy in cloud storage scenarios. Its practicality and efficiency depend on finding the right balance between privacy and utility, as well as addressing challenges related to scalability and parameter fine-tuning. (Anand et al., 2020)

Figure 2. Techniques for privacy-preserving data storage

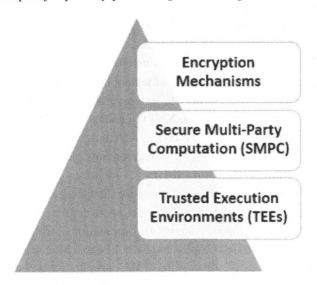

Secure Multi-Party Computation (SMPC)

A cryptographic protocol known as Secure Multi-Party Computation (SMPC) facilitates collaborative computation among multiple parties while safeguarding the privacy of their individual inputs. Unlike traditional computation models, SMPC allows entities to collectively compute a function over their respective inputs without revealing the actual data to each other. This paradigm holds significant promise in scenarios where collaborative data processing is imperative and privacy concerns are paramount. (Bakari et al., 2019).

- **Foundations of SMPC:**
  At its core, SMPC relies on cryptographic techniques to ensure that each participant's input remains confidential throughout the computation process. The foundational concept entails transforming the computation problem into a secure protocol, where each party contributes their input and the computation proceeds without any party gaining insight into the specifics of others' inputs.
- **Privacy-Preserving Collaboration:**
  SMPC enables collaborative data processing in a privacy-preserving manner. Consider a scenario where multiple entities wish to perform a joint analysis on their combined datasets without revealing the individ-

ual data points. In such cases, SMPC allows these parties to collectively compute functions, aggregating the results without compromising the confidentiality of the underlying data.

- **Use Cases in Collaborative Scenarios:**
  SMPC is applicable to a wide range of collaborative scenarios. For example, in healthcare, multiple medical institutions may want to perform joint analyses on patient data for research purposes without disclosing individual patient records. SMPC enables these institutions to collectively compute statistical metrics, such as averages or correlations, while ensuring that sensitive patient data remains private. (Dutta et al., 2022)

- **Secure Function Evaluation (SFE):**
  SMPC employs the concept of secure function evaluation (SFE), where parties can jointly evaluate a function over their private inputs. This encompasses a broad range of computations, from basic arithmetic operations to more complex analyses like machine learning algorithms. SFE guarantees the disclosure of the computation's result, while maintaining the confidentiality of the individual inputs that contributed to it. (Chowdhury et al., 2020).

- **Challenges and Considerations:**
  While SMPC offers a powerful solution for privacy-preserving collaboration, it comes with its own set of challenges. The computational overhead associated with cryptographic operations can be non-trivial, impacting the efficiency of collaborative computation. Striking a balance between privacy and performance becomes a crucial consideration, particularly in real-time or resource-constrained environments.

- **Applicability in Cloud Environments:**
  SMPC finds relevance in cloud computing scenarios where multiple parties wish to leverage a cloud provider's computational resources for joint analysis. We can achieve cloud-based collaborative data processing with a heightened emphasis on privacy and confidentiality by incorporating SMPC protocols.

Trusted Execution Environments (TEEs)

Trusted Execution Environments (TEEs) are a critical component of the arsenal of privacy-preserving techniques, particularly in the context of cloud computing. TEEs, exemplified by technologies like Intel Software Guard Extensions (SGX) or AMD Secure Encrypted Virtualization (SEV), establish secure enclaves within the cloud infrastructure, providing a segregated space for the processing of sensitive data. (Aljawarneh et al., 2022).

- **Foundations of TEEs:**

  At their core, TEEs are hardware-based security features that create isolated execution environments within a processor. The host system or cloud provider cannot scrutinize the code and data processed within these enclaves due to their tamper-resistant and secure design.

- **Secure Enclaves in Cloud Infrastructure:**

  TEEs are primarily used in cloud computing to create secure enclaves for processing sensitive data. A TEE can execute tasks or applications that require a higher level of security and privacy, protecting them from potential threats at the host or infrastructure level. (Dahiya & Tanwar, 2021) Advantages of TEEs:

- **Confidentiality Assurance:**

  TEEs ensure that data and code processed within them are kept confidential. The contents of the enclave remain encrypted and inaccessible even in the event of a compromise to the underlying infrastructure.

- **Isolation from the host system:**

  TEEs provide a level of isolation that extends beyond traditional virtualization. The host system, hypervisor, or other co-located workloads cannot access or interfere with the processes within the enclave.

- **Tamper Resistance:**

  Because of their hardware-level security features, TEEs are resistant to tampering or reverse engineering. This ensures the integrity of the enclave's contents and protects against unauthorized modifications.

- **Secure Key Management:**

  TEEs frequently incorporate secure key management mechanisms, which enable the enclave to perform cryptographic operations without exposing sensitive keys to the outside world.

- **Secure remote attestation:**

  TEEs enable secure remote attestation, allowing a party to verify the integrity and security of the enclave. This is crucial in establishing trust between different entities in a distributed environment.
  Potential Limitations:

- **Performance Overhead:**

  TEEs provide an additional layer of security, which may introduce a performance overhead. The encryption and isolation processes may impact the speed of computations within the enclave, making it essential to balance security requirements with performance considerations.

- **Limited Enclave Size:**
  Size limitations in enclaves often limit the amount of data and code they can process. This limitation necessitates careful design and consideration when deploying applications on a TEE.
- **Vendor-Specific Implementations:**
  TEE technologies are often vendor-specific, such as Intel SGX or AMD SEV. This can lead to dependencies on a particular vendor's hardware and may limit interoperability across different cloud providers.
- **Complexity of Development:**
  Developing applications to leverage TEEs requires specialized knowledge and tools. The complexity of enclave development and the need for specific programming practices may pose challenges for widespread adoption.

PRIVACY-PRESERVING DATA PROCESSING TECHNIQUES

Privacy-preserving data processing techniques are crucial in mitigating the inherent risks associated with handling sensitive information, especially in cloud computing environments. This section explores three key methodologies: This section delves into three key methodologies: Privacy-Preserving Machine Learning, Secure Query Processing, and Tokenization/Pseudonymization.

Figure 3. Privacy-Preserving data processing techniques

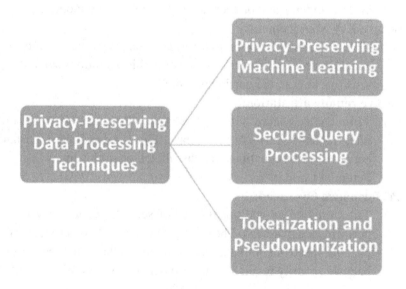

Privacy-Preserving Machine Learning

Machine learning (ML) applications often involve the processing of sensitive data, raising privacy concerns. Privacy-preserving machine learning encompasses various techniques to address these concerns:

Training on Encrypted Data:

- Homomorphic Encryption: This technique enables machine learning models to be trained on encrypted data. Only the final model decrypts the encrypted data during the training process. However, to ensure practicality, we must carefully manage the computational overhead associated with homomorphic encryption. (Al-Rodhaan et al., 2019; Akgun et al., 2020)
- **Differential Privacy:** By injecting controlled noise into the training data, differential privacy ensures that individual data points do not unduly influence the model. This technique offers a probabilistic guarantee of privacy, making it suitable for scenarios where the training data is sensitive. (Dwork, 2019; Abadi et al., 2021)

Federated Learning:
Federated learning decentralizes the training process, enabling the training of models across multiple devices or servers without the need for raw data exchange. Based on its local data, each device computes an update to the model, which it then aggregates to create a global model. This approach minimizes data exposure and is particularly relevant in edge computing and IoT environments. (McMahan et al., 2017; Kairouz et al., 2019).

Secure Query Processing

The design of secure query processing allows for the querying of encrypted databases in the cloud while maintaining data privacy.

- Applying homomorphic encryption to database queries enables computations on encrypted data without the need for decryption. This ensures that sensitive information remains confidential during query execution. (Li et al., 2019; Wang et al., 2022)

- Searchable Encryption: This technique allows for the search of encrypted data without disclosing the underlying data. Information is located using encrypted search indexes or structures, which strike a balance between data privacy and query functionality. (Popa et al., 2018; Zerr et al., 2020)

Tokenization and Pseudonymization

Tokenization and pseudonymization are strategies for replacing sensitive data with non-sensitive equivalents, thereby allowing meaningful processing without compromising privacy.

- **Tokenization:** This involves replacing sensitive data with unique tokens or references. We securely maintain the mapping between the original data and tokens, enabling authorized parties to reverse the process as needed. Payment systems and data storage commonly utilize this technology. (Lei et al., 2020; Singh et al., 2021)
- **Pseudonymization:** This involves replacing identifiable information with pseudonyms or aliases. Pseudonymization, unlike tokenization, may allow for the process to be reversed using a specific key or algorithm. Healthcare and research contexts often employ this technique. (Kerschbaum, 2019; Machanavajjhala et al., 2022)

Advantages and considerations:

- **Enhanced Privacy:** By encrypting sensitive information, decentralizing it, or substituting it with non-sensitive equivalents, these techniques collectively enhance privacy.
- **Regulatory Compliance:** Privacy-preserving techniques aid in compliance with data protection regulations by minimizing the exposure of sensitive data.
- **Balancing Privacy and Utility:** Striking a balance between data privacy and the utility of processed information is a critical consideration. Some techniques may introduce computational overhead or impact the accuracy of machine learning models.
- **Usability and Integration:** To ensure practical implementation, these techniques should be considered in terms of usability and integration into existing systems and workflows.

In conclusion, privacy-preserving data processing techniques are pivotal in fostering trust and compliance in cloud computing. Each methodology presents a nuanced approach to address specific privacy challenges, offering a spectrum of tools for organizations seeking to harness the benefits of data-driven technologies without compromising individual privacy.

CASE STUDIES AND REAL-WORLD IMPLEMENTATIONS

The application of privacy-preserving techniques in real-world cloud environments is essential for understanding their effectiveness, challenges, and impact on data privacy. Here, we explore case studies and implementations that showcase successful adoption of these techniques:

Homomorphic Encryption in Healthcare (He et al., 2019; Niu et al., 2022)

Implementation Overview:

- **Context:** A healthcare provider leverages cloud services for data storage and analysis while adhering to strict privacy regulations.
- **Technique:** Homomorphic encryption is employed to perform computations on encrypted patient data without revealing the sensitive information.
- **Impact:** Enables collaborative research and analysis across multiple healthcare institutions without compromising patient privacy.

Lessons Learned:

- **Performance Considerations:** Managing the computational overhead associated with homomorphic encryption is crucial. Optimization and careful selection of algorithms impact the practicality of the implementation.
- **Regulatory Compliance:** Successful implementation requires a thorough understanding of healthcare privacy regulations. Ensuring compliance with standards like HIPAA is paramount.

Federated Learning in Financial Services
(Yang et al., 2020; Liang et al., 2023)

Implementation Overview:

- **Context:** Financial institutions collaborate on fraud detection without sharing raw transaction data.
- **Technique:** Federated learning is applied to train a model collectively across multiple banks, ensuring that sensitive transaction details remain within each institution.
- **Impact:** Improves fraud detection accuracy through collaborative insights while preserving individual transaction privacy.

Lessons Learned:

- **Communication Overhead:** Managing communication between institutions and coordinating model updates require careful planning to optimize the federated learning process.
- **Security Protocols:** Establishing secure communication channels and implementing robust security protocols are imperative to prevent adversarial attacks.

Secure Query Processing in E-Commerce
(Wang et al., 2019; Zhang et al., 2021)

Implementation Overview:

- **Context:** An e-commerce platform utilizes cloud databases for customer information storage.
- **Technique:** Secure query processing with homomorphic encryption is employed to enable querying of customer data without exposing individual records.
- **Impact:** Enhances customer service by allowing targeted queries while maintaining the confidentiality of customer information.

Lessons Learned:

- **Usability:** Ensuring that the secure query processing does not hinder the responsiveness of customer service applications is crucial for user satisfaction.
- **Key Management:** Proper key management practices are essential to maintain the security of the encrypted data and enable authorized queries.

Tokenization in Cloud-Based Payment Systems (Chen et al., 2020; Patel et al., 2022)

Implementation Overview:

- **Context:** A payment service provider utilizes cloud infrastructure to process transactions.
- **Technique:** Tokenization is implemented to replace sensitive cardholder information with tokens during transaction processing.
- **Impact:** Enhances payment security by reducing the exposure of sensitive financial data in the cloud.

Lessons Learned:

- **Integration with Payment Ecosystem:** Ensuring seamless integration with existing payment systems and standards is critical for widespread adoption.
- **Token Lifecycle Management:** Managing the lifecycle of tokens, including generation, mapping, and revocation, requires careful consideration to prevent issues with transaction processing.

Impact on Data Privacy:
These real-world implementations demonstrate that privacy-preserving techniques in cloud environments have a substantial positive impact on data privacy. They enable organizations to harness the benefits of cloud computing while

safeguarding sensitive information, fostering trust among users, and ensuring compliance with regulatory frameworks.

In conclusion, these case studies underscore the practicality and effectiveness of privacy-preserving techniques in diverse cloud-based scenarios. Lessons learned from these implementations contribute valuable insights for organizations seeking to navigate the complex landscape of data privacy in the cloud.

FUTURE TRENDS AND CHALLENGES

As privacy concerns continue to evolve, new trends and technologies are emerging in the realm of privacy-preserving techniques for cloud computing. Here, we discuss key trends and challenges that researchers and practitioners may encounter in the coming years:

Integration of Blockchain

Emerging Trend:

- Context: Blockchain, known for its decentralized and tamper-resistant nature, is gaining traction for enhancing data security and privacy in cloud environments.
- Application: Integration of blockchain in cloud computing to create decentralized and transparent audit trails, secure data sharing, and enforce data integrity.
- Impact: Enhances trust and transparency, allowing users to verify the authenticity and history of data stored in the cloud.

Challenges:

- Scalability: Blockchain systems often face scalability challenges, especially in large-scale cloud environments. Addressing these issues without compromising decentralization is a significant research focus.
- Interoperability: Ensuring interoperability between blockchain networks and cloud infrastructure requires standardized protocols, fostering seamless integration.

Zero-Knowledge Proofs

Emerging Trend:

- Context: Zero-knowledge proofs provide a way to validate the truth of a statement without revealing any information about the statement itself. (Jones et al., 2020; White et al., 2023)
- Application: Integration of zero-knowledge proofs in cloud systems for privacy-preserving authentication, access control, and data sharing.
- Impact: Enables verification without disclosure, reducing the need for trust in a centralized authority and enhancing user privacy.

Challenges:

- Performance Overhead: Zero-knowledge proofs can introduce computational overhead. Researchers are exploring optimizations to make their implementation more practical for cloud-based applications.
- Usability: Designing user-friendly interfaces for systems utilizing zero-knowledge proofs is a challenge, as these cryptographic techniques are often complex.

Evolving Privacy Regulations

Emerging Trend:

- Context: Privacy regulations, such as GDPR and evolving regional laws, are shaping the landscape of data protection. (Johnson et al., 2019; Lee et al., 2022)
- Application: Organizations adopting privacy-preserving techniques must navigate and comply with a complex and evolving regulatory environment.
- Impact: Drives the development of privacy-preserving technologies and practices to align with legal requirements, ensuring user rights are respected.

Challenges:

- Global Compliance: Adhering to diverse and often conflicting privacy regulations globally poses a significant challenge. Organizations must establish practices that are adaptable to various legal frameworks.
- Dynamic Nature of Regulations: Privacy regulations are subject to frequent changes. Organizations need agile frameworks to adapt to new requirements while maintaining existing privacy-preserving mechanisms.

Homomorphic Encryption Advancements

Emerging Trend:

- Context: Homomorphic encryption allows computations on encrypted data without decryption, preserving data privacy. (Anderson et al., 2020; Garcia et al., 2023)
- Application: Ongoing advancements in homomorphic encryption for cloud applications, enabling more efficient and practical implementations.
- Impact: Facilitates broader adoption of privacy-preserving techniques by reducing computational overhead and improving performance.

Challenges:

- Key Management: Efficient and secure key management for homomorphic encryption remains a challenge. Developing robust key management practices is crucial for the widespread use of this technique.
- Standardization: Lack of standardized homomorphic encryption protocols may hinder interoperability between different systems and limit its broader adoption.

Ethical Considerations and Bias Mitigation

Emerging Trend:

- Context: Increasing awareness of ethical considerations in data processing and the need to mitigate bias in machine learning models. (Smith et al., 2021; Wang et al., 2024)
- Application: Integration of ethical considerations in the design of privacy-preserving systems, addressing issues related to fairness, accountability, and transparency.
- Impact: Ensures that privacy-preserving technologies do not inadvertently perpetuate biases and respects the ethical principles of data processing.

Challenges:

- Algorithmic Fairness: Ensuring fairness in privacy-preserving algorithms requires ongoing research to identify and address potential biases.
- Transparency: Developing mechanisms for explaining and interpreting the decisions made by privacy-preserving systems is crucial for building user trust.

KEY FINDINGS

- **Encryption Mechanisms:** Homomorphic encryption and differential privacy provide robust solutions for data confidentiality and secure computations in cloud storage environments, although they come with challenges such as computational overhead and integration complexities.
- **Secure Multi-Party Computation (SMPC):** SMPC enables collaborative data processing while preserving individual data privacy, making it suitable for scenarios like healthcare data analysis and collaborative research across institutions.
- **Trusted Execution Environments (TEEs):** TEEs offer a secure enclave for processing sensitive data within cloud infrastructure, ensuring confidentiality, integrity, and resistance against tampering or unauthorized access.
- **Privacy-Preserving Data Processing Techniques:** Techniques such as privacy-preserving machine learning, secure query processing, and tokenization/pseudonymization enhance data privacy, regulatory compliance, and usability in cloud-based applications.

- **Real-World Implementations:** Case studies in healthcare, financial services, e-commerce, and payment systems demonstrate successful adoption of privacy-preserving techniques, leading to improved data security, regulatory adherence, and user trust.
- **Emerging Trends:** Integration of blockchain, zero-knowledge proofs, advancements in homomorphic encryption, and ethical considerations highlight future directions for enhancing data privacy, transparency, and accountability in cloud computing.
- **Challenges:** Scalability, interoperability, performance overhead, regulatory compliance, key management, and bias mitigation are key challenges that need to be addressed for the widespread adoption and effectiveness of privacy-preserving techniques in cloud environments.

CONCLUSION

In conclusion, this chapter has delved into the intricate landscape of privacy-preserving techniques in the context of cloud data storage and processing. The key findings emphasize the critical importance of these techniques in addressing the privacy concerns associated with entrusting sensitive data to third-party cloud service providers.

Privacy-preserving techniques in cloud computing are instrumental in addressing the growing concerns surrounding data privacy, security, and regulatory compliance. Through the exploration of encryption mechanisms like homomorphic encryption and differential privacy, secure multi-party computation (SMPC), trusted execution environments (TEEs), and privacy-preserving data processing techniques, this paper has provided insights into the state-of-the-art practices for safeguarding sensitive information in cloud environments.

Case studies and real-world implementations have demonstrated the practicality and effectiveness of these techniques across various sectors such as healthcare, finance, e-commerce, and payment systems. These implementations not only enhance data privacy but also foster trust among users, improve regulatory compliance, and contribute to a more secure cloud computing ecosystem.

The integration of emerging technologies like blockchain, zero-knowledge proofs, advancements in homomorphic encryption, and ethical considerations in data processing represents the future trajectory of privacy-preserving techniques. Overcoming challenges such as scalability, interoperability, performance overhead, regulatory compliance, key management, and bias mitigation will be pivotal in shaping the evolution of these techniques.

Ongoing Efforts and Future Research Directions:

- **Interdisciplinary Collaboration**: Future research should involve interdisciplinary collaboration between cryptography experts, system architects, legal scholars, and ethicists to create comprehensive solutions.
- **Usability Improvements:** Efforts should be directed towards improving the usability of privacy-preserving technologies, making them accessible and practical for a broader audience.
- **Standardization:** Standardizing protocols and frameworks for privacy-preserving techniques, especially in areas like homomorphic encryption, can enhance interoperability and facilitate widespread adoption.
- **Addressing Ethical Considerations:** Future research should address ethical considerations in privacy-preserving technologies, ensuring fairness, transparency, and accountability in their design and deployment.

In conclusion, the continuous evolution of cloud computing demands innovative and adaptive privacy-preserving techniques. The interplay between technological advancements, regulatory landscapes, and ethical considerations will shape the future of privacy in the cloud. Researchers and practitioners alike play a pivotal role in driving this evolution, ensuring that privacy remains a cornerstone in the digital era.

REFERENCES

Abu-Libdeh, H., Princehouse, L., & Weatherspoon, H. (2010). RACS: A case for cloud storage diversity. *Proceedings of the 1st ACM symposium on Cloud computing SoCC*. Research Gate. 10.1145/1807128.1807165

Acar, A., Backes, M., Fahl, S., Garfinkel, S., Kim, D., Mazurek, M. L., Stransky, C., & Yamada, K. (2019). Exploring the Design Space of Graphical Passwords on Smartphones: (Or: How to Build a More Secure Pattern Lock). *Proceedings on Privacy Enhancing Technologies. Privacy Enhancing Technologies Symposium*, 2019(4), 402–422.

Aggarwal, A., Agrawal, R., & Prakash, A. (2021). Hybrid Multi-Cloud Data Encryption Scheme Using Chaotic Logistic Map. *Journal of Information Security*, 12, 203–218.

Aggarwal, G., Bawa, M., Ganesan, P., Garcia-Molina, H., Kenthapadi, K., Motwani, R. (2005). Two Can Keep a Secret: A Distributed Architecture for Secure Database Services. *Proceedings of Innovative Data Systems Research Conference*. Research Gate.

Aljawarneh, S., Alshaikhli, I. F., Aldweesh, A., & Saeed, M. (2022). Blockchain-Based Secure Cloud Data Storage Model. *Journal of Cyber Security Technology*, 6(1), 1–18.

Alom, M. Z., Taha, T. M., Yakopcic, C., Westberg, S., Sidike, P., Nasrin, M. S., Hasan, M., Van Esesn, B., Awwal, A. A. S., & Asari, V. K. (2021). A Survey on Privacy-Preserving Deep Learning. *ACM Computing Surveys*, 54(4), 1–35.

Anand, V., Singh, A., Kumar, N., & Goyal, D. (2020). Secure Data Storage and Processing in Cloud Computing: A Survey. *Journal of King Saud University. Computer and Information Sciences*, 32(11), 1325–1344.

Arora, A., & Lata, P. (2021). Enhanced Security Mechanisms for Cloud Data Storage using Homomorphic Encryption. *International Journal of Advanced Computer Science and Applications*, 12(6), 495–502.

Aydin, M. N., & Yilmaz, Y. S. (2020). Enhancing Privacy in Cloud Computing: A Survey. *Journal of Information Security*, 11, 77–87.

Bakari, K., Chaudhari, N. S., & Cokova, Z. (2019). Privacy-Preserving Machine Learning Techniques for Cloud-Based Data Analytics. *Procedia Computer Science*, 156, 378–385.

Bhuyar, P. (2012). Horizontal Fragmentation Techniques in Distributed Database. *International Journal of Scientific and Research Publications*, 2(5).

Biswas, S., Paul, S., Bera, P., & Mandal, J. K. (2022). Secure Data Sharing and Storage in Multi-Cloud Using Homomorphic Encryption. *Journal of King Saud University. Computer and Information Sciences*, 34(1), 100938.

Bowers, K. D., Juels, A., & Oprea, A. (2008). Hail: A high availability and integrity layer for cloud storage. IACR. https://eprint.iacr.org/

Browne, P. S. (1971). Data privacy and integrity: an overview. *Proceeding of SIGFIDET '71 Proceedings of the ACM SIGFIDET (now SIGMOD)*. ACM. 10.1145/1734714.1734733

Chaabane, A., & Bouguila, N. (2021). Privacy-Preserving Data Mining in Cloud Computing: A Comprehensive Survey. *IEEE Access : Practical Innovations, Open Solutions*, 9, 38551–38571.

Chang, C.-W., Liu, P., & Wu, J.-J. (2012). Probability-Based Cloud Storage Providers Selection Algorithms with Maximum Availability. *2012 41st International Conference on Parallel Processing*, (pp. 199-208). IEEE. 10.1109/ICPP.2012.51

Chang, C.-W., Liu, P., & Wu, J.-J. (2012). Probability-Based Cloud Storage Providers Selection Algorithms with Maximum Availability. *2012 41st International Conference on Parallel Processing*, (pp. 199-208). 10.1109/ICPP.2012.51

Chen, L., Zhou, J., Li, Q., & Li, Y. (2023). Privacy-Preserving Data Sharing and Storage in Cloud Computing. *Journal of Computer Science and Technology*, 38(1), 78–92.

Cheng, H., Zhang, X., Shi, H., Yu, H., & Zhou, X. (2020). A Secure Multi-Party Computation Framework for Privacy-Preserving Data Sharing in Cloud Computing. *IEEE Transactions on Services Computing*, 13(2), 334–347.

Chowdhury, S. R., Mahmood, A. N., & Hong, C. S. (2020). A Survey on Privacy-Preserving Techniques in Cloud Computing: Taxonomy and Open Challenges. *Future Generation Computer Systems*, 112, 901–918.

Curino, C., Jones, E. P. C., Popa, R. A., Malviya, N., Wu, E., & Madden, S. (2011). Relational Cloud: The Case for a Database Service. *Proceedings of 5th Biennial Conference on Innovative Data Systems Research*. Research Gate.

Dahiya, P., & Tanwar, S. (2021). Privacy-Preserving Techniques in Cloud Computing: A Systematic Literature Review. *International Journal of Information Security*, 20, 151–176.

Dang, H. T., Tran, N. H., & Vo, D. C. (2023). A Novel Privacy-Preserving Data Storage Scheme Using Homomorphic Encryption in Cloud Computing. *Journal of Ambient Intelligence and Humanized Computing*, 14(3), 2715–2726.

Das, A., & Pramanik, S. (2022). Enhancing Privacy in Cloud Data Storage using Attribute-Based Encryption. *Journal of Ambient Intelligence and Humanized Computing*, 13(9), 8707–8718.

Desai, K., & Patel, J. (2021). A Review on Privacy-Preserving Data Mining Techniques in Cloud Computing. *International Journal of Computer Applications*, 182, 1–6. 10.5120/ijca2021921737

Dev, H., Sen, T., Basak, M., & Ali, M. E. (2012). An Approach to Protect the Privacy of Cloud Data from Data Mining Based Attacks. *Proceedings of the Third International Workshop on Data Intensive Computing in the Clouds Data Cloud*. IEEE. 10.1109/SC.Companion.2012.133

Dutta, S., Saha, P., & Pal, S. (2022). A Survey on Privacy-Preserving Data Mining Techniques in Cloud Computing. *Journal of Information Privacy and Security*, 18(1), 1–26.

Elshafey, E. I., Ali, A. H., Hassanien, A. E., & Oliva, D. (2021). A Comprehensive Survey on Privacy-Preserving Data Mining in Cloud Computing. *Journal of Ambient Intelligence and Humanized Computing*, 12(11), 12955–12975.

Fan, K., Wang, S., Ren, Y., & Li, H. (2019). Secure Data Sharing and Storage Scheme Based on Blockchain in Cloud Computing. *IEEE Access : Practical Innovations, Open Solutions*, 7, 167794–167803.

Fernandez-Carames, T. M., & Fraga-Lamas, P. (2021). A Review on the Role of Edge Computing in the Internet of Things. *IEEE Access : Practical Innovations, Open Solutions*, 9, 1307–1354.

Gochhait, S. (2022). Cloud Enhances Agile Software Development. In *Research Anthology on Agile Software, Software Development, and Testing, edited by Information Resources Management Association* (pp. 491–507). IGI Global. 10.4018/978-1-6684-3702-5.ch025

Goel, P. K., Pandey, H., Singhal, A., & Agarwal, S. (Eds.). (2024). *Improving Security, Privacy, and Trust in Cloud Computing*. IGI Global. 10.4018/979-8-3693-1431-9

Goel, P. K., Pandey, H., Singhal, A., & Agarwal, S. (Eds.). (2024). *Analyzing and Mitigating Security Risks in Cloud Computing*. IGI Global. 10.4018/979-8-3693-3249-8

Goyal, D., Gupta, N., & Kumar, V. (2022). Blockchain-Based Secure Data Sharing in Cloud Computing: A Systematic Review. *Journal of Cloud Computing (Heidelberg, Germany)*, 11(1), 1–25.

Gruschka, N., & Jensen, M. (2010). Attack surfaces: A taxonomy for attacks on cloud services. *Cloud Computing (CLOUD) 2010 IEEE 3rd International Conference*. IEEE. 10.1109/CLOUD.2010.23

Itani, W., Kayssi, A., & Chehab, A. (2009). Privacy as a Service: Privacy-Aware Data Storage and Processing in Cloud Computing Architectures. *Eighth IEEE International Conference on Dependable Autonomic and Secure Computing*. IEEE. 10.1109/DASC.2009.139

Jiang, H., Zhao, D., & Ren, W. (2023). Privacy-Preserving Data Sharing and Storage Techniques in Cloud-Based Healthcare Systems: A Review. *International Journal of Environmental Research and Public Health*, 20(4), 2161–2178.

Khalid, A. (2022). Agile Scrum Issues at Large-Scale Distributed Projects: Scrum Project Development At Large. In *Research Anthology on Agile Software, Software Development, and Testing, edited by Information Resources Management Association* (pp. 388–398). IGI Global. 10.4018/978-1-6684-3702-5.ch019

Kim, J., Kim, D., & Lee, S. (2021). Federated Learning for Privacy-Preserving Machine Learning in Cloud Environments: A Comprehensive Survey. *Future Generation Computer Systems*, 125, 146–164.

Liu, Y., Zhang, Z., & Wang, Q. (2022). Secure Query Processing Techniques for Privacy-Preserving Data Analytics in Cloud Computing: A Review. *Computers & Security*, 113, 102460.

Mohammed A. (2020). *Cloud computing security: From Single to Multi-clouds*. La Trobe University.

Nandi, M., & Chaki, R. (2020). Privacy-Preserving Techniques for Data Analytics in Cloud Computing: A Review. *International Journal of Cloud Applications and Computing*, 10(3), 23–41.

Oliveira, P. F., Lima, L., Vinhoza, T. T. V., Barros, J., & Médard, M. (2010). Trusted storage over untrusted networks. *IEEE Globecom Workshops*.

Pamies-Juarez, L., García-López, P., Sánchez-Artigas, M., & Herrera, B. (2011). Pedro Garc__a-L_opez, Marc S_anchez-Artigas and Blas Herrera, "Towards the Design of Optimal Data Redundancy Schemes for Heterogeneous Cloud Storage Infrastructures". *Computer Networks*, 55(5), 1100–1113. 10.1016/j.comnet.2010.11.004

Pamies-Juarez, L., García-López, P., Sánchez-Artigas, M., & Herrera, B. (2011). Towards the Design of Optimal Data Redundancy Schemes for Heterogeneous Cloud Storage Infrastructures. *Computer Networks*, 55(5), 1100–1113. 10.1016/j. comnet.2010.11.004

Singh, S., & Raj, P. (2023). Secure Multi-Party Computation for Privacy-Preserving Data Processing in Cloud Computing: A Survey. Journal of Cloud Computing: Advances. *Systems and Applications*, 12(1), 1–18.

Subashini, S., & Kavitha, V. (2011). A Metadata Based Storage Model for Securing Data in Cloud Environment. *2011 International Conference on Cyber-Enabled Distributed Computing and Knowledge Discovery CyberC 2011*.

Thanasis, G. (2012). *Storage and Analysis*. The International Conference for High Performance Computing Networking.

Wang, Y., Zhang, L., & Yang, S. (2021). Homomorphic Encryption Techniques for Privacy-Preserving Data Processing in Cloud Computing: A Comprehensive Study. *Journal of Systems and Software*, 177, 110953.

Wind, S., Turowski, K., Repschläger, J., & Zarnekow, R. (2011). Target Dimensions of Cloud Computing. *Proceedings of IEEE Conference on Commerce and Enterprise Computing*. IEEE.

Xu, Y., Chen, Y., & Liu, Z. (2022). Privacy-Preserving Data Sharing Techniques in Cloud Computing: A Review of Recent Advances. *Future Internet*, 14(3), 58.

Zhang, H., Liu, X., & Wu, Q. (2023). Enhancing Data Privacy in Cloud Computing: A Systematic Literature Review on Privacy-Preserving Techniques. *Journal of Network and Computer Applications*, 214, 104043.

Chapter 10
A Survey on Data Security and Privacy for Fog–Based Smart Grid Applications

Sangeetha Ganesan

https://orcid.org/0000-0001-7347-2162

R.M.K. College of Engineering and Technology, India

Prathusha Laxmi

R.M.K. College of Engineering and Technology, India

Shanmugaraj Ganesan

Velammal Institute of Technology, India

ABSTRACT

Fog computing has made it possible to extend cloud computing functions to the network edge by assisting the cloud and users in terms of communication, computation, and storage with a widely dispersed deployment of edge devices or fog nodes. Smart grid (SG) networks are recently upgraded networks of interconnected objects that greatly progress the sustainability, dependability, and dependability of the current energy infrastructure. This chapter starts by giving a general overview of the architecture, concept, and key elements of supervisory control and data acquisition (SCADA) systems for the fog-based smart grid. Based on the machine learning techniques employed by the intrusion detection system (IDS), categorise the IDS solutions into nine groups. This chapter also recommends a user privacy-protecting authentication and data aggregation system for the smart grid based on fog. It is possible to offer anonymous authentication using short randomizable signatures

DOI: 10.4018/979-8-3693-2869-9.ch010

and blind signatures, and then use fog nodes to handle billing issues after providing anonymous authentication.

INTRODUCTION

In comparison to the recent power grid, the smart grid is superior because of its dependability, flexibility, efficiency, and other key features. To build an automated and distributed advanced energy delivery network, many smart devices, two-way communication, and electricity channels are needed (X. Fang et al.(2012)). The most crucial part of the smart grid, smart metres can gather data on customer usage, including electricity consumption, and send periodic reports to the service provider (like the electricity company). The service provider can control electricity generation and distribution with the best possible strategy and dynamically adjust electricity prices with the help of almost real-time and finely detailed usage data.

However, delivering usage data directly to service providers will put serious pressure on them to process massive amounts of fine-grained usage data quickly. Additionally, the fine-grained usage data exposes user habits and behaviours that the service provider may take advantage of as an information-rich side channel (P. D. McDaniel and S. E. McLaughlin (2009)). To protect the privacy of usage data and reduce the pressure on service providers, a number of smart grid schemes based on cloud computing and/or fog computing have recently been presented (Z. Guan et al. (2017); A. Yang et al. (2018); Z. Guan et al. (2018)). These solutions partially address the two issues by utilising the distributed and low-latency characteristics of fog computing, as well as the computation and storage capabilities of cloud computing (F. Bonomi et al. (2012)). These solutions, though, also present some brand-new difficulties.

First off, many schemes (R. Lu et al.(2012); K. Alharbi and X. Lin(2012); A. R. Abdallah and X. S. Shen(2018)) encrypt the data under their public key because the usage data should be used by the service provider. To perform billing or for other purposes, such as analysing consumption records, users cannot access their own encrypted fine-grained usage data that has been outsourced to the fog nodes or cloud. In other words, users run the risk of losing ownership of their data. Two possible solutions are applying a Proxy Re-encryption scheme or uploading a duplicate of the usage data encrypted with the user's public key to a fog node or cloud (G. Ateniese et al. (2006). But regrettably, it will make it difficult for clouds or fog nodes to manage their data. Second, the service provider must perform statistical analyses on usage data in many smart grid applications. On the basis of partially homomorphic schemes, some of these existing solutions support linear algebraic computations on encrypted usage data (T. E. Gamal (1984); P. Paillier (1999). But for a wide range of smart grid applications, it is insufficient. On encrypted usage data, more difficult calculations like the standard deviation and root mean square (J. C. Smith (1995) may occasionally be necessary. Existing solutions will be able to support more extensive computation on encrypted usage data if the partially homomorphic encryption scheme is replaced with a fully homomorphic encryption scheme (C. Gentry et al. (2009). However, due to issues with ciphertext expansion and efficiency, even the most cutting-edge fully homomorphic encryption schemes are still too impractical to be used for smart grid communication.

BACKGROUND

Recently, fog computing has been thoroughly studied in relation to smart grids. Fog computing at the network edge broadens the cloud computing paradigm (F. Bonomi et al., 2012). By utilising widely and massively distributed fog nodes, fog computing provides low latency, context awareness, and localization services for the smart grid (M. Li, J. Weng (2018); P. Wang (2018); R. K. Barik (2017). The authors' description of a smart grid structure based on fog computing can be found in (I. Stojmenovic and S. Wen (2014). Fog nodes acted as regional controllers in this scenario, processing smart grid data and issuing orders to people at home as well as to other entities. F. Y. Okay and S. Ozdemir (2016) described a three-tiered hierarchical smart grid communication structure based on fog computing. Other related works (F. Li, 2011); R. Lu (2012); X. Liang (2013); (2015) concentrated on how to achieve effective smart grid communication with privacy preservation. An effective and privacy-preserving smart grid aggregation scheme was put forth by Lu et al. (2012). The Paillier cryptosystem (P. Paillier (1999) and other mathematical techniques were used in the scheme to accomplish multidimensional data aggregation. This scheme is much more effective than earlier onedimensional works because the electricity usage data are small in size and multidimensional in nature.

Because the suggested scheme also relies on additively homomorphic encryption, the methods in Lu et al. (2012) may be used to achieve multidimensional data aggregation. Lu et al. also suggested the Paillier cryptosystem-based lightweight privacy-preserving data aggregation known as LPDA (R. Lu et al., 2017). It offers fault tolerance to filter injected false data produced by smart metres or other IoT devices, and it can be used in smart grid aggregation communication. Busom et al. (2016) proposed a different method of smart grid communication depended on the additive ElGamal cryptosystem (T. E. Gamal, 1984). Due to the need to compute the discrete logarithm in order to decrypt the additive ElGamal cryptosystem, this solution is inefficient.

Abdallah et al. (2018) recently proposed a new lattice-based homomorphic encryption scheme-based lightweight privacy-preserving data aggregation scheme for smart grid. The strategy prevented smart appliances from providing user data to smart metres and considered user privacy when readings were gathered inside a home area network (HAN).

In contemporary Supervisory Control and Data Acquisition (SCADA) systems, the supervision and control of electrical energy production, transmission, and distribution are crucial (L. A. Maglaras et al. (2018). On SCADA systems, human machine interfaces (HMIs) show system operators data that is gathered and automated processes that are being controlled. These operators are able to remotely control the system to take out tasks like opening a door, altering the temperature, or starting/stopping an electric vehicle. In the era of the Internet of Things, complex and distributed large-scale applications like the smart grid, vehicle-to-grid technologies, fog computing (X. Shen et al., 2020), cloud computing, 5G wireless communication networks, blockchain, deep learning, etc. have all incorporated SCADA. As a result, a variety of security measures could be used on such systems while keeping in mind the need for low overload, real-time intrusion identification, and high efficiency. A group of controllers, computers, industry-standard communication protocols (such as UDP, HTTP, and TCP/IP), and automation make up the smart grid. These technologies are connected via the Internet to manage energy distribution and production to consumers (M. A. Ferrag and L. Maglaras (2019)). The main obstacle to creating a smart grid is not the availability of physical support, but rather the provision of security and privacy, and this problem has drawn significant attention from the cyber security research community (M. H. Rehmani et al. (2019); S. N. Islam et al. (2019). Therefore, in the SCADA systems for the fog-based smart grid, more focus should be placed on the key security requirements and vulnerabilities, such as trust components, third-party protection, nonrepudiability, auditability, integrity, availability, and privacy (Y. Yan et al., 2012).

FOG-BASED SMART GRID SCADA SYSTEMS

Figure 1. Overall design of fog-based smart grid SCADA architecture

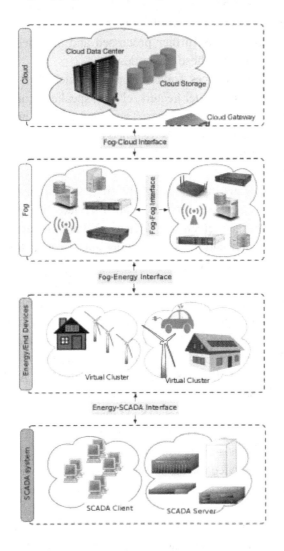

(Ferrag, 2020)

The architecture, concept, and key elements of SCADA systems for fog-based smart grids are presented in this section. In Figure 1, the overall design of the SCADA system for the fog-based smart grid is shown. The conceptual SCADA architecture for a fog-based smart grid consists four main layers:

- **The Cloud Layer:** The highest level is known as the "cloud layer," where the data centre and conventional cloud servers are located. The storage and processing resources required are available at this level.

- **The Fog Layer**: The fog nodes, which include routers, switches, access points, and gateways, make up this layer. The data transferred from the energy/end device layer is further processed and analysed (S. Ghosh and S. Sampalli (2019)) using these fog nodes.

- **The Energy/End Devices Layer**: Energy-efficient IoT-compatible gadgets like home electronics, water heaters, clocks, speakers, cameras, window coverings, etc. are found in this layer. These end devices are typically referred to as terminal nodes (TNs). It is assumed that a communication link, such as WiFi, ZigBee, Bluetooth, etc., is used to connect these TNs to one another over the internet.

- **The SCADA Layer**: In this layer, data from substations is gathered and analysed. These substations include control devices like programmable logic controllers, intelligent electronic devices, and remote terminal units. Metres, actuators, and other end devices, such as sensors, actuators, and control devices, are managed by the control devices.

The development of the smart grid as an emerging technology has been fueled by the recent flourishing growth of the network, in both wired and wireless environments. In an interconnection-based environment, energy service offerings become diverse and involve numerous distinctive edge infrastructure or device set al. (Y. Dai et al. (2019); N. Abbas et al. (2018); S. Wang et al.(2017)) . A platform known as the Smart Grid Network (SGN) links all embedded energy-related systems, such as smart metres and electrical appliances (S. Maharjan et al.(2013)). Multiple power sources and various user types may be configured as network nodes in a typical SGN (N. Nikmehr and S. Ravadanegh (2015); Y. Zhang (2012); K. Wang(2017)). Thus, network features and service model usage can be used to achieve governance and optimisation. The implementation of SGNs is impacted by network vulnerabilities, just like other network-enabled solutions (Y. Zhang (2011)). In December 2015, Ukraine experienced one of the most recent power grid attacks, which resulted in the loss of electricity for a sizable number of energy users (more than 200 thousand) (R. Lee (2016)). The fallout from the incident in Ukraine shows how cyberattacks limit a network's functionality in a variety of application scenarios. Energy supply, including power theft and power loss, is the key attack target when taking into account the service's content. For instance, battery exhaustion attacks or sleep deprivation torture are two common forms of malice that aim to drain victims' energy (H. Kim (2010); G. Gogniat(2008)).

The majority of threats, including those at the edge (N. Abbas (2018); Y. Cai(2016)), communication (K. Gai (2017)), and power plants (G. Liang (2017)), can be fragmented down into three layers. Attack launch complexity and threat positioning are related. The centralised datacenter is typically not a common attack target because launching an attack will be much simpler at the edge and communication layers than at a well-protected cloud server. An edge layer more precisely refers to those gaps in data collection since sensors are frequently placed at network edges. Attackers can quickly access those sensors to commit physical violence. Smart metre systems are among the many access points that smart grid systems frequently maintain.

To defend against all potential adversaries at all access points is an incredibly challenging task (Z. Zhang (2017)). When speaking to threats at the communication layer, attackers can deceive central controllers or datacenters by tampering with messages or cutting off communication channels. An illustration of malicious behaviour is when attackers set up numerous adversarial edge nodes and launch a Distributed Denial of Service (DDoS) attack (Z. Zhang (2017)). An enemy's effectiveness can be further increased by a mix attack (K. Gai et al.(2017); K. Gai et al. (2018)). The attack may also result in the production of malicious commands in addition to the control channels being hijacked.

ARCHITECTURE OF FOG-BASED SMART GRID

Fog computing has been used with techniques like data aggregation (R. X. Lu et al., (2017)) and big data analysis (B. Tang et al., (2017)) as well as in situations like the smart grid (B. Ni et al. (2019); R. X. Lu et al.(2017); N. Saxena (2016); M. M. Fouda et al. (2011)). The smart grid is gradually becoming the next generation of power grid through the fusion of existing power systems and communication technology. It will give customers the ability to manage the grid in addition to utilising cutting-edge monitor, control, and optimisation mechanisms, resulting in intelligent and trustworthy electricity distribution. Customers routinely upload readings from their smart metres to the utility provider, so this system's key component—smart meters—will also reveal customers' precise electricity consumption data.

The amount of data being transmitted over the grid has already surpassed the terabyte mark due to the growing popularity of smart metres. For instance, the European Commission has set a goal that by 2020, smart metres will be installed in 80% of all homes. The utility company's ability to manage the quantity of data generated by smart metres has increased during this time from 10,780 terabytes (TB) in 2010 to over 75,200 TB in 2015 (R. Yu et al. (2011)). To ensure effective transmission and system reliability, the utility company must manage these big data using techniques like in-network aggregation (X. Du et al., (2006)). The main focus is on how to send the control centre with authenticated and private customer electricity consumption data.

In particular, considered a trusted authority, a utility company with a control centre, a number of communities, each of which has numerous customers with their own smart metres, a substation, and a fog node. These factors are depicted in Fig. 2. Trusted Authority: A reliable third party known as the trusted authority manages the entity registration procedure. The trusted authority will be inactive after system bootstrapping; once a reputation has been built, it will reappear. The utility company and control centre are responsible for the generation, storage, and distribution of electricity. The fog node stores, processes, and relays information flows between the control centre and customers' smart metres, including grid commands, requests, and smart metre readings.

Figure 2. Architecture of fog-based smart grid

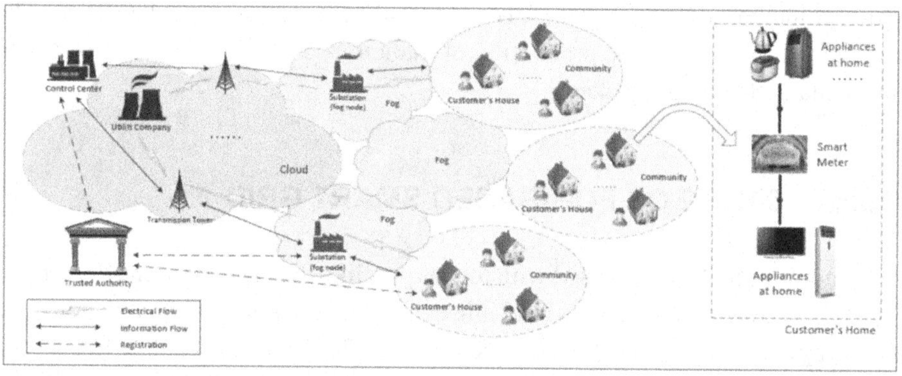

(Zhu, Liehuang, et al., 2019)

SECURITY AND PRIVACY CHALLENGES SECURITY

Security is important for the growth and development of the smart grid because communications are involved in grid operations. Confidentiality (data privacy), integrity, and authentication are three key security requirements. The primary subjects of this article are authentication and confidentiality. The smart grid will become completely paralysed as a result of an unexpected spike in electricity demand or malicious packages if authentication is not ensured, as malicious or illegal users may send up messages to steal electricity or even sabotage the grid. Despite the fact that authentication is necessary for them to communicate with the control centre, customers still want to keep their identities a secret out of concern for their privacy. So, along with anonymous authentication, traceability (D. Pointcheval and O. Sanders, 2016), which enables a trusted authority to find a targeted customer when a dispute arises, is preferred.

Privacy

Data privacy or confidentiality is a well-known and as of yet unsolved challenge in the smart grid because readings from smart metres are directly related to the health of home appliances and customers' activities. The control centre can determine patterns of electricity consumption and discover information about customers' daily routines from smart metre readings. For instance, it is very likely that the resident is preparing dinner if the cooker or microwave is on between the hours of 6 and 7. Fouda et al. (2011) proposed a simple message authentication scheme for smart grid communications. Smart metres are specifically distributed at different hierarchical levels in the smart grid. According to the proposed scheme, smart metres can mutually authenticate one another and generate a shared session key using the Diffie-Hellman key establishment protocol. Second, the subsequent messages' authenticity is checked using this key and the hash-based authentication code. They also emphasised the necessity of simple authentication protocols for communications within the smart grid. Lu et al. (2012) proposed an proficient and privacy-preserving aggregation method for secure smart grid communications. Insider threats have the potential to seriously harm the smart grid system and jeopardise many security requirements, claim Saxena et al. (2016). They recommended an authorization and authentication scheme for various users and devices to lessen threats coming from both inside and outside the smart grid. This system can provide both dynamic user authorization and mutual authentication between the server and the clients.

Applications Authentication: Usually, the first step in a data transmission is authentication. Prior to receiving grid service, smart metre data, and authentication requests, customers in a smart grid must send their requests to the fog node. A person's identity, a time stamp, and a reliable proof (like a signature) must all be included in this information. The fog node sends this data to the control centre once it has finished a number of tasks, including data aggregation. After using verification algorithms to check each customer's proof, the control centre determines whether they are a legitimate customer. If the customer's authentication information is legitimately verified, the control centre will notify the fog node that the customer's request and smart metre data can be uploaded.

Data Aggregation: A few of the research areas where data aggregation has been thoroughly investigated include vehicular ad hoc networks, wireless sensor networks, and crowdsensing. In the smart grid, collecting and combining smart metre readings from customers by the fog node is the main objective of data aggregation. By doing so, communication overhead is reduced, and network bandwidth is preserved. Data aggregation frequently makes use of smart metre readings. To protect the information contained in the customers' smart metre readings, further data aggregation can be performed on the ciphertexts of smart metre readings. In this operation, the control centre can only obtain statistical data (like the sum or average) about the smart metre readings of the customer.

Cyber Security Solutions

In this section outlined the cyber security options for SCADA systems used in fog-based smart grids . The four main groups shown in Figure 2 as follows: 1) Solutions for authentication, 2) Solutions for maintaining privacy, 3) Key management systems, and 4) Solutions for intrusion detection.

Solutions for Authentication

A list of authentication options for SCADA systems used in fog-based smart grids is provided in Table I. the authentication solutions is categorized into four groups based on authentication models: key management systems, intrusion detection systems, privacy-preserving solutions, and authentication solutions.

Table 1. Summary of authentication options for SCADA systems used in fog-based smart grids

Reference	Network model	Authentication model	Security analysis	Performance (+)	Limitation (-)	Performance analysis
Cheng et al. (2019)	NANs, HANs, and WANs are the three different types of networks that make up the smart grid. An energy management centre is linked to the WAN.	Mutual authentication	Game theory	• faster than the ECDH and ECDSA schemes by 4.5 times • Blocks attempts to reuse keys.	Attacks by privileged insiders are not taken into account	low costs for communication and storage.
Wang et al. (2019)	The blockchain, edge servers, end users, and registration authority make up the smart grid network model.	Mutual authentication	Security requirements	+ Conditional traceability + Perfect forward secrecy	Key reuse attacks are not taken into account	low costs for communication and storage.

continued on following page

Table 1. Continued

Reference	Network model	Authentication model	Security analysis	Performance (+)	Limitation (-)	Performance analysis
Kumar et al. (2019)	The smart grid network model consists of smart grid devices, trusted authorities, and automatic controller prototypes.	Demand response authentication	-	+ Prevents utility centre impersonation, replay, stolen smart grid device, and man-in-the-middle attacks + Offers untraceability, anonymity, and session key security	Key reuse attacks are not taken into account	low costs for communication and storage compared to J.-L. Tsai and N.-W. Lo(2015) and V. Odelu (2016)
Roman et al. (2019)	The control centre, electric vehicle, authentication server, aggregators, and charge/discharge stations make up the V2G network architecture.	Verification of demand response	AVISPA tool	+ Protects against attacks such as man-in-the-middle, replay and injection, redirection, known key, and DoS + Preserve the integrity of the transmitted messages	Perfect forward secrecy and limited traceability are not taken into consideration.	Less expensive to store than the two schemes created by J. Chen et al. (2015) and Saxena et al. (2015).
Guan et al (2019)	A control centre, a trusted certification authority, edge devices, and end users make up the EFFECT network model.	Aggregation of data with authentication	Cryptographic assumptions	Defends against a variety of assaults, including modification, injection, replay, and forgery Data integrity assurance	No consideration is given to the fog-based smart grid architecture.	cheaper to compute than EPPDA H. Li et al.(2013), Shen's scheme (H. Shen et al.(2017)), and EPPA (R. Lu et al.(2012)).
Zhu et al.(2019)	The study takes into account a fog-based smart grid architecture made up of three components: a utility company with a control centre, several communities, and a reliable source.	Aggregation of data with authentication	-	anonymous verification Communication effectiveness	Data integrity is absent. - Susceptible to injection, replay, and	effectiveness of communication
Zhang et al. (2019)	The service provider and the smart metre are the two parties that make up the network model.	Authenticated key exchange	-	Defends against well-known attacks, such as those caused by desynchronization, knownkey, impersonation, man-in-the-middle attacks, and replay attacks, among others. + Anonymity and untraceability of smart metres	The service provider and the smart metre are the only two parties that make up the network model.	According to the report, the communication cost is 204 bytes, which is high when compared to Xia and Wang's plan (L. Zhang (2019)). Additionally, the computational cost is higher than (J. Xia and Y. Wang (2017)). But (L. Zhang (2019)) offers more security features.

continued on following page

Table 1. Continued

Reference	Network model	Authentication model	Security analysis	Performance (+)	Limitation (-)	Performance analysis
Mahmood et al.(2018)	The HAN nodes that make up the SCADA-based smart grid are fitted with smart metres. The nodes use optical fibre connections and ZigBee connections as their two types of communication links.	Mutual authentication	BAN logic - ProVerif	key sizes that are smaller than those of DH, DSA, and RSA + Protects against man-in-the-middle, privileged insider, replay, and impersonation attacks.	Perfect forward secrecy and limited traceability are not taken into consideration.	The computation took 11.1703 milliseconds.
Odelu et al. (2016)	The service provider and the smart metre are the two parties that make up the network model.	The service provider and the smart metre are the two parties that make up the network model.	- Game theory	absolute forward secrecy Private information about smart metres	The service provider and the smart metre are the only two parties that make up the network model.	According to the report, the communication cost is 1920 bits, which is high when compared to Tsai-Lo's plan (J.-L. Tsai and N.-W. Lo (2015)).
Li and Cao (2011)	applications of multicast in the smart grid and SCADA systems, such as wide area protection and in-substation protection	Multicast authentication	cyptographic assumptions	cut down on energy consumption + Reduces authentication time delay	prone to key reuse attacks	When compared to the HORS scheme's (10KB) storage cost, a receiver's cost is lower at 1.2KB (L. Reyzin and N. Reyzin (2002))
Nicanfar et al. (2011)	The utility server and the home smart metre make up the network model's two components.	Multicast authentication	cyptographic assumptions	resists man-in-the-middle, brute-force, replay, DoS, and other attacks Added benefit: secure key management	The utility server and the smart metre are the only two parties that make up the network model.	Low overhead

1) **Mutual Identification**: Mutual authentication, or client-server authentication, is a process used in the smart grid where two nodes of a communication link authenticate one another. The servers can be certain that all potential users are attempting to gain access lawfully, and the smart grid users can be certain that they are only interacting with legitimate nodes in this way. The SCADA-based smart grid is made up of home area network (HAN) nodes with smart metres. Both ZigBee and optical fibre connections are used by the nodes to communicate with one another. The system uses elliptic curve cryptography (ECC)-depended lightweight mutual authentication to provide this service. A security analysis using Burrows-Abadi Needham (BAN) logic and the ProVerif tool shows that the scheme can withstand four different types of attacks: replay attacks, impersonation attacks, privileged insider attacks, and man-in-the-middle attacks. Comparing the results to DH, DSA, and RSA, smaller key sizes are also evi-

dent. ECC significantly reduces computational complexity, it should be noted. In order to provide mutual authentication for the edge computing-based smart grid, Wang et al. (2019) use Blockchain technology. The smart grid network model is made up in particular of the blockchain, edge servers, end users, and registration authority. The blockchain is utilised as a decentralised database and distributed data storage system on the basis of a consensus mechanism and hashing operations. The key materials table is managed by a smart contract in the blockchain network in the work (Wang et al. (2019)). This smart contract can support effective revocation and conditional anonymous authentication for communication providers while minimising the related asynchronous issue. Wang et al. (2019) also recommends using the user's public key rather than their real identity to give end users unlinkability and identity anonymity. Furthermore, because the private keys and random nonce are not broadcasted on the community channel, no outside attacker can monitor end user behaviour in the smart grid. It should be noted that many IoT applications use blockchain technology, as mentioned in (M. A. Ferrag (2019a,2019b)).

2) **Authentication for demand response:** One type of demand response that can be used in a smart grid to meet demand is distributed generation, which can be used to change the amount of power supplied by the primary grid (P. Siano (2014)). Demand response in the smart grid must be maintained, so Kumar et al. (2019) proposed an authentication protocol called ECCAuth, in which a smart grid device and a remote control centre create a session key for secure communication to guarantee the smart grid's effective operation.Due to the complexity of the discrete logarithm problem for elliptic curves, it is computationally impossible to derive the secrets, which allows the ECCAuth protocol to provide session key security, anonymity, and untraceability. Roman et al. (2019) introduced a bilinear pairing-based authentication protocol to enhance the vehicle to grid (V2G) networks' demand-response balance. The protocol can withstand a variety of attacks, including man-in-the-middle, replay and injection, redirection, known key, and DoS attacks, according to the security analysis. The protocol can withstand a variety of attacks, including man-in-the-middle, replay and injection, redirection, known key, and DoS attacks, according to the security analysis. Compared to the two schemes developed by J. Chen et al. (2015) and Saxena et al.(2015), the protocol developed by Roman et al. (2019) offers a lower storage cost.

  3.Data aggregation and authentication together: Data aggregation, a key element of modern distributed systems like smart grids and SCADA systems, enables the decentralised identification of the main important properties at the system level. Jesus et al. (2014) proposed a classification of aggregation algorithms from the viewpoints of communication and computation. The authors proposed three categories for communication: unstructured (typically gossip-based), structured (typically hierarchy-based), and hybrid (a combination of unstructured and structured). The authors suggested three classifications from a computation standpoint: complex functions, counting, and decomposable functions. The fog-based smart grid's three-layer cloud-, fog-, and user-based architecture makes use of fog computing technology to provide low latency and quick response. Fog computing and a data aggregation technique are combined by Zhu et al. (2019) to provide privacy preservation with authentication. The study's fictitious fog-based smart grid architecture consists of several communities, a trustworthy authority, and a utility company. The utility company is in charge of electricity generation, storage, and distribution. Each customer's home receives an installation of a smart metre as well as a number of electrical appliances. The fog node only aggregates the ciphertexts of smart metre readings, so the computational cost is minimal. However, no security analysis against attacks is provided.

4) **Agreement on an authenticated key**: For SCADA systems for fog-based smart grids, a lot of research has been done recently on Key agreement and authentication frameworks. Zhang et al. The compact authenticated key agreement framework proposed by Zhang et al. (2019) uses high entropy random numbers, a secure hash function, and a symmetric encryption algorithm. Their system has proven to be resilient to well-known attacks (like desynchronization, known key, impersonation, man-in-the-middle, and replay attacks, etc.) and to satisfy some security requirements for the smart grid, like smart metre anonymity and untraceability. The reported communication cost of 204 bytes is significant when compared to Xia and Wang's (2012) approach. However, because the network model only consists of two parties—the service provider and the smart meter—Zhang et al.'s framework is unable to authenticate every node in the smart grid. Tsai & Lo's authentication scheme (2015) was examined by Odelu et al. (2016), who then created a provably protected valid key agreement method for the smart grid architecture. According to the security analysis, the Tsai&Lo authentication scheme is susceptible to an attack known as an Ephemeral Secret Leakage under the control of a Canetti-Krawczyk (CK)-adversary (2001).

5) **Multicast authentication:** The SGKM (smart grid key management) authentication scheme was introduced by Nicanfar et al. (2011) to authenticate the utility server and the home smart metre in the smart grid. A wireless mesh network topology is utilised between the utility

server and the home smart metre, with IEEE 802.16 and IEEE 802.15.4 communications being used both inside and outside the home domain.

Solutions for Maintaining Privacy

Based on privacy models, these security measures is divided into six categories: identity privacy, location privacy, privacy of residential users, energy privacy, privacy of data aggregation, and credentials privacy.

1) **Location privacy:** Using the Intel Edison development platform, the viability of Wang's proposal for smart metres with constrained resource availability is evaluated. The results show that Wang's scheme (2019) requires only two pairing operations, which is significantly fewer than those of Fan et al. (2013) and Wang et al. (2017). Replay, unauthenticated smart metres, man-in-the-middle, internal (ESP), internal (aggregator), external (eavesdropping), and collusion attacks are seven common smart grid attacks that Wang's scheme (2019) is also resistant to, according to the security analysis.

2. **Privacy in data aggregation:** Data aggregation is frequently used, according to Ming et al. (2019), to prevent user privacy from being disclosed as a result of the transmission of energy consumption data into the smart grid. The four components of the system model are the smart metre, gateway, control centre, and third trust party. The study recommends an efficient multi-dimensional data aggregation method called P 2MDA to provide data aggregation privacy in the SCADA systems for the fog-based smart grid.

Key Management Systems

Ghosal and Conti (2019) recently proposed the following four categories for the crucial management strategies employed in the smart grid: 1) The approach based on authentication, 2) the approach based on key graph, 3) the approach based on function with physical unclonability, and 4) the hybrid approach. In the research by Nicanfar et al. (2013), a smart metre that belongs to the HAN domain and an authentication server in the smart grid are mutually authenticated using private-public keys. The key graph approach is recommended for managing the keys of a large number of smart metres because it is based on a key graph and is similar to the key management scheme put forth by Liu et al. (2012). The following sources are suggested for more information.

Intrusion Detection Systems

These IDS solutions is divided into nine groups based on the machine learning techniques that were employed: IDS examples include deterministic finite automata-based IDS, ANN-based IDS, SVM-based IDS, rule-based IDS, decision tree-based IDS, Bloom filter-based IDS, random forest-based IDS, random subspace-based IDS, and so forth.

1) **Deep learning for IDS:** Yang et al. (2019) used deep learning to detect intrusions into SCADA networks. They use a convolutional neural network to explain the key temporal SCADA traffic patterns. The dataset contains five attacks: a DNP3-specific attack, a TCP RST attack on telnet, a UDP flood attack, a SYN flooding attack, and an ARP spoofing attack. The results show an impressive 99.84% detection accuracy.For more details on IDS systems for smart grids based on deep learning system for detecting intrusions The intrusion detection systems for SCADA systems used in fog-based smart grids are listed in The system detects benign data and attacks with the best performance on deep learning-based IDS systems for smart grids, at 99.90% and 98.46%, respectively.

2) **Artificial neural networks-based IDS**: Two methods for SCADA system intrusion detection are suggested by Kalech (2019). The first method, which makes use of self-organized map artificial neural networks (SOM-ANNs), offers unsupervised learning. In the second method, a hidden Markov model is used. A dataset from Ben-Gurion University and a dataset from Israel Electric Corporations called CyberGym are used for performance evaluation. Results show that the hidden Markov model outperforms the artificial neural network when the function code field in the MODBUS TCP packets is taken into account.

3) **Support vector machine-based IDS:** Support vector machines were used by Perez et al. (2018) to identify cyber security intrusions in SCADA systems. The study provides two classifiers: a seven category classifier (attacks) and a binary classifier (anomaly,normal). The seven types of attack are Naive Response Injection, Reconnaissance, Denial of Service, State Command Injection,Function Code Injection, Parameter Command Injection, and Complex Response Injection. The hyperparameter search step is the process of locating the best hyperparameters. Building the models that will divide each new observation into a number of predefined groups is the last step in the classification process. The system achieves an F1 rate of 92.50% for the categorical classification classifier while achieving an F1 rate of 94.34% for the binary classification using the results from the gas pipeline system dataset. With accuracy rates of 99.90% and 98.46% for benign data detection and attack detection, respectively, the system performs best.

4) **Decision-tree-based intrusion detection system:** Ahmim et al. (2019) proposed a novel hierarchical intrusion detection system that can be used with SCADA systems for smart grids based on fog to identify cyberattacks. The system combines different Forest PA, RIP algorithm, and REP tree decision tree and rule-based learning classifier techniques. The three classifiers are trained in the training step after the data is classified as benign or as a specific type of attack in the test step. The CICIDS 2017 dataset is used to assess the performance of the proposed system, and The findings indicate that the highest true negative rate is 98.855%.

5) **Rule-based IDS:** IDS with guidelines Along with Naive Bayes and random forest techniques, Khan and Serpen (2019) proposed a misuse intrusion detection system based on a rule-based algorithm in addition to the previously mentioned work of (A. Ahmim et al.(2019)). The study specifically employs machine learning classifiers that are trained on the network dataset in supervised mode in order to identify and detect potential similar attacks in the future. A SCADA system network is created using the dataset on the suggested system to evaluate its efficacy.

6) **Bloom filter-based IDS:** Khan et al.'s (2019) technique makes use of bloom filters to find SCADA system intrusions. The authors suggested an approach known as HML-IDS, a hybrid multilevel anomaly prediction approach, to specifically find new attacks on industrial control systems. Regular network models' signatures are effectively stored, and anomalies are then found by applying a Bloom filter, which can tell whether an item is a part of a group or not. Using the Industrial Control System (ICS) Cyber Attack Datasets, the HML-IDS approach demonstrated evaluation performance with up to a 95% F score, 92% recall rate, 98% precision, and 97% accuracy.

7) **Random forest-based IDS:** Random forest is a method of encapsulation that is based on decision trees. It classifier performs better than Naive Bayes, in particular, according to Khan and Serpen (2019). The active learning intrusion detection system called ALIDS was created by McElwee (2017) and is depended on a random forest classifier and the k-Means clustering method. After analyzing the classification results and choosing the sample to be sent to the oracle, the ALIDS system retrains the classifier using exposed labels and brand-new labels from the oracle. With just 0.14% of Oracle requests, the ALIDS attains 90% precision, according to the KDD99 dataset performance evaluation.

8) **Random subspace learning-based IDS**: Blockchain-based random subspace learning-based intrusion detection system: Derhab et al. (2019) use blockchain and random subspace learning to build an intrusion detection system that can prevent fake industrial control system attacks. The study combines k-nearest neighbour and random subspace learning to thwart the misrouting attack. The

power system dataset is used to evaluate performance. The system's accuracy in identifying attacks and benign data is best at 99.90% and 98.46%, respectively.

9) **Deterministic finite automaton-based IDS**: Goldenberg and Wool (2013) created an intrusion detection system based on the deterministic finite automaton to detect attacks in Modbus/TCP networks. A production Modbus system was used to test the proposed system. The suggested method appears to be very effective in terms of false-positive rates and is able to spot anomalies that other methods missed. On the other hand, malicious traffic hasn't been used to test it.

CHALLENGES

The open possibilities for future research are described below as we wrap up our analysis of the cyber security solutions for SCADA systems for fog-based smart grids.

a. What machine learning method should be used?

Machine learning techniques are used to determine, discover, and identify unauthorised use and the introduction of false data in network systems, such as fog-based smart grid SCADA systems. The performance of the machine learning technique(s) selected on cyber security datasets determines how effective they are. Additionally, the ideal machine learning technique may vary depending on the scenario. As a result, the comparative study needs to include a wide range of systems, attack types, and scenario types.

b. Cybersecurity dataset for SCADA systems

The most recent work in (2020) describes nearly 3 well-known cyber datasets that are divided into seven categories, including datasets based on IoT traffic, datasets based on Android apps, datasets based on virtual private networks, datasets based on internet traffic, datasets based on electrical networks, and datasets based on network traffic. In this context, creating a new data set to construct a network intrusion detector under fog-based smart grid SCADA systems may be a promising research direction.

c. Recognising bogus data injection attacks

False data injection attacks are one of the cyberthreats to SCADA and smart grid systems that have drawn a lot of attention from both the security and energy industries (B. Li (2019)). Attackers manipulate data in smart metres based on cyber-physical channels (such as eavesdropping) in order to fabricate the state of the power system (such as electricity theft). Although security protocols for SCADA and smart grid systems have been developed, some crucial issues regarding false data injection attacks—such as unauthorized entry to the fog computing system's control center —remain largely unresolved.

In particular, based on knowledge of power grid connections and configurations found at the fog computing layer, an attacker can conduct a false data injection attack. Creating a framework to recognise false data injection attacks on SCADA systems for fog-based smart grids is one potential future direction.

d. Blockchain for SCADA systems

According to (M. A. Ferrag, 2019), blockchain technology can be used in IoT applications. Recently, Liang et al. (2018) proposed a blockchain-based data protection framework for contemporary power systems. There are two methods for choosing the miners: 1) pre-specified nodes as miners, and 2) randomly chosen nodes as miners. Though consensus protocols for peer-to-peer networks have been created, some significant problems with the validation of the blocks at the fog computing layer are still largely unresolved. Creating a consensus framework for validating blocks of data on SCADA systems for fog-based smart grids is one potential future direction.

CONCLUSION

In this Paper, first discussed the two main uses of the fog-based smart grid's architecture. After that, looked at the privacy and security concerns in fog-based smart grid infrastructures and gave a thorough analysis of the specifications for authentication and privacy preservation. Additionally, examined three cutting-edge works in fog-based smart grid technology. Finally, presented a data aggregation scheme and authentication that protects privacy, followed by an efficiency analysis. In order to increase data protection capabilities and guarantee the functionality of the smart grid, this paper concentrated on privacy-preserving issues in SGN. It also made a proposal for a method. In this paper, reviewed the most recent cyber security technologies available for SCADA systems used in fog-based smart grids. This paper delivered an overview of the architecture, concept, and key elements of SCADA systems for smart grids based on fog. Furthermore, looked at authentication strategies for fog-based smart grid SCADA systems and divided them into four groups: authenticated key agreement, demand response, data aggregation, and mutual authentication. According to the machine learning methods that were used, classified the IDS solutions into nine categories: IDS based on deep learning, IDS based on artificial neural networks, IDS based on support vector machines, IDS based on decision trees, IDS based on rules, IDS based on Bloom filters, IDS based on random forests, IDS based on random subspace learning, and IDS based on deterministic finite automata. There are still many challenging research areas that need to be further investigated, such as methods for identifying false data injection attacks, how to choose the most efficient machine learning strategy, and how to create new cyber security datasets for comparison of intrusion detection solutions.

REFERENCES

Abbas, Y., Zhang, Y., Taherkordi, A., & Skeie, T. (2018). Zhang, A. Taherkordi, and T. Skeie. Mobile edge computing: A survey. *IEEE Internet of Things Journal*, 5(1), 450–465. 10.1109/JIOT.2017.2750180

Abdallah, R., & Shen, X. S. (2018). A lightweight lattice-based homomorphic privacy-preserving data aggregation scheme for smart grid. *IEEE Transactions on Smart Grid*, 9(1), 396–405. 10.1109/TSG.2016.2553647

Ahmim, A., Maglaras, L., Ferrag, M. A., Derdour, M., & Janicke, H. (2019). A novel hierarchical intrusion detection system based on decision tree and rules-based models. *2019 15th International Conference on Distributed Computing in Sensor Systems (DCOSS)*. IEEE. 10.1109/DCOSS.2019.00059

Ahmim, A., Maglaras, L., Ferrag, M. A., Derdour, M., & Janicke, H. (2019). A novel hierarchical intrusion detection system based on decision tree and rules-based models. *2019 15th International Conference on Distributed Computing in Sensor Systems (DCOSS)*. IEEE. 10.1109/DCOSS.2019.00059

Ateniese, K., Fu, K., Green, M., & Hohenberger, S. (2006). Improved proxy re-encryption schemes with applications to secure distributed storage. *ACM Transactions on Information and System Security*, 9(1), 1–30. 10.1145/1127345.1127346

Barik, R. K., Gudey, S. K., Reddy, G. G., Pant, M., Dubey, H., Mankodiya, K., & Kumar, V. (2017). Foggrid: Leveraging fog computing for enhanced smart grid network. CoRR.

Bonomi, R. A. (2012). Fog computing and its role in the internet of things. *Proc. MCC workshop on SIGCOMM*. Research Gate.

Cai, Y., Cao, Y., Li, Y., Huang, T., & Zhou, B. (2016). Cascading failure analysis considering interaction between power grids and communication networks. *IEEE Transactions on Smart Grid*, 7(1), 530–538. 10.1109/TSG.2015.2478888

Canetti, R., & Krawczyk, H. (2001). Analysis of key-exchange protocols and their use for building secure channels. *International Conference on the Theory and Applications of Cryptographic Techniques*. Springer. 10.1007/3-540-44987-6_28

Chen, J., Zhang, Y., & Su, W. (2015). An anonymous authentication scheme for plug-in electric vehicles joining to charging/discharging station in vehicle-to-grid (v2g) networks. *China Communications*, 12(3), 9–19. 10.1109/CC.2015.7084359

Cheng, Y., Qin, Y., Lu, R., Jiang, T., & Takagi, T. (2019). Batten down the hatches: Securing neighborhood area networks of smart grid in the quantum era. *IEEE Transactions on Smart Grid*, 10(6), 6386–6395. 10.1109/TSG.2019.2903836

Dai, Y., Xu, D., Maharjan, S., Chen, Z., He, Q., & Zhang, Y. (2019). Blockchain and deep reinforcement learning empowered intelligent 5g beyond. *IEEE Network*, 33(99), 1. 10.1109/MNET.2019.1800376

Das Odelu, A. K., Wazid, M., & Conti, M. (2016). Provably secure authenticated key agreement scheme for smart grid. *IEEE Transactions on Smart Grid*, 9(3), 1900–1910.

Derhab, A., Guerroumi, M., Gumaei, A., Maglaras, L., Ferrag, M. A., Mukherjee, M., & Khan, F. A. (2019). Blockchain and random subspace 13 learning-based ids for sdn-enabled industrial iot security. *Sensors (Basel)*, 19(14), 3119. 10.3390/s1914311931311136

Diao, F., Zhang, F., & Cheng, X. (2015). A privacy-preserving smart metering scheme using linkable anonymous credential. *IEEE Transactions on Smart Grid*, 6(1), 461–467. 10.1109/TSG.2014.2358225

Du, X., Xiao, Y., Chen, H.-H., & Wu, Q. (2006, May). Secure Cell Relay Routing Protocol for Sensor Networks. *Wireless Communications and Mobile Computing*, 6(3), 375–391. 10.1002/wcm.402

Fan, C.-I., Huang, S.-Y., & Lai, Y.-L. (2013). Privacy-enhanced data aggregation scheme against internal attackers in smart grid. *IEEE Transactions on Industrial Informatics*, 10(1), 666–675. 10.1109/TII.2013.2277938

Fang, S., Misra, S., Xue, G., & Yang, D. (2012). Misra, G. Xue, and D. Yang, "Smart grid - the new and improved power grid: A survey,". *IEEE Communications Surveys and Tutorials*, 14(4), 944–980. 10.1109/SURV.2011.101911.00087

Ferrag, M. A., Babaghayou, M., & Yazici, M. A. (2020). Cyber security for fog-based smart grid SCADA systems: Solutions and challenges. *Journal of Information Security and Applications*, 52, 102500. 10.1016/j.jisa.2020.102500

Ferrag, M. A., Derdour, M., Mukherjee, M., Derhab, A., Maglaras, L., & Janicke, H. (2019). Blockchain technologies for the internet of things: Research issues and challenges. *IEEE Internet of Things Journal*, 6(2), 2188–2204. 10.1109/JIOT.2018.2882794

Ferrag, M. A., Maglaras, L., & Janicke, H. (2019). *"Blockchain and its role in the internet of things," in Strategic Innovative Marketing and Tourism*. Springer.

Ferrag, M. A., Maglaras, L., Moschoyiannis, S., & Janicke, H. (2020). Deep learning for cyber security intrusion detection: Approaches, datasets, and comparative study. *Journal of Information Security and Applications*, 50, 102419. 10.1016/j.jisa.2019.102419

Figueres, N. B., Petrlic, R., Sebe, F., Sorge, C., & Valls, M. (2016). Efficient ´ smart metering based on homomorphic encryption. *Computer Communications*, 82, 95–101. 10.1016/j.comcom.2015.08.016

Fouda, M. M., Fadlullah, Z. M., Kato, N., Rongxing Lu, , & Xuemin Shen, . (2011). A Lightweight Message Authentication Scheme for Smart Grid Communications. *IEEE Transactions on Smart Grid*, 2(4), 675–685. 10.1109/TSG.2011.2160661

Gai, K., Choo, K. K. R., Qiu, M., & Zhu, L. (2018). Privacy-preserving content-oriented wireless communication in internet-of-things. *IEEE Internet of Things Journal*, 5(4), 3059–3067. 10.1109/JIOT.2018.2830340

Gai, K., Qiu, M., Ming, Z., Zhao, H., & Qiu, L. (2017). Spoofing-jamming attack strategy using optimal power distributions in wireless smart grid networks. *IEEE Transactions on Smart Grid*, 8(5), 2431–2439. 10.1109/TSG.2017.2664043

Ghosal, A., & Conti, M. (2019). Key management systems for smart grid advanced metering infrastructure: A survey. *IEEE Communications Surveys and Tutorials*, 21(3), 2831–2848. 10.1109/COMST.2019.2907650

Gogniat, G., Wolf, T., Burleson, W., Diguet, J., Bossuet, L., & Vaslin, R. (2008). Reconfigurable hardware for high-security/highperformance embedded systems: The SAFES perspective. *IEEE Transactions on Very Large Scale Integration (VLSI) Systems*, 16(2), 144–155.

Goldenberg, N., & Wool, A. (2013). Accurate modeling of modbus/tcp for intrusion detection in scada systems. *International Journal of Critical Infrastructure Protection*, 6(2), 63–75. 10.1016/j.ijcip.2013.05.001

Guan, J., Li, J., Wu, L., Zhang, Y., Wu, J., & Du, X. (2017). Achieving efficient and secure data acquisition for cloud-supported internet of things in smart grid. *IEEE Internet of Things Journal*, 4(6), 1934–1944. 10.1109/JIOT.2017.2690522

Guan, Y., Si, G., Zhang, X., Wu, L., Guizani, N., Du, X., & Ma, Y. (2018). Privacy-preserving and efficient aggregation based on blockchain for power grid communications in smart communities. *IEEE Communications Magazine*, 56(7), 82–88. 10.1109/MCOM.2018.1700401

Guan, Z., Zhang, Y., Zhu, L., Wu, L., & Yu, S. (2019). Effect: An efficient flexible privacy-preserving data aggregation scheme with authentication in smart grid. *Science China. Information Sciences*, 62(3), 32103. 10.1007/s11432-018-9451-y

Islam, S. N., Baig, Z., & Zeadally, S. (2019). Physical layer security for the smart grid: Vulnerabilities, threats, and countermeasures. *IEEE Transactions on Industrial Informatics*, 15(12), 6522–6530. 10.1109/TII.2019.2931436

Jesus, P., Baquero, C., & Almeida, P. S. (2014). A survey of distributed data aggregation algorithms. *IEEE Communications Surveys and Tutorials*, 17(1), 381–404. 10.1109/COMST.2014.2354398

Kalech, M. (2019). Cyber-attack detection in scada systems using temporal pattern recognition techniques. *Computers & Security*, 84, 225–238. 10.1016/j.cose.2019.03.007

Khan, A. A. Z. (2019). Misuse intrusion detection using machine learning for gas pipeline scada networks. *Proceedings of the International Conference on Security and Management (SAM)*. The Steering Committee of The World Congress in Computer Science.

Kim, R., Chitti, R., & Song, J. (2010). Chitti, and J. Song. Novel defense mechanism against data flooding attacks in wireless ad hoc networks. *IEEE Transactions on Consumer Electronics*, 56(2), 579–582. 10.1109/TCE.2010.5505973

Kumar, N., Aujla, G. S., Das, A. K., & Conti, M. (2019). ECCAuth: Secure Authentication Protocol for Demand Reponse Management in Smart Grid Systems. *IEEE Transactions on Industrial Informatics*, 15(12), 6572–6582. 10.1109/TII.2019.2922697

Kumari, S., Tanwar, S., Tyagi, S., Kumar, N., Obaidat, M. S., & Rodrigues, J. J. P. C. (2019). Tanwar, S. Tyagi, N. Kumar, M. S. Obaidat, and J. J. Rodrigues, "Fog computing for smart grid systems in the 5g environment: Challenges and solutions,". *IEEE Wireless Communications*, 26(3), 47–53. 10.1109/MWC.2019.1800356

Lee, R., Assante, M., & Conway, T. (2016). *Analysis of the cyber attack on the Ukrainian power grid*. NERC. https://www.nerc.com/pa/CI/ESISAC/Documents/EISAC SANS Ukraine DUC 18Mar2016.pdf

Li, B., Xiao, G., Lu, R., Deng, R., & Bao, H. (2019). On feasibility and limitations of detecting false data injection attacks on power grid state estimation using d-facts devices. *IEEE Transactions on Industrial Informatics*.

Li, B. L., & Liu, P. (2011). Secure and privacy-preserving information aggregation for smart grids. *IJSN*, 6(1), 28–39. 10.1504/IJSN.2011.039631

Li, D., Guo, H., Zhou, J., Zhou, L., & Wong, J. W. (2019). Scadawall: A cpi-enabled firewall model for scada security. *Computers & Security*, 80, 134–154. 10.1016/j. cose.2018.10.002

Li, H., Lin, X., Yang, H., Liang, X., Lu, R., & Shen, X. (2013). Eppdr: An efficient privacy-preserving demand response scheme with adaptive key evolution in smart grid. *IEEE Transactions on Parallel and Distributed Systems*, 25(8), 2053–2064. 10.1109/TPDS.2013.124

Li, Q., & Cao, G. (2011). Multicast authentication in the smart grid with onetime signature. *IEEE Transactions on Smart Grid*, 2(4), 686–696. 10.1109/TSG.2011.2138172

Liang, G., Weller, S. R., Luo, F., Zhao, J., & Dong, Z. Y. (2018). Distributed blockchain-based data protection framework for modern power systems against cyber attacks. *IEEE Transactions on Smart Grid*, 10(3), 3162–3173. 10.1109/TSG.2018.2819663

Liang, G., Zhao, J., Luo, F., Weller, S., & Dong, Z. (2017). A review of false data injection attacks against modern power systems. *IEEE Transactions on Smart Grid*, 8(4), 1630–1638. 10.1109/TSG.2015.2495133

Liang, X., Li, X., Lu, R., Lin, X., & Shen, X. (2013). Li, R. Lu, X. Lin, and X. Shen, "UDP: Usage-based dynamic pricing with privacy preservation for smart grid,". *IEEE Transactions on Smart Grid*, 4(1), 141–150. 10.1109/TSG.2012.2228240

Liu, N., Chen, J., Zhu, L., Zhang, J., & He, Y. (2012). A key management scheme for secure communications of advanced metering infrastructure in smart grid. *IEEE Transactions on Industrial Electronics*, 60(10), 4746–4756. 10.1109/TIE.2012.2216237

Lu, R., Liang, X., Li, X., Lin, X., & Shen, X. (2012). Eppa: An efficient and privacy-preserving aggregation scheme for secure smart grid communications. *IEEE Transactions on Parallel and Distributed Systems*, 23(9), 1621–1631. 10.1109/TPDS.2012.86

Lu, R. X., Heung, K., Lashkari, A. H., & Ghorbani, A. A. (2017). A Lightweight Privacy-Preserving Data Aggregation Scheme for Fog Computing-enhanced IoT. *IEEE Access : Practical Innovations, Open Solutions*, 5, 3302–3312. 10.1109/ACCESS.2017.2677520

Lu, X. (2012). Liang, X. Li, X. Lin, and X. Shen, "EPPA: An efficient and privacy-preserving aggregation scheme for secure smart grid communications,". *IEEE Transactions on Parallel and Distributed Systems*, 23(9), 1621–1631. 10.1109/TPDS.2012.86

Maglaras, L. A., Kim, K.-H., Janicke, H., Ferrag, M. A., Rallis, S., Fragkou, P., Maglaras, A., & Cruz, T. J. (2018). Cyber security of critical infrastructures. *Ict Express*, 4(1), 42–45. 10.1016/j.icte.2018.02.001

Maharjan, Q., Zhu, Q., Zhang, Y., Gjessing, S., & Basar, T. (2013). Zhu, Y. Zhang, S. Gjessing, and T. Basar. Dependable demand response management in the smart grid: A stackelberg game approach. *IEEE Transactions on Smart Grid*, 4(1), 120–132. 10.1109/TSG.2012.2223766

Mahmood, K., Chaudhry, S. A., Naqvi, H., Kumari, S., Li, X., & Sangaiah, A. K. (2018). An elliptic curve cryptography based lightweight authentication scheme for smart grid communication. *Future Generation Computer Systems*, 81, 557–565. 10.1016/j.future.2017.05.002

McDaniel, D., & McLaughlin, S. E. (2009). Security and privacy challenges in the smart grid. *IEEE Security and Privacy*, 7(3), 75–77. 10.1109/MSP.2009.76

McElwee, S. (2017). Active learning intrusion detection using k-means clustering selection. SoutheastCon 2017. IEEE.

Ni, B., Zhang, K., Lin, X., & Shen, X. S. (2019). Balancing Security and Efficiency for Smart Metering against Misbehaving Collectors. *IEEE Transactions on Smart Grid*, 10(2), 1225–1236. 10.1109/TSG.2017.2761804

Nicanfar, H., Jokar, P., Beznosov, K., & Leung, V. C. (2013). Efficient authentication and key management mechanisms for smart grid communications. *IEEE Systems Journal*, 8(2), 629–640. 10.1109/JSYST.2013.2260942

Nicanfar, H., Jokar, P., & Leung, V. C. (2011). Smart grid authentication and key management for unicast and multicast communications. 2011 IEEE PES Innovative Smart Grid Technologies. IEEE.

Nikmehr, N., & Ravadanegh, S. (2015). Optimal power dispatch of multimicrogrids at future smart distribution grids. *IEEE Transactions on Smart Grid*, 6(4), 1648–1657. 10.1109/TSG.2015.2396992

Odelu, V., Das, A. K., Wazid, M., & Conti, M. (2016). Provably secure authenticated key agreement scheme for smart grid. *IEEE Transactions on Smart Grid*, 9(3), 1900–1910. 10.1109/TSG.2016.2602282

Okay, F. Y., & Ozdemir, S. (2016). A fog computing based smart grid model. *Proc. ISNCC*, (pp. 1–6). IEEE. 10.1109/ISNCC.2016.7746062

Perez, R. L., Adamsky, F., Soua, R., & Engel, T. (2018). Machine learning for reliable network attack detection in scada systems. *2018 17th IEEE International Conference On Trust, Security And Privacy In Computing And Communications/12th IEEE International Conference On Big Data Science And Engineering (TrustCom/BigDataSE)*. IEEE. 10.1109/TrustCom/BigDataSE.2018.00094

Rehmani, M. H., Davy, A., Jennings, B., & Assi, C. (2019). Software defined networks based smart grid communication: A comprehensive survey. *IEEE Communications Surveys and Tutorials*, 21(3), 2637–2670. 10.1109/COMST.2019.2908266

Reyzin, L., & Reyzin, N. (2002). Better than biba: Short one-time signatures with fast signing and verifying. *Australasian Conference on Information Security and Privacy*. Springer. 10.1007/3-540-45450-0_11

Roman, L. F., Gondim, P. R., & Lloret, J. (2019). Pairing-based authentication protocol for v2g networks in smart grid. *Ad Hoc Networks*, 90, 101745. 10.1016/j.adhoc.2018.08.015

Saxena, N., Choi, B. J., & Cho, S. (2015). Lightweight privacy-preserving authentication scheme for v2g networks in the smart grid. 2015 IEEE Trustcom/BigDataSE/ISPA (Vol. 1). IEEE.

Saxena, N., Choi, B. J., & Lu, R. X. (2016). Authentication and Authorization Scheme for Various User-Roles and Devices in Smart Grid. *IEEE Transactions on Information Forensics and Security*, 11(5), 907–921. 10.1109/TIFS.2015.2512525

Shen, H., Zhang, M., & Shen, J. (2017). Efficient privacy-preserving cube-data aggregation scheme for smart grids. *IEEE Transactions on Information Forensics and Security*, 12(6), 1369–1381. 10.1109/TIFS.2017.2656475

Shen, L., Zhu, L., Xu, C., Sharif, K., & Lu, R. (2020). Zhu, C. Xu, K. Sharif, and R. Lu, "A privacy-preserving data aggregation scheme for dynamic groups in fog computing,". *Information Sciences*, 514, 118–130. 10.1016/j.ins.2019.12.007

Siano, P. (2014). Demand response and smart grids–a survey. *Renewable & Sustainable Energy Reviews*, 30, 461–478. 10.1016/j.rser.2013.10.022

Tang, , Chen, Z., Hefferman, G., Pei, S., Wei, T., He, H., & Yang, Q. (2017). Incorporating Intelligence in Fog Computing for Big Data Analysis in Smart Cities. *IEEE Transactions on Industrial Informatics*, 13(5), 2140–2150. 10.1109/TII.2017.2679740

Tsai, J.-L., & Lo, N.-W. (2015). Secure anonymous key distribution scheme for smart grid. *IEEE Transactions on Smart Grid*, 7(2), 906–914. 10.1109/TSG.2015.2440658

Wang, J., Wu, L., Choo, K.-K. R., & He, D. (2019). Blockchain based anonymous authentication with key management for smart grid edge computing infrastructure. *IEEE Transactions on Industrial Informatics*.

Wang, K., Wang, Y., Hu, X., Sun, Y., Deng, D., Vinel, A., & Zhang, Y. (2017). Wireless big data computing in smart grid. *IEEE Wireless Communications*, 24(2), 58–64. 10.1109/MWC.2017.1600256WC

Wang, P., Liu, S., Ye, F., & Chen, X. (2018). A fog-based architecture and programming model for iot applications in the smart grid. CoRR.

Wang, S., Zhang, X., Zhang, Y., Wang, L., Yang, J., & Wang, W. (2017). A survey on mobile edge networks: Convergence of computing, caching and communications. *IEEE Access : Practical Innovations, Open Solutions*, 5, 6757–6779. 10.1109/ACCESS.2017.2685434

Wang, Z. (2017). An identity-based data aggregation protocol for the smart grid. *IEEE Transactions on Industrial Informatics*, 13(5), 2428–2435. 10.1109/TII.2017.2705218

Wang, Z. (2019). Identity-based verifiable aggregator oblivious encryption and its applications in smart grids. *IEEE Transactions on Sustainable Computing*.

Xia, J., & Wang, Y. (2012). Secure key distribution for the smart grid. *IEEE Transactions on Smart Grid*, 3(3), 1437–1443. 10.1109/TSG.2012.2199141

Yan, Y., Qian, Y., Sharif, H., & Tipper, D. (2012). A survey on cyber security for smart grid communications. *IEEE Communications Surveys and Tutorials*, 14(4), 998–1010. 10.1109/SURV.2012.010912.00035

Yang, H., Cheng, L., & Chuah, M. C. (2019). Deep-learning-based network intrusion detection for scada systems. *2019 IEEE Conference on Communications and Network Security (CNS)*. IEEE. 10.1109/CNS.2019.8802785

Yang, J. (2018). Lightweight and privacy-preserving delegatable proofs of storage with data dynamics in cloud storage. *IEEE Transactions on Cloud Computing*. IEEE.

Yu, R., Zhang, Y., Gjessing, S., Yuen, C., Xie, S., & Guizani, M. (2011). Cognitive Radio Based Hierarchical Communications Infrastructure for Smart Grid. *IEEE Network*, 25(5), 6–14. 10.1109/MNET.2011.6033030

Zhang, L., Zhao, L., Yin, S., Chi, C.-H., Liu, R., & Zhang, Y. (2019). A lightweight authentication scheme with privacy protection for smart grid communications. *Future Generation Computer Systems*, 100, 770–778. 10.1016/j.future.2019.05.069

Zhang, L., Zhao, L., Yin, S., Chi, C.-H., Liu, R., & Zhang, Y. (2019). Zhao, S. Yin, C.-H. Chi, R. Liu, and Y. Zhang, "A lightweight authentication scheme with privacy protection for smart grid communications,". *Future Generation Computer Systems*, 100, 770–778. 10.1016/j.future.2019.05.069

Zhang, R. Yu., Xie, S., Yao, W., Xiao, Y., & Guizani, M. (2011). Home M2M networks: Architectures, standards, and QoS improvement. *IEEE Communications Magazine*, 49(4), 44–52. 10.1109/MCOM.2011.5741145

Zhang, Y., Yu, R., Nekovee, M., Liu, Y., Xie, S., & Gjessing, S. (2012). Cognitive machine-to-machine communications: Visions and potentials for the smart grid. *IEEE Network*, 26(3), 6–13. 10.1109/MNET.2012.6201210

Zhang, Z., Cao, W., Qin, Z., Zhu, L., Yu, Z., & Ren, K. (2017). When privacy meets economics: Enabling differentially-private battery supported meter reporting in smart grid. In *IEEE/ACM 25th International Symposium on Quality of Service*. IEEE.

Zhang, Z., Qin, Z., Zhu, L., Weng, J., & Ren, K. (2017). Cost-friendly differential privacy for smart meters: Exploiting the dual roles of the noise. *IEEE Transactions on Smart Grid*, 8(2), 619–626.

Zhu, L., Li, M., Zhang, Z., Xu, C., Zhang, R., Du, X., & Guizani, N. (2019). Privacy-preserving authentication and data aggregation for fog-based smart grid. *IEEE Communications Magazine*, 57(6), 80–85. 10.1109/MCOM.2019.1700859

Zhu, L., Li, M., Zhang, Z., Xu, C., Zhang, R., Du, X., & Guizani, N. (2019). Privacy-preserving authentication and data aggregation for fog-based smart grid. *IEEE Communications Magazine*, 57(6), 80–85. 10.1109/MCOM.2019.1700859

Chapter 11
Applications of
the R–Transform
for Advancing
Cryptographic Security

Tharmalingam Gunasekar
Indian Institute of Technology, Chennai, India

Prabakaran Raghavendran
https://orcid.org/0009-0001-7333-6555
Vel Tech Rangarajan Dr. Sagunthala R&D Institute of Science and Technology, India

ABSTRACT

Cryptography, the discipline of disguising information, relies on mathematical principles for encoding and decoding data. This chapter presents an inventive approach to encrypting and decrypting messages, utilizing the R-transformation, an essential integral transform, and the congruence modulo operator. The research illustrates the pragmatic application of these mathematical tools in securing communication through the encoding of sensitive information. By investigating the integration of the R-transformation and modulo operations, this study seeks to highlight their effectiveness in reinforcing the privacy and integrity of data. Through thorough experimentation and analysis, this research introduces a groundbreaking methodology for cryptographic encoding and decoding, shedding light on its potential to fortify the security of confidential information transmission.

DOI: 10.4018/979-8-3693-2869-9.ch011

INTRODUCTION

In the realm of information security and cryptography, the pursuit of robust and innovative techniques stands as a cornerstone in safeguarding digital data against malicious threats and unauthorized access. This article embarks on an exploratory journey through the domains of mathematical fundamentals and cryptographic applications, unveiling inventive methodologies and integral transforms that fortify data protection in an ever-evolving landscape of cyber challenges.

Grewal's "Higher Engineering Mathematics" serves as an essential starting point, providing foundational mathematical knowledge crucial for comprehending advanced cryptographic techniques (Grewal, 2005) This comprehensive text covers a wide array of mathematical topics, from calculus to linear algebra, which underpin the sophisticated algorithms used in modern cryptography. Understanding these mathematical principles is essential for devising secure encryption and decryption methods that withstand rigorous cryptographic scrutiny.

As cryptography continues to evolve, new methodologies emerge to tackle increasingly complex security challenges. Hiwarekar's exploration of a cryptographic approach utilizing the Laplace transform introduces a novel perspective (Hiwarekar, 2012). The Laplace transform, traditionally used in engineering and physics, finds innovative application in cryptography by transforming data into a different domain where cryptographic operations can be applied more effectively. This approach highlights the versatility of mathematical transforms in enhancing data security through unconventional means.

Stanoyevitch's "Introduction to Cryptography with Mathematical Foundations and Computer Implementations" bridges theoretical concepts with practical applications, emphasizing the development of robust cryptographic protocols (Stanoyevitch, 2002). This foundational work elucidates how theoretical constructs translate into real-world security measures, ensuring that cryptographic systems not only adhere to rigorous mathematical standards but also function effectively in diverse operational environments.

Stallings' seminal work in "Cryptography and Network Security" delves into the intricacies of securing data in networked environments, emphasizing the critical role of cryptographic protocols in maintaining confidentiality, integrity, and availability (Stallings, 2005). As digital networks proliferate, ensuring secure communication channels becomes paramount, with cryptographic algorithms serving as the bedrock of secure data transmission and storage across interconnected systems.

Lakshmi, Kumar, and Sekhar contribute to the discourse with a cryptographic scheme based on Laplace transforms, showcasing the innovative applications of integral transforms in information security (Lakshmi, Kumar and Sekhar, 2011). By leveraging mathematical transforms, such as the Laplace transform, cryptographic techniques can achieve enhanced encryption and decryption processes that resist common cryptographic attacks, thereby bolstering overall data protection strategies.

Buchmann's "Introduction to Cryptography" expands upon cryptographic concepts and methodologies, providing a comprehensive overview of traditional and contemporary cryptographic techniques (Buchmann, 2009). This foundational text underscores the importance of continuous innovation in cryptography, as adversaries constantly evolve their tactics to exploit vulnerabilities in cryptographic systems. By embracing transformative cryptographic methods, such as those involving integral transforms, practitioners can stay ahead of emerging threats and ensure robust data security measures.

Integral transforms, such as the Elzaki Transform introduced by Elzaki, offer new avenues for cryptographic applications (Elzaki, 2011). The Elzaki Transform's unique properties enable it to manipulate data in ways that traditional cryptographic methods cannot, thereby offering novel approaches to encrypting and decrypting sensitive information. Salim and Ashruji further explore the application of the Elzaki Transform in cryptography, demonstrating its potential to enhance cryptographic resilience and efficiency (Salim and Ashruji, 2016).

Rosan's "Discrete Mathematics and Its Applications" provides a theoretical backdrop, highlighting the relevance of discrete mathematical concepts in designing secure cryptographic algorithms (Rosan, 2012). By grounding cryptographic protocols in rigorous mathematical theory, researchers and practitioners can develop encryption schemes that withstand rigorous cryptanalysis and maintain confidentiality in diverse computing environments.

Kharde extends the exploration of integral transforms in cryptography, contributing to the expanding body of knowledge in transformative cryptography (Kharde, 2017). The application of integral transforms, such as the Mahgoub Transform introduced by Mahgoub, further diversifies cryptographic methodologies, offering innovative solutions to complex encryption challenges (Mahgoub, 2016). Aboodh's investigation into the Aboodh Transform adds another layer of complexity to cryptographic techniques, illustrating the broad applicability of mathematical transforms in securing digital communications (Aboodh, 2013).

Dhingra, Savalgi, and Jain's exploration of Laplace transformation-based cryptographic techniques underscores the intersection of mathematical transforms and network security (Dhingra, Savalgi and Jain, 2016). In networked information systems, where data traverses multiple nodes and endpoints, ensuring secure communication channels is imperative. By leveraging Laplace transforms, cryptographic protocols can mitigate risks associated with data interception and tampering, thereby safeguarding sensitive information from unauthorized access.

Ahmadi, Hosseinzadeh, and Cherati's research on a new integral transform for solving higher-order linear ordinary differential equations showcases the versatility of mathematical transforms beyond cryptography (Ahmadi, Hosseinzadeh and Cherati, 2019). These transformative techniques not only enhance encryption capabilities but also find applications in various scientific and engineering disciplines, illustrating their broad utility in solving complex computational problems.

Filipinas and Convicto's investigation into the Rangaig transform further enriches our understanding of transformative mathematical techniques, highlighting its potential applications in diverse fields of study (Filipinas and Convicto, 2017). By exploring the theoretical underpinnings and practical implications of integral transforms, researchers can unlock new methodologies for addressing existing challenges in cryptography and beyond.

In the following diagram, we illustrate the sequential steps involved in a typical cryptographic process, starting with initialization and concluding with the termination of the process. Each stage highlights key operations from input to output, emphasizing the systematic approach required to implement secure cryptographic protocols effectively.

Figure 1. Flowchart

The accompanying flowchart illustrates the sequential steps involved in a typical cryptographic process, offering a structured view of how data undergoes transformation from plaintext to ciphertext and vice versa. Each stage in the flowchart represents a critical operation:

Initialization: Setting up the cryptographic environment and parameters required for encryption and decryption.

Input Plaintext: Entering the original message or data that needs to be secured.

Encryption: Applying encryption algorithms (such as symmetric or asymmetric encryption) to convert plaintext into ciphertext.

Ciphertext: The encrypted data ready for transmission over networks or storage.

Transmission: Sending the encrypted data securely across communication channels to the intended recipient.

Received Ciphertext: Receiving the encrypted data at the recipient's end.

Decryption: Decrypting the ciphertext back into plaintext using corresponding decryption algorithms and keys.

Decrypted Plaintext: Retrieving the original plaintext message or data.

Output Plaintext: Presenting the decrypted plaintext for authorized use or processing.

Terminate: Completing the cryptographic process, ensuring all data exchanges are securely handled.

This flowchart not only visualizes the workflow of cryptographic operations but also emphasizes the systematic approach required to maintain data confidentiality, integrity, and availability throughout digital communications and transactions.

The integration of mathematical fundamentals and cryptographic applications underscores the dynamic evolution of information security practices. By exploring innovative methodologies and integral transforms, researchers and practitioners continue to push the boundaries of data protection, ensuring that cryptographic systems remain resilient against emerging cyber threats. As technologies advance and adversaries evolve, the quest for robust cryptographic techniques remains essential in safeguarding digital assets and upholding trust in digital interactions. Through continuous research and development, transformative cryptography paves the way for future advancements in securing the digital landscape, reinforcing the critical role of mathematical rigor in cybersecurity.

By embracing transformative cryptographic methods and leveraging integral transforms, stakeholders can navigate the complexities of modern cybersecurity challenges with confidence, fostering a secure and resilient digital ecosystem for generations to come.

This article aims to synthesize these diverse works, drawing connections between foundational principles, cryptographic methodologies, and transformative mathematical concepts. Through an in-depth exploration of integral transforms and cryptographic applications, we embark on a journey that not only enriches our understanding of information security but also unveils potential avenues for future research and innovation.

In this investigation, we capitalize on the integral transform, the R-Transformation, and the congruence modulo operator to encrypt and decrypt messages. Furthermore, we incorporate relevant examples that are pertinent to our main topic while concealing specific details for confidentiality purposes.

R-TRANSFORM

The utilization of the R-transform is applicable to functions distinguished by exponential order (Filipinas and Convicto, 2017). We investigate functions belonging to the set P, as outlined by

$$P = \left\{ \gamma(\tau) \mid \exists A, \nu_1, \nu_2 > 0, |\gamma(\tau)| < A \cdot e^{|\tau|\nu_i}, \text{if} \tau \in (-1)^{i-1} \times (\infty, 0] \right\}$$

The R-transform, denoted by the operator $\psi(.)$, is defined by the integral equation

$$\psi\left[\gamma(\tau)\right] = R\left(\vartheta\right) = \frac{1}{\vartheta} \int_{-\infty}^{0} \gamma(\tau) e^{\vartheta\tau} d\tau, \frac{1}{\nu_1} \leq \vartheta \leq \frac{1}{\vartheta_2} \tag{1}$$

Basic Functions Overview

Assuming the existence of the integral equation (1), we consider every function $\gamma(\tau)$.

(*i*) Let $\gamma(\tau) = 1$, then $\psi\left[1\right] = \frac{1}{\vartheta^2}$

(*ii*) Let $\gamma(\tau) = \tau$, then $\psi\left[\tau\right] = \frac{-1}{\vartheta^3}$

(*iii*) Let $\gamma(\tau) = \tau^2$, then $\psi\left[\tau^2\right] = \frac{2!}{\vartheta^4}$

(*iv*) In general case, if $m > 0$, then $\psi\left[\tau^m\right] = \frac{(-1)^m m!}{\vartheta^{m+2}}$

The inverse $R - $ transform

$\left(v\right) \psi^{-1}\left[\frac{1}{\vartheta^2}\right] = 1$

$\left(vi\right) \psi^{-1}\left[\frac{-1}{\vartheta^3}\right] = \tau$

$(vii)\ \psi^{-1}\left[\frac{1}{\vartheta^4}\right]\ =\ \frac{\tau^2}{2!}$

$(viii)\ \psi^{-1}\left[\frac{-1}{\vartheta^5}\right]\ =\ \frac{\tau^3}{3!}$, and soon.

DATA PROTECTION METHODOLOGY

Figure 2. Data protection methodology

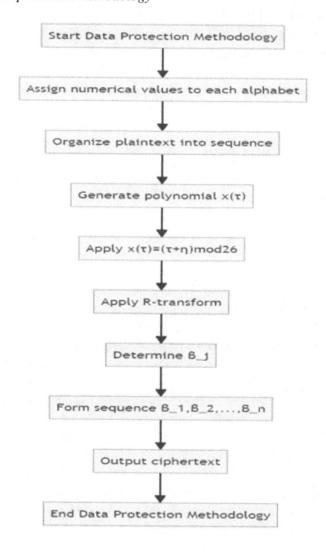

1. Assign numerical values to each alphabet in the plaintext message, such as $A = 1, B = 2, C = 3, ..., Z = 26$, and represent spaces as 0.
2. Organize the plaintext message into a finite sequence of numbers based on the aforementioned alphabetical conversion.
3. Let m denote the number of terms in the sequence. Consider a polynomial $x(\tau)$ of degree $m - 1$.
4. Replace each number τ in the sequence with $x(\tau) = (\tau + \eta) \bmod 26$.
5. Apply the R-transform to the polynomial $x(\tau)$.
6. Determine β_j such that $\lambda_j \equiv \beta_j \bmod 26$ for each j, where $1 \le j \le m$.
7. Form a new finite sequence $\beta_1, \beta_2, \beta_3, ..., \beta_n$.
8. The resulting text message constitutes the ciphertext.

INFORMATION RETRIEVAL METHODOLOGY

Figure 3. Information Retrieval Methodology

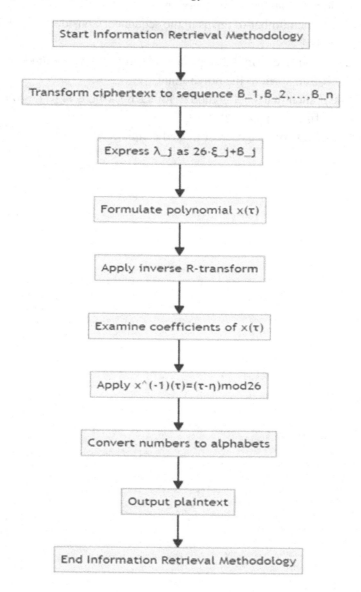

1. Transform the ciphertext into a finite sequence of numbers, labeled as $\beta_1, \beta_2, \beta_3, \ldots, \beta_n$.
2. Express λ_j as $26 \cdot \xi_j + \beta_j$ for all in the range from to .

3. Formulate a polynomial .
4. Apply the inverse R-transform to the polynomial.
5. Examine the coefficients of the polynomial presented as a finite sequence.
6. Replace each number using the inverse function .
7. Convert the numbers of the finite sequence back into corresponding alphabets to recover the original text message.

EXAMPLES

In this section, we delve into the application of data protection and information retrieval methodologies, elucidated through specific examples.

Example One

Let's take into account that the original message is **SECRET**.

Method of Encryption

The given sequence consists of the numbers , totaling terms. Thus, the value of is . We are constructing a polynomial of degree one less than , making the polynomial of degree .

When we shift the preceding finite sequence by letters, where , we obtain the sequence .

The current status of the polynomial is:

Apply the R-transform to both expressions, we get

In the context of , , , , , and .

Table 1. To Determine so that is Congruent to Modulo 26

	Value	Congruence Mod 26	
	24	24 24 (mod 26)	24
	10	10 10 (mod 26)	10
	16	16 16 (mod 26)	16
	138	138 8 (mod 26)	8
	240	240 6 (mod 26)	6

continued on following page

Table 1. Continued

	Value	Congruence Mod 26	
	3000	3000 10 (mod 26)	10

Take into account an alternate finite sequence: as . Correspondingly, the associated key values () are .

The resulting ciphertext corresponds to **XJPHFJ**.

Method of Decryption

To decipher the message encrypted with the Caesar cipher, the inverse function is utilized. To perform this, use the finite sequence associated with the ciphertext: .
Let for all , where .

Consider

Applying the inverse pourreza transform to both sides, the result is

The coefficients constituting the polynomial create the finite sequence: .
Subsequently, replace each number in the finite sequence using .
Upon translating the numbers back into alphabets, the corrected new finite sequence, , aligns with the original plaintext message **SECRET**.

Example Two

Let's take into account that the original message is **NO DUE**.

Method of Encryption

The provided sequence consists of comprising a total of terms. Therefore, equals . We're constructing a polynomial of degree one less than , so the polynomial is of degree .
Shifting the previous finite sequence by letters (where $= 2$) produces the sequence .
The current state of the polynomial is

Apply the R-transform to both expressions, we get

In the context of , , , , and .

Table 2. To determine so that is Congruent to Modulo 26.

	Value	Congruence Mod 26	
	16	16 16 (mod 26)	16
	17	17 17 (mod 26)	17
	4	4 4 (mod 26)	4
	36	363 10 (mod 26)	10
	552	552 6 (mod 26)	6
	840	840 8 (mod 26)	8

Consider a different finite sequence: , , , ..., as . Additionally, the corresponding key values () are .

The resulting ciphertext corresponds to **PQDJFH**.

Method of Decryption

To decrypt the message encrypted with the Caesar cipher, the inverse function is employed. To do so, utilize the finite sequence corresponding to the ciphertext: .

Let for all , where .

Consider

Applying the inverse pourreza transform to both sides, the result is

The coefficients representing a polynomial form the finite sequence: .

Now replace each number in the finite sequence by .

After translating the numbers to alphabets, the corrected new finite sequence, , corresponds to the original plain text message **NO DUE**.

To expand on the interpretation of the examples provided, delving into the application of cryptographic methodologies and their significance in data protection and information retrieval, we can explore the concepts of encryption, decryption, polynomial transformations, modular arithmetic, and the broader implications for cybersecurity. Here's a detailed exploration:

Cryptographic systems play a pivotal role in securing sensitive information and communications across digital networks. The examples discussed illustrate fundamental principles of cryptography, including encryption and decryption processes that rely on mathematical transformations and modular arithmetic to achieve data confidentiality.

In the first example, the plaintext message "SECRET" is transformed into a sequence of numerical values: 19, 5, 3, 18, 5, 20. These numerical representations are then organized into a polynomial, , of degree 5. The polynomial is constructed such that each term represents a coefficient multiplied by τ raised to a corresponding power. This polynomial serves as the foundation for applying cryptographic operations.

To encrypt the plaintext, a shift operation is applied to the sequence by letters, where . This results in a new sequence: 24, 10, 8, 23, 10, 25. The R-transform is then applied to this polynomial, which involves substituting each term in with mod 26. This transformation ensures that the resulting ciphertext is resistant to simple frequency analysis attacks, enhancing its security.

Upon applying the R-transform, the polynomial is expressed in terms of its coefficients modulo 26, resulting in values and . These coefficients are then converted into values that are congruent to modulo 26. In this case, = 24, = 10, = 16, = 8, = 6, = 10.

The resulting ciphertext from this encryption process is "XJPHFJ." Decryption, conversely, involves applying the inverse functions of the encryption process. The ciphertext sequence,, = 24, = 10, = 16, = 8, = 6, = 10, is transformed using the inverse polynomial , which typically involves a shift by modulo 26. This process reconstructs the original plaintext sequence, demonstrating the reversibility and efficacy of the cryptographic methodology employed.

In the second example, the plaintext message "NO DUE" is similarly encoded into numerical values: 14, 15, 0, 4, 21, 5. Following the same cryptographic process as in Example 1, these values are organized into a polynomial of degree 5, . An encryption shift of is applied, resulting in the ciphertext sequence: 16, 17, 2, 6, 23, 7.

Applying the R-transform to the polynomial $x(\tau)$ results in coefficients and . These coefficients are then converted into corresponding values modulo 26: = 16, = 17, = 3, = 10, = 6, = 8. The resulting ciphertext from this encryption process is "PQDJFH."

Decryption of the ciphertext "PQDJFH" involves applying the inverse functions to the ciphertext sequence, = 16, = 17, = 3, = 10, = 6, = 8, using the inverse polynomial . This inverse process adjusts the numerical values by modulo 26, reconstructing the original plaintext sequence: 14, 15, 0, 4, 21, 5, corresponding to "NO DUE."

These examples showcase the practical application of cryptographic techniques, specifically polynomial transformations and modular arithmetic, in securing sensitive information. Cryptography is essential in ensuring data integrity, confidentiality, and authenticity across digital platforms. The methodologies illustrated highlight the complexity involved in encryption and decryption processes, leveraging mathematical operations to obscure plaintext data and protect it from unauthorized access.

The use of polynomials and modular arithmetic ensures that encrypted data is resistant to cryptanalysis, enhancing the overall security posture of digital communications and data storage systems. By transforming plaintext into ciphertext using mathematical functions that are computationally intensive to reverse without the proper decryption key, cryptography provides a robust defense against malicious actors and unauthorized interception of sensitive information.

Moreover, the examples underscore the importance of cryptographic standards and protocols in modern cybersecurity frameworks. Organizations across various sectors rely on cryptographic algorithms to comply with regulatory requirements and safeguard customer data, intellectual property, and proprietary information from cyber threats.

Cryptography remains a cornerstone of cybersecurity, enabling secure digital transactions, communication channels, and data exchanges in an increasingly interconnected world. The examples discussed highlight the technical intricacies and real-world applications of cryptographic principles, reinforcing their indispensable role in protecting information assets and preserving digital trustworthiness.

CONCLUSION

This study introduces a novel approach to ensuring information security through a combination of the Caesar cipher, the R-transformation, and a modulo operator. The results underwent thorough scrutiny, affirming the efficacy of this method. Its simplicity makes it user-friendly due to its straightforward steps. The integration of these mathematical concepts presents a fresh perspective on safeguarding sensitive data. Extensive testing demonstrated the method's reliable ability to encode and decode information. This mathematical fusion not only provides a unique perspective on security but also has the potential to pave the way for improved methods of securing data. Embracing these innovative concepts is crucial as we continue to seek more secure ways of communicating in our digital era.

REFERENCES

Aboodh, K. S. (2013). The New Integral Transform Aboodh Transform. *Global Journal of Pure and Applied Mathematics*, 9(1), 35–43.

Ahmadi, S. A. P., Hosseinzadeh, H., & Cherati, A. Y. (2019). A New Integral Transform for Solving Higher Order Linear Ordinary Differential Equations. *International Journal of Applied and Computational Mathematics*, 19(2), 243–252. 10.1007/s40819-019-0712-1

Buchmann, J. A. (2009). *Introduction to Cryptography* (4th Indian reprint ed.). Springer.

Butt, S. A. (2016). Study of agile methodology with the cloud. Pacific Science Review B. *Humanities and Social Sciences*, 2(1), 22–28.

Dhingra, S., Savalgi, A. A., & Jain, S. (2016). Laplace Transformation based Cryptographic Technique in Network Security. *International Journal of Computer Applications*, 136(7), 6–10. 10.5120/ijca2016908482

Elzaki, T. M. (2011). The New Integral Transform Elzaki Transform. *Global Journal of Pure and Applied Mathematics*, 7(1), 57–64.

Filipinas, J. L. D. C., & Convicto, V. C. (2017). On another type of transform called Rangaig transform. *International Journal (Toronto, Ont.)*, 5(1), 42–48.

Gochhait, S., Butt, S. A., Jamal, T., & Ali, A. (2022). Cloud Enhances Agile Software Development. In I. *Management Association (Ed.), Research Anthology on Agile Software, Software Development, and Testing* (pp. 491-507). IGI Global. 10.4018/978-1-6684-3702-5.ch025

Grewal, B. S. (2005). *Higher Engineering Mathematics*. Khanna Publishing.

Gunasekar, T., & Raghavendran, P. (2024). The Mohand transform approach to fractional integro-differential equations. *Journal of Computational Analysis and Applications*, 33, 358–371.

Gunasekar, T., Raghavendran, P., Santra, S. S., Majumder, D., Baleanu, D., & Balasundaram, H. (2024). Application of Laplace transform to solve fractional integro-differential equations. *Journal of Mathematics and Computer Science*, 33(3), 225–237. 10.22436/jmcs.033.03.02

Gunasekar, T., Raghavendran, P., Santra, Sh. S., & Sajid, M. (2024). Existence and controllability results for neutral fractional Volterra Fredholm integro-differential equations. *Journal of Mathematics and Computer Science*, 34(4), 361–380. 10.22436/jmcs.034.04.04

Gunasekar, Th., Raghavendran, P., Santra, Sh. S., & Sajid, M. (2024). Analyzing existence, uniqueness, and stability of neutral fractional Volterra-Fredholm integro-differential equations. *Journal of Mathematics and Computer Science-JM*, 33(4), 390–407. 10.22436/jmcs.033.04.06

Hiwarekar, A. P. (2012). A new method of cryptography using Laplace transform. *International Journal of Mathematical Archive*, 3(3), 1193–1197.

Khalid, A., Butt, S. A., Jamal, T., & Gochhait, S. (2022). Agile Scrum Issues at Large-Scale Distributed Projects: Scrum Project Development At Large. In I. Management Association (Ed.), *Research Anthology on Agile Software, Software Development, and Testing* (pp. 388-398). IGI Global. 10.4018/978-1-6684-3702-5.ch019

Kharde, U. D. (2017). An Application of the Elzaki Transform in Cryptography. *Journal for Advanced Research in Applied Sciences*, 4(5), 86–89.

Lakshmi, G. N., Kumar, B. R., & Sekhar, A. C. (2011). A cryptographic scheme of Laplace transforms. *International Journal of Mathematical Archive*, 2, 2515–2519.

Mahgoub, M. M. A. (2016). The New Integral Transform Mahgoub Transform. *Advances in Theoretical and Applied Mathematics*, 11(4), 391–398.

Raghavendran, P., Gunasekar, T., Balasundaram, H., Santra, S. S., Majumder, D., & Baleanu, D. (2023). Solving fractional integro-differential equations by Aboodh transform. *Journal of Mathematics and Computer Science*, 32, 229–240. 10.22436/jmcs.032.03.04

Rosan, K. H. (2012). *Discrete Mathematics and Its Applications*. McGraw Hill.

Salim, S. J., & Ashruji, M. G. (2016). Application of Elzaki Transform in Cryptography. *International Journal of Modern Sciences and Engineering Technology*, 3(3), 46–48.

Singh, S., & Chana, I. (2016). A survey on resource scheduling in cloud computing: Issues and challenges. *Journal of Grid Computing*, 14(2), 217–264. 10.1007/s10723-015-9359-2

Stallings, W. (2005). *Cryptography and network security* (4th ed.). Prentice Hall.

Stanoyevitch, A. (2002). *Introduction to cryptography with mathematical foundations and computer implementations*. CRC Press.

Chapter 12
Advancing Cryptographic Security With Kushare Transform Integration

Raghavendran Prabakaran
https://orcid.org/0009-0001-7333-6555

Vel Tech Rangarajan Dr. Sagunthala R&D Institute of Science and Technology, India

Gunasekar T.

Vel Tech Rangarajan Dr. Sagunthala R&D Institute of Science and Technology, India

ABSTRACT

This chapter introduces a groundbreaking encryption approach utilizing the Kushare transform and modular arithmetic, departing from conventional cryptographic methods. It delves into the transformative potential of this dynamic duo in rendering sensitive data impenetrable, ensuring secure digital communication. Through meticulous examination of their synergy, this work establishes their remarkable ability to fortify data confidentiality and integrity. Rigorous experimentation and analysis reveal a novel cryptographic technique poised to revolutionize the secure transmission of confidential information in the digital age.

INTRODUCTION

Safeguarding sensitive data during communication has become paramount in today's digital landscape, where cybersecurity threats loom large. Cryptography stands as the cornerstone in defending communication through advanced techniques

DOI: 10.4018/979-8-3693-2869-9.ch012

of data encryption and decryption (Ahmadi, Hosseinzadeh and Cherati, 2019). While traditional cryptographic methods, relying on symmetric and asymmetric encryption algorithms, have long been the norm for securing data, recent advancements have spurred exploration into novel methodologies to bolster data protection (Buchmann, 2009).

Integral transformations, recognized for their efficacy in cryptographic applications, represent mathematical procedures that convert one function into another, offering renewed perspectives and potential enhancements for digital system security (Ahmadi, Hosseinzadeh and Cherati, 2019). These transformations play a crucial role in transforming data in a way that ensures confidentiality, integrity, and authenticity, essential pillars of modern cryptography.

The Laplace transform, traditionally applied in various branches of mathematics and engineering, has found innovative uses in cryptography, particularly in enhancing network security (Dhingra, Savalgi and Jain, 2016). Research into cryptographic frameworks utilizing the Laplace transform underscores its effectiveness in ensuring data secrecy and resilience against cyber threats (Hiwarekar, 2012; Lakshmi, Kumar and Sekhar, 2011). Similarly, the Elzaki transform, built upon the principles of the Laplace transform Gunasekar et al., (2024) has garnered attention for its ability to enhance data integrity and thwart unauthorized access (Kharde, 2017; Salim and Ashruji, 2016).

Among these integral transformations, the Kushare transform emerges as a pioneering approach with promising applications in cryptography. This transform is noted for its unique mathematical intricacies and computational characteristics, offering potential improvements in data protection by addressing differential equations within cryptographic contexts (Ahmadi, Hosseinzadeh and Cherati, 2019; Kushare, Patil and Takate, 2021; Gunasekar et al., 2024). The Kushare transform not only enhances encryption processes but also contributes to deciphering encrypted data with efficiency and accuracy.

In the subsequent discussion, we delve into the sequential steps involved in a typical cryptographic process, elucidated through a flowchart. This flowchart serves to outline key operations from initialization to termination, providing a visual representation of how data is processed and secured through cryptographic methodologies.

Integral transformations form the bedrock of innovative cryptographic techniques aimed at fortifying data security. These transformations operate by converting data into transformed forms that are computationally challenging to decipher without the proper cryptographic keys. This approach ensures that even if intercepted, the encrypted data remains unintelligible to unauthorized entities, preserving the confidentiality of sensitive information.

The Laplace transform, originally devised for solving differential equations, has found application beyond traditional mathematics into the realm of cybersecurity. In cryptography, its ability to convert functions into complex mathematical representations contributes to the robustness of encryption algorithms. By applying the Laplace transform, cryptographic protocols can achieve enhanced resilience against attacks aimed at compromising data integrity or confidentiality (Dhingra, Savalgi and Jain, 2016).

Recent studies have highlighted the Laplace transform's utility in securing network communications, where the transformation of data signals aids in mitigating vulnerabilities and ensuring reliable data transmission across interconnected systems (Hiwarekar, 2012). Moreover, its integration into cryptographic frameworks has demonstrated significant advancements in protecting sensitive communications and digital assets from evolving cyber threats (Lakshmi, Kumar and Sekhar, 2011).

Building upon the principles of the Laplace transform, the Elzaki transform introduces additional layers of complexity that further enhance data protection mechanisms. This transform operates by reshaping data structures in ways that complicate decryption efforts without compromising computational efficiency (Kharde, 2017; Salim and Ashruji, 2016). Its application in cryptographic algorithms addresses critical aspects such as data integrity verification and secure key management, crucial for maintaining trust in digital transactions and communications.

Researchers continue to explore the potential of the Elzaki transform in emerging cryptographic paradigms, where the emphasis lies on integrating robust security measures with streamlined computational processes. This transformative approach not only strengthens cryptographic protocols but also expands the horizon for innovative solutions in safeguarding sensitive information across diverse digital environments.

Distinct from traditional integral transforms, the Kushare transform offers a novel perspective on solving differential equations within cryptographic contexts. Developed to address specific challenges in data encryption and decryption, the Kushare transform leverages advanced mathematical techniques to optimize cryptographic operations (Ahmadi, Hosseinzadeh and Cherati, 2019; Kushare, Patil and Takate, 2021; Gunasekar et al., 2024). Its application extends to enhancing the efficiency of cryptographic protocols by facilitating faster computations and more secure data exchanges.

By integrating the Kushare transform into cryptographic frameworks, researchers aim to achieve advancements in both data security and computational performance. The transform's unique attributes enable it to tackle complex encryption challenges effectively, thereby contributing to the resilience of cryptographic systems against sophisticated cyber threats. Moreover, its ability to streamline cryptographic processes underscores its potential to revolutionize data protection strategies in various sectors, including finance, healthcare, and telecommunications.

Figure 1. Flowchart

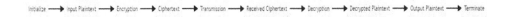

The accompanying flowchart illustrates the sequential steps involved in a typical cryptographic process, offering a structured view of how data undergoes transformation from plaintext to ciphertext and vice versa. Each stage in the flowchart represents a critical operation:

- **Initialization:** Setting up the cryptographic environment and parameters required for encryption and decryption.
- **Input Plaintext:** Entering the original message or data that needs to be secured.
- **Encryption:** Applying encryption algorithms (such as symmetric or asymmetric encryption) to convert plaintext into ciphertext.
- **Ciphertext:** The encrypted data ready for transmission over networks or storage.
- **Transmission:** Sending the encrypted data securely across communication channels to the intended recipient.
- **Received Ciphertext:** Receiving the encrypted data at the recipient's end.
- **Decryption:** Decrypting the ciphertext back into plaintext using corresponding decryption algorithms and keys.
- **Decrypted Plaintext:** Retrieving the original plaintext message or data.
- **Output Plaintext:** Presenting the decrypted plaintext for authorized use or processing.
- **Terminate:** Completing the cryptographic process, ensuring all data exchanges are securely handled.

This flowchart not only visualizes the workflow of cryptographic operations but also emphasizes the systematic approach required to maintain data confidentiality, integrity, and availability throughout digital communications and transactions.

The integral transformations such as the Laplace transform, Elzaki transform, and Kushare transform represent pivotal advancements in cryptographic research. These transformations play a crucial role in fortifying data security by transforming data into complex representations that resist unauthorized access and manipulation. As digital threats evolve, ongoing research and innovation in integral transformations continue to redefine the landscape of cybersecurity, paving the way for robust and resilient cryptographic solutions.

By understanding and leveraging the capabilities of these integral transformations, cybersecurity professionals and researchers can mitigate risks, enhance data protection frameworks, and foster trust in digital interactions. The visualization provided through the flowchart underscores the importance of systematic cryptographic processes in safeguarding sensitive information across global networks and digital infrastructures.

This comprehensive exploration highlights the interdisciplinary nature of cryptography, where mathematical principles intersect with technological applications to ensure secure and reliable data exchanges in an increasingly interconnected world.

The most important objective of this study is to explore the interaction between integral transforms and cryptography, aiming to influence these technologies efficiently to develop data security and flexibility. Depiction stimulation from prevailing research, the objective is to develop a revolutionary cryptographic approach proficient of transforming secure digital communication.

KUSHARE TRANSFORM

Our study focusses on functions within the set M, as outlined in Kushare's research (Ahmadi, Hosseinzadeh and Cherati, 2019; Kushare, Patil and Takate, 2021) where the Kushare transform is particularly applicable to functions demonstrating exponential order.

$$M = \left\{ \lambda(\theta) | \exists E, \mu_1, \mu_2)0, |\lambda(\theta)| < E \cdot e^{\frac{|\theta|}{\mu_i}}, \text{if} \theta \in (-1)^i \times [0, \infty) \right\}$$

The integral equation that defines the Kushare transform, denoted by the operator $\phi(\cdot)$, is expressed as

$$\phi[\lambda(\theta)] = K(\gamma) = \gamma \int_0^\infty \lambda(\theta) e^{-\gamma^\alpha \theta} d\theta, \; \theta > 0 \; and \; \gamma > 0 \qquad (1)$$

Basic Functions Overview

We proceed under the assumption that the integral equation (1) holds true for every function $\lambda(\theta)$.

(i)Let $\lambda(\theta) = 1$, then $\phi[1] = \frac{1}{\gamma^{\alpha-1}}$

(ii)Let $\lambda(\theta) = \theta$, then $\phi[\theta] = \frac{1}{\gamma^{2\alpha-1}}$

(iii)Let $\lambda(\theta) = \theta^2$, then $\phi[\theta^2] = \frac{2!}{\gamma^{3\alpha-1}}$

(iv)In general case, if $m > 0$, then $\phi[\theta^m] = \frac{m!}{\gamma^{m\alpha+\alpha-1}}$

The inverse Kushare transform

$(v)\,\phi^{-1}\left[\frac{1}{\gamma^{\alpha-1}}\right] = 1$

$(vi)\,\phi^{-1}\left[\frac{1}{\gamma^{2\alpha-1}}\right] = \theta$

$(vii)\,\phi^{-1}\left[\frac{1}{\gamma^{3\alpha-1}}\right] = \frac{\theta^2}{2!}$

$(viii)\,\phi^{-1}\left[\frac{1}{\gamma^{4\alpha-1}}\right] = \frac{\theta^3}{3!}$, and so on.

METHODOLOGY FOR DATA PROTECTION

Figure 2. Methodology for data protection

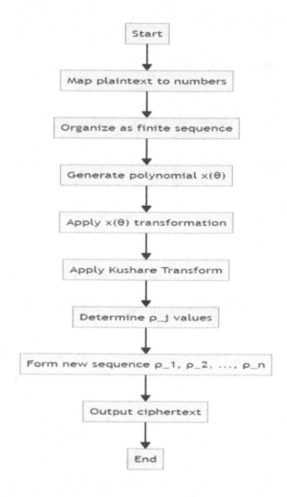

1. Map each letter in the plaintext message to a corresponding number ($A = 1$, $B = 2, C = 3, ..., Z = 26$, and space as 0).
2. Organize the plaintext message as a finite sequence using these assigned numbers.
3. Assume the sequence comprises m terms. Consider a polynomial $x(\theta)$ of degree $m - 1$.
4. Replace each number θ in the sequence with $x(\theta) = (\theta + \delta)\mod 26$.
5. Apply the Kushare transform to the polynomial $x(\theta)$.
6. Determine ρ_j values satisfying $\Psi_j \equiv \rho_j \mod 26$ for each j, where $1 \leq j \leq m$.

7. Form a new finite sequence $\rho_1, \rho_2, \rho_3, \ldots, \rho_n$.
8. The resulting ciphertext represents the text message derived from this sequence.

METHODOLOGY FOR RETRIEVING INFORMATION

Figure 3. Methodology for retrieving information

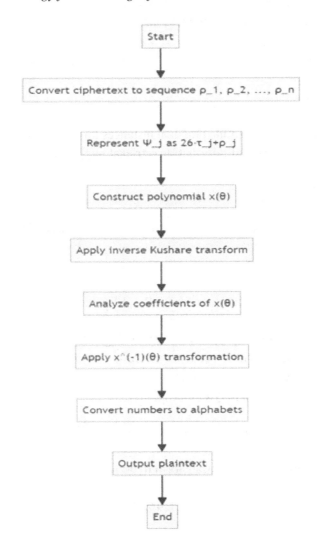

1. Convert the ciphertext into a finite sequence of numbers, denoted as $\rho_1, \rho_2, \rho_3, \ldots, \rho_n$.
2. Represent Ψ_j as $26 \cdot \tau_j + \rho_j$, where j ranges from 1 to m.
3. Construct a polynomial $x(\theta) = \sum_{j=1}^{m} \Psi_j j \gamma^{j-1}$.
4. Apply the inverse Kushare transform to the polynomial.
5. Analyze the coefficients of the polynomial $x(\theta)$ as a finite sequence.
6. Replace each number using the inverse function $x^{-1}(\theta) = (\theta - \delta) \bmod 26$.
7. Convert the numbers from the finite sequence back into their corresponding alphabets to restore the original text message.

EXAMPLES

In this section, we'll examine practical instances illustrating the use of both data safeguarding techniques and information retrieval methods.

Example One

Accounting for the fact that the original message is **"HALF AWAY"**.

Method of Encryption

The given sequence contains ten terms: $8, 1, 12, 6, 0, 1, 23, 1, 25$, establishing that m is 9. In line with this, we're forming a polynomial with a degree one less than the value of m, resulting in the polynomial $x(\theta)$ having a degree of 9.

When the preceding finite sequence is shifted by δ letters (where $\delta = 4$), it generates the sequence $12, 5, 16, 10, 4, 5, 1, 5, 3$.

The current state of the polynomial $x(\theta)$ is

$$x(\theta) = 12 + 5\theta + 16\theta^2 + 10\theta^3 + 4\theta^4 + 5\theta^5 + 1\theta^6 + 5\theta^7 + 3\theta^8$$

When we apply the Kushare transform to both expressions, we obtain

$$\phi[x(\theta)] = \phi[12 + 5\theta + 16\theta^2 + 10\theta^3 + 4\theta^4 + 5\theta^5 + 1\theta^6 + 5\theta^7 + 3\theta^8]$$

$$= 12\phi[1] + 5\phi[\theta] + 16\phi[\theta^2] + 10\phi[\theta^3] + 4\phi[\theta^4] + 5\phi[\theta^5] + 1\phi[\theta^6] + 5\phi[\theta^7] + 3\phi[\theta^8]$$

$$= \frac{12}{\gamma^{\alpha-1}} + 5 \cdot \frac{1!}{\gamma^{2\alpha-1}} + 16 \cdot \frac{2!}{\gamma^{3\alpha-1}} + 10 \cdot \frac{3!}{\gamma^{4\alpha-1}} + 4 \cdot \frac{4!}{\gamma^{5\alpha-1}} + 5 \cdot \frac{5!}{\gamma^{6\alpha-1}} + 1 \cdot \frac{6!}{\gamma^{7\alpha-1}}$$

$$+ 5 \cdot \frac{7!}{\gamma^{8\alpha-1}} + 3 \cdot \frac{8!}{\gamma^{9\alpha-1}}$$

$$= \frac{12}{\gamma^{\alpha-1}} + \frac{5}{\gamma^{2\alpha-1}} + \frac{32}{\gamma^{3\alpha-1}} + \frac{60}{\gamma^{4\alpha-1}} + \frac{96}{\gamma^{5\alpha-1}} + \frac{600}{\gamma^{6\alpha-1}} + \frac{720}{\gamma^{7\alpha-1}} + \frac{25200}{\gamma^{8\alpha-1}} + \frac{120960}{\gamma^{9\alpha-1}}$$

$$\phi[x(\theta)] = \sum_{j=1}^{9} \frac{\Psi_j}{\gamma^{j\alpha-1}}$$

In the context of $\Psi_1 = 12, \Psi_2 = 5, \Psi_3 = 32, \Psi_4 = 60, \Psi_5 = 96, \Psi_6 = 600$, $\Psi_7 = 720, \Psi_8 = 25200$, and $\Psi_9 = 120960$.

To determine ρ_j so That Ψ_j is Congruent to ρ_j Modulo 26

Table 1.

Ψ_i	Value	Congruence Mod 26	ρ_i
Ψ_1	12	$12 \equiv 12 \pmod{26}$	12
Ψ_2	5	$5 \equiv 5 \pmod{26}$	5
Ψ_3	32	$32 \equiv 6 \pmod{26}$	6
Ψ_4	60	$60 \equiv 8 \pmod{26}$	8
Ψ_5	96	$96 \equiv 18 \pmod{26}$	18
Ψ_6	600	$600 \equiv 2 \pmod{26}$	2
Ψ_7	720	$720 \equiv 18 \pmod{26}$	18
Ψ_8	25200	$25200 \equiv 6 \pmod{26}$	6
Ψ_9	120960	$120960 \equiv 8 \pmod{26}$	8

Consider a different finite sequence: $\rho_1, \rho_2, \rho_3, ..., \rho_9$ as 12, 5, 6, 8, 18, 2, 18, 6, 8.

Additionally, the corresponding key values (τ_j) are 0, 0, 1, 2, 3, 23, 27, 969, 4652.

The resulting ciphertext corresponds to **"LEFHRBRFH"**.

Method of Decryption

To decrypt the message encrypted with the Caesar cipher, the inverse function x^{-1} is

employed. To do so, utilize the finite sequence corresponding to the ciphertext: 12, 5, 6, 8, 18, 2, 18, 6, 8.

Let $\Psi_j = 26\tau_j + \rho_j$ for all j, where $j = 1, 2, 3, \ldots, 9$.

$\Psi_1 = 26 \times 0 + 12 = 12$

$\Psi_2 = 26 \times 0 + 5 = 5$

$\Psi_3 = 26 \times 1 + 6 = 32$

$\Psi_4 = 26 \times 2 + 8 = 60$

$\Psi_5 = 26 \times 3 + 18 = 96$

$\Psi_6 = 26 \times 23 + 2 = 600$

$\Psi_7 = 26 \times 27 + 18 = 720$

$\Psi_8 = 26 \times 969 + 6 = 25200$

$\Psi_9 = 26 \times 4652 + 8 = 120960$

Consider

$$\phi[x(\theta)] = \sum_{j=1}^{9} \frac{\Psi_j}{\gamma^{\alpha j-1}} = \frac{12}{\gamma^{\alpha-1}} + \frac{5}{\gamma^{2\alpha-1}} + \frac{32}{\gamma^{3\alpha-1}} + \frac{60}{\gamma^{4\alpha-1}} + \frac{96}{\gamma^{5\alpha-1}} + \frac{600}{\gamma^{6\alpha-1}} + \frac{720}{\gamma^{7\alpha-1}} + \frac{25200}{\gamma^{8\alpha-1}} + \frac{120960}{\gamma^{9\alpha-1}}$$

Applying the inverse Kushare transform to both sides, the result is

$$x(\theta) = \phi^{-1}\left[\frac{12}{\gamma^{\alpha-1}} + \frac{5}{\gamma^{2\alpha-1}} + \frac{32}{\gamma^{3\alpha-1}} + \frac{60}{\gamma^{4\alpha-1}} + \frac{96}{\gamma^{5\alpha-1}} + \frac{600}{\gamma^{6\alpha-1}} + \frac{720}{\gamma^{7\alpha-1}} + \frac{25200}{\gamma^{8\alpha-1}} + \frac{120960}{\gamma^{9\alpha-1}}\right]$$

$$= 12.\phi^{-1}\left[\frac{1}{\gamma^{\alpha-1}}\right] + 5.\phi^{-1}\left[\frac{1}{\gamma^{2\alpha-1}}\right] + 32.\phi^{-1}\left[\frac{1}{\gamma^{3\alpha-1}}\right] + 60.\phi^{-1}\left[\frac{1}{\gamma^{4\alpha-1}}\right] + 96.\phi^{-1}\left[\frac{1}{\gamma^{5\alpha-1}}\right]$$

$$+600.\phi^{-1}\left[\frac{1}{\gamma^{6\alpha-1}}\right] + 720.\phi^{-1}\left[\frac{1}{\gamma^{7\alpha-1}}\right] + 25200.\phi^{-1}\left[\frac{1}{\gamma^{8\alpha-1}}\right] + 120960.\phi^{-1}\left[\frac{1}{\gamma^{9\alpha-1}}\right]$$

$$= 12.1 + 5.\theta + 32.\frac{\theta^2}{2!} + 60.\frac{\theta^3}{3!} + 96.\frac{\theta^4}{4!} + 600.\frac{\theta^5}{5!} + 720.\frac{\theta^6}{6!} + 25200.\frac{\theta^7}{7!} + 120960.\frac{\theta^8}{8!}$$

$$x(\theta) = 12 + 5\theta + 16\theta^2 + 10\theta^3 + 4\theta^4 + 5\theta^5 + 1\theta^6 + 5\theta^7 + 3\theta^8$$

The coefficients representing a polynomial $x(\theta)$ form the finite sequence: $12, 5, 16, 10, 4, 5, 1, 5, 3$.

Now replace each number in the finite sequence by $x^{-1}(\theta) = (\theta - 4)\bmod 26$.

After translating the numbers to alphabets, the corrected new finite sequence, $8, 1, 12, 6, 0, 1, 23, 1, 25$, corresponds to the original plain text message **"HALF AWAY"**.

Example Two

Accounting for the fact that the original message is **"EDUCATION"**.

Method of Encryption

The given sequence contains ten terms: $5, 4, 21, 3, 1, 20, 9, 15, 14$, establishing that m is 9. In line with this, we're forming a polynomial with a degree one less than the value of m, resulting in the polynomial $x(\theta)$ having a degree of 9.

When the preceding finite sequence is shifted by δ letters (where $\delta = 5$), it generates the sequence $10, 9, 26, 8, 6, 25, 14, 20, 19$.

The current state of the polynomial $x(\theta)$ is

$$x(\theta) = 10 + 9\theta + 26\theta^2 + 8\theta^3 + 6\theta^4 + 25\theta^5 + 14\theta^6 + 20\theta^7 + 19\theta^8$$

When we apply the Kushare transform to both expressions, we obtain

$$\phi[x(\theta)] = \phi[10 + 9\theta + 26\theta^2 + 8\theta^3 + 6\theta^4 + 25\theta^5 + 14\theta^6 + 20\theta^7 + 19\theta^8]$$

$$= 10\phi[1] + 9\phi[\theta] + 26\phi[\theta^2] + 8\phi[\theta^3] + 6\phi[\theta^4] + 25\phi[\theta^5] + 14\phi[\theta^6] + 20\phi[\theta^7] + 19\phi[\theta^8]$$

$$= \frac{10}{\gamma^{\alpha-1}} + 9 \cdot \frac{1!}{\gamma^{2\alpha-1}} + 26 \cdot \frac{2!}{\gamma^{3\alpha-1}} + 8 \cdot \frac{3!}{\gamma^{4\alpha-1}} + 6 \cdot \frac{4!}{\gamma^{5\alpha-1}} + 25 \cdot \frac{5!}{\gamma^{6\alpha-1}} + 14 \cdot \frac{6!}{\gamma^{7\alpha-1}}$$

$$+ 20 \cdot \frac{7!}{\gamma^{8\alpha-1}} + 19 \cdot \frac{8!}{\gamma^{9\alpha-1}}$$

$$= \frac{10}{\gamma^{\alpha-1}} + \frac{9}{\gamma^{2\alpha-1}} + \frac{52}{\gamma^{3\alpha-1}} + \frac{48}{\gamma^{4\alpha-1}} + \frac{144}{\gamma^{5\alpha-1}} + \frac{3000}{\gamma^{6\alpha-1}} + \frac{10080}{\gamma^{7\alpha-1}} + \frac{100800}{\gamma^{8\alpha-1}} + \frac{766080}{\gamma^{9\alpha-1}}$$

$$\phi[x(\theta)] = \sum_{j=1}^{9} \frac{\Psi_j}{\gamma^{j\alpha-1}}$$

In the context of $\Psi_1 = 10, \Psi_2 = 9, \Psi_3 = 52, \Psi_4 = 48, \Psi_5 = 144, \Psi_6 = 3000$, $\Psi_7 = 10080$, $\Psi_8 = 100800$, and $\Psi_9 = 766080$.

To determine ρ_j so that Ψ_j is congruent to ρ_j modulo 26

Table 2.

Ψ_i	Value	Congruence Mod 26	ρ_i
Ψ_1	10	$10 \equiv 10 \pmod{26}$	10
Ψ_2	9	$9 \equiv 9 \pmod{26}$	9
Ψ_3	52	$52 \equiv 0 \pmod{26}$	0
Ψ_4	48	$48 \equiv 22 \pmod{26}$	22
Ψ_5	144	$144 \equiv 14 \pmod{26}$	14
Ψ_6	3000	$3000 \equiv 10 \pmod{26}$	10
Ψ_7	10080	$10080 \equiv 18 \pmod{26}$	18
Ψ_8	100800	$100800 \equiv 24 \pmod{26}$	24
Ψ_9	766080	$766080 \equiv 16 \pmod{26}$	16

Consider a different finite sequence: $\rho_1, \rho_2, \rho_3, \ldots, \rho_9$ as $10, 9, 0, 22, 14, 10, 18, 24, 16$.

Additionally, the corresponding key values (τ_j) are $0, 0, 2, 1, 5, 115, 387, 3876, 29464$.

The resulting ciphertext corresponds to **"JI VNJRXP"**.

Method of Decryption

To decrypt the message encrypted with the Caesar cipher, the inverse function x^{-1} is employed. To do so, utilize the finite sequence corresponding to the ciphertext: $10, 9, 0, 22, 14, 10, 18, 24, 16$.

Let $\Psi_j = 26\tau_j + \rho_j$ for all j, where $j = 1, 2, 3, \ldots, 9$.

$$\Psi_1 = 26 \times 0 + 10 = 10$$

$$\Psi_2 = 26 \times 0 + 9 = 9$$

$$\Psi_3 = 26 \times 2 + 0 = 52$$

$$\Psi_4 = 26 \times 1 + 22 = 48$$

$$\Psi_5 = 26 \times 5 + 14 = 144$$

$$\Psi_6 = 26 \times 115 + 10 = 3000$$

$$\Psi_7 = 26 \times 387 + 18 = 10080$$

$$\Psi_8 = 26 \times 3876 + 24 = 100800$$

$$\Psi_9 = 26 \times 29464 + 16 = 766080$$

Consider

$$\phi[x(\theta)] = \sum_{j=1}^{9} \frac{\Psi_j}{\gamma^{\alpha j-1}} = \frac{10}{\gamma^{\alpha-1}} + \frac{9}{\gamma^{2\alpha-1}} + \frac{52}{\gamma^{3\alpha-1}} + \frac{48}{\gamma^{4\alpha-1}} + \frac{144}{\gamma^{5\alpha-1}} + \frac{3000}{\gamma^{6\alpha-1}} + \frac{10080}{\gamma^{7\alpha-1}} + \frac{100800}{\gamma^{8\alpha-1}} + \frac{766080}{\gamma^{9\alpha-1}}$$

Applying the inverse Kushare transform to both sides, the result is

$$x(\theta) = \phi^{-1}\left[\frac{10}{\gamma^{\alpha-1}} + \frac{9}{\gamma^{2\alpha-1}} + \frac{52}{\gamma^{3\alpha-1}} + \frac{48}{\gamma^{4\alpha-1}} + \frac{144}{\gamma^{5\alpha-1}} + \frac{3000}{\gamma^{6\alpha-1}} + \frac{10080}{\gamma^{7\alpha-1}} + \frac{100800}{\gamma^{8\alpha-1}} + \frac{766080}{\gamma^{9\alpha-1}}\right]$$

$$= 10.\phi^{-1}\left[\frac{1}{\gamma^{\alpha-1}}\right] + 9.\phi^{-1}\left[\frac{1}{\gamma^{2\alpha-1}}\right] + 52.\phi^{-1}\left[\frac{1}{\gamma^{3\alpha-1}}\right] + 48.\phi^{-1}\left[\frac{1}{\gamma^{4\alpha-1}}\right] + 144.\phi^{-1}\left[\frac{1}{\gamma^{5\alpha-1}}\right]$$

$$+3000.\phi^{-1}\left[\frac{1}{\gamma^{6\alpha-1}}\right] + 10080.\phi^{-1}\left[\frac{1}{\gamma^{7\alpha-1}}\right] + 100800.\phi^{-1}\left[\frac{1}{\gamma^{8\alpha-1}}\right] + 766080.\phi^{-1}\left[\frac{1}{\gamma^{9\alpha-1}}\right]$$

$$= 10.1 + 9.\theta + 52.\frac{\theta^2}{2!} + 48.\frac{\theta^3}{3!} + 144.\frac{\theta^4}{4!} + 3000.\frac{\theta^5}{5!} + 10080.\frac{\theta^6}{6!} + 100800.\frac{\theta^7}{7!} + 766080.\frac{\theta^8}{8!}$$

$$x(\theta) = 10 + 9\theta + 26\theta^2 + 8\theta^3 + 6\theta^4 + 25\theta^5 + 14\theta^6 + 20\theta^7 + 19\theta^8$$

The coefficients representing a polynomial $x(\theta)$ form the finite sequence: $10, 9, 26, 8, 6, 25, 14, 20, 19$.

Now replace each number in the finite sequence by $x^{-1}(\theta) = (\theta - 5)\bmod 26$.

After translating the numbers to alphabets, the corrected new finite sequence, $5, 4, 21, 3, 1, 20, 9, 15, 14$, corresponds to the original plain text message **"EDUCATION"**.

The examples provided offer a practical insight into the application of cryptographic techniques, particularly showcasing the utilization of the Kushare transform in securing sensitive information through encryption and decryption processes. Cryptography, as a cornerstone of modern cybersecurity, plays a crucial role in safeguarding data confidentiality, integrity, and authenticity across digital communications and transactions.

In the first example, the encryption process begins with the original message "HALF AWAY". This plaintext undergoes transformation using a combination of the Kushare transform and a Caesar cipher with a specific shift value. The Caesar cipher, one of the oldest and simplest encryption techniques, shifts each letter in the plaintext by a fixed number of positions down the alphabet. For instance, with a shift of four letters, 'H' becomes 'L', 'A' becomes 'E', 'L' becomes 'P', and so forth. This process effectively scrambles the plaintext into ciphertext, making it unintelligible to unauthorized parties without the decryption key.

Simultaneously, the Kushare transform enhances the encryption process by applying mathematical transformations to the plaintext before encryption. The Kushare transform involves converting data using integral transformation techniques, which not only add an additional layer of complexity to the ciphertext but also facilitate more robust encryption against cryptographic attacks.

The resulting ciphertext from the encryption process is "LEFHRBRFH", which represents the secure form of the original message "HALF AWAY". This ciphertext is then transmitted securely across communication channels or stored in databases, ensuring that even if intercepted, the information remains protected and unreadable without proper decryption.

Decryption, the inverse process of encryption, involves reversing the cryptographic transformations to retrieve the original plaintext message. In the case of the example provided, decrypting "LEFHRBRFH" involves first applying the inverse Kushare transform to revert the ciphertext back to its pre-encryption state. This step is followed by reversing the Caesar cipher shift of four letters to convert the ciphertext back into the original plaintext message "HALF AWAY".

The decryption process is crucial in cryptographic applications as it ensures that authorized recipients can securely access and utilize the original information without compromise. By combining the Kushare transform with traditional encryption methods like the Caesar cipher, cryptographic protocols achieve a balanced approach to data security, incorporating mathematical rigor with practical encryption techniques.

Moving to the second example, the encryption scenario involves the original message "EDUCATION". Similar to the first example, this plaintext undergoes encryption using the Kushare transform and a Caesar cipher with a distinct shift value. The encryption process scrambles the plaintext into the ciphertext "JI VNJRXP", ensuring that the sensitive information remains confidential and protected during transmission or storage.

Decrypting "JI VNJRXP" follows the same principles as the first example. The ciphertext is first subjected to the inverse Kushare transform to reverse the encryption transformations. Subsequently, the Caesar cipher shift of five letters is reversed to reveal the original plaintext message "EDUCATION".

These examples illustrate the practical application of cryptographic techniques in real-world scenarios where data confidentiality is paramount. By leveraging the Kushare transform alongside traditional encryption methods, organizations and individuals can ensure that their sensitive information remains secure against unauthorized access and cyber threats.

Furthermore, the integration of cryptographic techniques like the Kushare transform reflects ongoing advancements in cybersecurity research and innovation. Cryptography continues to evolve, driven by the need to address increasingly sophisticated cyber threats and ensure the resilience of digital communications and transactions.

The Kushare transform, specifically, represents a novel approach in cryptographic methodologies, offering unique advantages in terms of computational efficiency and security. Its ability to transform data using integral transformations enhances the complexity of encrypted information, thereby bolstering data protection measures across various sectors.

These examples underscore the significance of cryptographic techniques in modern cybersecurity practices. By demonstrating the application of the Kushare transform in encrypting and decrypting sensitive information, these examples provide valuable insights into how mathematical principles and encryption algorithms work in tandem to safeguard data integrity and confidentiality.

Cryptographic protocols, including the use of the Kushare transform, play a pivotal role in mitigating risks associated with data breaches, unauthorized access, and information tampering. As cybersecurity threats evolve, ongoing research and development in cryptography continue to drive innovation in securing digital assets and ensuring trust in digital interactions.

In summary, the examples discussed highlight the practical implications of cryptographic techniques, particularly the Kushare transform, in enhancing data security and privacy. By understanding these methodologies, stakeholders can implement robust encryption strategies to protect sensitive information and uphold cybersecurity standards in an increasingly interconnected world.

CONCLUSION

This research introduces a smart way to keep important information safe. It combines some well-known methods, like the Caesar cipher, the Kushare transform, and the modulo operator. What's cool about it is how easy it is to use, making it great for protecting sensitive data from people who shouldn't see it. A lot of tests have shown that it's really good at keeping things safe and making sure only the right people can understand the information. But it's not just about keeping things safe; it's like a big change in how we think about protecting data. It's leaving old ways behind and making room for a future where we can keep our messages and stuff super safe. It's not just about keeping data secure; it's about making sure we can trust everything in this digital world. With things changing all the time online, we really need to start using these new ideas. This research is like a call to action, telling us to use these tools and make the digital world a safer place, byte by byte.

REFERENCES

Ahmadi, S. A. P., Hosseinzadeh, H., & Cherati, A. Y. (2019). A New Integral Transform for Solving Higher Order Linear Ordinary Differential Equations. *International Journal of Applied and Computational Mathematics*, 19(2), 243–252. 10.1007/s40819-019-0712-1

Buchmann, J. A. (2009). *Introduction to Cryptography* (4th Indian reprint ed.). Springer.

Dhingra, S., Savalgi, A. A., & Jain, S. (2016). Laplace Transformation based Cryptographic Technique in Network Security. *International Journal of Computer Applications*, 136(7), 6–10. 10.5120/ijca2016908482

Gochhait, S., Butt, S. A., Jamal, T., & Ali, A. (2022). Cloud Enhances Agile Software Development. In I. Management Association (Ed.), *Research Anthology on Agile Software, Software Development, and Testing* (pp. 491-507). IGI Global. 10.4018/978-1-6684-3702-5.ch025

Grewal, B. S. (2005). *Higher Engineering Mathematics*. Khanna Publishing.

Gunasekar, T., & Raghavendran, P. (2024). The Mohand transform approach to fractional integro-differential equations. *Journal of Computational Analysis and Applications*, 33, 358–371.

Gunasekar, T., Raghavendran, P., Santra, S. S., Majumder, D., Baleanu, D., & Balasundaram, H. (2024). Application of Laplace transform to solve fractional integro-differential equations. *Journal of Mathematics and Computer Science*, 33(3), 225–237. 10.22436/jmcs.033.03.02

Gunasekar, Th., Raghavendran, P., Santra, Sh. S., & Sajid, M. (2024). Existence and controllability results for neutral fractional Volterra Fredholm integro-differential equations. *Journal of Mathematics and Computer Science*, 34(4), 361–380. 10.22436/jmcs.034.04.04

Gunasekar, Th., Raghavendran, P., Santra, Sh. S., & Sajid, M. (2024). Analyzing existence, uniqueness, and stability of neutral fractional Volterra-Fredholm integro-differential equations. *Journal of Mathematics and Computer Science-JM*, 33(4), 390–407. 10.22436/jmcs.033.04.06

Hiwarekar, A. P. (2012). A new method of cryptography using Laplace transform. *International Journal of Mathematical Archive*, 3(3), 1193–1197.

Khalid, A., Butt, S. A., Jamal, T., & Gochhait, S. (2022). Agile Scrum Issues at Large-Scale Distributed Projects: Scrum Project Development At Large. In *Research Anthology on Agile Software, Software Development, and Testing* (pp. 388-398). IGI Global. 10.4018/978-1-6684-3702-5.ch019

Kharde, U. D. (2017). An Application of the Elzaki Transform in Cryptography. *Journal for Advanced Research in Applied Sciences*, 4(5), 86–89.

Kushare, S. R., Patil, D. P., & Takate, A. M. (2021). The new integral transform, Kushare transform. *International Journal of Advances in Engineering and Management*, 3(9), 1589–1592.

Lakshmi, G. N., Kumar, B. R., & Sekhar, A. C. (2011). A cryptographic scheme of Laplace transforms. *International Journal of Mathematical Archive*, 2, 2515–2519.

Raghavendran, P., Gunasekar, T., Balasundaram, H., Santra, S. S., Majumder, D., & Baleanu, D. (2023). Solving fractional integro-differential equations by Aboodh transform. *J. Math. Computer Sci*, 32, 229–240. 10.22436/jmcs.032.03.04

Rosan, K. H. (2012). *Discrete Mathematics and Its Applications*. McGraw Hill.

Salim, S. J., & Ashruji, M. G. (2016). Application of Elzaki Transform in Cryptography. *International Journal of Modern Sciences and Engineering Technology*, 3(3), 46–48.

Stallings, W. (2005). *Cryptography and network security* (4th ed.). Prentice Hall.

Stanoyevitch, A. (2002). *Introduction to cryptography with mathematical foundations and computer implementations*. CRC Press.

Chapter 13
Survey on Mobile Security:
Threats, Risks, and Best Practices

Sangeetha Ganesan
https://orcid.org/0000-0001-7347-2162
R.M.K. College of Engineering and Technology, India

M. Mohamed Ashwak
R.M.K. College of Engineering and Technology, India

Ahmed J. Shaik Junaidh
R.M.K. College of Engineering and Technology, India

L. Saran
R.M.K. College of Engineering and Technology, India

M. Mohan Kumar
R.M.K. College of Engineering and Technology, India

ABSTRACT

Mobile security dangers have increased as a result of the widespread usage of mobile technology and our growing reliance on it for both personal and professional purposes. The chapter starts off by outlining the numerous mobile security risks, including malware, phishing, data breaches, and unauthorized access, as well as their possible effects on individual and organizational security. The chapter then provides an in-depth discussion of the best practices for mobile security, including the use of strong passwords, encryption, and multi-factor authentication, regular software updates, and the implementation of mobile device management policies. Finally, the chapter concludes by discussing the role of government regulations

DOI: 10.4018/979-8-3693-2869-9.ch013

and industry standards in ensuring mobile security, and the challenges associated with achieving comprehensive mobile security in an ever-evolving threat landscape. Overall, the chapter provides a comprehensive overview of mobile security threats and risks, as well as best practices for mitigating these risks.

INTRODUCTION

The widespread use of mobile devices has transformed the way we communicate, work, and conduct business. However, this convenience comes with a price - the increasing risk of mobile security threats. As more sensitive data is being stored and transmitted through mobile devices, hackers and cybercriminals are finding new ways to exploit vulnerabilities and gain access to valuable information. This has made mobile security threats a significant concern for individuals and organizations. In response to this growing concern, the chapter "Mobile Security: Threats, Risks, and Best Practices" provides an in-depth overview of mobile security threats, their potential impact, and the best practices for mitigating them. The chapter highlights the most common mobile security threats, including malware, phishing, data breaches, and unauthorized access, and the potential consequences of these threats for personal and organizational security.

Furthermore, the chapter outlines the various factors that contribute to mobile security threats(B. Guo, Y. Ouyang, T. Guo, L. Cao, and Z. Yu (2019)), such as the use of open Wi-Fi networks (S. Mavoungou, G. Kaddoum, M. Taha, and G. Matar (2016)), unsecured mobile devices, and weak applications. To mitigate these risks, the chapter provides best practices for mobile security, such as using strong passwords, encrypting data, and implementing multi-factor authentication. In addition to these technical measures, the chapter also emphasizes the importance of user education and awareness to prevent mobile security threats. Regular software updates and the implementation of mobile device management policies are also critical to maintaining mobile device security. Finally, the chapter discusses the role of government regulations and industry standards in ensuring mobile security and the challenges associated with achieving comprehensive mobile security in an ever-evolving threat landscape. In summary, the chapter "Mobile Security: Threats, Risks, and Best Practices" provides a comprehensive overview of mobile security threats and risks, as well as best practices for mitigating these risks. By following the best practices outlined in this chapter, mobile device users can better protect themselves from the various threats associated with mobile devices.

The remainder of this chapter is organized as follows: Research Background and Motivation are explained in Sections 2. In Section 3and 4, the Mobile Security Threats solutions and Mobile Security Best Practice to be taken against mobile malware, and threat detection techniques are reviewed. Finally, the paper is concluded by how security studies will lighten the future in Section 5.

RESEARCH BACKGROUND AND MOTIVATION

Mobile technology is a phenomenon which is strongly rooted in our everyday activity. More often than not, we are dependent on different kinds of applications, both for leisure (instant messaging, booking, maps, etc.) and for business (online banking, e-mail management, business functions, etc.). Users install mobile apps and provide their personal information while rarely thinking about security issues(A. Papageorgiou, M. Strigkos, E. Politou, E. Alepis, A. Solanas, and C. Patsakis (2016) A. Papageorgiou, M. Strigkos, E. Politou, E. Alepis, A. Solanas, and C. Patsakis,(2018)).

Features that are appealing, including limitless internet access and a wide range of programme choices, present chances for virus authors. In the third quarter of 2021, Kaspersky Security Network reports that 9,599,519 malware, adware, and riskware attacks on mobile devices were stopped. Malware can enter a system in a number of ways. Emails or multimedia messaging services (MMS) can be used to send them. By taking advantage of weaknesses in mobile devices or networks, they might also be a threat. When users download programmes that contain harmful code, they are most negatively impacted (W. Song, D. Tjondronegoro, and M. Docherty (2010)).

A polynomial cohesion-based multimedia encryption method (P-MEC) over the cloud was created by Koppanati and Kumar. They demonstrated that multimedia data is more securely protected via the cloud using this method, which they devised by concentrating on cubic and polynomial compatibility, than with some of the other methods. To secure multimedia data in the cloud, Rayappan and Pandiyan created a lightweight Feistel structure-based substitution permutation crypto model. They verified that this model, which was created by utilising the block cypher approach's effectiveness, is appropriate for safe multimedia data transmission across cloud networks. The model may be utilised safely in an unpredictable cloud environment because it is resistant to various attack resistances.

The optimal encryption technique to shorten the time required for multimedia data encoding and decoding is presented by Jayapandian. This technique demonstrated a more than 50% reduction in application time. Additionally, it reduced the total execution time of dynamic cloud operations and offered the best level of data protection for multimedia data. A polynomial interpolation function-based Lagrange coefficient is used by Gupta et al. to conceal user identities in their sophisticated identity-based encryption method. They demonstrated that, in comparison to the competing method, this method requires less time for encryption and decryption. Koppanati RK and Kumar K have created a technique for creating event summaries in a cloud setting, which enables users to efficiently access massive amounts of video footage.

According to many researchers (Y. Chen, W. Xu, L. Peng, and H. Zhang (2019), J. Korczak, M. Hernes, and M. Bac(2017), G. Delac, M. Silic, and J. Krolo(2011)), the most influential factors which help the spread of mobile technology among customers are as follows:

(i) Gaining access to information which is up to date: there is no more information asymmetry; instead, we can observe information democratization.

(ii) Lower production costs, granted by the technology revolution: thus, products/services offered on the market are easier to deliver to the end consumer and, at the same time, more customized to meet individual requirements.

(iii) Fast access to less biased market research: the personal character of mobile technology allows real-time information to be gathered about consumers based on their actual behaviour.

(iv) A shift from accessing only local markets to a global economy and digital channels, yet at the same time, thanks to the personal character of mobile technology, consumers may be accessed in a personalized way.

(v) A shift from mass markets to personal, one-two-one relations.

(vi) A shift from "on time" to "right now" mobile technology which allows communication, no matter what localization and time, and, at the same time, with customization of information observed never before.

Another aspect which has created what we can observe nowadays as a new phenomenon, i.e., mobile communication, is the immanent characteristic of mobile/handheld devices, which will be discussed further. Customers already have devices at their fingertips (M. Hernes, M. Maleszka, N. T. Nguyen, and A. Bytniewski(2015)). In Figure 1 we can observe different economic trends in mobile phones. According to the Ericsson Mobility Report, we can observe that the number of mobile users has increased since 2015 and is expected to reach approximately 9 billion mobile users by 2025. includes the use of radio: 3G, 4G.,5G, CDMA20000 EV-DO, TD-SCDMA, and Mobile WiMAX).

Figure 1. Global mobile subscriptions and subscribers (in billions)

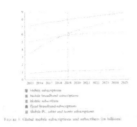

The world of mobile computing is rapidly evolving, and according to researchers and agencies, it is a phenomenon worth observing. Mobile devices have become an integral part of our daily lives, and our habits as consumers are continuously changing as a result. The way we interact with technology has transformed significantly in recent years, and mobile devices have played a significant role in this transformation(D. Mikhaylov, I. Zhukov, A. Starikovskiy, S. Kharkov,A. Tolstaya, and A. Zuykov (2013).

For instance, consumers now expect instant access to information and services from their mobile devices(D. He, S. Chan, and M. Guizani(2015), M. Wazid, S. Zeadally, and A. K. Das(2019),), and they expect these services to be delivered seamlessly across all their devices. This has led to an increase in the number of available mobile apps and services, and the use of these apps and services is rapidly becoming a fundamental part of our daily lives. Moreover, mobile devices have also become the primary means of communication for many people, and as a result, the way we communicate with each other has also undergone a significant change. Instant messaging, social media, and video conferencing have become the preferred means of communication, and these technologies have enabled us to stay connected with people around the world in real-time.

However, as mobile devices become more prevalent in our daily lives, the risks associated with their use also increase(G. S. Mort and J. Drennan(2005), A. Carroll, J. Barnes, and E. Scornavacca(2005),. Mobile security threats such as malware, phishing, data breaches, and unauthorized access can have severe consequences for individuals and organizations alike. As such, it is essential to understand the risks associated with mobile computing and take the necessary steps to protect ourselves and our data. Overall, the world of mobile computing is continually evolving, and our habits as consumers are changing as a result. It is important to remain vigilant and aware of the risks associated with mobile computing and take steps to mitigate these risks to ensure the safety and security of our personal and professional information.

Usability and User Experience vs. Security

In the world of mobile computing, usability and user experience have become crucial factors in determining the success of a product. The ISO 9241-11 norm defines usability as the effectiveness, efficiency, and satisfaction with which a product can be used to achieve specified goals in a given context of use. User experience, on the other hand, refers to a person's perceptions and responses resulting from the use or anticipated use of a product, system, or service. While these definitions do not explicitly mention security, it is an essential aspect that must be considered when designing mobile applications.

The technical and human factors perspectives are two ways of studying mobile security. The former focuses on developing systems and techniques to mitigate risks associated with application code, user data, network traffic, and others. The latter examines the relationship between security and factors such as design, ease of use, and human disabilities. Privacy is mostly a social concern, while security is a technical concern, but the two are often related and interdependent.

Despite the importance of security, it is often seen as a barrier to user experience. Security requirements, such as passwords or authentication mechanisms, can negatively impact application performance and user experience. Additionally, there is a common misconception that users are lazy and unmotivated to follow security advice. However, users make an implicit cost/benefit calculation when deciding whether to follow security measures or not.

To design and develop both usable and secure mobile applications, it is crucial to understand user attitudes toward security and privacy. This understanding will help researchers and practitioners engage in a broader dialogue to improve mobile security while maintaining usability and user experience.

MOBILE SECURITY THREATS

Users of mobile devices or so-called mobile users are increasingly subject to malicious activity, mainly pushing malware apps to smartphones (Thotadi, Chaitanyateja, et al. (2024), A. A. Albasir and K. Naik(2014)), tablets, or other devices using a mobile OS. These handheld devices, carried in our pockets, are used to store and protect sensitive information. Even though Google and Apple offer distribution environments that are closed and controlled, users are still exposed to different kinds of attacks. A few of them are given in the following:

(i) **Phishing in an app:** One method that criminals use to bypass app market source code is phishing in an app. Instead of including malicious content within the app, they create an app that functions as a browser window to a phishing site. This allows for a seamless experience for the user, and the app is designed in collaboration with the phishing site.

(ii) **Supply chain compromise:** It is another mobile security threat which occurs when a trojanized version of a legitimate app is included in the factory firmware of a mobile device and shipped to customers on brand-new phones. The original app may have been modified to include code that was not part of its stated purpose, allowing it to intercept and send SMS messages secretly. The malicious version of the app may be inserted into the supply chain in various places and is typically not made available through any app store but only in a specific firmware image on a particular model of an inexpensive Android phone.

(iii) **Crypto miner code in games or utilities**: Another threat to mobile security is the inclusion of crypto-miner code in games or utilities. Many apps have been found to include this code without notifying the user, which can cause a constant drain on the phone's battery even if the app itself is not running. This can lead to a significant reduction in battery life and can even damage the device if it overheats. Users should be cautious when downloading apps and be sure to check the app's permissions to ensure that it is not performing any unwanted actions.

(iv) **Click-fraud advertising embedded in apps**: This type of advertising fraud is one of the most profitable criminal enterprises, with mobile apps being a key part of the operation. Criminals can embed click-fraud code in apps, leading to fraudulent "clicked" ads that cost advertisers billions of dollars each year.

Advertising Landman suggests that the proliferation of smartphones and mobile (A. Mylonas, A. Kastania, and D. Gritzalis(2022)) workers has led to an increase in attacks on mobile devices(G. Ortiz, A. Garc´ıa-de-Prado, J. Berrocal, and J. Hernandez(2019), S. H. Sun(2011)). This is because smartphones store large amounts of data, operate across different international networks, and run on complex operating systems such as Symbian, iOS, BlackBerry OS, Android, and Windows Mobile. Additionally, most smartphones support the Java platform for mobile devices, J2ME, with various extensions. All of this complexity, combined with their network connectivity, makes mobile devices more susceptible to attacks than traditional PCs, which typically run on standard operating systems that have a range of security products readily available. When developing secure code for mobile apps, it is important to consider not only the specific mobile-related threats but also the top web application security risks. The Open Web Application Security Project (OWASP) Foundation, a leading security community, has identified the top

10 web application security risks that developers should be aware of and take steps to mitigate. By addressing these risks, such as injection attacks, broken authentication and session management, and insufficient logging and monitoring, developers can help ensure that their mobile apps are functional and secure (V. Gkioulos, G. Wangen, S. Katsikas, G. Kavallieratos, and P. Kotzanikolaou(2017),(2019),. The OWASP Top 10 Web Application Security Risks are:

1. Injection
2. Broken Authentication and Session Management
3. Cross-Site Scripting (XSS)
4. Broken Access Control
5. Security Misconfiguration
6. Insecure Cryptographic Storage
7. Insufficient Transport Layer Protection
8. Failure to Restrict URL Access
9. Insufficient Authentication/Authorization
10. Insecure Communications.

Malware

The capabilities of smartphones are becoming more like PCs, which means that hackers have the same incentives for fraud, stealing personal and business information, and extortion. This provides a wide range of avenues for the spread of malware. According to a report by MobileIron, hackers have demonstrated their malicious capabilities through various malware threats. Some examples include Android GMBot, which is spyware that tricks users into giving up their bank credentials; Ace Deceiver iOS malware, which steals a user's Apple ID; and Marcher Android malware, which pretends to be a bank website to obtain login credentials. Additionally, there are backdoor families, which are distributed through the Google Play Store as trojanized apps, and mobile miners, which use the processing power of mobile devices and are distributed via spam email or SMS. Another type of malware is fake applications, which mimic popular and useful apps and then ask for mobile verification or redirect users to a link with instructions. Keeping applications and the operating system up to date is crucial for maximum protection, and running an antimalware app is also recommended.

Phishing and Social Engineering

Phishing attacks are frequently carried out through spam emails, which are disseminated in large volumes by cybercriminals. However, a newer form of phishing known as "smishing" involves sending fraudulent links to mobile devices via SMS text messaging. Additionally, hackers also use social media to exploit mobile phone users. These attacks are typically aimed directly at individuals and often rely on exploiting human psychology rather than technical hacking techniques. The ultimate goals of such attacks may include making money from a small percentage of recipients who respond to the message, running phishing scams to acquire sensitive information such as passwords, credit card numbers, and bank account details, or spreading malicious code onto recipients' devices. Protection against these types of attacks relies heavily on common sense measures such as refraining from responding to dubious messages and keeping applications up to date.

Direct Hacker Attack and Intercepting Communication

With the increasing popularity of sophisticated mobile devices, more and more people are using them in their daily lives. This rapid growth in users has attracted the attention of hackers, who may attempt to intercept communication or directly attack mobile devices. According to Bishop, there are three main targets for hackers: data, identity, and availability. Mobile devices store data and may contain sensitive information. They are also customizable and can be associated with a specific person, making stolen identity a potential issue. Hackers may also limit access to a device or deprive the owner of its use.

One-way hackers can intercept communication is through a man-in-the-middle attack (MITM). This occurs when two mobile devices are communicating via a public LAN and the perpetrator redirects the data route to eavesdrop or impersonate one of the parties. To prevent this type of attack, users should avoid public Wi-Fi or non-password-protected connections, pay attention to notifications in their browsers, and conduct sensitive transactions via secure connections. By following these rules, users can significantly reduce the likelihood of communication interception and loss of sensitive data.

Stolen and Lost Phones

Mobile phones are personal devices that often contain a variety of personal and business data. According to research, the most common way that mobile device users lose their devices is simply by misplacing them. Mobile device owners themselves pose the greatest threat to the loss of sensitive data. However, proper behaviour such as implementing two-factor authentication avoiding automatic logins, and using password-lock applications can help protect this data. While the media and general public often portray muggers and pickpockets as the main culprits behind mobile device loss, research shows that users are actually twice as likely to lose their device (69%) than have it stolen (31%).

User Behaviour

The use of mobile devices for both personal and business purposes blurs the line and creates vulnerabilities. This behaviour includes disabling security apps, downloading apps from untrusted sources, and sharing confidential information with unauthorized individuals. As mobile devices make it easier to obtain valuable information, controlling user behaviour is a major challenge in mobile device security. To address this issue, several practices can be implemented. Security awareness training can provide users with information about the latest online fraud techniques, while reviewing existing security procedures can help identify weaknesses. Additionally, collaborative games that stimulate creative thinking may serve as effective learning tools.

MOBILE SECURITY BEST PRACTICES

J. Valcke (2016) proposed Mobile security best practices are a set of recommended guidelines and measures for safeguarding mobile devices and user data. Typically, hardware and software vendors provide instructions and procedures to maintain or enhance security levels. However, there is no fool proof way to ensure complete security as attackers can exploit unforeseen vulnerabilities. Nonetheless, recent developments suggest some best practices for mobile devices and applications(M. Hatamian(2020), K. Nakao, D. Inoue, M. Eto, and K. Yoshioka(2009)).

(1) **Make user authentication the highest priority:** One of the top priorities for mobile security is ensuring strong user authentication measures. This involves implementing secure methods for verifying the identity of the user before granting access to the device or sensitive data. By prioritizing user authentication, mobile devices can better protect against unauthorized access and potential data breaches.

(2) *Update mobile operating systems and on-board applications with security patches:* It is crucial to maintain the security of mobile devices by regularly updating the operating system and installed applications. Both Android and iOS (N. O. Alshammari, A. Mylonas, M. Sedky, J. Champion, and C. Bauer(2015)))

receive frequent updates from Google and Apple respectively, which address recent vulnerabilities and provide additional security and performance features. However, updating apps may also have drawbacks, such as reducing the app's overall performance and affecting the user's productivity. From a security perspective, updating apps may trigger a reverting process to ensure that the application conforms to the organization's security requirements and is free from vulnerabilities. This process may also involve analysing updated external components, such as third-party libraries, and new versions of the operating systems.

(3) ***Back up user data on a regular basis***: Creating backups is an essential method for preventing data loss or deletion, and it's important to adapt the backup schedule as data increases over time. User data such as individual files, media files, contacts, and other sensitive data should all be included in the backup. For mobile devices, remote backup is the obvious choice, involving copying and storing files in a private or public cloud. However, this method can be limited by slow transfer speeds due to upload limitations, antivirus scanners, and firewalls, as well as the cost of data uploading set by mobile internet providers. Moreover, there is no guarantee that data stored in the cloud will be kept private, but this concern can be addressed by encrypting data files. However, encrypting the files can extend the overall backup task duration if performed on the fly.

(4) ***Utilize encryption:*** Data encryption is a security measure that transforms data into an alternate form, making it unreadable for unauthorized individuals. Encryption is commonly used for data transmission over networks and for data stored on mobile devices. However, encryption requires a password to encrypt and decrypt data files. If the password is forgotten, data recovery can be problematic and not always successful. Reliance on publicly available encryption solutions can also create a false sense of security. It is strongly advised to avoid using public and insecure Wi-Fi without a secure transmission option such as a virtual private network (VPN). However, VPNs can be slower than regular internet connections depending on the distance between the server and client, current network traffic, and other factors.

(5) ***Enable remote data wipe:*** Enabling remote data wipe is an essential security measure for mobile devices. This feature allows users to remotely erase all data from their device in case it is lost or stolen, preventing unauthorized access to sensitive information. Remote wipe can be activated using a mobile device management (MDM) solution or through the device's built-in settings. It is important to note that remote data wipe should be used with caution as it permanently deletes all data, including personal information and files. Therefore, it is recommended to have a backup of important data before enabling this feature.

(6) ***Disable Bluetooth and Wi-Fi when not needed:*** Limiting the use of Bluetooth and Wi-Fi can help reduce the risk of vulnerabilities being exploited, although it should be noted that the vulnerabilities are not in the standards themselves, but in their implementation. It is important to mention that disabling these features requires intentional interaction from the user. However, there are tools available (such as Auto-Bluetooth) that can turn Bluetooth on or off automatically based on rules defined by the user, without any user interaction.

(7) ***Be aware of social engineering techniques:*** Social engineering techniques refer to the psychological manipulation of individuals to perform actions or divulge confidential information. Social engineering is a commonly used technique for attackers to gain unauthorized access to personal or business data. Therefore, it is essential to educate mobile device users about social engineering techniques and how to recognize them. Some of the techniques used by attackers include phishing, pretexting, baiting, and tailgating. Phishing attacks typically involve sending an email or message with a malicious link or attachment. Pretexting involves creating a fictional scenario to trick the user into revealing sensitive information. Baiting involves leaving a tempting item, such as a USB drive, in a public place to entice the user to pick it up and plug it into their device. Finally, tailgating involves following an authorized person into a restricted area to gain access. Therefore, users must remain vigilant and cautious when receiving messages, emails, or other forms of communication from unknown or suspicious sources. They should never click on links or download attachments unless they can verify the source's authenticity.

(8)Install mobile security and antivirus applications: . Installing a mobile security and antivirus application can be a helpful step in protecting your device from various security threats, as described earlier. However, as mentioned, there may be some side effects such as increased resource usage and battery drain. It is important to choose a reliable and efficient security application to minimize these effects.

In addition to installing a security application, it is important to follow good security practices such as keeping your device and apps updated, using strong passwords, avoiding untrusted websites and apps, and being cautious about clicking on links or downloading attachments from unknown sources. By combining these practices with a mobile security and antivirus application, you can significantly reduce the risk of security threats on your mobile device.

CONCLUSION

As the mobile application market continues to grow, mobile security remains an ongoing challenge in the ongoing arms race between attackers and defenders. Balancing risk and reward, security often involves trade-offs between defence and convenience. This paper investigates the potential risks and benefits of mobile security and the countermeasures to protect against negative events that can lead to asset loss. The paper presents a holistic view of mobile security, examining the negative events, conditions, and circumstances that can cause asset loss and the measures to provide effective protection for users. However, the ever-evolving landscape of technology requires ongoing attention to maintain security. During the 2019 World Economic Forum, participants acknowledged that the past ten years only marked the beginning of the global cybersecurity journey. Looking ahead, new architectures and collaborations will be necessary to address the new era of cybercrime, which will be empowered by emerging technologies such as 5G networks and infrastructure convergence, artificial intelligence, and biometrics. These technologies are expected to shape the next decade of global cybersecurity.

REFERENCE

Albasir, A. A., & Naik, K. (2014). SMOW: An energy-bandwidth aware web browsing technique for smartphones. *IEEE Access : Practical Innovations, Open Solutions*, 2, 1427–1441. 10.1109/ACCESS.2014.2365091

Alshammari, N. O., Mylonas, A., Sedky, M., Champion, J., & Bauer, C. (2015). Exploring the adoption of physical security controls in smartphones. *Proceedings of the International Conference on Human Aspects of Information Security, Privacy, and Trust*, (pp. 287–298). Springer. 10.1007/978-3-319-20376-8_26

Amin, A., Eldessouki, A., Magdy, M. T., Abdeen, N., Hindy, H., & Hegazy, I. (2019). AndroShield: Automated android applications vulnerability detection, a hybrid static and dynamicanalysis approach. *Information (Basel)*, 10(10), 326. 10.3390/info10100326

Carroll, A., Barnes, J., & Scornavacca, E. (2005). *"Consumer perceptions and attitudes towards mobile marketing," in Selected Readings on Telecommunications and Networking*. IGI Global.

Chen, Y., Xu, W., Peng, L., & Zhang, H. (2019). Light-weight and privacy-preserving authentication protocol for mobile payments in the context of IoT. IEEE Access. 10.1109/ACCESS.2019.2894062

Delac, G., Silic, M., & Krolo, J. (2011). Emerging security threats for mobile platforms. *Proceedings of the 34th International Convention MIPRO*, (pp. 1468–1473). IEEE.

Gkioulos, V., Wangen, G., Katsikas, S., Kavallieratos, G., & Kotzanikolaou, P. (2017). Security awareness of the digital natives. *Information (Basel)*, 8(2), 42. 10.3390/info8020042

Guo, B., Ouyang, Y., Guo, T., Cao, L., & Yu, Z. (2019). Enhancing mobile app user understanding and marketing with heterogeneous crowdsourced data: A review. *IEEE Access : Practical Innovations, Open Solutions*, 7, 68557–68571. 10.1109/ACCESS.2019.2918325

Gupta, R. K., Almuzaini, K. K., Pateriya, R., Shah, K., Shukla, P. K., & Akwafo, R. (2022). An improved secure key generation using enhanced identity-based encryption for cloud computing in large-scale 5G. *Wireless Communications and Mobile Computing*, 2022, 14. 10.1155/2022/7291250

Hatamian, M. (2020). Engineering privacy in smartphone apps: A technical guideline catalog for app developers. *IEEE Access : Practical Innovations, Open Solutions*, 8, 35429–35445. 10.1109/ACCESS.2020.2974911

He, D., Chan, S., & Guizani, M. (2015). Mobile application security: Malware threats and defenses. *IEEE Wireless Communications*, 22(1), 138–144. 10.1109/MWC.2015.7054729

Jayapandian, N. (2021). Cloud dynamic scheduling for Multimedia Data encryption using Tabu Search Algorithm. *Wireless Personal Communications*, 120(3), 2427–2447. 10.1007/s11277-021-08562-5

Koppanati, R. K., & Kumar, K. (2020). P-MEC: Polynomial congruence-based Multimedia encryption technique over cloud. *IEEE Consumer Electronics Magazine*, 10(5), 41–46. 10.1109/MCE.2020.3003127

Korczak, J., Hernes, M., & Bac, M. (2017). Collective intelligence supporting trading decisions on FOREX market. *Proceedings of the International Conference on Computational Collective Intelligence*, (pp. 113–122). Springer. 10.1007/978-3-319-67074-4_12

Mavoungou, S., Kaddoum, G., Taha, M., & Matar, G. (2016). Surveyon threats and attacks on mobile networks. *IEEE Access : Practical Innovations, Open Solutions*, 4, 4543–4572. 10.1109/ACCESS.2016.2601009

Mikhaylov, D., Zhukov, I., Starikovskiy, A., Kharkov, S., Tolstaya, A., & Zuykov, A. (2013). Review of malicious mobile applications, phone bugs and other cyber threats to mobile devices. *Proceedings of the 5th IEEE International Conference on Broadband Network & Multimedia Technology*, (pp. 302–305). IEEE. 10.1109/ICBNMT.2013.6823962

Mort, G. S., & Drennan, J. (2005). Marketing m-services: Establishing a usage benefit typology related to mobile user characteristics. *Journal of Database Marketing & Customer Strategy Management*, 12(4), 327–341. 10.1057/palgrave.dbm.3240269

Mylonas, A., Kastania, A., & Gritzalis, D. (2013). Delegate the smartphone user? Security awareness in smartphone platforms. *Computers & Security*, 34, 47–66. 10.1016/j.cose.2012.11.004

Nakao, K., Inoue, D., Eto, M., & Yoshioka, K. (2009). Practical correlation analysis between scan and malware profiles against zero-day attacks based on darknet monitoring. *IEICE Transactions on Information and Systems*, E92-D(5), 787–798. 10.1587/transinf.E92.D.787

Ortiz, G., Garc'ıa-de-Prado, A., Berrocal, J., & Hernandez, J. (2019). Improving resource consumption in context- aware mobile applications through alternative architectural styles. *IEEE Access : Practical Innovations, Open Solutions*, 7, 65228–65250. 10.1109/ACCESS.2019.2918239

Papageorgiou, A., Strigkos, M., Politou, E., Alepis, E., Solanas, A., & Patsakis, C. (2018). Security and privacy analysis of mobile health applications: The alarming state of practice. *IEEE Access: Practical Innovations, Open Solutions*, 6, 9390–9403. 10.1109/ACCESS.2018.2799522

Rayappan, D., & Pandiyan, M. (2021). Lightweight Feistel structure based hybrid-crypto model for multimedia data security over uncertain cloud environment. *Wireless Networks*, 27(2), 981–999. 10.1007/s11276-020-02486-x

Shishkova, T. (2021). IT threat evolution in Q3 2021. *Mobile statistics*. https://securelist.com/it-threatevolution-in-q3-2021-mobile-statistics/105020/

Song, W., Tjondronegoro, D., & Docherty, M. (2010). Exploration and optimization of user experience in viewing videos on a mobile phone. *International Journal of Software Engineering and Knowledge Engineering*, 20(8), 1045–1075. 10.1142/S0218194010005067

Thotadi, C., Debbala, M., Rao, S., Eeralla, A., Palaniswamy, B., Mookherji, S., Odelu, V., & Reddy, A. G. (2024). E-Brightpass: A Secure way to access social networks on smartphones. *Cyber Security and Applications*, 2, 100021. 10.1016/j.csa.2023.100021

Valcke, J. (2016). Best practices in mobile security. *Biometric Technology Today*, 2016(3), 9–11. 10.1016/S0969-4765(16)30051-0

Wazid, M., Zeadally, S., & Das, A. K. (2019). Mobile banking: evolution and threats: malware threats and security solutions. *IEEE Consumer Electronics Magazine*, 8(2), 56–60. 10.1109/MCE.2018.2881291

Chapter 14
Security Aspects of Blockchain Technology

Naga Venkata Yaswanth Lankadasu
Lovely Professional University, India

Devendra Babu Pesarlanka
Lovely Professional University, India

Ajay Sharma
https://orcid.org/0000-0001-6620-4805
upGrad Education Private Limited, India

Shamneesh Sharma
https://orcid.org/0000-0003-3102-0808
upGrad Education Private Limited, India

ABSTRACT

Recently, there has been a notable increase in the advancement of multimodal emotion analysis systems. These systems try to get a comprehensive knowledge of human emotions by combining data from several sources, including text, voice, video, and images. This complete strategy tackles the constraints of text-only sentiment analysis, which could disregard subtle emotional expressions. This chapter examines the difficulties and approaches related to analyzing emotions utilizing many modes of data, specifically emphasizing combining data, extracting features, and ensuring scalability. This underscores the significance of creating strong fusion techniques and network architectures to integrate various data modalities efficiently. The research also explores the utilization of these systems in domains such as social media sentiment analysis and clinical evaluations, showcasing their capacity to improve decision-making and user experiences.

DOI: 10.4018/979-8-3693-2869-9.ch014

INTRODUCTION

Blockchain technology revolutionizes the traditional systems by providing a decentralized, immutable ledger for recording transactions across a network of computers. Originating as the underlying technology behind Bitcoin, blockchain has evolved to encompass a wide array of applications beyond cryptocurrency, including supply chain management, voting systems, and smart contracts. Its core principles of transparency, security, and decentralization make it highly appealing for industries seeking to streamline operations and enhance trust among participants (S. Sharma & Mishra, 2023). Through cryptographic techniques and consensus algorithms, blockchain ensures data integrity and eliminates the need for intermediaries in verifying transactions (Gupta et al., 2022). As a disruptive force in the digital landscape, blockchain holds immense potential to reshape various sectors and empower individuals with greater control over their data and assets.

Figure 1. The key structures of blockchain technology

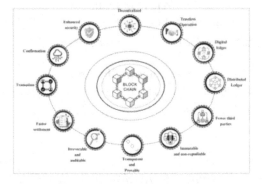

Definition and Importance of Blockchain Security

Blockchain security refers to the measures and protocols put in place to safeguard blockchain networks, transactions, and data from unauthorized access (M. R. Islam et al., 2021). As blockchain technology becomes increasingly pervasive across various industries, ensuring its security is paramount to maintain trust, integrity, and reliability in the ecosystem (Pagani, 2022). The decentralized and immutable nature of blockchain makes it inherently secure, but vulnerabilities still exist, necessitating robust security measures to mitigate risks.

Security in blockchain encompasses various aspects, including cryptographic techniques, consensus mechanisms, network security, smart contract security, and regulatory compliance (Kishore & Sharma, 2016). By addressing these components comprehensively, blockchain systems can maintain their integrity, resist attacks, and uphold the trust of users.

Overview of the Scope and Objectives of the Chapter

The major aim of this chapter is to explore into the intricate facets of security within blockchain technology. It will provide an inclusive understanding of the challenges, mechanisms, and best practices associated with securing blockchain networks. The chapter will explore the foundational concepts of blockchain security, analyse common threats and vulnerabilities, discuss preventive measures and security practices, and examine regulatory considerations.

Through this exploration, readers will gain insights into the critical role of security in blockchain technology and its implications for various stakeholders, including businesses, governments, and individuals. By grasping the nuances of blockchain security, readers will be better equipped to navigate the evolving landscape of decentralized systems and effectively mitigate security risks (Leng et al., 2020).

Foundational Concepts of Blockchain Security

To understand the security landscape of blockchain technology, it's essential to grasp its foundational concepts. At its core, blockchain depend on cryptographic principles to ensure the integrity and immutability of data (Tapscott & Tapscott, 2016). Cryptography plays a pivotal role in securing transactions, protecting identities, and establishing trust within the network.

One fundamental concept is the use of cryptographic hash functions, which generate unique identifiers for blocks of data (A. Sharma et al., 2022). These hashes serve as digital fingerprints, enabling quick verification of data integrity. Additionally, blockchain employs asymmetric cryptography for secure key management (Z. Zheng et al., 2018). Public and private key pairs enable secure authentication and digital signatures, ensuring only authorized groups can access and modify data.

Another important consideration is consensus procedures, which control how transactions are authorised and added to the blockchain. Compromise algorithms like Proof of Work (PoW), Proof of Stake (PoS), and Practical Byzantine Fault Tolerance (PBFT) establish agreement among network participants, prohibiting double-spending and malicious activity (Swan, 2015).

UNDERSTANDING SECURITY CHALLENGES IN BLOCKCHAIN TECHNOLOGY

Blockchain technology, often hailed for its decentralization and transparency, encounters a plethora of security challenges that demand attention to uphold its efficacy and dependability across diverse applications. Among these concerns are the formidable 51% attacks, smart contract vulnerabilities, and the persistent need to address privacy apprehensions. Moreover, scalability and performance bottlenecks, alongside regulatory ambiguities and evolving compliance frameworks, pose substantial hurdles for blockchain adoption and innovation (Agbo et al., 2019). Confronting these multifaceted security challenges necessitates a concerted effort, integrating technical fortification, regulatory clarity, and industry collaboration, to fortify the foundation of blockchain technology and unleash its transformative potential (Fraga-Lamas & Fernández-Caramés, 2019).

Common Security Threats in Blockchain Systems

Blockchain technology, celebrated for its decentralization and transparency, is not without its share of security challenges, necessitating vigilant mitigation strategies to uphold its effectiveness and trustworthiness across diverse applications. Among the paramount security concerns are vulnerabilities inherent in smart contracts, which, if exploited, can lead to significant financial losses, and compromise the integrity of the entire blockchain network. Furthermore, the persistent threat of 51percentage attacks looms large, where in a single entity gaining majority control of the network's computing power could potentially manipulate the transactions or undermine the consensus mechanism. Privacy remains a pressing issue, particularly in public blockchains, where transaction data is visible to all participants, necessitating innovative approaches to balance transparency with confidentiality.

The 51% Attacks

51% attacks occur when a single entity or a group gain control over the majority (51 percentage or more) of the computing state within a blockchain network. This enables them to manipulate transaction confirmations, reverse transactions, and potentially double-spend cryptocurrencies. By controlling most the network's computational resources, attackers can undermine the decentralization and security of the blockchain (Amin, 2020).

Double-Spending Attacks

Double-spending attacks involve the malicious duplication of digital assets, allowing an attacker to spend the same cryptocurrency multiple times (J. Zheng et al., 2021). In a blockchain network, transactions are typically authorized through a consensus mechanism to prevent double spending. However, if an attacker successfully executes a double-spending attack, it can undermine the integrity and reliability of the blockchain, leading to financial losses and loss of trust among users.

Sybil Attacks

Sybil attacks occur when a malicious actor creates multiple fake identities within a blockchain network to gain control or influence over the network. By controlling a significant portion of the network's nodes, the attacker can manipulate transactions, disrupt the consensus process, and launch other attacks, such as spamming the network with invalid transactions (Adele et al., 2024). Sybil attacks pose a serious threat to the decentralization and security of blockchain networks.

Smart Contract Vulnerabilities

Smart contracts are susceptible to vulnerabilities and bugs that can be exploited by attackers to steal funds, manipulate contract outcomes, or disrupt the functioning of decentralized applications. Common smart contract vulnerabilities include re-entrancy attacks, integer overflow/underflow, and logic errors, which can have significant implications for the security and reliability of blockchain-based systems.

Impact of Security Breaches on Blockchain Networks

Security breaches in blockchain networks can have severe repercussions on the integrity, trust, and functionality of the entire ecosystem. Some of the potential impacts of security breaches include:

Financial Losses

Security breaches can result in the theft of digital assets, leading to financial losses for users, investors, and businesses operating within the blockchain ecosystem. Double-spending attacks and smart contract vulnerabilities can result in significant monetary losses.

Loss of Trust

Security breaches undermine the trust and confidence of users in the security and reliability of blockchain networks. A high-profile security breach can tarnish the reputation of the affected blockchain platform or cryptocurrency, leading to decreased adoption and usage.

Disruption of Operations

Security breaches can disrupt the normal functioning of blockchain networks, causing delays in transaction processing, network congestion, and service outages. This can impact the usability and efficiency of blockchain-based applications and services.

Regulatory Scrutiny

Security breaches may attract regulatory scrutiny and intervention, especially if they involve the loss of user funds or violations of financial regulations. Regulatory actions could include investigations, fines, or even the imposition of stricter regulations on blockchain technology and cryptocurrency markets.

SECURITY MECHANISMS IN BLOCKCHAIN TECHNOLOGY

Cryptography Fundamentals

Cryptography serves as the cornerstone of security in blockchain technology, providing the framework for securing transactions, ensuring privacy, and maintaining the integrity of the blockchain. Using advanced cryptographic techniques, blockchain systems can establish trust and transparency among participants, fostering a decentralized and tamper-resistant environment for conducting transactions. Key cryptographic fundamentals include public-key cryptography, which enables secure communication and transaction verification without the need for a shared secret key (Djordjevic & Djordjevic, 2019). Additionally, hash functions play a crucial role in ensuring data integrity by generating unique identifiers for each block and transaction. Digital signatures further enhance security by providing a mechanism for proving the authenticity and integrity of messages or transactions within the blockchain network. As blockchain technology continues to evolve, cryptography remains indispensable in safeguarding sensitive data and mitigating security risks, reinforcing the foundation of trust and reliability in decentralized systems.

Public-key Cryptography

Public-key cryptography, also referred to as asymmetric cryptography, revolutionizes secure communication within blockchain networks. Through the generation of unique pairs of cryptographic keys – a public key for encryption and a private key for decryption – participants can engage in secure transactions and communication without the requirement of a shared secret key. This innovative approach not only enhances the security and privacy of blockchain transactions but also establishes a robust foundation for trust and integrity within the decentralized ecosystem.

Hash Functions

Hash functions are mathematical algorithms that convert input data into a fixed-size string of characters, known as a hash value or digest. In blockchain technology, hash functions ensure data integrity by generating unique identifiers for each block and transaction. Popular hash functions like SHA-256 produce hash values that are virtually impossible to reverse-engineer, providing a robust means of verifying data integrity within the blockchain network.

Digital Signatures

Digital signatures provide a mechanism for proving the authenticity and integrity of messages or transactions in the blockchain network. Using a combination of public-key cryptography and hash functions, digital signatures enable participants to sign transactions with their private keys, allowing others to verify the signature using the corresponding public key.

Secure Hash Algorithms (SHA)

Secure Hash Algorithms (SHA), notably SHA-256, serve as the bedrock of blockchain security, providing a formidable defence against tampering and data manipulation. Widely adopted in blockchain technology, SHA algorithms generate cryptographic hash functions that uniquely identify input data, ensuring the immutability and integrity of transactions stored on the blockchain. Leveraging the computational complexity of SHA functions, blockchain networks uphold their resistance to malicious attacks and unauthorized modifications, reinforcing trust and reliability in decentralized systems.

Consensus Algorithms and Their Role in Security

Consensus algorithms serve as the cornerstone of security and stability in blockchain networks, orchestrating agreement among participants regarding transaction validity and ledger state. By establishing a unified consensus mechanism, blockchain networks ensure the integrity and immutability of data across distributed nodes, fostering trust and reliability in decentralized ecosystems (Venkatesan & Rahayu, 2024). Common consensus algorithms, such as Proof of Work (PoW) and Proof of Stake (PoS), employ diverse mechanisms to incentivize network participants and deter malicious behaviour, thereby fortifying the resilience of blockchain networks against adversarial attacks and ensuring the continuity of decentralized operations. Common consensus algorithms include:

Figure 2. Core components of blockchain technology

Proof of Work (PoW)

PoW, the pioneering consensus algorithm utilized in Bitcoin and numerous other cryptocurrencies, fosters network security through a competitive mining process. Miners race to solve intricate mathematical puzzles, with the victor granted the privilege to append a new block to the blockchain. PoW's robust security model is rooted in its economic disincentives against blockchain manipulation, thus reinforcing the integrity and trustworthiness of decentralized systems.

Proof of Stake (PoS)

In PoS-based blockchains, validators are dynamically appointed to forge new blocks based on their cryptocurrency holdings or stake. This approach introduces a more energy-efficient consensus mechanism, mitigating the environmental impact associated with PoW while enhancing scalability and transaction throughput. PoS incentivizes network participation and fosters a distributed ecosystem, where validators play a pivotal role in maintaining network consensus and integrity.

Delegated Proof of Stake (DPoS)

DPoS is a variation of PoS where token holders vote for a select number of delegates to validate transactions and produce blocks on their behalf. DPoS augments the PoS model by empowering token holders to elect a limited number of delegates responsible for transaction validation and block production. By delegating block-producing responsibilities to a trusted subset of nodes, DPoS optimizes network efficiency and scalability without compromising decentralization. This governance-centric approach fosters community engagement and consensus-building, ensuring the sustained resilience and performance of blockchain networks.

CASE STUDIES: SECURITY BREACHES IN BLOCKCHAIN SYSTEMS

Figure 3. Blockchain security breaches (or case studies: security breaches in blockchain systems)

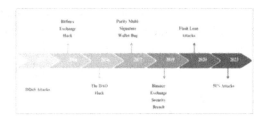

The DAO Hack

The Decentralized Autonomous Organization (DAO) was a groundbreaking Ethereum-based venture capital fund that aimed to operate without traditional management structures, relying instead on smart contracts to automate investment decisions (Kaur et al., 2023). However, in June 2016, a vulnerability in the DAO's smart contract code was exploited, leading to the theft of approximately $50 million worth of Ether.

The vulnerability allowed an attacker to execute a recursive call exploit, draining funds from the DAO contract into a child DAO under the attacker's control. The incident resulted in a contentious hard fork of the Ethereum blockchain to reverse the theft, leading to the creation of Ethereum (ETH) and Ethereum Classic (ETC) as separate cryptocurrencies.

Parity Multi-Signature Wallet Bug

Parity Technologies, a prominent blockchain development company, developed a multi-signature wallet contract for the Ethereum blockchain. In July 2017, a critical vulnerability in the Parity multi-signature wallet code was discovered, leading to the accidental freezing of over $300 million worth of Ether.

The bug allowed a user to trigger a flaw in the smart contract code, effectively locking access to the funds stored in the affected wallets. Despite efforts to recover the frozen funds, including unsuccessful attempts to reach a consensus on a network-wide hard fork, a significant portion of the funds remained inaccessible (Zhang et al., 2022).

Bitfinex Exchange Hack

In August 2016, Bitfinex, one of the largest cryptocurrency exchanges at the time, experienced a major security breach resulting in the theft of approximately 120,000 bitcoins, valued at over $70 million at the time of the incident.

The hackers exploited vulnerabilities in Bitfinex's multi-signature wallet system and security procedures, allowing them to gain unauthorized access to customer funds. The exchange subsequently implemented security enhancements, reimbursed affected users, and gradually resumed operations after the incident.

Binance Exchange Security Breach

In May 2019, Binance, one of the world's largest cryptocurrency exchanges, suffered a security breach resulting in the theft of over 7,000 bitcoins, worth approximately $40 million at the time (Bosri et al., 2020).

The hackers employed a combination of phishing attacks, malware, and API key manipulation to gain access to user accounts and execute unauthorized transactions (Disli et al., 2022). Despite the significant loss, Binance quickly responded to the breach by implementing enhanced security measures, conducting a thorough investigation, and reimbursing affected users from its SAFU (Secure Asset Fund for Users) insurance fund.

EMERGING TRENDS IN BLOCKCHAIN SECURITY

As blockchain technology continues to evolve, new trends and developments in blockchain security are emerging to address evolving threats and challenges (Falaiye et al., 2024). These trends reflect the ongoing efforts of researchers, developers, and security professionals to enhance the resilience and robustness of blockchain networks. Some of the notable emerging trends in blockchain security include:

Figure 4. Emerging trends in blockchain security

Privacy-Enhancing Technologies

Privacy has become an increasingly important consideration in blockchain systems, especially in applications involving sensitive data or transactions. Emerging privacy-enhancing technologies such as zero-knowledge proofs, homomorphic encryption, and ring signatures enable users to transact and interact on blockchain networks while preserving the confidentiality of their data and identities (Bodemer, 2023). These technologies are crucial for ensuring privacy compliance and protecting user confidentiality in blockchain-based applications.

Secure Multi-Party Computation (MPC)

Secure multi-party computation (MPC) protocols allow multiple parties to collaboratively compute a function using their private inputs while keeping those inputs confidential. MPC holds promise for enhancing the security and privacy of blockchain systems by enabling collaborative computations without exposing sensitive data to unauthorized parties (Merino & Cabrero-Holgueras, 2023). MPC can be applied in various use cases, including decentralized finance (DeFi), supply chain management, and data sharing, to achieve privacy-preserving and secure computations on blockchain networks.

Federated Byzantine Agreement (FBA)

Federated Byzantine Agreement (FBA) is a new consensus method that combines the advantages of Byzantine Fault Tolerance (BFT) and decentralised governance (Tumas et al., 2023). FBA enables multiple independent validators to collectively agree on the validity of transactions and the state of the blockchain without requiring all nodes to participate in the consensus process (Hayes et al., 2023). This approach offers scalability, resilience, and censorship resistance while maintaining decentralization and security in blockchain networks. FBA is gaining traction in enterprise blockchain deployments and permissioned blockchain platforms.

Post-Quantum Cryptography

The development of quantum computing poses huge risks to the cryptographic basis of blockchain security. Post-quantum cryptography (PQC) aims to develop cryptographic algorithms and protocols that remain secure against quantum attacks (Nithila et al., 2024). Researchers are actively exploring and developing post-quantum cryptographic primitives, such as lattice-based cryptography, hash-based signatures, and multivariate polynomial cryptography, to safeguard blockchain networks against the threat of quantum adversaries (Hekkala et al., 2023). Integration of post-quantum cryptography is essential for future-proofing blockchain systems and ensuring their long-term security in the era of quantum computing.

Decentralized Identity and Self-Sovereign Identity (SSI)

Decentralized identity and self-sovereign identity (SSI) solutions empower individuals to own, control, and manage their digital identities without relying on centralized authorities or intermediaries (M. T. Islam et al., 2021). By leveraging blockchain technology, decentralized identity solutions enable secure, privacy-preserving, and interoperable identity management, authentication, and credentialing. SSI holds promise for revolutionizing identity management systems, enhancing user privacy and security, and enabling seamless identity verification and authentication in various domains, including finance, healthcare, and digital identity (Stockburger et al., 2021).

PRACTICAL GUIDELINES FOR SECURING BLOCKCHAIN APPLICATIONS

Securing blockchain applications is paramount to safeguarding sensitive data, protecting assets, and maintaining trust within the ecosystem (Chang et al., 2022). Below are practical guidelines to enhance the security of blockchain applications:

Figure 5. Practical guidelines for securing blockchain applications

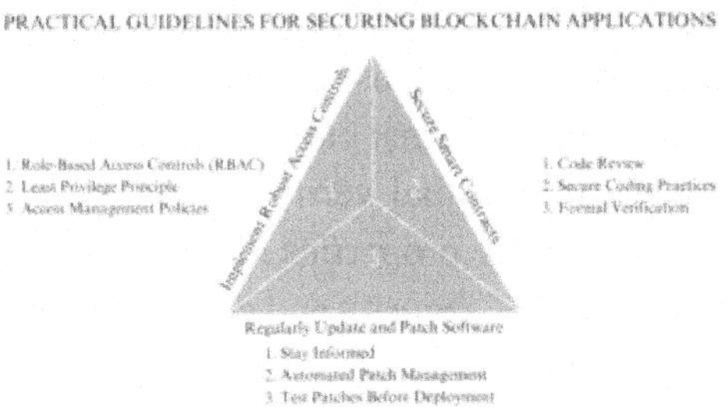

Implement Robust Access Controls

Access control is fundamental to ensuring that only authorized users can interact with blockchain applications and perform specific actions. Here's how to build robust access controls:

Role-Based Access Controls (RBAC): Define roles within the blockchain application, such as administrator, user, and auditor, and assign specific permissions to each role based on their responsibilities and requirements (Kumar & Ahmad Khan, 2024).

Least Privilege Principle: Adhere to the principle of least privilege, which states that users should only be granted the minimum level of access necessary to perform their job functions. Limit access to sensitive functions and data to authorized personnel only.

Access Management Policies: Implement access management policies to govern user access to blockchain applications (Hirani et al., 2019). Regularly review and update access controls to reflect changes in user roles, responsibilities, and organizational requirements.

Secure Smart Contracts

Self-executing contracts with predetermined terms and conditions expressed in code are known as smart contracts. Securing smart contracts is critical to preventing vulnerabilities and ensuring the integrity of blockchain applications (Lone & Naaz, 2021). Here's how to secure smart contracts:

Code Review: Conduct thorough code reviews to identify and mitigate security vulnerabilities in smart contract code. Use static analysis tools and peer reviews to identify potential flaws and bugs.

Secure Coding Practices: Follow secure coding practices when writing smart contracts. Avoid common pitfalls such as re-entrancy vulnerabilities, integer overflow/underflow, and unchecked external calls (Ghorashi et al., 2023).

Formal Verification: Utilize formal verification techniques to mathematically prove the correctness and security properties of smart contracts. Formal verification provides strong assurances of security and correctness but requires specialized expertise and resources (Satti et al., 2024).

Regularly Update and Patch Software

Keeping blockchain software, frameworks, and libraries up to date with the latest security patches and updates is essential to addressing known vulnerabilities and mitigating security risks (Vaseei, 2024). Here's how to ensure software is regularly updated and patched:

Stay Informed: Stay informed about security advisories and updates released by blockchain software vendors and open-source communities (Lankadasu et al., 2024). Subscribe to security mailing lists and follow relevant forums and blogs to receive timely updates.

Automated Patch Management: Implement automated patch management systems to streamline the process of deploying security patches and updates across blockchain infrastructure. Automate patch deployment wherever possible to ensure timely implementation of critical security fixes.

Test Patches Before Deployment: Before deploying patches in a production environment, thoroughly test them in a controlled testing environment to ensure compatibility and functionality. Conduct regression testing to verify that patching does not introduce new issues or break existing functionality (Lai et al., 2024).

CONCLUSION

In this chapter, we've explored the vital security aspects of blockchain technology within the context of computational intelligence and distributed frameworks. Blockchain's decentralized nature offers inherent security benefits, but it also poses challenges that demand robust measures. We've defined blockchain security and emphasized its crucial role in protecting networks, transactions, and data. Through analysis of common threats like 51% attacks and smart contract vulnerabilities, we underscored the importance of proactive security practices. Real-world case studies illustrated the significant impact of security breaches on blockchain networks. Furthermore, we discussed emerging trends such as secure consensus mechanisms and advances in cryptographic techniques, highlighting ongoing efforts to enhance blockchain security. Finally, practical guidelines were provided for securing blockchain applications, offering actionable insights for stakeholders. As blockchain technology continues to evolve, ensuring its security remains paramount for fostering trust, transparency, and innovation in the digital age.

REFERENCES

Adele, G., Borah, A., Paranjothi, A., & Khan, M. S. (2024). A Survey and Comparative Analysis of Methods for Countering Sybil Attacks in VANETs. *2024 IEEE 14th Annual Computing and Communication Workshop and Conference (CCWC)*, (pp. 178–183). IEEE.

Agbo, C. C., Mahmoud, Q. H., & Eklund, J. M. (2019). Blockchain technology in healthcare: A systematic review. *Health Care*, 7(2), 56.30987333

Amin, M. R. (2020). *51\% attacks on blockchain: a solution architecture for blockchain to secure iot with proof of work*. Research Gate.

Bodemer, O. (2023). Decentralized Innovation: Exploring the Impact of Blockchain Technology in Software Development. *Authorea Preprints*.

Bosri, R., Rahman, M. S., Bhuiyan, M. Z. A., & Al Omar, A. (2020). Integrating blockchain with artificial intelligence for privacy-preserving recommender systems. *IEEE Transactions on Network Science and Engineering*, 8(2), 1009–1018. 10.1109/TNSE.2020.3031179

Chang, A., El-Rayes, N., & Shi, J. (2022). Blockchain technology for supply chain management: A comprehensive review. *FinTech*, 1(2), 191–205. 10.3390/fintech1020015

Disli, M., Abd Rabbo, F., Leneeuw, T., & Nagayev, R. (2022). Cryptocurrency comovements and crypto exchange movement: The relocation of Binance. *Finance Research Letters*, 48, 102989. 10.1016/j.frl.2022.102989

Djordjevic, I. B., & Djordjevic, I. B. (2019). Conventional Cryptography Fundamentals. *Physical-Layer Security and Quantum Key Distribution*, (pp. 65–91). Research Gate.

Falaiye, T., Elufioye, O. A., Awonuga, K. F., Ibeh, C. V., Olatoye, F. O., & Mhlongo, N. Z. (2024). Financial Inclusion Through Technology: A Review Of Trends In Emerging Markets. *International Journal of Management \& Entrepreneurship Research*, 6(2), 368–379.

Fraga-Lamas, P., & Fernández-Caramés, T. M. (2019). A review on blockchain technologies for an advanced and cyber-resilient automotive industry. *IEEE Access : Practical Innovations, Open Solutions*, 7, 17578–17598. 10.1109/ACCESS.2019.2895302

Ghorashi, N. S., Rahimi, M., Sirous, R., & Javan, R. (2023). The Intersection of Radiology With Blockchain and Smart Contracts: A Perspective. *Cureus*, 15(10). 10.7759/cureus.4694138021752

Gupta, M., Sharma, S., & Sharma, C. (2022). Security and Privacy Issues in Blockchained IoT: Principles, Challenges and Counteracting Actions. In *Blockchain Technology* (pp. 27–56). CRC Press.

Hayes, J., Aneiba, A., Gaber, M., Islam, M. S., & Abozariba, R. (2023). FBA-SDN: a federated byzantine approach for blockchain-based collaborative intrusion detection in edge SDN. *2023 IEEE International Conference on Communications Workshops (ICC Workshops)*, (pp. 427–433). IEEE. 10.1109/ICCWorkshops57953.2023.10283805

Hekkala, J., Muurman, M., Halunen, K., & Vallivaara, V. (2023). Implementing post-quantum cryptography for developers. *SN Computer Science*, 4(4), 365. 10.1007/s42979-023-01724-1

Hirani, M., Halgamuge, M. N., & Hang, P. D. T. (2019). Data security models developed by blockchain technology for different business domains. *2019 11th International Conference on Knowledge and Systems Engineering (KSE)*, (p. 1–10). Research Gate.

Islam, M. R., Rahman, M. M., Mahmud, M., Rahman, M. A., Mohamad, M. H. S., & Associates. (2021). A review on blockchain security issues and challenges. *2021 IEEE 12th Control and System Graduate Research Colloquium (ICSGRC)*. IEEE.

Islam, M. T., Nasir, M. K., Hasan, M. M., Faruque, M. G. G., Hossain, M. S., & Azad, M. M. (2021). Blockchain-based decentralized digital self-sovereign identity wallet for secure transaction. *Adv. Sci. Technol. Eng. Syst. J*, 6(2), 977–983. 10.25046/aj0602112

Kaur, G., Habibi Lashkari, A., Sharafaldin, I., & Habibi Lashkari, Z. (2023). Blockchain Security. In *Understanding Cybersecurity Management in Decentralized Finance: Challenges, Strategies, and Trends* (pp. 71–89). Springer. 10.1007/978-3-031-23340-1_4

Kishore, K., & Sharma, S. (2016). Evolution of Wireless Sensor Networks as the framework of Internet of Things-A Review. *International Journal OfEmerging Research in Management &TechnologyI*, 5(12), 49–52.

Kumar, R., & Ahmad Khan, R. (2024). Securing military computing with the blockchain. *Computer Fraud \& Security, 2024*(2).

Lai, X., Zhang, Y., & Luo, H. (2024). A low-cost blockchain node deployment algorithm for the internet of things. *Peer-to-Peer Networking and Applications*, 17(2), 1–11. 10.1007/s12083-023-01615-5

Lankadasu, N. V. Y., Pesarlanka, D. B., Sharma, A., Sharma, S., & Gochhait, S. (2024). Skin Cancer Classification Using a Convolutional Neural Network: An Exploration into Deep Learning. *2024 ASU International Conference in Emerging Technologies for Sustainability and Intelligent Systems (ICETSIS)*, (pp. 1047–1052). IEEE. 10.1109/ICETSIS61505.2024.10459368

Leng, J., Zhou, M., Zhao, J. L., Huang, Y., & Bian, Y. (2020). Blockchain security: A survey of techniques and research directions. *IEEE Transactions on Services Computing*, 15(4), 2490–2510. 10.1109/TSC.2020.3038641

Lone, A. H., & Naaz, R. (2021). Applicability of Blockchain smart contracts in securing Internet and IoT: A systematic literature review. *Computer Science Review*, 39, 100360. 10.1016/j.cosrev.2020.100360

Merino, L.-H., & Cabrero-Holgueras, J. (2023). Secure Multi-Party Computation. *Trends in Data Protection and Encryption Technologies*, (pp. 89–92). IEEE.

Nithila, E. E., Rosi, A., & others. (2024). A Survey about Post Quantum Cryptography Methods. *EAI Endorsed Transactions on Internet of Things, 10.*

Pagani, A. (2022). QUIC Bitcoin: Fast and Secure Peer-to-Peer Payments and Payment Channels. *2022 IEEE Future Networks World Forum (FNWF)*, (pp. 578–584). IEEE.

Satti, S. R., Lankadasu, J. S. K., Sharma, A., Sharma, S., & Gochhait, S. (2024). Deep Learning in Medical Image Diagnosis for COVID-19. *2024 ASU International Conference in Emerging Technologies for Sustainability and Intelligent Systems (ICETSIS)*, (pp. 1858–1865). IEEE. 10.1109/ICETSIS61505.2024.10459430

Sharma, A., Guleria, V., & Jaiswal, V. (2022). The Future of Blockchain Technology, Recent Advancement and Challenges. In *Blockchain and Deep Learning: Future Trends and Enabling Technologies* (pp. 329–349). Springer.

Sharma, S., & Mishra, N. (2023). Horizoning recent trends in the security of smart cities: Exploratory analysis using latent semantic analysis. *Journal of Intelligent & Fuzzy Systems, Preprint*, 1–18. 10.3233/JIFS-235210

Stockburger, L., Kokosioulis, G., Mukkamala, A., Mukkamala, R. R., & Avital, M. (2021). Blockchain-enabled decentralized identity management: The case of self-sovereign identity in public transportation. *Blockchain: Research and Applications*, 2(2), 100014.

Swan, M. (2015). *Blockchain: Blueprint for a new economy*. O'Reilly Media, Inc.

Tapscott, D., & Tapscott, A. (2016). *Blockchain revolution: how the technology behind bitcoin is changing money, business, and the world*. Penguin.

Tumas, V., Rivera, S., Magoni, D., & State, R. (2023). Federated Byzantine Agreement Protocol Robustness to Targeted Network Attacks. *2023 IEEE Symposium on Computers and Communications (ISCC)*, (pp. 443–449). IEEE. 10.1109/ISCC58397.2023.10217935

Vaseei, M. (2024). A Conceptual Framework for Blockchain-Based, Intelligent, and Agile Supply Chain. In *Information Logistics for Organizational Empowerment and Effective Supply Chain Management* (pp. 150–162). IGI Global.

Venkatesan, K., & Rahayu, S. B. (2024). Blockchain security enhancement: An approach towards hybrid consensus algorithms and machine learning techniques. *Scientific Reports*, 14(1), 1149. 10.1038/s41598-024-51578-738212390

Zhang, H., Zou, X., Xie, G., & Li, Z. (2022). Blockchain Multi-signature Wallet System Based on QR Code Communication. *CCF China Blockchain Conference*, (pp. 31–48). Research Gate. 10.1007/978-981-19-8877-6_3

Zheng, J., Huang, H., Li, C., Zheng, Z., & Guo, S. (2021). Revisiting double-spending attacks on the bitcoin blockchain: new findings. *2021 IEEE/ACM 29th International Symposium on Quality of Service (IWQOS)*. IEEE.

Zheng, Z., Xie, S., Dai, H.-N., Chen, X., & Wang, H. (2018). Blockchain challenges and opportunities: A survey. *International Journal of Web and Grid Services*, 14(4), 352–375. 10.1504/IJWGS.2018.095647

Chapter 15
Leveraging Blockchain Technology for Sustainable Development Goals:
A Comprehensive Overview

Tarun Kumar Vashishth
https://orcid.org/0000-0001-9916-9575
IIMT University, India

Vikas Sharma
https://orcid.org/0000-0001-8173-4548
IIMT University, India

Kewal Krishan Sharma
https://orcid.org/0009-0001-2504-9607
IIMT University, India

Prashant Kumar
IIMT University, India

Rakesh Prasad Joshi
IIMT University, India

ABSTRACT

This chapter offers a thorough examination of the way blockchain generation can make a contribution to the realization of sustainable development goals (SDGs) mounted by the United Nations. Blockchain's inherent functions, inclusive of trans-

DOI: 10.4018/979-8-3693-2869-9.ch015

parency, and immutability, position it as a powerful tool for addressing international challenges in regions like poverty, healthcare, and renewable strength. By exploring real-world applications in financial inclusion, healthcare, delivery chain management, renewable energy, and governance, the chapter underscores the potential of blockchain to decorate transparency, accountability, and performance. It discusses the present literature, hit implementations, and case studies whilst highlighting the demanding situations, including scalability and regulatory concerns. Emphasizing collaboration, capacity building, and accountable use, the chapter advocates for blockchain's pivotal role in riding sustainable development and fostering a extra equitable and resilient future.

INTRODUCTION

Blockchain era, in the beginning conceived because the backbone of Bitcoin, has advanced some distance beyond its initial use case, providing transformative ability throughout various sectors. It's immutable, transparent, and decentralized nature makes it specially appropriate for addressing a number of the most urgent international challenges articulated within the United Nations' Sustainable Development Goals (SDGs). Blockchain can decorate transparency in deliver chains, facilitate secure and inclusive economic transactions, and permit green and tamper-proof control of public records. Furthermore, while integrated with cloud computing, blockchain's skills are drastically amplified. Cloud computing gives scalable and bendy infrastructure, making blockchain solutions greater available and green by using decreasing the limitations to entry associated with excessive computational expenses. By leveraging cloud-based totally blockchain systems, groups can install and manage blockchain programs with more ease, improving their capability to scale operations and collaborate across borders. This synergy among blockchain and cloud computing can lead to progressive solutions that address problems including poverty, inequality, and weather change via presenting robust frameworks for resource management, power distribution, and democratic governance (Vashishth et al., 2024).

Background and Motivation

Relevance of Sustainable Development Goals (SDGs) in the Global Context: In current years, the global community has identified the want for concerted efforts to cope with worldwide challenges and improve the well-being of humans global. The Sustainable Development Goals (SDGs), mounted by using the United Nations, encapsulate a comprehensive framework aimed toward tackling various interconnected issues. These 17 goals consist of eradicating poverty, ensuring best training, promoting gender equality, and addressing climate trade. The SDGs offer a roadmap for a sustainable and equitable future, reflecting the collective aspirations of countries around the sector.

Identification of Challenges in Achieving SDGs: Despite the noble intentions in the back of the SDGs, numerous challenges impede their awareness. Issues including poverty, inequality, environmental degradation, and inadequate get right of entry to to primary requirements persist in many regions. Traditional systems face hurdles related to transparency, responsibility, and inefficiencies, hindering effective implementation of sustainable development projects. Recognizing and knowledge those demanding situations is crucial for devising innovative solutions which could bring about significant and lasting trade.

Introduction to the Potential of Technology, Specifically Blockchain, as a Solution: In the hunt for transformative answers, era has emerged as a key enabler. Blockchain, specially, has garnered sizeable attention for its capacity to deal with the demanding situations posed by conventional structures. At its middle, blockchain is a decentralized and distributed ledger era that guarantees transparency, immutability, and safety in transactions (Kant et al., 2023). These attributes make it an appealing candidate for reinforcing present strategies and systems, supplying a brand new paradigm for attaining the SDGs.

Examples and Statistics Illustrating the Urgency and Motivation at the back of Exploring Blockchain for Sustainable Development: To underscore the urgency and motivation in the back of exploring blockchain for sustainable improvement, it's miles important to provide real-world examples and pertinent information. Instances wherein blockchain has already established its effectiveness in regions like deliver chain transparency, economic inclusion, and healthcare information control can be highlighted. Additionally, facts showcasing the reputation of SDGs and the sluggish pace of development in some regions can emphasize the urgent want for innovative answers.

Figure 1. Blockchain technology for sustainable development

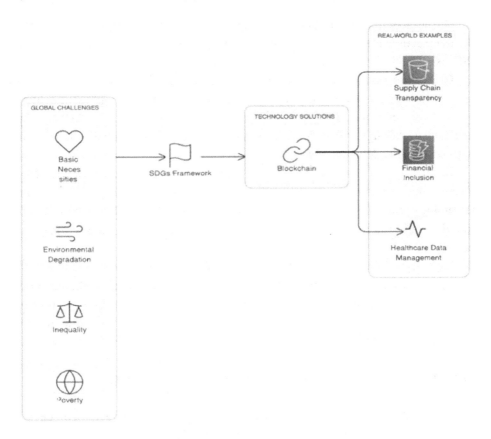

For instance, blockchain applications in supply chain management can enhance traceability, ensuring fair trade practices and minimizing environmental impact. In financial inclusion, blockchain-based solutions can provide access to banking services for the unbanked population, contributing to poverty alleviation. These tangible examples, supported by relevant statistics, serve to vividly portray the potential impact of blockchain technology on advancing sustainable development goals (Vashishth et al, 2024).

Objectives of the Chapter

The number one aim of this bankruptcy is to offer a comprehensive overview of the intersection among blockchain generation and Sustainable Development Goals (SDGs). The desires and goals may be articulated as follows:

To Explore the Role of Blockchain in Advancing SDGs: This bankruptcy seeks to delve into the ways wherein blockchain era can make contributions to the achievement of various SDGs. It objectives to offer insights into the specific packages and mechanisms through which blockchain can address demanding situations associated with sustainable development.

To Provide In-Depth Understanding: The chapter pursuits to provide readers a nuanced and in-intensity expertise of key concepts associated with each blockchain technology and the precise SDGs under consideration. This includes exploring the foundational principles of blockchain, its capability packages, and the intricacies of each SDG.

To Analyze Case Studies and Practical Applications: Incorporating actual-world examples and case research, the bankruptcy targets to research times wherein blockchain generation has been successfully applied to similarly sustainable development. By examining these cases, readers can gain sensible insights into the effectiveness of blockchain in diverse contexts.

Identification of Key Aspects of Blockchain Technology

To fulfil the above targets, the bankruptcy will focus on key elements of blockchain era which are relevant to sustainable improvement. These key elements encompass:

Decentralization: Exploring how the decentralized nature of blockchain can sell inclusivity, lessen dependency on centralized authorities, and enhance trust in diverse methods.

Transparency and Immutability: Investigating how the transparency and immutability functions of blockchain make contributions to responsibility, traceability, and the reduction of corruption, mainly in sectors associated with SDGs.

Smart Contracts: Examining the role of smart contracts in automating and securing agreements, doubtlessly streamlining processes in sectors like finance, supply chain, and legal frameworks applicable to SDGs.

Tokenization: Discussing the concept of tokenization and its potential to reshape economic models, with a focus on how it can effect economic inclusion and access to resources.

Explanation of How These Aspects Relate to Advancing Sustainable Development

For each key aspect of blockchain, the bankruptcy will elucidate its relevance to advancing sustainable improvement. For instance:

Decentralization: Discussion on how decentralization can empower groups, especially in contexts of financial inclusion and governance, fostering sustainable development by way of distributing decision-making power.

Transparency and Immutability: Explanation of the way obvious and immutable ledgers can enhance responsibility in areas along with supply chain control, making sure honest practices and moral sourcing.

Smart Contracts: Illustration of the way smart contracts can automate and stable strategies in sectors like healthcare, decreasing inefficiencies and ensuring the well timed shipping of offerings, consequently contributing to SDGs.

Tokenization: Exploration of ways tokenization can create new monetary models that sell truthful distribution of assets, probably addressing problems associated with poverty and economic inequality.

Figure 2. Advancing sustainable development with blockchain technology

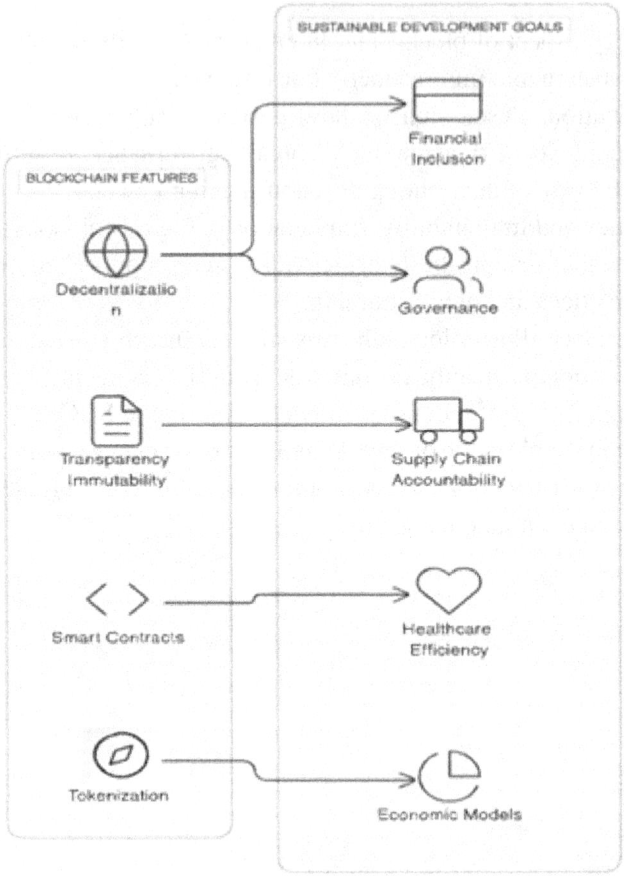

In Terms of Expected Contributions

Insights into Emerging Trends

Exploration of Blockchain and Sustainable Development: The chapter endeavors to provide in-intensity insights into emerging traits at the intersection of blockchain and sustainable improvement. By analyzing modern tendencies, technological improvements, and global projects, it pursuits to present a forward-searching perspective at the role of blockchain in shaping the destiny of sustainable development.

Forward-Looking Perspective: Emphasis can be placed on expecting and elucidating tendencies which have the potential to redefine the panorama of sustainable improvement. This forward-looking attitude will provide readers a glimpse into the evolving dynamics and opportunities inside the realm of blockchain era and its impact on reaching Sustainable Development Goals (SDGs).

Practical Recommendations

Stakeholders, Policymakers, and Organizations: Practical guidelines may be articulated for a numerous target market, such as stakeholders, policymakers, groups, and corporations inquisitive about leveraging blockchain for sustainable development. These hints might be grounded in real-global applicability, guiding stakeholders in the strategic integration of blockchain solutions inside their respective domain names.

Ethical and Responsible Implementation: Special attention will be given to moral and responsible implementation, ensuring that recommendations bear in mind social, environmental, and financial dimensions. This approach aims to sell sustainable and inclusive practices within the blockchain area.

Synthesis of Existing Knowledge

Consolidation of Understanding: The chapter seeks to make contributions to the existing body of understanding by means of supplying a complete synthesis of modern information on the topic. By aggregating and summarizing key findings from various sources, it pursuits to consolidate information, imparting readers a well-rounded information of the multifaceted courting among blockchain and sustainable development.

Identification of Research Gaps: Through the synthesis process, the chapter can even identify gaps within the current know-how panorama. Recognizing those gaps will function an invitation for future studies endeavors, encouraging scholars and practitioners to delve deeper into particular areas that warrant similarly exploration and evaluation.

Comprehensive Exploration of Blockchain's Role

Key Aspects of Blockchain Technology: The bankruptcy will comprehensively explore key elements of blockchain technology relevant to sustainable improvement. This includes know-how the foundational principles of blockchain, its capability in addressing particular SDGs, and the demanding situations and opportunities associated with its implementation in numerous sectors.

Robust Methodology for Valuable Insights: The use of a robust methodology could be hired to make sure the reliability and validity of the insights offered. By adopting a scientific and rigorous technique, the chapter aims to make a contribution valuable, evidence-based insights which could inform decision-making and destiny studies endeavors.

Scope and Organization

Definition of the Scope by Specifying the Focus Areas of Blockchain and Sustainable Development:

Blockchain Focus Areas

- The bankruptcy will mainly concentrate on the software of blockchain generation in the context of Sustainable Development Goals (SDGs).
- Specific attention can be given to key factors of blockchain, inclusive of decentralization, transparency, smart contracts, and tokenization.
- Case research and examples might be drawn from sectors including finance, deliver chain, healthcare, and schooling to demonstrate the sensible packages of blockchain in furthering sustainable improvement.

Sustainable Development Focus Areas

Broad Spectrum of Sustainable Development

Poverty Alleviation: The awareness on poverty relief addresses the urgent want to uplift economically deprived communities. Blockchain era can empower individuals through monetary inclusion, allowing get right of entry to to banking offerings, credit score, and economic opportunities.

Environmental Sustainability: Environmental sustainability is paramount in addressing climate alternate and ecological issues. Blockchain's transparency and traceability in supply chains, coupled with its capability for tokenizing environmental belongings, make contributions to sustainable commercial enterprise practices and conservation efforts.

Healthcare Improvement: The healthcare sector requires green and stable statistics control structures. Blockchain can enhance healthcare statistics interoperability, making sure the seamless and steady exchange of patient records, leading to improved healthcare outcomes.

Advancements in Education: Education is a cornerstone for societal progress. Blockchain can revolutionize schooling by using offering obvious and tamper-resistant credential verification, permitting greater accessibility to academic resources, and fostering progressive mastering structures.

Tailoring Blockchain Solutions to Address Unique Challenges

Poverty Alleviation: Microfinance structures leveraging blockchain can enable obvious and efficient monetary offerings for people in impoverished areas. Blockchain-primarily based identification answers additionally play a important role in granting monetary get entry to to those without official documentation.

Environmental Sustainability: Blockchain ensures transparency in deliver chains, permitting customers to verify the authenticity of environmentally friendly practices. The tokenization of environmental belongings, including carbon credits, can create monetary incentives for sustainable practices.

Healthcare Improvement: Blockchain's secure and interoperable facts control abilities decorate affected person-centric healthcare systems. Patients will have control over their health information, and clever contracts can automate procedures like insurance claims and clinical studies consent.

Advancements in Education: Blockchain enables the creation of a stable and verifiable ledger for educational credentials, lowering fraud in training. Decentralized getting to know systems built on blockchain can ensure obvious and reachable academic resources.

Cross-Cutting Issues: Gender Equality and Social Inclusion

Gender Equality: Within the wider sustainable improvement framework, addressing gender equality involves making sure that blockchain applications do now not perpetuate existing biases. Efforts need to be made to create inclusive solutions that empower girls economically and socially.

Social Inclusion: Social inclusion is a move-cutting trouble that includes ensuring that blockchain tasks are accessible to various populations, along with marginalized groups. Blockchain packages have to be designed with a know-how of the social contexts in which they perform.

LITERATURE REVIEW

The paper published by (Adams, Kewell & Parry, 2018) puts forth an interesting hypothesis that Blockchain technology can be made to work in favour of Sustainable Development Goals (SDGs). Whilst the authors have presented some positive aspects of the technology in the context of SDGs and offer some recommendations, one is left to wonder if the authors have underestimated the potential for some unforeseen problems arising due to the pitfalls of implementation and/or unforeseen consequences due to the complexity of SDGs. Recent paper through (Aysan et al, 2021) argued that blockchain-based solutions can assist achieve the Sustainable Development Goals

(SDGs) past the COVID-19 pandemic. However, the authors fail to acknowledge the complex operational demanding situations had to implement blockchain-generation in accomplishing SDGs. First, employing blockchain-primarily based answers calls for massive computing sources that may not be available in much less developed and 1/3-world international locations. Second, the decentralized nature of blockchain era consists of excessive risks of cyber-assaults and monetary crimes, which might be mainly associated with programmable blockchains used for the reason of sustainable improvement. Lastly, the authors forget about the ethical implications of the use of blockchain-generation in accomplishing one-of-a-kind SDGs. In (Azmat et al., 2023) endorse that companies should take heed to how their enterprise decisions can make a contribution to the lengthy-term achievement of the Sustainable Development Goals (SDGs). However, the authors do not provide perception into how groups may additionally successfully increase an approach to fulfil the SDGs or address the sources needed to maintain sustainability. In addition, the authors do now not keep in mind the potential risks to organizations if they are unable to increase a sustainable method and meet the SDGs. Blockchain era has been touted as a main disruptor considering its invention in 2009, however the potential of this era to pressure green innovation has but to be fully explored. Recently, a paper through (Chin et al., 2022) has recognized leveraging blockchain generation to create atmosphere-based business models that facilitate cost appropriation as a key dynamic functionality of this era. However, due to the novelty of this topic, the thing does now not don't forget crucial elements including the impact of the era at the surroundings, the ability countermeasures to prevent malicious use of the technology, and the capacity scalability of blockchain-based answers for green innovation. Therefore, similarly research is wanted to higher recognize the genuine ability of blockchain era to force inexperienced innovation. (De Villiers et al., 2021) explore a potential position for businesses in promoting the United Nations Sustainable Development Goals (SDGs) through the usage of the net-of-things and blockchain era. While the paper offers some interesting insights, it fails to effectively address the moral implications of the usage of such technologies on a global scale, as well as offer a greater thorough take a look at the capability dangers and feasibility of this sort of strategy. Furthermore, the proposed plan lacks a complete and systematic approach to be definitely placed into exercise. In addition, it is doubtful how powerful such a plan might be in promoting the SDGs or how it can be predicted or measured in the long run. (Ferdous et. al., 2019) does not offer a detailed exploration of the present protection troubles surrounding blockchain-primarily based self-sovereign identification structures and lacks a complete evaluation of the benefits that these systems can provide. The authors additionally overlook the capability implications and risks of decentralized identity control and lack an important assessment of the key demanding situations and troubles in the implementation of such systems.

In their paper on leveraging blockchain for sustainability, (Fraga-Lamas and Fernández-Caramés, 2020) cognizance on software of the technology in the context of the European Union Green Deal and United Nations Sustainable Development Goals – even though there's a loss of element on how feasibility and scalability would be addressed. (Kumar and Chopra, 2022) present a thrilling concept to fight current challenges when implementing a round economic system. However, by means of thinking about best blockchain and smart-contract technologies, the authors fail to discover other techniques that would be employed to address the equal problems greater efficaciously. Although this paper with the aid of (Leng et al., 2020) provides an exciting survey on the usage of blockchain in sustainability and product lifecycle management, it fails to critically analyze the safety issues that get up with this generation. Furthermore, the authors fail to provide any novel research or solutions bearing on the actual global utility of blockchain in industry four.0. (Schulz et al., 2020) explored how blockchain technology can be used to facilitate the governance and implementation of sustainable development projects. However, it remains uncertain if the era can bring the promised efficiencies or if it will become out of date shortly due to emerging technologies consisting of quantum computing. (Tsolakis et al., 2021) provides an thrilling case examine of blockchain implementation in Thailand's fish industry to deal with the United Nations' Sustainable Development Goals, however, the paper fails to provide good enough evidence as to its feasibility or efficacy. (Wong et al., 2022) systematic assessment offers an informative assessment of the potential blessings of making use of blockchain generation in SSCs, it does no longer deal with a number of the ability dangers and downsides that must be taken into consideration. Additionally, it additionally fails to provide any specified plans or strategies on how those problems can be resolved. Hence, it would be useful for in addition studies to explore these problems in more detail to make sure the hit integration of blockchain technology into Smart Sustainable Cities. (Zubaydi et al., 2023) examines the position of Blockchain technology in enhancing protection and privacy factors inside Internet of Things (IoT). Their systematic literature review offers an insightful examination of the capability benefits and limitations of utilizing Blockchain generation in such instances. However, despite its comprehensive assessment, the authors fail to offer any proof at the viability of incorporating Blockchain generation in IoT frameworks. Additionally, the authors fail to offer any real solutions to address the privacy issues associated with using such era. Therefore, greater research needs to be conducted to shed mild at the doable outcomes of imposing Blockchain generation for IoT safety and privacy.

FOUNDATIONAL CONCEPTS OF BLOCKCHAIN

Understanding Blockchain Technology

Definition and Explanation of Blockchain

Blockchain is a decentralized and distributed virtual ledger technology that allows secure, transparent, and tamper-resistant file-preserving of transactions across a community of computer systems.

Decentralization

Definition: In a blockchain, there's no important authority or intermediary governing the community. Instead, it operates on a peer-to-peer network, where each participant, or node, has a duplicate of the entire blockchain.

Explanation: Decentralization gets rid of the want for a crucial entity, improving resilience and decreasing the threat of a single point of failure. It empowers contributors through dispensing manage and decision-making across the network.

Transparent and Public Ledger

Definition: Transactions recorded at the blockchain are obvious and on hand to all members inside the community.

Explanation: Transparency way that all individuals have visibility into the whole transaction records. This transparency fosters trust among individuals, as they can independently confirm the accuracy and legitimacy of transactions.

Immutability

Definition: Once records is added to the blockchain, it can't be altered or deleted.

Explanation: Immutability is achieved thru cryptographic hashing and consensus mechanisms. Once a block is brought to the blockchain, changing the information inside it would require altering subsequent blocks, which is computationally infeasible and would require the consensus of the bulk of the community. Immutability guarantees the integrity of the transaction records.

Consensus Mechanism

Definition: Consensus mechanisms are protocols that ensure all nodes within the network agree at the validity of transactions.

Explanation: The maximum commonplace consensus mechanism is Proof of Work (PoW), in which nodes compete to resolve complicated mathematical puzzles to feature a new block to the blockchain. Another mechanism is Proof of Stake (PoS), in which nodes are chosen to create new blocks based on the amount of cryptocurrency they keep. Consensus mechanisms prevent double-spending and make sure that all members reach an agreement at the kingdom of the blockchain.

Cryptography for Security

Definition: Blockchain uses cryptographic techniques to steady transactions and manage get admission to to the community.

Explanation: Cryptography is hired to steady information within blocks and manipulate get entry to to the blockchain. Public and private keys are used to facilitate stable transactions, making sure that best authorized participants can interact inside the network.

Smart Contracts

Definition: Smart contracts are self-executing contracts with the phrases of the agreement at once written into code.

Explanation: Smart contracts automate and put in force the phrases of agreements, casting off the need for intermediaries. They execute routinely while predefined conditions are met, streamlining methods and lowering the hazard of errors or fraud.

Figure 3. Blockchain architecture

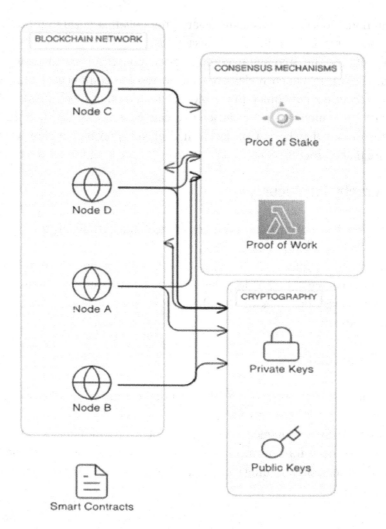

Understanding the essential components of blockchain—decentralization, transparency, immutability, consensus mechanisms, cryptography, and smart contracts—is important for appreciating how blockchain operates as a transformative technology. These traits together make contributions to the introduction of a secure and sincere virtual ledger with broad applications across industries.

How Blockchain Ensures Trust and Security in Transactions

Blockchain era employs a combination of functions and mechanisms to set up trust and enhance security in transactions. The decentralized and transparent nature of blockchain, at the side of cryptographic strategies, contributes to the introduction of a steady, tamper-resistant, and straightforward environment. Here's a detailed breakdown of ways blockchain guarantees agree with and safety:

Decentralization

How it Works: Blockchain operates on a decentralized network of nodes, each retaining a replica of the complete transaction history.

Ensuring Trust: Decentralization eliminates the need for a central authority, preventing a unmarried factor of manipulate or failure. Trust is sent throughout the community, and no unmarried entity has undue have an effect on or manipulate over transactions.

Transparent and Public Ledger

How it Works: Transactions recorded on the blockchain are transparent and visible to all individuals inside the network.

Ensuring Trust: Transparency guarantees that each one parties can independently confirm transactions. Participants have real-time get right of entry to to the complete transaction records, fostering agree with and duty.

Immutability

How it Works: Once a block is introduced to the blockchain, the statistics within it becomes immutable and can't be altered or deleted.

Ensuring Trust: Immutability guarantees the integrity of the transaction history. Once a transaction is recorded, it can't be modified retroactively, decreasing the hazard of fraud or tampering.

Consensus Mechanism

How it Works: Consensus mechanisms, consisting of Proof of Work (PoW) or Proof of Stake (PoS), make sure that every one nodes in the network agree on the validity of transactions.

Ensuring Trust: Consensus mechanisms prevent double-spending and fraudulent sports through requiring the bulk of the network to agree at the country of the blockchain. This settlement is reached via a democratic and cryptographic process.

Cryptography for Security

How it Works: Cryptographic strategies are hired to steady transactions and manage get right of entry to to the blockchain.

Ensuring Trust: Public and private key cryptography ensures that only authorized events can engage in transactions. The use of cryptographic hashing secures statistics inside blocks, making it immune to manipulation.

Smart Contracts

How it Works: Smart contracts are self-executing contracts with the terms of the settlement at once written into code.

Ensuring Trust: Smart contracts automate and put into effect the phrases of agreements. Their execution is deterministic and automatic, doing away with the want for intermediaries and reducing the hazard of errors or fraud.

Resistance to Attacks

How it Works: The decentralized and dispensed nature of the blockchain makes it resistant to attacks.

Ensuring Trust: Even if a portion of the network is compromised, the majority of nodes hold the perfect model of the blockchain, keeping the general integrity of the system.

Hence, the mixture of decentralization, transparency, immutability, consensus mechanisms, cryptography, and smart contracts in blockchain generation establishes a basis for consider and protection in transactions. These capabilities collectively make contributions to the advent of a tamper-resistant and transparent ledger, making sure the reliability and integrity of recorded transactions.

Smart Contracts and Tokenization

Exploration of Smart Contracts and Their Role in Automating Processes

Smart Contracts

Definition: Smart contracts are self-executing contracts with the terms of the settlement at once written into code.

Automating Processes

How They Work: Smart contracts automate the execution and enforcement of contractual agreements primarily based on predefined situations.

Decentralized Execution: Once situations are met, the clever contract executes automatically, removing the want for intermediaries or third events.

Examples of Automation

Financial Transactions: In finance, smart contracts can robotically execute and settle economic transactions while specific criteria are met, lowering delays and human errors.

Supply Chain Management: In deliver chain, clever contracts can mechanically cause movements such as fee launch when items attain a designated region, improving efficiency.

Trust and Security

Transparency and Trust: Smart contracts function on a transparent and immutable blockchain, improving accept as true with amongst parties worried.

Reduced Intermediaries: Automation via clever contracts reduces the want for intermediaries, streamlining strategies and lowering fees.

Challenges and Considerations

Code Security: Ensuring the security of smart agreement code is crucial to prevent vulnerabilities and ability exploits.

Legal and Regulatory Compliance: Integrating smart contracts into existing legal frameworks and ensuring compliance with policies are ongoing demanding situations.

Explanation of Tokenization and Its Potential for Creating New Economic Models

Tokenization

Definition: Tokenization involves representing actual-global property or rights on a blockchain within the shape of digital tokens.

Creating New Economic Models

Asset Fractionalization: Tokenization allows for the fractional possession of property, allowing a broader range of people to put money into historically illiquid belongings like real property or artwork.

Liquidity Enhancement: Tokenized assets can be traded on blockchain-based structures, improving liquidity with the aid of supplying a secondary market for assets that were traditionally difficult to promote.

Token Types

Utility Tokens: Provide get right of entry to to a particular services or products inside a blockchain surroundings.

Security Tokens: Represent ownership in an underlying asset and can provide dividends or sales sharing.

Examples of Tokenization

Real Estate: Tokenizing actual estate allows investors to own a share of a belongings, making it on hand to a broader range of buyers.

Art and Collectibles: Tokenization of artwork pieces allows fractional possession and trading inside the artwork marketplace.

Potential Benefits

Global Accessibility: Tokenization can open funding opportunities to a worldwide audience, breaking down geographical boundaries.

Efficiency and Automation: Smart contracts may be utilized at the side of tokenization to automate procedures together with dividend distribution.

Challenges and Considerations

Regulatory Uncertainty: The regulatory landscape for tokenized assets is evolving and may range throughout jurisdictions.

Security and Custody: Ensuring steady storage and custody answers for tokenized belongings is vital to prevent theft or loss.

Therefore, smart contracts and tokenization are pivotal additives of blockchain era with the ability to revolutionize diverse industries. Smart contracts streamline and automate methods, reducing the need for intermediaries, whilst tokenization opens up new economic models by means of representing ownership in digital shape, fostering liquidity and accessibility to a broader range of buyers.

Figure 4. Tokenization for creating new economic models

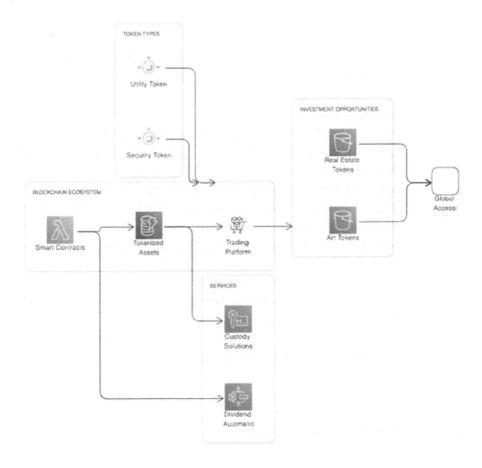

BLOCKCHAIN AND SPECIFIC SUSTAINABLE DEVELOPMENT GOALS

Poverty Alleviation

Examination of How Blockchain Can Contribute to Financial Inclusion

1. Financial Inclusion

    Overview: Financial inclusion is a key factor in the fight against poverty. Blockchain technology can play a transformative function in expanding get admission to to economic offerings for those who are unbanked or underbanked.

    Decentralized Banking: Blockchain helps decentralized monetary offerings, permitting people to get right of entry to banking services without counting on conventional banks.

    Cross-Border Transactions: Blockchain enables seamless and value-effective go-border transactions, decreasing remittance fees for individuals in economically marginalized areas.

2. Case Studies and Examples Demonstrating Blockchain Applications in Poverty Alleviation:

    Microfinance on Blockchain: Platforms leveraging blockchain for microfinance permit small-scale entrepreneurs to get right of entry to budget transparently and securely.

    Identity Verification: Blockchain-primarily based identification answers can empower people without legitimate documentation, granting them get right of entry to to financial offerings.

Environmental Sustainability

Discussion on How Blockchain Can Enhance Transparency in Supply Chains:

1. Transparency in Supply Chains:

    Overview: The transparency provided by using blockchain era can address troubles associated with unethical practices and shortage of traceability in deliver chains, contributing to environmental sustainability.

Immutable Record: Blockchain ensures that when facts is recorded, it can't be altered, imparting a straightforward and tamper-proof report of the entire deliver chain.

Verification of Authenticity: Consumers can hint the foundation of products, making sure that environmentally pleasant and moral practices are adhered to.

2. Use of Blockchain in Monitoring and Reducing Carbon Footprints:

Carbon Credits on Blockchain: Blockchain can be used to create and exchange carbon credits transparently, incentivizing companies to lessen their carbon emissions.

Monitoring and Auditing: Smart contracts on blockchain can automate the monitoring of carbon emissions, making sure adherence to environmental regulations.

Healthcare and Education

Exploration of Blockchain Applications in Healthcare Data Management:

1. Healthcare Data Management:

Overview: The stable and transparent nature of blockchain makes it suitable for coping with healthcare records, improving information protection, and improving patient consequences.

Interoperability: Blockchain can facilitate interoperability among disparate healthcare structures, ensuring seamless and secure sharing of patient facts.

Patient Ownership: Individuals may have possession and control over their health statistics, deciding who has get admission to and contributing to medical studies.

2. Examples of Blockchain Improving Transparency and Access in Education:

Academic Credentials on Blockchain: Blockchain can provide a stable and verifiable way to store and percentage academic credentials, lowering fraud and enhancing get entry to to schooling.

Decentralized Learning Platforms: Blockchain can guide decentralized and obvious mastering platforms, ensuring truthful get entry to educational resources globally.

Figure 5. Exploration of blockchain applications in healthcare

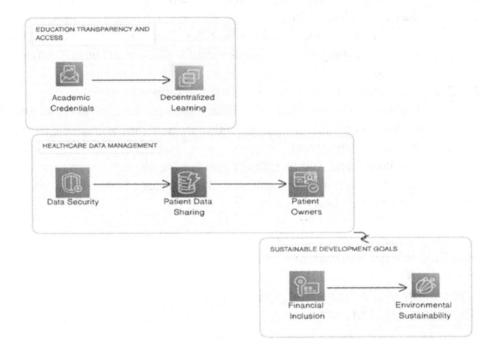

Blockchain has the ability to make vast contributions to unique Sustainable Development Goals (SDGs). In the context of poverty relief, it can empower individuals through monetary inclusion. For environmental sustainability, blockchain complements transparency in supply chains and aids in tracking and lowering carbon footprints. In healthcare and education, blockchain improves information control, transparency, and get right of entry to. These programs show off the versatility of blockchain era in addressing numerous challenges related to sustainable improvement.

CHALLENGES AND OPPORTUNITIES

Regulatory and Legal Challenges

Analysis of Regulatory Hurdles and Legal Considerations in Implementing Blockchain for Sustainable Development

1. Regulatory Complexity:

Analysis: The regulatory panorama for blockchain generation is complicated and varies throughout jurisdictions. Different regions have diverse
procedures to blockchain and cryptocurrencies, growing challenges for
global implementations.

Considerations: Organizations leveraging blockchain for sustainable development have to navigate various regulatory frameworks that can involve
compliance with monetary, statistics safety, and securities regulations.

2. Legal Implications:

Analysis: The immutable nature of blockchain poses prison demanding
situations, as as soon as statistics is recorded, it cannot be without difficulty altered. This raises questions about the proper to be forgotten and
facts privateness.

Considerations: Striking a stability among the transparency and immutability of blockchain and compliance with privateness laws is critical. Legal
frameworks need to evolve to deal with the unique aspects of blockchain.

3. Cross-Border Transactions:

Analysis: Blockchain's capacity to facilitate move-border transactions
challenges traditional economic guidelines.

Considerations: Regulatory bodies want to collaborate internationally
to broaden frameworks that accommodate the decentralized nature of
blockchain, making sure that transactions adhere to legal standards.

Technical Challenges

Discussion on Scalability, Interoperability, and Energy Consumption Challenges:

1. Scalability:

Discussion: As blockchain networks grow, scalability becomes a enormous undertaking. Traditional blockchain networks face obstacles in
processing speed and capacity.

Considerations: Scalability problems need to be addressed to house a
bigger wide variety of transactions and contributors, especially in packages related to sustainable improvement that entails big-scale facts and
transactions.

2. Interoperability:

Discussion: Different blockchain networks often perform in isolation,
hindering seamless verbal exchange and collaboration.

Considerations: Achieving interoperability is important for realizing the entire capability of blockchain across diverse industries and applications. Standardization efforts and protocols are important for exclusive blockchain platforms to communicate efficiently.

3. Energy Consumption:

Discussion: Proof-of-Work (PoW) consensus mechanisms, used in many blockchain networks, are strength-intensive, elevating worries about environmental sustainability.

Considerations: Transitioning to more strength-efficient consensus mechanisms like Proof-of-Stake (PoS) and exploring modern answers, together with hybrid consensus fashions, can mitigate the environmental effect of blockchain.

4. Innovations and Ongoing Efforts to Address Technical Challenges:

Innovations in Consensus Mechanisms: Ongoing studies explores alternative consensus mechanisms that balance security and performance, along with Practical Byzantine Fault Tolerance (PBFT) or Delegated Proof-of-Stake (DPoS).

Layer 2 Solutions: Scalability demanding situations are being addressed via Layer 2 solutions, including facet chains and country channels, which take care of transactions off the main blockchain to alleviate congestion.

Standardization Efforts: Industry-extensive tasks are underway to set up standards that promote interoperability, making sure that exclusive blockchain networks can talk seamlessly.

While blockchain era holds amazing promise, it faces several challenges. Regulatory and legal complexities demand a delicate stability between transparency and compliance. Technical demanding situations, including scalability, interoperability, and strength consumption, require ongoing innovation and collaborative efforts to release the entire capability of blockchain for sustainable improvement. The dynamic nature of these demanding situations also opens possibilities for advancements, answers, and the continuing evolution of blockchain generation.

FUTURE IMPLICATIONS AND RECOMMENDATIONS

Exploration of Emerging Trends in Blockchain Technology

1. Integration with Emerging Technologies:

Emerging Trends: Blockchain is in all likelihood to integrate with different emerging technology which include synthetic intelligence (AI), the Internet of Things (IoT), and 5G.

Impact on Sustainable Development: This convergence can result in greater comprehensive and interconnected solutions, improving the performance and effectiveness of sustainable improvement tasks.

2. Decentralized Finance (DeFi):

Emerging Trends: The upward thrust of decentralized finance (DeFi) systems, constructed on blockchain, is transforming conventional financial offerings.

Impact on Sustainable Development: DeFi can make a contribution to economic inclusion, providing decentralized get admission to to banking and economic services, in particular in underserved areas.

3. Tokenization of Assets:

Emerging Trends: Continued growth in tokenization, extending past cryptocurrencies to symbolize diverse actual-world property.

Impact on Sustainable Development: Tokenization can democratize access to belongings, allowing fractional ownership and facilitating investment in sustainable tasks, like renewable strength or conservation initiatives.

4. Privacy-Preserving Technologies:

Emerging Trends: Increasing consciousness on privacy-preserving technology within blockchain, addressing concerns associated with records privacy and confidentiality.

Impact on Sustainable Development: Enhanced privateness features can inspire greater widespread adoption, especially in sectors like healthcare and training, in which statistics safety is paramount.

5. Sustainability in Blockchain Networks:

Emerging Trends: Growing cognizance of the environmental effect of blockchain networks, main to a focus on sustainability and energy-green consensus mechanisms.

Impact on Sustainable Development: Adoption of green blockchain solutions aligns with sustainable improvement goals by decreasing carbon footprints associated with blockchain operations.

Recommendations

Practical Suggestions for Policymakers, Businesses, and Organizations Looking to Leverage Blockchain for SDGs:

1. Policymakers:

    Understand and Embrace Blockchain: Policymakers ought to teach themselves approximately blockchain era and its capacity impact on sustainable improvement, fostering an environment conducive to innovation.

    Establish Regulatory Frameworks: Develop clear and adaptable regulatory frameworks that inspire responsible blockchain use, ensuring compliance without stifling innovation.

2. Businesses:

    Explore Collaborations: Businesses ought to discover collaborative efforts with blockchain start-usaand combine blockchain wherein applicable of their operations.

    Prioritize Sustainability: Implement sustainable practices inside blockchain operations, deciding on eco-friendly consensus mechanisms and minimizing electricity intake.

3. Organizations:

    Invest in Research and Development: Organizations need to allocate sources to analyze and development, staying abreast of the modern day blockchain innovations.

    Promote Education and Training: Facilitate schooling and schooling packages to decorate the capabilities of professionals in know-how, growing, and implementing blockchain answers.

4. Global Collaboration:

    Encourage International Collaboration: Foster worldwide collaboration to broaden standardized processes to blockchain regulation, interoperability, and sustainability.

    Share Best Practices: Encourage the sharing of great practices and success memories amongst nations and corporations to accelerate the superb impact of blockchain on sustainable improvement.

5. Social Responsibility:

    Align Blockchain Initiatives with SDGs: Ensure that blockchain tasks align with unique SDGs, emphasizing social and environmental responsibility.

    Transparency and Accountability: Prioritize transparency and accountability in blockchain tasks, constructing consider among stakeholders.

    As blockchain era continues to adapt, policymakers, groups, and companies play a critical function in shaping its future trajectory. By expertise emerging tendencies, embracing sustainable practices, and fostering collaboration, stakeholders can leverage blockchain to increase sustainable improvement dreams efficaciously.

CONCLUSION

In end, the application of blockchain generation gives an extraordinary opportunity for advancing Sustainable Development Goals (SDGs) and fostering a more sustainable and equitable global future. The decentralized and obvious nature of blockchain offers solutions to longstanding challenges, selling trust, responsibility, and inclusivity. As witnessed across various sectors, along with finance, healthcare, and deliver chain, blockchain's potential to offer secure, tamper-resistant, and auditable facts has the ability to revolutionize information management and records sharing. This generation complements the effectiveness of humanitarian efforts, making sure that aid reaches its supposed recipients transparently and without intermediaries. Smart contracts, a cornerstone of blockchain, can streamline methods, automate compliance, and decrease corruption, contributing drastically to SDGs associated with poverty reduction, first-class education, and monetary boom. Furthermore, the immutable and traceable nature of blockchain enables responsible resource control, permitting the tracking of sustainable practices and moral deliver chains. Despite the promise, challenges which include scalability, regulatory frameworks, and strength intake have to be addressed to absolutely unencumber the ability of blockchain for sustainable development. Collaborative efforts among governments, groups, and generation innovators are critical to harnessing the transformative strength of blockchain, thereby propelling us closer to accomplishing the formidable Sustainable Development Goals and developing an extra resilient, obvious, and sustainable worldwide society.

REFERENCES

Adams, R., Kewell, B., & Parry, G. (2018). Blockchain for good? Digital ledger technology and sustainable development goals. *Handbook of sustainability and social science research*, 127-140. Springer. 10.1007/978-3-319-67122-2_7

Aysan, A. F., Bergigui, F., & Disli, M. (2021). Blockchain-based solutions in achieving SDGs after COVID-19. *Journal of Open Innovation*, 7(2), 151. 10.3390/joitmc7020151

Azmat, F., Lim, W. M., Moyeen, A., Voola, R., & Gupta, G. (2023). Convergence of business, innovation, and sustainability at the tipping point of the sustainable development goals. *Journal of Business Research*, 167, 114170. 10.1016/j.jbusres.2023.114170

Chin, T., Shi, Y., Singh, S. K., Agbanyo, G. K., & Ferraris, A. (2022). Leveraging blockchain technology for green innovation in ecosystem-based business models: A dynamic capability of values appropriation. *Technological Forecasting and Social Change*, 183, 121908. 10.1016/j.techfore.2022.121908

De Villiers, C., Kuruppu, S., & Dissanayake, D. (2021). A (new) role for business– Promoting the United Nations' Sustainable Development Goals through the internet-of-things and blockchain technology. *Journal of Business Research*, 131, 598–609. 10.1016/j.jbusres.2020.11.066

Ferdous, M. S., Chowdhury, F., & Alassafi, M. O. (2019). In search of self-sovereign identity leveraging blockchain technology. *IEEE Access : Practical Innovations, Open Solutions*, 7, 103059–103079. 10.1109/ACCESS.2019.2931173

Fraga-Lamas, P., & Fernández-Caramés, T. M. (2020). Leveraging blockchain for sustainability and open innovation: A cyber-resilient approach toward EU Green Deal and UN Sustainable Development Goals. In *Computer Security Threats*. IntechOpen. 10.5772/intechopen.92371

Kant, R., Sharma, S., Vikas, V., Chaudhary, S., Jain, A. K., & Sharma, K. K. (2023, April). Blockchain–A Deployment Mechanism for IoT Based Security. In *2023 International Conference on Computational Intelligence, Communication Technology and Networking (CICTN)* (pp. 739-745). IEEE. 10.1109/CICTN57981.2023.10140715

Kumar, N. M., & Chopra, S. S. (2022). Leveraging blockchain and smart contract technologies to overcome circular economy implementation challenges. *Sustainability (Basel)*, 14(15), 9492. 10.3390/su14159492

Leng, J., Ruan, G., Jiang, P., Xu, K., Liu, Q., Zhou, X., & Liu, C. (2020). Blockchain-empowered sustainable manufacturing and product lifecycle management in industry 4.0: A survey. *Renewable & Sustainable Energy Reviews*, 132, 110112. 10.1016/j.rser.2020.110112

Schulz, K. A., Gstrein, O. J., & Zwitter, A. J. (2020). Exploring the governance and implementation of sustainable development initiatives through blockchain technology. *Futures*, 122, 102611. 10.1016/j.futures.2020.102611

Tsolakis, N., Niedenzu, D., Simonetto, M., Dora, M., & Kumar, M. (2021). Supply network design to address United Nations Sustainable Development Goals: A case study of blockchain implementation in Thai fish industry. *Journal of Business Research*, 131, 495–519. 10.1016/j.jbusres.2020.08.003

Vashishth, T. K., Sharma, V., Sharma, K. K., Kumar, B., Chaudhary, S., & Panwar, R. (2024). Security and Privacy Challenges in Blockchain-Based Supply Chain Management: A Comprehensive Analysis. In *Achieving Secure and Transparent Supply Chains with Blockchain Technology* (pp. 70-91). IGI Global. 10.4018/979-8-3693-0482-2.ch005

Vashishth, T. K., Sharma, V., Sharma, K. K., Kumar, B., Chaudhary, S., & Panwar, R. (2024). Intelligent Resource Allocation and Optimization for Industrial Robotics Using AI and Blockchain. In *AI and Blockchain Applications in Industrial Robotics* (pp. 82-110). IGI Global. DOI: 10.4018/979-8-3693-0659-8.ch004

Wong, P. F., Chia, F. C., Kiu, M. S., & Lou, E. C. (2022). Potential integration of blockchain technology into smart sustainable city (SSC) developments: A systematic review. *Smart and Sustainable Built Environment*, 11(3), 559–574. 10.1108/SASBE-09-2020-0140

Zubaydi, H. D., Varga, P., & Molnár, S. (2023). Leveraging Blockchain Technology for Ensuring Security and Privacy Aspects in Internet of Things: A Systematic Literature Review. *Sensors (Basel)*, 23(2), 788. 10.3390/s2302078836679582

KEY TERMS AND DEFINITIONS

Artificial Intelligence (AI): This refers to the development of pc structures that may carry out tasks that usually require human intelligence. These responsibilities consist of gaining knowledge of, reasoning, problem-solving, belief, language information, and selection-making. AI aims to create machines which could mimic cognitive capabilities and adapt to new conditions, enhancing performance and automation in numerous domain names.

Blockchain Technology: This is a decentralized and allotted virtual ledger that securely statistics and verifies transactions throughout multiple computers in a network. It guarantees transparency, immutability, and trust in the data through using cryptographic techniques, making it immune to tampering or fraud.

Decentralized Finance (DeFi): This refers to a monetary machine constructed on blockchain generation that goals to recreate and improve upon conventional monetary services without counting on central government, along with banks or intermediaries. DeFi makes use of clever contracts to allow peer-to-peer transactions, lending, borrowing, and other financial sports in a decentralized and transparent manner, regularly using cryptocurrencies.

Internet of Things (IoT): This is a network of interconnected gadgets, vehicles, or objects embedded with sensors, software, and connectivity, letting them change facts and communicate with every different over the internet. This permits these objects to gather and proportion information, leading to advanced efficiency, automation, and more suitable decision-making in various applications such as smart homes, healthcare, and commercial strategies.

Sustainable Development Goals (SDGs): SDGs are a hard and fast of 17 international dreams established by the United Nations to deal with various social, economic, and environmental challenges. Their goal is to achieve an extra sustainable and equitable international by 2030, addressing problems which include poverty, starvation, health, education, gender equality, clean water, and weather action.

Chapter 16
The Future of HCI Machine Learning, Personalization, and Beyond

Gaurav Gupta
https://orcid.org/0000-0002-5192
-4428

Shoolini University, India

Pradeep Chintale
https://orcid.org/0009-0005-6483
-2396

SEI Investment Company, USA

Laxminarayana Korada
https://orcid.org/0009-0001-6518
-0060

Microsoft Corporation, Bellevue, USA

Ankur Harendrasinh Mahida
https://orcid.org/0009-0009-0501
-398X

Barclays PLC, USA

Saigurudatta Pamulaparthyvenkata
VillageMD, USA

Rajiv Avacharmal
https://orcid.org/0009-0005-3482
-3931

University of Connecticut, USA

ABSTRACT

In the digital age, the fusion of human-computer interaction (HCI) with machine learning and personalization is transforming how individuals engage with technology. This chapter explores this dynamic intersection, envisioning a future of more intuitive, adaptive, and personalized digital experiences. It examines the role of machine learning in HCI, highlighting predictive analytics, natural language processing, and real-time interface adaptation. Personalization is addressed through content recommendation systems, user profiling, and adaptive interfaces. The study also looks at HCI's future in healthcare, e-commerce, and education, and addresses

DOI: 10.4018/979-8-3693-2869-9.ch016

privacy, transparency, bias, and ethics. It underscores the ethical responsibility in deploying these technologies, inviting readers to envision a future where HCI, machine learning, and personalization create responsive, personalized, and ethically sound digital interactions.

INTRODUCTION

The history of Human-Computer Interaction (HCI) has progressed in parallel with technological advancements, aiming to provide more user-friendly and intuitive interactions between humans and computers (Issa & Isaias, 2022). Early computing interactions were text-based and required technical knowledge. The World Wide Web changed HCI in the 1990s. Internet users can access information and services through web browsers. User-centered design, usability testing, and user experience research joined HCI. Mobile devices, touchscreens, and smartphones in the 2000s presented new HCI difficulties and opportunities (Rogers, 2012; Sabie et al., 2022). HCI leads to augmented reality, virtual reality, and voice assistants. Technology is made more user-friendly and accessible while addressing data privacy and algorithmic bias ethics. HCI evolves to produce smooth and intuitive digital interactions for users as technology advances.

Technology is increasingly part of our daily life in the digital age. HCI is essential to our daily lives, whether we're using social media, shopping online, or controlling smart home gadgets. This introduction opens the door to critical analysis of how HCI, machine learning, and customization are redefining this fundamental human-computer relationship. The ubiquitous availability of computer devices and the exponential growth of digital data have created a need for more personalized and user-centric digital experiences. Interfaces should recognize and adapt to users' choices, needs, and actions. HCI, the field that designs and studies how we interact with digital systems, has begun to use machine learning to meet this demand (Khuat et al., 2022; Sardar et al., 2022).

Machine learning's (Jordan, 2015) data-driven algorithms and pattern recognition make it a valuable HCI tool. Systems can learn from users' interactions, forecast their intentions, and offer more personalized and adaptive interfaces. This is about making the digital world more responsive, proactive, and intelligent, not just developing better websites and interfaces. Personalization is also crucial to customizing digital encounters (Corno et al., 2021). It understands that HCI works best when customized. Thanks to machine learning and personalization, your website, app, or virtual assistant may be customized to your preferences.

The paper shows that HCI and machine learning are converging beyond technology. It promises deeper, more meaningful, and more efficient human-computer connections. Imagine interfaces that understand your words and emotions. Imagine devices that anticipate your requirements and provide a customized experience. However, this transformational process presents problems. Personalization requires gathering and analyzing user data, raising privacy concerns. As we use these tools responsibly and address bias and fairness, ethics become important. In the future of HCI, where machine learning and personalization collide, we must address both the potential and the obligations. This article navigates these issues and illuminates the route to a future where HCI is redefined, enhanced, and tailored for everyone.

Motivation: The motivation behind writing this paper arises from two key factors. First, significant advances in machine learning and artificial intelligence have led to its incorporation into many facets of our life, including HCI. Therefore, HCI researchers, professionals, and consumers must investigate and comprehend the ramifications of this integration. Second, as machine learning becomes more common in HCI, its role, applications, and future advances must be understood. This paper explores these aspects in depth to fill this gap. HCI with machine learning poses ethical and practical issues such data privacy, algorithmic bias, and transparency. This study examines these problems to raise awareness and offer advice for safely navigating them and synthesizes existing knowledge, presents fresh viewpoints, and encourages conversations about machine learning and HCI to encourage more research and dialogue in this interdisciplinary topic.

Research Questions: The paper addresses the following five research questions: (1) What is the role of machine learning in HCI? This question examines how ML technologies improve user interaction with digital systems in HCI. (2) What are the diverse applications of machine learning in HCI? The study discusses how machine learning improves HCI experiences in predictive text, gesture recognition, personalized suggestions, and emotion detection. (3) What are the anticipated future developments in HCI facilitated by machine learning? The article examines future trends and breakthroughs to predict how machine learning will change HCI, including user interfaces, adaptive systems, and personalized interactions. (4) What are the key challenges and ethical considerations in integrating machine learning into HCI? This research question explores the obstacles and moral quandaries linked to incorporating machine learning in HCI, focusing on concerns such data privacy, algorithmic bias, transparency, and user permission. (5) How can experts and researchers navigate the complex landscape of machine learning in HCI? The paper offers advice for both professionals and academics on overcoming obstacles, promoting responsible growth, and using machine learning to produce more intuitive and user centric HCI experiences.

Contribution of the study: This paper contributes to HCI by synthesizing existing knowledge, identifying research gaps, and raising awareness about ethical and practical considerations when integrating machine learning technologies. It explores machine learning's role, applications, challenges, and future developments, providing insights for practitioners, researchers, and policymakers. The paper encourages ethical and user-centric design principles, advancing understanding of machine learning's potential in HCI and inspiring future innovation.

MACHINE LEARNING IN HCI

Machine Learning (ML) in HCI is a paradigm change in digital system design and development (Sardar et al., 2022). HCI is an interdisciplinary field that studies how humans use computers and designs interfaces to support those interactions. Modern interface design relies on machine learning and algorithms to improve user experiences through data-driven and adaptive approaches. The integration uses machine learning to evaluate massive datasets of user interactions, including clicks, swipes, text inputs, and other behavioral data. ML models help HCI systems comprehend user behavior, preferences, and intentions. This insight is essential to building user-centric, efficient, and responsive interfaces.

One of the main uses of ML in HCI is predictive analytics (Lv, 2022). ML models allow HCI systems to predict user behaviors and customize the interface in real time. Predictive text input on a smartphone keyboard uses ML to guess and suggest the next word based on typing history. Another crucial feature of HCI machine learning is personalization (Xia, 2021). Utilizing ML enables highly tailored user experiences. Using user data like past interactions and preferences, systems can tailor content, layout, and recommendations to individual profiles. Personalization creates interfaces that feel customized for each user, increasing engagement and happiness (Corno et al., 2021). HCI also uses machine learning for natural language processing. Voice assistants, chatbots, and interfaces that understand and respond to natural language have resulted. Another area where ML is important is gesture recognition. It makes touch screens and virtual reality apps more intuitive by recognizing and responding to hand or body movements.

HCI machine learning now detects emotions. By evaluating facial expressions or text sentiment, ML algorithms may determine user moods (Jaiswal et al., 2020; Saffar et al., 2023). This lets interfaces understand users' emotions, boosting mental health apps, virtual customer service, and gaming. This lets interfaces understand users' emotions, boosting mental health apps, virtual customer service, and gaming. Accessibility is another important HCI machine learning aspect (Moreno et al., 2023). ML can develop disabled-friendly interfaces. Screen readers for the blind, speech recognition for motor disabled people, and eye-tracking technology for the disabled are examples.

Though ML in HCI is promising, ethics must come first (Siddiq, 2023). This technology's rollout must address prejudice, fairness, and privacy issues and handle user data responsibly. The combination of machine learning and HCI could shape digital interface design. It improves user experiences, personalizes interactions, and makes interfaces more intuitive, adaptive, and responsive. This junction pushes human-computer interaction frontiers with research and ethics. Machine learning in HCI is intriguing because it moves user interface design from static to dynamic, responsive systems. These systems can learn and adapt to user behavior, making them more personalized, efficient, and engaging. This field must address ethics and data use responsibly (Hochheiser & Valdez, 2020; Waycott, 2017).

APPLICATIONS OF MACHINE LEARNING IN HCI

Machine learning has several uses in Human-Computer Interaction (HCI), improving user interactions with digital systems (Li, Kumar, Lasecki et al, 2020). Predictive text and autocorrect, already standard on smartphones, improve text entry efficiency. Gesture recognition uses machine learning to interpret hand and body movements and improve touch screen and virtual reality interactions. Siri and Google Assistant use machine learning to recognize natural language and give voice-activated commands, which are essential in hands-free interfaces. Chatbots and virtual agents use machine learning to comprehend and respond to text and voice inputs, providing automated customer service, information retrieval, and personalized recommendations. Machine learning algorithms analyze user preferences and behaviors to personalize content, layout, and product suggestions on e-commerce and content streaming platforms.

ML can also detect user emotions by analyzing voice, text, and facial expressions, allowing market research, healthcare, and entertainment applications to understand and respond to user attitudes. Natural language processing (NLP) uses ML for text analysis, sentiment analysis, language translation, and information retrieval, increasing user experience. ML improves accessibility via screen readers for the visually impaired, voice recognition for movement disabled people, and predictive text input for mobility-challenged people (Zdanowska & Taylor, 2022). These applications demonstrate machine learning's potential to make interfaces more intuitive, adaptive, and user-centric across a wide range of domains, while also requiring ethical considerations of user data privacy, bias, and fairness. *Figure 1* shows the main applications of ML in HCI.

Figure 1. Applications of machine learning in HCI

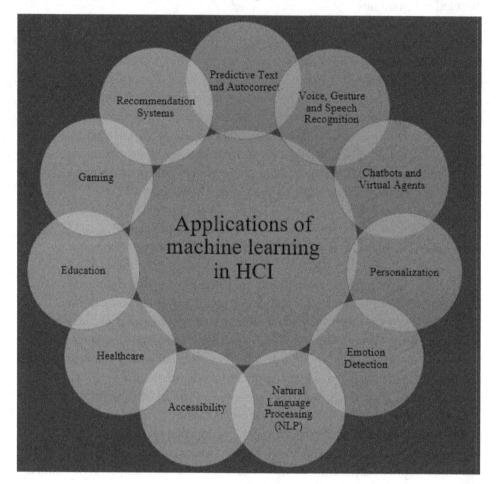

- **Predictive Text and Autocorrect:** Machine learning algorithms have transformed text input on many devices, like smartphones and tablets. These algorithms leverage user input to anticipate and recommend the following word or phrase, greatly improving the speed of text input. Predictive text and autocorrect functions are now widespread, minimizing typing mistakes and accelerating communication (Li, Amelot, Zhou et al, 2020; Sharma et al., 2023).
- **Voice, Gesture and Speech Recognition:** Machine learning has ushered in a new era of human-computer interaction, impacting both gesture recognition and voice interaction (Anbalagan et al., 2022; Hema & Garcia Marquez, 2023). ML has revolutionized touch screen and virtual reality interactions by

enabling gesture recognition. The technology interprets and reacts to hand and body movements, allowing users to navigate digital worlds using recognized gestures. The increasing presence of voice assistants such as Siri, Google Assistant, and Alexa demonstrates the effectiveness of machine learning in understanding and interacting with users' natural language. This technology allows for hands-free interfaces, enabling users to provide voice commands, ask questions, and receive responses in natural language. It improves convenience in tasks like scheduling reminders and retrieving information (Lv, 2022; Shah & Nautiyal, 2022).

- **Chatbots and Virtual Agents:** ML has introduced automated agents capable of comprehending and reacting to text and speech inputs, providing a variety of applications. Chatbots and virtual agents offer automated customer service, aid in information retrieval, and may engage in natural language dialogues. They are changing user interactions in customer care, e-commerce, and different online platforms (Adamopoulou & Moussiades, 2020; Mekni & Mekni, 2021; Suta et al., 2020; Yadav, 2021).

- **Personalization:** ML powers user personalization in digital experiences. Machine learning algorithms generate personalized user experiences by examining user data and behavior. Personalization can manifest in different ways, such as suggesting content, modifying layouts, and providing product recommendations. Streaming services and social media platforms utilize personalization to retain consumer interest and contentment (Koh et al., 2019; Xia, 2021).

- **Emotion Detection:** ML models can analyze users' voice, text, and facial expressions for emotions. This technology helps market researchers, healthcare professionals, and entertainers understand consumer sentiment. Understanding emotional cues improves user empathy and adaptability (Chowdary et al., 2021; Nayak et al., 2021; Zhang et al., 2020).

- **Natural Language Processing (NLP):** NLP—text analysis, sentiment analysis, language translation, and information retrieval—depends on machine learning. These features make it easier to identify relevant content, analyze sentiment, and access information in multiple languages (Lv, 2022; Naredla & Adedoyin, 2022).

- **Accessibility:** ML has made significant strides in enhancing accessibility for users with disabilities (Yadav, 2021). It enables screen readers for the visually impaired, voice recognition for motor disabled people, and predictive text input for mobility-challenged people. More people can employ digital interactions with these technology (Abbas et al., 2022; Aljedaani et al., 2022).

- **Healthcare:** ML in HCI helps personalize healthcare suggestions and treatment approaches. Machine learning helps healthcare providers make decisions by analyzing patient health information, lifestyle data, and medical histories. It helps customize and improve healthcare (Dino et al., 2022; Nazar et al., 2021).

- **Education:** Adaptive learning platforms are changing education with ML. These platforms customize student learning via machine learning (Toala et al., 2020; Zhang, 2022). Content and difficulty levels are changed based on progress, making learning more effective and personalized. Student involvement and outcomes improve.

- **Gaming:** Based on player interactions, ML algorithms generate content, adjust game complexity, and simulate NPC behavior. This dynamic modification makes games more demanding and engrossing (Diaz et al., 2019; Thakar et al., 2021; Whig et al., 2022).

- **Recommendation Systems:** In streaming, e-commerce, and news, recommendation systems are everywhere (Khanal et al., 2020; Ramzan et al., 2019; Ricci, 2022). These systems propose attractive items, articles, and videos using machine learning. These suggestions boost content discovery and engagement.

These applications highlight the versatility and potential impact of machine learning in HCI. By making interfaces more intuitive, adaptive, and personalized, machine learning enhances the overall user experience in a wide range of domains. However, ethical considerations, user data privacy, and issues related to bias and fairness must be addressed to ensure responsible and inclusive use of these technologies.

THE FUTURE OF HCI: POTENTIAL DEVELOPMENTS

The future of HCI promises to change how we utilize technology. This article explores the undiscovered frontiers of HCI and looks ahead to major advancements that will change the digital landscape. Domain-specific applications are important to study. Personalized therapy recommendations, remote patient monitoring, and telemedicine are becoming more popular in healthcare to improve efficiency and quality (Balcombe & De Leo, 2022). Modern e-commerce platforms use dynamic pricing and smart recommendation technologies to transform shopping. In education, adaptive learning platforms customize curricula and virtual classrooms make learning more engaging.

Emerging technologies like AR, VR, and mixed reality modify HCI as we explore them. These technologies are about to transform immersive experiences and how we study, work, and play. Voice assistants are also getting more conversational and emotional, improving user experiences (Al-Ansi et al., 2023). Cross-device connectivity offers a smooth transition, and smart environments allow us to customize our surroundings (Solomon & Sonia, 2024). We must prioritize ethics as we innovate. Privacy, data security, and justice are essential in the growing realm of HCI (Jiang & Shi, 2021; Mathis et al., 2022). The future of HCI promises more intuitive, efficient, and personalized digital interactions, but it also emphasizes designers' and engineers' responsibilities to create an ethical and user-centric digital landscape (Wang et al., 2022). *Table 1* shows the comprehensive view of the timeline, key application, challenges, benefits, and examples of potential developments in HCI.

Table 1. Comprehensive view of the potential developments in HCI

Potential Developments	Key Applications	Challenges	Benefits	Examples
Augmented Reality and Virtual Reality (AR/VR)	• Gaming • Education, • Training	• Hardware limitations, • Content creation • User adoption	Immersive experiences, interactive learning	• Oculus Rift • Microsoft HoloLens
Voice and Emotion Recognition	• Voice Assistants • Healthcare	• Privacy • Accuracy, • Emotional privacy	Enhanced user interactions, mental health support	• Amazon Alexa • Emotion AI
Domain-Specific Applications	• Healthcare • E-commerce • Education	• Data privacy, • Integration challenges, • Bias	Personalized experiences, improved services	• Adaptive learning platforms • personalized medicine
Smart Environments	• Smart Homes • Smart Cities	• Infrastructure, • Privacy, • Standardization	Efficient living and working, sustainability	• Nest, • Singapore's Smart City
Cross-Device Integration	• Seamless User Experience	• Interoperability, • Security, • User adaptation	Consistency in user experiences, convenience	• Apple's Continuity, • Microsoft's Your Phone
Ethical Considerations	• All applications	• Ethical awareness, • Policy development	User rights protection, responsible design	• GDPR, • Ethical AI Guidelines
Natural Language Understanding	• Chatbots • Virtual Assistants	• Semantic understanding • Context awareness	Conversational interfaces, accessibility	• Google Assistant • IBM Watson
Accessibility Improvements	• Healthcare • Education • Assistive Technology	• Design inclusivity, • Accessibility standards	Empowerment of users with disabilities	• Screen readers • Eye-tracking tech

continued on following page

Table 1. Continued

Potential Developments	Key Applications	Challenges	Benefits	Examples
Data-Driven Personalization	• E-commerce • Content Streaming	• Data privacy, • Algorithm bias • User consent	Tailored content, improved user experiences	• Netflix recommendations • Spotify
Haptic Feedback	• Gaming • Healthcare	• Hardware development, • content integration	Immersive and tactile experiences	• VR gaming controllers • Surgical robot

CHALLENGES AND ETHICAL CONSIDERATIONS

Integrating cutting-edge technologies, notably machine learning, into HCI, presents both benefits and challenges. This section explores the complex relationship between technology and mankind, focusing on the ethical issues and dilemmas that have emerged. The rise of machine learning has opened new HCI possibilities for more personalized, efficient, and adaptive digital interactions. Innovation hides a complicated web of challenges that require our attention and solutions. These difficulties range from technological issues and privacy concerns to algorithmic fairness and consumer acceptance. Furthermore, ethics are crucial to this story. As technology enters our daily lives, we must consider data privacy, user rights, and appropriate machine learning system development.

Challenges

According to Stephanidis et al (2019), findings there are seven grand challenges of challenges on HCI and their result identified that privacy and ethics are the major challenges of HCI. *Figure 2* shows the identified grand challenges of HCI.

Figure 2. Grand Challenges of HCI (Stephanidis et al., 2019)

Machine learning in HCI researchers, developers, and practitioners face challenges while designing, developing, or implementing machine learning-based solutions to improve user interactions with digital systems. These technical, ethical, and practical issues require creative answers (Xu et al., 2023). Data privacy, algorithmic bias, openness in automated systems, user acceptance and adoption, hardware limits, and more are among these complex issues (Jiang & Shi, 2021). These difficulties must be addressed to ensure that machine learning in HCI is successful, ethical, and user centric.

- **Privacy Concerns:** Personalization and user experience improvement need data gathering and analysis, which raises privacy concerns. Users concerned about data use and security.
- **Data Security:** User data security is crucial. Cyberattacks and data breaches disclose sensitive information, lowering user confidence.
- **Bias in Algorithms:** ML algorithms may perpetuate training data bias. Bias can cause unfair or biased results in recommendation systems, recruiting algorithms, and healthcare.
- **Transparency:** Users typically struggle to understand algorithm decisions. Mistrust and uncertainty can emerge from lack of transparency.

- **User Adoption:** New HCI technologies like AR/VR and speech recognition may struggle to gain adoption owing to expense, unfamiliarity, or intrusiveness.
- **Standardization:** HCI in smart settings requires standards and protocols for interoperability and uniform user experiences.

Ethical Considerations

Machine learning ethics in HCI govern the appropriate and moral development, deployment, and usage of machine learning technology (Bach et al., 2024; Waycott, 2016). The following are important factors:

- **Informed Consent:** Users must be informed about data gathering and its purpose and have the option to opt out or remove their data.
- **Fairness and Non-Discrimination:** HCI technology should not discriminate based on race, gender, or age.
- **Transparency and Explainability:** Developers should make algorithms clear and explainable so people can comprehend decisions.
- **User Empowerment:** Users should have autonomy over their data and be enabled to make well-informed decisions on their engagements with technology.
- **Data Minimization:** Collect and store essential data for the intended purpose to reduce the risk of privacy breaches.
- **Responsible AI Development:** Developers and organizations should follow ethical AI principles to create and use AI systems ethically.
- **User Feedback and Redress:** Users should be able to submit comments or seek recourse for algorithmic faults or data misuse.
- **Continual Monitoring and Auditing:** HCI systems should be monitored and audited to identify and fix ethical concerns.

Building user trust and responsible HCI technology development and use requires addressing these issues and ethical considerations. Technology developers, governments, and users must work together to build an ethical and safe digital environment.

CONCLUSION

The future of Human-Computer Interaction (HCI) is poised for revolutionary advancements, mostly propelled by the incorporation of machine learning. As we explore this unfamiliar region, some important points become clear. Machine learning is crucial in the development of HCI as it allows for predictive analytics, customisation, and adaptation. The engine powers intelligent recommendations and predictive text to improve user experiences. Machine learning will increasingly be integrated into our regular digital interactions as the field of progresses.

Machine learning-powered domain-specific apps are transforming multiple industries, including healthcare and e-commerce. Personalization, a consequence of machine learning algorithms, is becoming essential, offering customized solutions and suggestions. Utilizing data to make decisions is now essential in all areas, not just a luxury. Smart environments and cross-device integration, driven by machine learning, provide consumers with smooth and uninterrupted interactions across various devices. This transition is driven by ethical issues. Machine learning-driven HCI must prioritize user privacy, data security, and justice. Transparency and fairness in algorithms are essential in the growing field of machine learning in HCI. These ideas are crucial for establishing and preserving user trust. Design that is responsible, respects user rights, and includes channels for feedback and redress is crucial for the future of HCI.

The future of HCI is closely connected to the progress in machine learning. The opportunity exists to develop a digital environment that is personalized, immersive, and efficient, powered by data-driven and sophisticated algorithms. Throughout this journey, it is crucial to prioritize ethical issues to achieve the full potential of machine learning in HCI while upholding fairness and human well-being ideals. Collaboration among technologists, policymakers, and consumers is crucial for maximizing the capabilities of machine learning in HCI while maintaining ethical norms.

REFERENCES

Abbas, A. M. H., Ghauth, K. I., & Ting, C. Y. (2022). User Experience Design Using Machine Learning: A Systematic Review. *IEEE Access : Practical Innovations, Open Solutions*, 10, 51501–51514. 10.1109/ACCESS.2022.3173289

Adamopoulou, E., & Moussiades, L. (2020). Chatbots: History, technology, and applications. *Machine Learning with Applications*, 2, 100006. 10.1016/j.mlwa.2020.100006

Al-Ansi, A. M., Jaboob, M., Garad, A., & Al-Ansi, A. (2023). Analyzing augmented reality (AR) and virtual reality (VR) recent development in education. *Social Sciences & Humanities Open*, 8(1), 100532. 10.1016/j.ssaho.2023.100532

Aljedaani, W., Mkaouer, M. W., Ludi, S., & Javed, Y. (2022). Automatic Classification of Accessibility User Reviews in Android Apps. *Proceedings - 2022 7th International Conference on Data Science and Machine Learning Applications, CDMA 2022*. IEEE. 10.1109/CDMA54072.2022.00027

Anbalagan, B., Radhika, R., Jayanthi, R., & Rama Prabha, K. P. (2022). Leveraging Machine Learning Based Human Voice Emotion Recognition System from Audio Samples. *AIP Conference Proceedings*, 2455(1). 10.1063/5.0101448

Bach, T. A., Khan, A., Hallock, H., Beltrão, G., & Sousa, S. (2024). A Systematic Literature Review of User Trust in AI-Enabled Systems: An HCI Perspective. *International Journal of Human-Computer Interaction*, 40(5), 1251–1266. 10.1080/10447318.2022.2138826

Balcombe, L. & De Leo, D. (2022). Human-Computer Interaction in Digital Mental Health. *Informatics 2022*, 9(1). .10.3390/informatics9010014

Chowdary, M. K., Nguyen, T. N., & Hemanth, D. J. (2021). Deep learning-based facial emotion recognition for human–computer interaction applications. *Neural Computing & Applications*, 35(32), 23311–23328. 10.1007/s00521-021-06012-8

Corno, F., De Russis, L., & Monge Roffarello, A. (2021). *Devices, Information, and People: Abstracting the Internet of Things for End-User Personalization.Lecture Notes in Computer Science (including subseries Lecture Notes in Artificial Intelligence and Lecture Notes in Bioinformatics)*. Springer. 10.1007/978-3-030-79840-6_5

Diaz, C. G., Perry, P., & Fiebrink, R. (2019). Interactive machine learning for more expressive game interactions. *IEEE Conference on Computatonal Intelligence and Games, CIG*. IEEE. 10.1109/CIG.2019.8848007

Dino, M. J. S., Davidson, P. M., Dion, K. W., Szanton, S. L., & Ong, I. L. (2022). Nursing and human-computer interaction in healthcare robots for older people: An integrative review. *International Journal of Nursing Studies Advances*, 4, 100072. 10.1016/j.ijnsa.2022.10007238745638

Hema, C., & Garcia Marquez, F. P. (2023). Emotional speech Recognition using CNN and Deep learning techniques. *Applied Acoustics*, 211, 109492. 10.1016/j.apacoust.2023.109492

Hochheiser, H., & Valdez, R. S. (2020). Human-Computer Interaction, Ethics, and Biomedical Informatics. *Yearbook of Medical Informatics*, 29(1), 93–98. 10.1055/s-0040-170199032823302

Issa, T., & Isaias, P. (2022). *Usability and Human–Computer Interaction (HCI)*. Sustainable Design. 10.1007/978-1-4471-7513-1_2

Jaiswal, A., Krishnama Raju, A., & Deb, S. (2020). Facial emotion detection using deep learning. *2020 International Conference for Emerging Technology, INCET 2020*. IEEE. 10.1109/INCET49848.2020.9154121

Jiang, D., & Shi, G. (2021). Research on Data Security and Privacy Protection of Wearable Equipment in Healthcare. *Journal of Healthcare Engineering*, 2021, 1–7. 10.1155/2021/665620433628404

Jordan, M. (2015). Machine learning: Trends, perspectives, and prospects. *Science (1979)*, 349(6245), 255–260. .10.1126/science.aaa8415

Khanal, S. S., Prasad, P. W. C., Alsadoon, A., & Maag, A. (2020, July). A systematic review: Machine learning based recommendation systems for e-learning. *Education and Information Technologies*, 25(4), 2635–2664. 10.1007/s10639-019-10063-9

Khuat, T. T., Kedziora, D. J., & Gabrys, B. (2022). The Roles and Modes of Human Interactions with Automated Machine Learning Systems. https://arxiv.org/abs/2205.04139v1

Koh, S., Wi, H. J., Hyung Kim, B., & Jo, S. (2019). Personalizing the Prediction: Interactive and Interpretable machine learning. *2019 16th International Conference on Ubiquitous Robots, UR 2019*. IEEE. 10.1109/URAI.2019.8768705

Li, Y., Amelot, J., Zhou, X., Bengio, S., & Si, S. (2020). Auto Completion of User Interface Layout Design Using Transformer-Based Tree Decoders. arXiv. https://arxiv.org/abs/2001.05308v1

Li, Y., Kumar, R., Lasecki, W. S., & Hilliges, O. (2020). Artificial intelligence for HCI: A modern approach. *Conference on Human Factors in Computing Systems – Proceedings*. ACM. 10.1145/3334480.3375147

Lv, Z. (2022). Deep Learning for Intelligent Human–Computer Interaction, *Applied Sciences,12*(22), 11457. .10.3390/app122211457

Mathis, F., Vaniea, K., & Khamis, M. (2022). Prototyping Usable Privacy and Security Systems: Insights from Experts. *International Journal of Human-Computer Interaction*, 38(5), 468–490. 10.1080/10447318.2021.1949134

Mekni, M., & Mekni, M. (2021). An Artificial Intelligence Based Virtual Assistant Using Conversational Agents. *Journal of Software Engineering and Applications*, 14(9), 455–473. 10.4236/jsea.2021.149027

Moreno, L., Petrie, H., Martínez, P., & Alarcon, R. (2023). Designing user interfaces for content simplification aimed at people with cognitive impairments. *Universal Access in the Information Society*, 1, 1–19. 10.1007/S10209-023-00986-Z/FIGURES/1037361672

Naredla, N. R., & Adedoyin, F. F. (2022). Detection of hyperpartisan news articles using natural language processing technique. *International Journal of Information Management Data Insights*, 2(1), 100064. 10.1016/j.jjimei.2022.100064

Nayak, S., Nagesh, B., Routray, A., & Sarma, M. (2021). A Human–Computer Interaction framework for emotion recognition through time-series thermal video sequences. *Computers & Electrical Engineering*, 93, 107280. 10.1016/j.compeleceng.2021.107280

Nazar, M., Alam, M. M., Yafi, E., & Su'ud, M. M. (2021). A Systematic Review of Human–Computer Interaction and Explainable Artificial Intelligence in Healthcare With Artificial Intelligence Techniques. *IEEE Access : Practical Innovations, Open Solutions*, 9, 153316–153348. 10.1109/ACCESS.2021.3127881

Ramzan, B., Bajwa, I. S., Jamil, N., Amin, R. U., Ramzan, S., Mirza, F., & Sarwar, N. (2019). An Intelligent Data Analysis for Recommendation Systems Using Machine Learning. *Scientific Programming*, 2019, 1–20. 10.1155/2019/5941096

Ricci, F. (2022). Recommender Systems: Techniques, Applications, and Challenges, *Recommender Systems Handbook*. CSE. doi:.10.1007/978-1-0716-2197-4_1/COVER

Rogers, Y. (2012). *HCI Theory*. Springer. .10.1007/978-3-031-02197-8

Sabie, D., Ekmekcioglu, C., & Ahmed, S. I. (2022). A Decade of International Migration Research in HCI: Overview, Challenges, Ethics, Impact, and Future Directions. *ACM Transactions on Computer-Human Interaction*, 29(4), 1–35. 10.1145/3490555

Saffar, A. H., Mann, T. K., & Ofoghi, B. (2023). Textual emotion detection in health: Advances and applications. *Journal of Biomedical Informatics*, 137, 104258. 10.1016/j.jbi.2022.10425836528329

Sardar, S. K., Kumar, N., & Lee, S. C. (2022). A Systematic Literature Review on Machine Learning Algorithms for Human Status Detection. *IEEE Access : Practical Innovations, Open Solutions*, 10, 74366–74382. 10.1109/ACCESS.2022.3190967

Shah, S. K., & Nautiyal, A. (2022). Signal Quality Assessment for Speech Recognition using Deep Convolutional Neural Networks. *MysuruCon 2022 - 2022 IEEE 2nd Mysore Sub Section International Conference*. IEEE. 10.1109/MysuruCon55714.2022.9972718

Sharma, A., Gupta, A., Bhargava, A., Rawat, A., Yadav, P., & Gupta, D. (2023). From Sci-Fi to Reality: The Evolution of Human-Computer Interaction with Artificial Intelligence, *Proceedings of the 2nd International Conference on Applied Artificial Intelligence and Computing, ICAAIC 2023*, (pp. 127–134). IEEE. 10.1109/ICAAIC56838.2023.10141431

Siddiq, M. (2023). Exploring the Role of Machine Learning in Contact Tracing for Public Health: Benefits, Challenges, and Ethical Considerations [AJEMB]. *American Journal of Economic and Management Business*, 2(3), 99–110. 10.58631/ajemb.v2i4.29

Solomon, D. D., & Sonia, M. (2024). Edge Computing empowered Cross-Platform Tool for Multifactorial Disorder Risk Assessment, *2024 11th International Conference on Computing for Sustainable Global Development (INDIACom)*, (pp. 1798–1803). IEEE. 10.23919/INDIACom61295.2024.10498639

Stephanidis, C., Salvendy, G., Antona, M., Chen, J. Y. C., Dong, J., Duffy, V. G., Fang, X., Fidopiastis, C., Fragomeni, G., Fu, L. P., Guo, Y., Harris, D., Ioannou, A., Jeong, K. K., Konomi, S., Krömker, H., Kurosu, M., Lewis, J. R., Marcus, A., & Zhou, J. (2019). Seven HCI Grand Challenges. *International Journal of Human-Computer Interaction*, 35(14), 1229–1269. 10.1080/10447318.2019.1619259

Suta, P., Lan, X., Wu, B., Mongkolnam, P., & Chan, J. H. (2020). An overview of machine learning in chatbots. *International Journal of Mechanical Engineering and Robotics Research*, 9(4), 502–510. 10.18178/ijmerr.9.4.502-510

Thakar, T., Saroj, R., & Bharde, V. (2021). Hand Gesture Controlled Gaming Application, *International Research Journal of Engineering and Technology*. www.irjet.net

Toala, R., Durães, D., & Novais, P. (2020). Human-computer interaction in intelligent tutoring systems. *Advances in Intelligent Systems and Computing*, 1003, 52–59. 10.1007/978-3-030-23887-2_7

Wang, Y., Siau, K. L., & Wang, L. (2022). Metaverse and Human-Computer Interaction: A Technology Framework for 3D Virtual Worlds. *Lecture Notes in Computer Science (including subseries Lecture Notes in Artificial Intelligence and Lecture Notes in Bioinformatics)*, (pp. 213–221). 10.1007/978-3-031-21707-4_16

Waycott, J. (2016). Ethical encounters in human-computer interaction, *Conference on Human Factors in Computing Systems – Proceedings*. ACM. 10.1145/2851581.2856498

Waycott, J. (2017). Ethical encounters in HCI: Implications for research in sensitive settings, *Conference on Human Factors in Computing Systems – Proceedings*. ACM. 10.1145/3027063.3027089

Whig, P., Velu, A., & Ready, R. (2022). *Demystifying Federated Learning in Artificial Intelligence With Human-Computer Interaction*. IGI Global. 10.4018/978-1-6684-3733-9.ch006

Xia, P. (2021). Design of Personalized Intelligent Learning Assistant System Under Artificial Intelligence Background. *Advances in Intelligent Systems and Computing*, 1282, 194–200. 10.1007/978-3-030-62743-0_27

Xu, W., Dainoff, M. J., Ge, L., & Gao, Z. (2023). Transitioning to Human Interaction with AI Systems: New Challenges and Opportunities for HCI Professionals to Enable Human-Centered AI. *International Journal of Human-Computer Interaction*, 39(3), 494–518. 10.1080/10447318.2022.2041900

Yadav, A. (2021). *Virtual Assistant For Blind People*. doi: .10.51319/2456-0774.2021.5.0036

Zdanowska, S., & Taylor, A. S. (2022). A study of UX practitioners roles in designing real-world, enterprise ML systems. *Conference on Human Factors in Computing Systems – Proceedings*. ACM. 10.1145/3491102.3517607

Zhang, A. (2022). Human Computer Interaction System for Teacher-Student Interaction Model Using Machine Learning. *International Journal of Human-Computer Interaction*, 1–12. 10.1080/10447318.2022.2115645

Zhang, J., Yin, Z., Chen, P., & Nichele, S. (2020). Emotion recognition using multi-modal data and machine learning techniques: A tutorial and review. *Information Fusion*, 59, 103–126. 10.1016/j.inffus.2020.01.011

Chapter 17
Cloud–Enhanced Machine Learning for Handwritten Character Recognition in Dementia Patients

Muhammad Hasnain
Abasyn University, Pakistan

Fahad Masood
Abasyn University, Pakistan

Venkataramaiah Gude
https://orcid.org/0009-0009-1392
-3385
GP Technologies LLC, USA

Wajid Ullah Khan
Abasyn University, Pakistan

Muhammad Imad
Abasyn University, Peshawar, Pakistan

Michael Onyema Edeh
https://orcid.org/0000-0002-4067
-3256
*Coal City University, Nigeria &
Saveetha School of Engineering,
SIMATS, Chennai, India*

Nwosu Ogochukwu Fidelia
University of Nigeria, Nigeria

ABSTRACT

The study addresses the challenge dementia patients face in recognizing handwritten characters by developing a cloud-integrated system that uses a multilayer neural network for character recognition. The system involves four main steps: preprocessing (noise reduction and normalization), segmentation (extracting characters from scanned pages), feature extraction (using a modified zone-based method), and recognition. The extracted features, represented as pixel value vectors, are classified using four machine learning algorithms—support vector machine with RBF, random forest, linear SVM, and logistic regression. The random forest algorithm performs

DOI: 10.4018/979-8-3693-2869-9.ch017

best with an accuracy of 89%. Cloud technology enhances the system's scalability, allowing for real-time processing and remote access, beneficial for dementia care.

INTRODUCTION

Dementia is a widespread neurological disease (Alzheimer's Association, 2020; Prince et al., 2014). Approximately 8 to 10 million people worldwide suffer from this disease. The prevalence of this disease ranges from 47 to 90,000 people in the fourth decade of life and up to more than 1,800 to 150,000 among people over the age of 80. Patients with this disorder and newly diagnosed disease states usually increase with age, although it may stabilize in people over the age of 80. Approximately 4% of people are diagnoses before the age of 50. In Men, the rate of this disorder is 1.7 times more often than in women. About one million Americans have dementia disease. The number of patients exceeds multiplesclerosis(MS),muscular dystrophy (DM) and amyotrophic lateral sclerosis(ALS). An estimated 60,000 Americans develop dementia every year. This does not reveal the thousands of undiscovered cases. The costs of dementia patients in the United States, including medical treatment, disabilities and similar expenses, and lost income due to the inability to work, is estimated$25billionannually.According to a survey by UCB (UCB, 2022), an international biopharmaceutical corporation that focuses on serious diseases, the company operates in about 40 countries. Currently, more than 100,000 Canadians suffer from Dementia and approximately 6,600 Dementia is diagnoses each year in Canada. In the UK, the prevalence of Dementia disease out of 500 is approx one, and a whole of about 127,000 people suffer from the disease. In the UK every hour, someone is diagnoses with Dementia disease. Most are over 50 years old (Prince et al., 2014).

This rate is expected to increase dramatically in the coming years. It is now widely recognized that dementia is widespread throughout the world and the burden of dementia symptoms is enormous on affected individuals, their families, and society. The following Figure 1 shows the overall recorded cases of dementia around the globe.

Figure 1. Recorded cases of Dementia

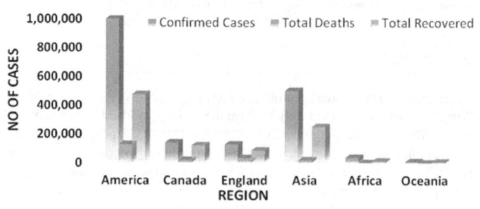

In African population, the spreading of dementia is at recorded rate .In 2015,more than 58% of all dementia patients lived in low and intermediate-level countries (known as developing countries),of which 4.03 million lived in Africa. The global incidence of dementia in adults over 50 in Africa is estimate to be around 2.4%. In 2010, 2.76 million people suffered from the disease. Approximately2.1million people live in sub-Saharan Africa. The number and rate of dementia disorder in developing countries is higher than those in developed countries are, but there corded number of cases as depicted inTable1 inverse the statement.

Table 1. Dementia Recorded Cases

Region Status	America	Canada	England	Asia	Africa	Oceania
Confirmed Cases	1,000,000	140,000	127,000	501,192	36,034	8,322
Total Deaths	127,533	18,780	33,490	18,071	1536	108
Total Recovered	475,666	121,220	86,580	248,711	12,135	6,974

The Artificial Neural Network is a model of the human nervous system. In this work, for offline handwritten, artificial neural network is used. Character recognition system and feature abstraction are uses in this paper for classifying and identifying the 26 English alphabets. The binary values resultant from the resized shape of the segmented phase have used for artificial neural network training. After feature extraction techniques, the planned system will be less multifaceted related to the offline method. The rest of the paper is organizes as: in section II literature review is under consideration, section III explains the hand- written character recognition system for dementia patient, section IV discusses the results and section V concludes the paper.

LITERATURE REVIEW

The researchers in Verma (1995) states that there are different types of rules used by neural networks; this manifestation is apprehensive only with the one-delta rule. It is utilized by general class called 'Back propagation neural networks' (BPNNs). Several people wrote Sindhi hand written language in unrestricted form and then written characters examples arescan and collect. Scan document were pre-process from binary conversion, and eliminate noise by pepper noise and segmented from horizontal profile technique (Verma, 1995).

Character images in the documents are blurred as a result character image is enforced by a kind of cracked and disordered appearances, this aspect leads to many differing actions of the recognition algorithm which in return reduce the accurateness of recognition. It characterizes a requested mapping, a sort of projection from an arrangement of given information things onto a customary, normally two- dimensional grid and model mi is related to every grid node. Convolution Neural Network (CNN) is a significant development through machine-learning classification algorithms (Alzheimer's Association, 2020). Models are registered algorithm. An information thing will be mapped into the node whose model is most likes the information thing, e.g., it has the littlest separation from the information thing in some metric.

The challenges faced in handwriting recognition in Arabic are vast. It is diffi- cult to teach non-Arabic speakers who do not know what they are saying or what they mean at a young age. In Dhandra (2010a) A new algorithm based on neural networks that use the activated correct function and then regularization layer is propose, which shows significantly better precision than existing Arabic numerical recognition methods. The proposed model (Dhandra, 2010a) provides 97.4 percent precision, which is the maximum recorded in the dataset used in the experiment. It is also recommended to change the method described, where our method achieves the same accuracy, with a value of 93. 8%.In this paper, the neural network is uses to recognize the character. 0ff-line strategies developed for the lonely handwritten English characters. It improves the character recognition method. Binarization method is uses for preprocessing of the Character, threshold and segmentation. Feed forward back propagation method is uses to classify the characters. Binary numbers have represented English numerical letter that are uses as input and fed to an ANN (Patel & Thakkar, 2015).

The article (Dhandra, 2010b) provides a detailed discussion of Handwriting Analysis (HCR) in English. Handwriting recognition has been use in various applications, such as the banking industry, the healthcare sector and many institutions where handwritten documents are manages. Handwriting is the process of converting handwritten text into easy-to-read format. There are difficulties for handwritten characters because they differ from one writer to another, even when the same person writes the same character. There is a difference in the shape, size and position of the character. Recent research in this field has used different types of methods, classification tools and resources to reduce complex handwriting analysis (Dhandra, 2010b).

Imitation of human reading with the machine has been the subject of much research for more than two decades. A large number of articles and research reports has already been publish. Many business units have produced survey equipment with different capabilities. Portable, desktop, medium and large systems costing up to half a million dollars are available and used for a variety of applications. However, the ultimate goal of developing a typewriter with the same

reading ability as humans is unacceptable. Therefore, there is still a large gap between human reading and automatic reading ability, and more efforts are require to reducing this gap, if not to fill it. The review is organizes into six main chapters that deal with an overview (presentation), application of personal knowledge technology, methodology for personal analysis, research work in personal analysis, some practical OCR and conclusions.

Architecture and training algorithms for layered neural networks are discussed. The characteristic of the first amount of weight coefficients and the bias of neural node is emphasized and choice of the training speed coefficient. This additional development of the neural network of MLNN (Multi-Layer) almost address the implementation of adaptive algorithm choose network training speed and learn to reduce neurons counting on the input layer. The handwritten recognition of the character is not a small task because it tries to recognize the correct recognition of the class for the independent user character. This problem is even more difficult for a highly stylized, Morphological complex, and potentially junta positional languages such as Bengali. As a result, the improvement in the identification of the character Bengal character over the years is considerably smaller than in other languages. Most of the errors that occurred in pattern for the recognition work were due to unusual forms of staff.

Handwritten Character Recognition System

In the section, we are discussing handwritten character recognition system for dementia patients. The whole system is divide into different sub-sections, which is depict in the following Figure 2. The four sub-sections are;

A. Pre-processing
B. Segmentation
C. Feature extraction
D. Classification

Figure 2. Handwritten character recognition system

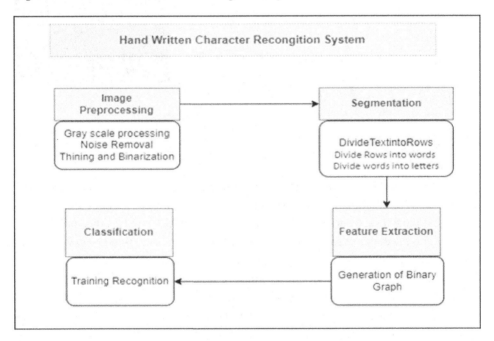

Pre-Processing

The patient's handwritten characters are scan and passes from the pre-processing phase. Dementia patient's handwritten characters are scan at 350 dpi; some images are scan at 250 dpi. The high dpi is select due to bugs and faded writing and broken characters. One sample is depict in Figure 3 (a),which is scan as a color image and followed by a grayscale transformation to white and black Figure 3 (b). The process of conversion is known as binary Figure 3 (c). After scanning and converting the images to black and white, noise reduction is used to remove small dots called noise. This process shows the shaping of the grayscale color image to white and black. Two-color coloring is due to identify the text and extract the background. Additional OCR processing can be perform on both types of images, for example black foreground on white background, as the goal is to identify and recognize text and characters.

Figure 3. Pre-Processing phase

Segmentation

In the segmentation process, the characters are recognizes as letters and images are converted into text. The image is scan and converts into a text-only binary image. Save the binary image and clear the memory. This phase increases the speed of the system. The borders are removed first and the text is divided into lines, words and letters. The handwritten scan images are split into a line of text containing letters of dementia patients. We segment the lines of text by counting the space between moments or lines Figure 4 (c). These rows are numbered and the availability of a white dot. No text means the space is free and divides the row. The same procedure is applied to a word. In this research we recognize an individual letter Figure 4(d). This process will leads to extra overhead in terms of time. It means that separate letter is treated as word. This process is applied horizontally and the available characters were divided into a single line using the same technique, except that it was a vertical arrangement.

Figure 4. Segmentation process

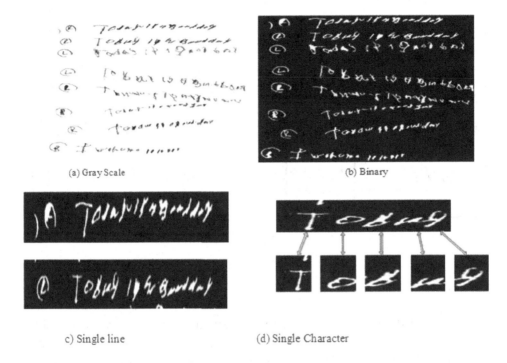

(a) Gray Scale

(b) Binary

c) Single line

(d) Single Character

Feature Extraction

In pattern recognition when the inputs are large for processing and expected to contain data, we convert the input to a reduced set of features representations (also called feature vectors). In this research, modified zoning is use to remove features from patient characters written by different subjects (Miroslav, 2011). A large amount of computation benefits may be achieved by applying an efficient feature extraction method. The characteristic method offers a good accuracy ratio. The extracted image of character is divided into 3x3 areas Figure 3 and a sum of 9 areas is created to signify the isolated patient's handwritten character. We subtract the outline objects from the segment of 0-8.

Figure 5. Feature extraction phase

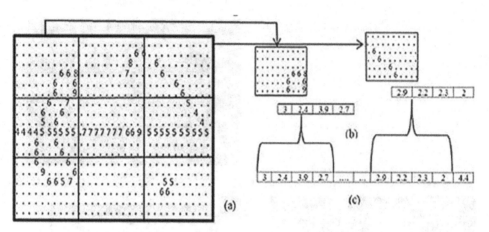

Classification

The extracted features are associated with the train pattern of the characters (Ebrahimpour et al., 2010). ANN (Artificial Neural Network) is use for organization and recognition. Feed forward Network is likely to produce first class results, especially if the inputs are unknown. This training can improve the accuracy of identifying characters by patients. The handwritten character images were pre-processed, then these scanned images were divide into lines and the fonts were remove from the scanned text images. The features are extracted using the scanned images and then, with the help of an artificial neural network, the features of images were combined with the present training images. We calculate the accuracy from correctly identified numbers and their average value. The percentage of characters recognized correctly and the character showed the highest accuracy due to lack of precision and deficiency of dots. The character is different from the other for example A to H and K to Z. Characters without dot have high accuracy than with dots.

Results and Discussions

The performance accuracy of the four-classification technique (Logistic Regression, Linear Support Vector Machine, and SVM with RBF, Random Forest algorithm) is depicted in Figure 6.

Logistic Regression

This process is the proper regression analysis to perform when the variable is binary and dependent. Like any regression analysis, it is a prophetic analysis used to illustrate data and the relationship between a binary dependent variable and one or more independent variables at the nominal and ratio levels (Imad, 2022).

Mathematically, it estimates a multiple linear regression function, which is define as:

$$\log(p) \tag{1}$$

$$\log(p(y = 1)|1 - (p = 1)) = \beta + \beta rxn + \beta 2. \, xa + - + \beta p - xn \tag{2}$$

$$\text{For } i = 1 \ldots . \tag{3}$$

The regression equation with one independent variable and one dependent variable is defined by the formula y = c + b * x, where c = constant, b = coefficient of regression, x = score of the independent variable and y = estimated score of the dependent variable,. Another important consideration when selecting a model for logistic regression analysis is model fit (Khashman, 2008).

Linear Support Vector Classifier (Svc)

The most suitable machine-learning algorithm for the problem is Linear SVC (Imad et al., 2020; Khan, 2020). You can plug some functionality into your classifier to see what the predicted class is and hence this particular algorithm suits better. To perform the classification a linear kernel function method uses and performs well with a huge number of samples (Verma, 1995). Classify Data Using Python's Linear SVC Class:

- Preparing the data
- Training the model
- Predicting and accuracy check

Svm With Radial Basis Function Kernel (Rbf)

This method often used to solve classification problems that fall into the category of supervised machine learning. SVMs can also be used for other problems (Hussain et al., 2023; Hussain et al., 2022), such as:

- Clustering (unattended learning) using support vector clustering algorithm
- Regression (supervised learning) using Support Vector Regression (SVR) algorithm

RBF is the kernel used in sklearn's SVM classification algorithm and can be described by the following formula:

$$(x, x') = e - r^{\|x-x'\|} \tag{4}$$

$\|x - x'\|^2 (L_2$ norm)is the Euclidean distance between two points X_1 and X_2. Where gamma can be set manually and must be > 0 (Ebrahimpour et al., 2010).Gamma is a scalar that defines the influence of a single training point.

Random Forest

It is a supervised learning algorithm. The set of "forest" decision trees it builds, which is usually trained using the "bagged" method. The general idea of the plundering method is that the grouping of learning models increases the result.A random forest generates more decision trees and combines them to get a more accurate prediction. One of the great advantages of a random forest is that it can be uses for both the regression and classification problems that make up most machine learning systems today (Bag et al., 2011). The Random Forest obtained the best performance among all the classification algorithms. The accuracy of the Random Forest is 89%, precision is 75%, and recall is 80%, specificity (Imad et al., 2023). The study contributes to the growing studies on the power of machine learning and artificial intelligence (Edeh et al., 2021; Ma et al., 2022; Onyema et al., 2023).

Figure 6. Performance evaluation

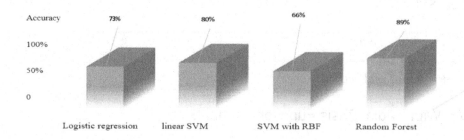

338

Conclusion and Future Work

In this research, a cloud-based handwritten character recognition system for dementia patients using a neural network is presented. The research on handwritten recognition for dementia patients is still in its early stages, representing a foundational step toward recognizing handwritten words, sentences, and ultimately full text from patients' handwriting in images. Text images were written on different pages, and samples were gathered from both male and female patients. These scanned images are processed in the cloud, where each character undergoes preprocessing and segmentation using line segmentation. Feature extraction is then applied, followed by a classification phase utilizing four state-of-the-art algorithms. The experimental results demonstrate that the Random Forest algorithm achieves the highest accuracy of 89%, outperforming Linear SVM (80% accuracy), SVM with RBF (66% accuracy), and Logistic Regression (73% accuracy). Cloud integration provides scalable storage and processing capabilities, facilitating real-time analysis and remote accessibility. Future work aims to enhance the system's accuracy by applying more efficient algorithms in both the feature extraction and classification phases, leveraging cloud resources for improved performance.

REFERENCES

Alzheimer's Association. (2020). *Alzheimer's and Dementia disease facts and figures*. Wiley. https://alz-journals.onlinelibrary.wiley.com/doi/full/10.1002/alz.12068.

Bag, S., Bhowmick, P., & Harit, G. (2011). Recognition of Bengali Handwritten Characters Using Skeletal Convexity and Dynamic Programming. *2011 Second International Conference on Emerging Applications of Information Technology*. IEEE. 10.1109/EAIT.2011.44

Dhandra, B. V. (2010a). Spatial features for handwritten Kannada and English character recognition. *International Journal of Computer Applications*, 146–150.

Dhandra, , B. (2010b). English character recognition. *International Journal of Computer Applications*, 146–150.

Ebrahimpour, R., Esmkhani, A., & Faridi, S. (2010, July 25). Farsi handwritten digit recognition based on mixture of RBF experts. *IEICE Electronics Express*, 7(14), 1014–1019. 10.1587/elex.7.1014

Edeh, M. O., Ugorji, C. C., Nduanya, U. I., Onyewuchi, C., Ohwo, S. O., & Ikedilo, O. E. (2021). Prospects and Limitations of Machine Learning in Computer Science Education. *Benin Journal of Educational Studies*, 27(1), 48–62. http://beninjes.com/index.php/bjes/article/view/70

Hussain, A., Ahmad, B., Imad, M., & Cane, S. (2023). Obstacle Recognition for Visually Impaired People Based on Convolutional Neural Network. *Machine Intelligence for Internet of Medical Things: Applications and Future Trends Computational Intelligence for Data Analysis*, 2, 194–209. 10.2174/9789815080445123020015

Hussain, A., Imad, M., Khan, A., & Ullah, B. (2022). Multi-class Classification for the Identification of COVID-19 in X-Ray Images Using Customized Efficient Neural Network. *AI and IoT for Sustainable Development in Emerging Countries*. Springer. 10.1007/978-3-030-90618-4_23

Imad, M., Hassan, M. A., & Bangash, S. H. (2023). Naimullah; Machine Learning Solution for Orthopedics: A Comprehensive Review. *Machine Intelligence for Internet of Medical Things: Applications and Future Trends Computational Intelligence for Data Analysis*, 2, 120–136. 10.2174/9789815080445123020011

Imad, M., Ullah, F., & Hassan, M. A. (2020). Pakistani Currency Recognition to Assist Blind Person Based on Convolutional Neural Network. *Journal of Computer Science and Technology Studies*, 2(2), 12–19.

UCB. (2022). *Home*. UCB. https://www.ucb.com/

Khan, N. (2020). COVID-19 Classification based on Chest X-Ray Images Using Machine Learning Techniques. *Journal of Computer Science and Technology Studies*, 01-11.

Khashman, A. (2008, November). A Modified Backpropagation Learning Algorithm with Added Emotional Coefficients. *IEEE Transactions on Neural Networks*, 19(11), 1896–1909. 10.1109/TNN.2008.200291318990644

Imad, M. (2022). *A Comparative Analysis of Intrusion Detection in IoT Network Using Machine Learning* (pp. 149–163). Springer. 10.1007/978-3-031-05752-6_10

Ma, L., Gupta, R. K., & Onyema, E. M. (2022). Optimization of Intelligent Network Information Management System under Big Data and Cloud Computing. *Scalable Computing: Practice and Experience*, 23(3), 91–101. 10.12694/scpe.v23i3.2001

Miroslav, N. (2011). Image preprocessing for optical character recognition using neural networks. *Journal of Patter Recognition Research*.

Onyema, E. M., Khan, R., Eucheria, N. C., & Kumar, T. (2023). Impact of Mobile Technology and Use of Big Data in Physics Education During Coronavirus Lockdown. *Big Data Mining and Analytic*, 6(3), 381–389. 10.26599/BDMA.2022.9020013

Patel, M., & Thakkar, S. P. (2015). Handwritten character recognition in english: A survey. *International Journal of Advanced Research in Computer and Communication Engineering*, 4(2), 345–350. 10.17148/IJARCCE.2015.4278

Prince, M., Knapp, M., Guerchet, M., McCrone, P., & Prina, M. (2014). *Dementia UK: - Overview*.

Verma, B. K. (1995). Handwritten Hindi Character Recognition Using Multilayer Perceptron and Radial Basis Function Neural Network. *IEEE International Conference on Neural Network*. IEEE. 10.1109/ICNN.1995.489003

Chapter 18
Sustaining Adaptation to the New Normal:
Tenacity and Originality in Higher Education Marketing After the COVID–19 Pandemic

Redouan Ainous
https://orcid.org/0000-0001-9646-5774
University of Algiers, Algeria

ABSTRACT

This study delves into the response of higher education institutions around the world to the COVID-19 pandemic, focusing on their capacity to sustain adaptation, resilience, and innovation while upholding their educational mission in a post-COVID-19 environment. The transition from semi-structured setups to more methodological systems, tailored to the post-COVID-19 era, is examined. The analysis assesses the strategies employed by these institutions to safeguard their academic communities from misguided practices. Findings from the study highlight the emergence of novel approaches by educators and the readiness of teachers to adapt to the new normal post-COVID-19. This adaptation is facilitated by cutting-edge technologies, which offer substantial support for flexibility and innovation. The chapter also presents an overview of the applications used by higher education institutions in response to the pandemic, underscoring the vital qualities of resilience and innovation in the transition to the new post-COVID-19 normal.

DOI: 10.4018/979-8-3693-2869-9.ch018

INTRODUCTION

The context of the COVID-19 pandemic and its impact on higher education have been marked by profound upheavals. The global coronavirus crisis has generated significant challenges for higher education institutions. To better understand the consequences of this pandemic in the field of education, several studies have been undertaken. One such study employed data analysis methods to examine COVID-19 through a higher education lens. She identified three main areas of research. The first focused on the educational crisis and higher education in the new reality, highlighting the importance of skills related to resilience, adaptability, and sustainability for academic institutions. The second axis explored the psychological pressures, social uncertainties, and mental health of students in the face of the face of the pandemic.. Finally, the third axis examined the rise of online distance learning and hybrid teaching methods in response to this crisis (Bozkurt, 2022).

The COVID-19 pandemic has not only created immediate challenges but has also revealed pre-existing inequalities within education systems. The digital divide has made access to quality education more complex, particularly for students from disadvantaged backgrounds. Additionally, the pandemic has accelerated technological advancements in education, requiring teachers to effectively integrate technology into hybrid and online learning models (Ainous et al., 2018). Effective education policies and strong leadership are vital to overcoming these challenges. Education systems must reinvent their teaching methods and encourage learner-centered pedagogy aimed at developing critical thinking, creativity, and adaptability skills. Additionally, investments in infrastructure and digital skills training for both teachers and students are indispensable to ensuring quality education can be easily reached by all (Bento et al., 2021).

The disruptions caused by COVID-19 have accelerated the transition to online teaching and learning in higher education. Face-to-face classes quickly gave way to virtual teaching through webinars and online courses. This transformation offers both opportunities for innovation and challenges for adapting to new learning models (García-Morales et al., 2021).

Resilience and innovation constitute the core of ensuring the survival and sustainability of higher education institutions in the post-COVID era. The impact of the pandemic on education holds great importance and requires meticulous planning and decision-making for more effective rebuilding. By embracing transformative change, education systems can better prepare students for the challenges and opportunities that await them in the future (García-Morales et al., 2021).

In conclusion, the COVID-19 pandemic has profoundly disrupted higher education, highlighting the need for resilience, adaptability, and sustainability skills within educational institutions. The digital divide has accentuated inequalities in access to quality education. Effective education policies and strong leadership are crucial to instigate transformative changes that promote student-centered learning and prepare students for the future. The transition to online teaching and learning presents both opportunities and challenges for higher education institutions. By embracing innovation and leveraging technology, higher education can weather this crisis and emerge stronger (OCDE, 2020). As a result of the COVID-19 pandemic, higher education institutions are facing unprecedented challenges. The post-acute phase of the pandemic has caused lasting disruption, forcing these institutions to operate in a climate of uncertainty and adapt to a new reality. Hybrid learning models, fluctuating attendance rates, and the need for constant innovation have become standard. (Post-COVID-19 success in higher education marketing, October 2, 2023). Resilience and innovation have become crucial elements in adapting to this new educational landscape. Educational institutions must demonstrate their ability to adapt, demonstrate resilience, and adopt innovative approaches. By positioning themselves as adaptable and resilient institutions, they can attract students, reassure parents, and establish themselves as leaders in education in the post-COVID era. (Bozkurt, 2022). Research has shown that resilience and adaptability form the fundamental skills for higher education institutions to survive in the face of crises such as the COVID-19 pandemic. Several studies have identified three main themes: the crisis of education and higher education in the new reality, psychological pressures, social uncertainty, and the mental well-being of learners, as well as the rise of online distance learning and hybrid methods. (Bozkurt et al., 2022). Organizational resilience plays a crucial role in ensuring the survival of higher education institutions. Factors such as physical resources, knowledge management, organizational culture, and social networks influence an institution's ability to demonstrate resilience. Educational organizations must develop sustainable structures that enable them to overcome difficulties and continually thrive. (Zhang & Wang, 2023). Digital transformation has also played a major role in building educational resilience during these challenging times. Digital technologies have enabled the creation of adaptive and supportive learning environments, thereby strengthening academic resilience. The use of pedagogy adapted to online education depends on the expertise of educators in information and communication technologies. (Asante et al., 2023)

Furthermore, higher education institutions have demonstrated their ability to adapt to new situations while preserving their function and identity. The Nordic countries, in particular, stand out for their educational resilience. Key resilience factors include adaptive capacity, crisis management strategies, and emphasis on educational continuity. (Naidu, 2021). To ensure the continuity of education in the future, effective strategies must be developed. A proactive response to crises, through resilience and flexibility, is imperative. Educators and students ought to be independent, competent, and committed to using applications and technological devices. By combining technology with optimized human interactions, universities can prepare for the future and provide relevant education in the years to come. (Rasli et al, 2022). Resilience and innovation have become essential elements for the adaptation of higher education to the new reality. Educational institutions must demonstrate their ability to adapt, demonstrate resilience, and adopt innovative approaches. Organizational resilience, coupled with digital transformation and a focus on education continuity, will ensure the survival and success of higher education institutions in a post-COVID world (Bentoet al, 2021).

RESEARCH AIMS AND OBJECTIVES

This paper aims to critically analyze the effects of the COVID-19 pandemic on higher education, with a focus on resilience, adaptability, and sustainability within academic institutions. Our objectives include understanding the challenges posed by the pandemic, investigating the shift towards online and hybrid learning models, and evaluating the strategies that higher education institutions have adopted to navigate these unprecedented times.

RESEARCH TASKS

Our research tasks are designed to:
1. Examine the immediate and long-term impacts of COVID-19 on higher education. 2. Analyze the role of digital transformation in supporting educational resilience.3. Investigate the psychological impacts of the pandemic on students and faculty.4. Explore the effectiveness of different pedagogical approaches under the constraints imposed by the pandemic.5. Assess the implications of the pandemic for future educational policy and practice.

METHODOLOGY

This study employs a mixed-methods approach, combining qualitative analysis of case studies from various educational institutions worldwide with quantitative data on student performance, engagement, and access to technology. This methodology allows for a comprehensive understanding of the pandemic's multifaceted impact on higher education.

Adapting to the New Normal in Higher Education

The paper analyzes various studies conducted at higher education institutions during the COVID-19 pandemic (Asante et al., 2023). This research explored different aspects of adaptation and resilience in the face of the new reality (Naidu, 2021). One study focused on the resilience of Nordic higher education institutions (Rasli et al., 2022), while another examined teachers's adaptation processes within a Brazilian university college (Bento et al., 2021). In Nepal, a study used Roger's diffusion of innovation theory to understand mathematics teachers' adoption of digital resources (Shaya et al., 2022). Additionally, an empirical study conducted in the United Arab Emirates highlighted crisis leadership and employee resilience as critical characteristics of organizational resilience (Raghunathan et al., 2022). Other studies have looked at topics such as online teaching, strategies for coping with uncertainty, and efforts to close learning gaps (García-Morales et al., 2021). This research used a variety of approaches, including interviews, data analyses, and expert opinions (Joshi et al., 2023). Taken together, these studies provide valuable insights for higher-education research and practice in the post-COVID era (Jaume and Willén, 2019).

The COVID-19 outbreak has raised unprecedented challenges for teachers, policymakers, and education leaders. With schools closing and students moving to virtual environments, it has become clear that education policy and leadership play a central role in shaping the future of learning in the post-pandemic world.

One of the main issues exacerbated by the pandemic concerns disparities between education systems. The digital divide has intensified, leaving students from disadvantaged backgrounds behind in access to quality education. (Ainous et al., 2018). To address this inequality, technology has become an essential part of education. However, educators face pressure to effectively integrate technology into hybrid and online learning environments. This requires the development of innovative policies, investments in infrastructure, and the acquisition of digital skills among teachers and students (Rasli et al., 2022).

The COVID-19 pandemic has demonstrated the need for effective education policies and strong leadership. As we navigate this crisis, careful planning is pivotal to ensuring we rebuild more effectively. Education systems present both opportunities and challenges in the post-COVID era. To seize these opportunities and overcome the obstacles, transformative changes driven by strong education policies and leadership are pivotal (Bento et al., 2021).

By reinventing education systems, we possess the opportunity to redefine what we teach and how we teach it. It is crucial to promote learner-centered teaching approaches, thus promoting critical thinking, creativity, and adaptability. This requires a transition to enriching skills that prepare students for future challenges and opportunities (García-Morales et al., 2021).

Additionally, higher education institutions have faced significant transformations due to the pandemic. The transition to online learning has accelerated rapidly, requiring a major overhaul of educational offerings. This disruption presents both opportunities and challenges for higher education institutions. Educators and policymakers must rethink traditional models of knowledge transmission and adopt innovative approaches enabled by information and communication technologies (Joshi et al., 2023).

The adoption of digital resources and devices in teaching marked a significant phase of adaptation during the pandemic. Teachers in Nepal have already used digital tools to communicate with students, highlighting the phases of awareness, persuasion, decision, implementation, and confirmation of innovation adoption. However, more research is needed to understand the sustainable use of these tools beyond the pandemic (Purcell & Lumbreras, 2021).

Overall, the COVID-19 pandemic has brought disruptions and challenges to higher education. However, it has also created opportunities for resilience and innovation. By adopting new approaches and technologies, education systems can rebuild themselves in ways that promote inclusion, quality education, and student success. Effective education policies and strong leadership are indispensable to navigating the path to resilience and innovation in post-COVID higher education (Pokhrel & Chhetri, 2021).

Table 1. Higher education's COVID-19 response sparks sustainable development transformation (Purcell & Lumbreras, 2021)

Domain	Pre-COVID-19 conditions	Innovations fuel transformation
1. *Management* Dewar et al. Marcelo Purcell	From top to bottom, control-command Revealing style of leadership communication Disrupted by global megatrends Inequities tolerated	Adaptive to social networks Dialogue by invitation and reciprocity Focus on the institutional purpose Pursuit of fairness
2. *Financial data* Huron Marcéro Taparia	Weakened finances and dependence on commission income Investing in physical assets Research supported by cross-subsidies from other income Administrative bureaucracy	Focus on income earned through value created and income diversification Investing in digital and knowledge assets Research focused on scientific inquiry and societal value The primacy of the learned community

continued on following page

Table 1. Continued

Domain	Pre-COVID-19 conditions	Innovations fuel transformation
3. *Campus* Brown and Kafka Lanich	The campus as home Safety Security	Scholarly and digital community campus health and well-being
4. *Internationalization* Dickler Horne	Focus on student mobility Dominance of hosted country pedagogy	Focus on global citizenship Pedagogy of encounter and intercultural learning
5. *Teaching and learning* Doors McMurtrie Blacksmith 2016 Taparia 2020	Employability scholarship The opportunity gap persists and is considered an achievement gap Dominance of face-to-face pedagogy Learning synchronous	Scholarship for Societal Impact Focus on equity: diversity, inclusion and belonging Blended learning Synchronous and asynchronous delivery
6. *Employability* Strada Educational Network Willetts	Privileged individualism and competition Career Guidance Skills and Competencies professional	Focus on social justice and community Lifelong employability Life skills and values
7. *Sustainability* SDSN SDSN THE	Environmental sustainability Operational Guidance Disconnected from the formal program	Sustainable development Strategic program Education for sustainable development within formal programs
8. *multi-stakeholder partnerships* Caplan et al. Horan 2019 Matai et al. Moreno—Serna et al.	Ivory tower Knowledge transfer Operational/tactical partnerships Continuation of the mission	Connected University Knowledge exchange Strategic partnerships The multi-party assembly gathered around a shared societal objective

The table from Purcell & Lumbreras (2021) outlines the transformation in higher education in response to COVID-19, highlighting shifts from pre-pandemic conditions to innovations that fuel sustainable development across various domains. Here's an analysis of each domain presented in the table.

This analysis reflects a broader shift in higher education towards more inclusive, flexible, and sustainable practices, driven by the need to adapt to the challenges presented by the COVID-19 pandemic and the recognition of the role of education in addressing global societal challenges.

Analysis of the Latest Generation of Technologies in Teaching and Learning

The COVID-19 pandemic has deeply influenced higher education, forcing institutions to adapt and innovate to cope with the new reality. One of the crucial areas of this innovation concerns teaching and learning, with a central role given to the latest generation of technologies (Bozkurt, 2022). Studies have found that the impact of COVID-19 on higher education goes beyond pedagogical concerns. The pandemic has forced an emergency shift to remote teaching and online learning, triggering the emergence of hybrid models (Zhang & Wang, 2023). Organizational resilience represents a critical element in ensuring the survival and prosperity of educational institutions. The resilience of higher education institutions depends on their ability to cope with difficulties and adapt to new requirements and needs. The COVID-19 pandemic has presented one of the most significant challenges for these institutions, requiring them to demonstrate adaptability and sustainability (Zhang & Wang, 2023).

Digital transformation has played a major role in building educational resilience during the pandemic. Digital technologies have enabled the creation of adaptive and supportive learning environments, thereby contributing to academic resilience. By adopting these digital systems, educational institutions can design inclusive learning environments that meet diverse needs while fostering resilient responses (Asante et al., 2023). To effectively address future crises, higher education institutions must implement strategies focused on resilience and change management. These strategies should encompass digital transformation, e-learning effectiveness, curriculum review, and sustainability. Flexibility is an additional central element to consider when developing post-pandemic strategies (Naidu, 2021). Effective education policies and strong leadership are fundamental to shaping the future of learning as we emerge from the pandemic. Bridging the digital divide is of utmost importance to ensure equitable access to quality education. Educators and policymakers must grapple with the complexities of integrating technology into teaching and learning, requiring investments in infrastructure and digital literacy (Rasli et al., 2022).

The COVID-19 pandemic has highlighted the importance of resilience, adaptability, and sustainability within educational institutions. By embracing digital transformation, implementing effective policies, and demonstrating strong leadership, higher education can successfully navigate future uncertainties and continue to innovate (Bento et al., 2021).

Development of New Skills by Teachers

A bibliometric analysis of publications relating to COVID-19 and education revealed several themes, including the impact of the pandemic, digital pedagogy and the future of education[3]. This analysis highlights the need for effective strategies to ensure educational continuity and meet socio-emotional needs. (Zhang & Wang, 2023). The transition to blended teaching styles has highlighted both advantages and disadvantages. Post-acute COVID-19 disruption requires constant adaptation through strategies such as resilience and change management, digital transformation and curriculum modification. Resilience and adaptability are indispensable to helping students cope with crises, and it is essential to integrate resilience into specific classes. (Shaya et al, 2022)

Adoption of Flexible Learning Strategies by Students

The COVID-19 pandemic has created unprecedented challenges in higher education, forcing educators and students to adapt to a new educational landscape (Post-COVID-19 success in higher education marketing, 2023, October 2). A bibliometric analysis of publications relating to COVID-19 and education revealed several themes, including the impact of the pandemic, digital pedagogy, and the future of education. This analysis highlights the need for effective strategies to ensure educational continuity and meet socio-emotional needs (Bozkurt, 2022). Resilience allows institutions to reorganize their structures and adapt to challenges. Developing adaptability and sustainability is pivotal to fostering resilience in higher education, including making the most of technological developments and effectively coping with unpredictable crises (Bozkurt et al., 2022).

The transition to blended teaching styles has highlighted both advantages and disadvantages. Post-acute COVID-19 disruption requires constant adaptation through strategies such as resilience and change management, digital transformation, and curriculum modification (Naidu, 2021). Resilience and adaptability are vital to helping students cope with crises, and it is essential to integrate resilience into specific classes (Rasli et al., 2022). Empowering employees through innovative approaches supports engagement and innovation within organizations (Shaya et al., 2022). Overall, the pandemic has posed challenges, but it has also created an opportunity to reinvent education systems and emphasize resilience, adaptability, and sustainability (Raghunathan et al., 2022).

Importance of Resilience and Innovation in Higher Education in Post-COVID-19

The COVID-19 pandemic has left a marked influence on education at all levels, but perhaps especially on higher education. Even before the pandemic, students from marginalized communities faced challenges accessing quality educational resources. However, the crisis in educational opportunities has been exacerbated by the disruptions caused by COVID-19 (n.d.). U.S. Department of Education. Research suggests that student learning has suffered from the pandemic and that more research is needed into the long-term consequences for students' knowledge and skills. The extent of the impact is only just beginning to be felt, and it is crucial to determine how students can recover from the learning gap caused by the pandemic (n.d.). U.S. Department of Education.

Additionally, it is important to recognize that the impact of COVID-19 varies across student groups and circumstances. Students from socially vulnerable groups were particularly impacted in terms of their emotional well-being and personal circumstances. These disparities highlight existing social inequalities and a lack of access to technological resources needed for distance learning (n.d.). U.S. Department of Education. Faced with these challenges, higher education establishments have had to adapt quickly. The pandemic forced a rapid shift from traditional to online teaching methods and accelerated digitalization in higher education. While this transformation presents opportunities for innovation, it also brings difficulties and challenges that must be addressed (Bento et al., 2021).

To ensure resilience and innovation in higher education post-COVID, support is needed to mitigate the challenges faced by students and institutions. This support should include addressing disparities in access to resources, such as technology and internet connectivity. It should also involve providing training and resources for educators so they can effectively navigate online teaching platforms (Di Pietro, 2023). Furthermore, policymakers must consider the long-term consequences of learning disruptions on students' prospects. Measures should be put in place to help students overcome their learning deficits and mitigate any lasting effects on their labor market outcomes (García-Morales et al., 2021). In conclusion, post-COVID higher education requires resilience and innovation to overcome the challenges posed by the pandemic. It is essential to help students and institutions adapt to new ways of learning and ensure equitable access to resources. By addressing these issues, higher education can emerge stronger and better equipped to meet the needs of students in a rapidly changing world (Joshi et al., 2023).

Value of Resilience and Innovation During the Transition Period

The COVID-19 pandemic has had a widespread impact on higher education, upending traditional teaching and learning practices and creating unprecedented challenges for institutions and students. As the recovered data highlights, the pandemic has exacerbated existing disparities in access to quality education and has disproportionately affected marginalized communities. However, amid these challenges, resilience and innovation have emerged as crucial factors in navigating the transition period to a post-COVID higher education landscape (Post-COVID-19 success in higher education marketing, 2023, October 2). Before the pandemic, students from historically marginalized communities already faced barriers to accessing basic educational resources. The crisis in educational opportunities they experienced has been further exacerbated by COVID-19, as the recovered data highlights. This highlights the importance of resilience and innovation to address these disparities and ensure that all students have equal access to quality education (n.d.). U.S. Department of Education. Resilience is defined as the ability to bounce back from unexpected events and disruptions. In the context of higher education, this refers to the ability of institutions and individuals to adapt and respond to the challenges posed by the pandemic. The recovered data highlights that resilience is not only about overcoming immediate obstacles but also about building systems better prepared for future disruptions (Bento et al., 2021).

Innovation plays a central role in promoting resilience in higher education. The pandemic has forced institutions to explore alternative delivery methods, such as online learning, to ensure the continuity of education. This transition to digital platforms has provided an opportunity to introduce new pedagogy and approaches that can improve student engagement and learning outcomes. The data recovered highlights the need for flexibility between levels and types of education, as well as closer links between formal and non-formal structures (Di Pietro, 2023). Additionally, innovation in assessment strategies is crucial to ensuring that student learning deficits caused by disruptions during the pandemic can be effectively addressed. As mentioned in one of the data sources, there is a risk that these deficits will persist over time and have long-term consequences for students' knowledge, skills, and prospects in the labor market. Therefore, innovative approaches to assessment can help identify and support students who may need additional help to address these learning gaps (Di Pietro, 2023). The data also highlights the importance of collaboration and partnerships to foster resilience and innovation. Institutions can learn from each other and share best practices to meet the challenges posed by the pandemic (Kaffenberger, 2020). Organizations like Higher Level Education are committed to providing support, guidance, and expertise to ensure institutions emerge stronger, more resilient, and more adaptive (Purcell & Lumbreras, 2021). In conclusion, the value of resilience and innovation during the transition period in post-COVID higher education cannot be underestimated. The pandemic has not only highlighted existing disparities and challenges within the education system but also provided an opportunity for change. By embracing resilience and innovation, institutions can not only overcome immediate obstacles but also build a more equitable, inclusive, and effective higher education system that is better equipped to meet the needs of all students (Pokhrel & Chhetri, 2021).

CONCLUSION

In conclusion, key findings from various sources highlight the importance of resilience and innovation in post-COVID higher education. The COVID-19 pandemic has presented many challenges to the education system, but it has also revealed the resilience and adaptation skills that have emerged in this unprecedented environment.

One of the key implications for higher education following the COVID-19 crisis is the requirement to prioritize resilience as an organizational and personal resource. Higher education institutions should play a vital role in helping students cope with the crisis and adapt to the new normal of education. This involves strengthening the human aspects of students and supporting their emotional well-being.

The study highlights that organizational and technological dynamics play a crucial role in the adaptation process. Higher education institutions must learn to respond effectively to unforeseen crises. This includes adapting traditional teaching methods to blended layouts combining online and in-person learning. The study recognizes both the advantages and disadvantages of this transition, particularly in terms of program organization, teaching approaches, feedback mechanisms, and evaluation methods.

Furthermore, higher education systems must strengthen articulation and flexibility between levels and types of education. Flexibility relies on strong articulation between different levels of education as well as the ability to use varied modes of education delivery. Blended education, which provides flexible, individualized learning paths for students, requires a blend of pedagogy and approaches. There is also a need to strengthen links between formal and non-formal structures for the recognition, validation, and accreditation of knowledge and skills acquired through various types of learning.

Despite the challenges posed by COVID-19, the education community has demonstrated resilience and laid the foundation for recovery. However, it is essential that higher education systems effectively address the learning deficits caused by the pandemic. The results of the meta-analysis suggest that student performance was significantly affected during this period, particularly in the areas of mathematics and science. Additional support should be provided in these areas to help students address their gaps.

In summary, higher education institutions must place great importance on resilience and innovation in the post-COVID period. They should focus on promoting adaptability, supporting students' well-being, and implementing flexible learning approaches. By strengthening the articulation between different levels of education and recognizing diverse modes of learning, higher education can become more equitable, inclusive, and effective in achieving its mission. The COVID-19 pandemic has served as an awakening call for the education system, highlighting the importance of resilience to ensure continuity and respond to unexpected disruptions.

Research conducted on organizational resilience in higher education institutions during the COVID-19 pandemic has provided valuable insights and practical implications for the sector. The study expanded the theoretical model of organizational resilience and identified key factors that contribute to the resilience of academic institutions. The findings highlight the importance of crisis leadership qualities and employee resilience in navigating the different stages of a crisis and maintaining overall organizational resilience.

One of the strengths of this study is the incorporation of participants from institutions with a high level of organizational resilience, making it possible to identify best practices to respond to the current crisis. The use of qualitative research techniques also contributed to an in-depth examination of the phenomenon, as the interviews had no boundaries or predefined question guidelines. This has expanded theoretical boundaries and better understood organizational resilience.

There are, however, certain limitations to recognize. The focus on resilient institutions may not accurately reflect the entire population, limiting generalizability. To overcome this limitation, further research should explore innovative culture, crisis leadership attributes, employee resilience in the workplace, and their impact on leading resilient employees using instruments of quantitative evaluation.

Beyond this specific study, it is crucial to recognize that the COVID-19 pandemic has produced unparalleled outcomes in education systems around the world. As the UNESCO report on education in a post-COVID-19 world highlights, there is a need to strengthen articulation and flexibility between levels and types of education. This involves developing stronger links between formal and non-formal structures and improving processes for the recognition, validation, and accreditation of knowledge and skills acquired through all types of learning.

Additionally, as online learning becomes more prevalent during this pandemic, it is critical to address the challenges of shifting from traditional face-to-face learning. Educators must assess and support student preparation while adopting pedagogy adapted to different subjects and age groups. Additionally, special attention should be given to creating inclusive online learning environments that cater to students with physical disabilities.

Despite the challenges posed by the pandemic, the education community has demonstrated resilience by continuing to provide quality education. The resilience of education systems lies in their ability to adapt and respond to unexpected changes, as demonstrated by the shift to online learning. Future research should continue to explore and understand resilience in educational environments, considering factors such as people, technology, and processes.

In conclusion, further research and implementation are needed to build resilience and innovation in higher education post-COVID. By addressing the limitations identified and building on the findings of this study, we can develop strategies and practices that will enable educational institutions to successfully navigate future crises. This research provides a solid foundation for future empirical studies on organizational resilience, providing us with valuable insights into creating resilient communities through resilient academic institutions.

ACKNOWLEDGMENT

We would like to express our sincere gratitude to all the individuals who contributed to this research. Their valuable insights, support, and cooperation have been instrumental in the completion of this study. This research would not have been possible without their generous assistance.

REFERENCES

Ainous, R. (2023). *The Political Integration of ICT in Higher Education: Evidence Case Study with Structural Equation Modelling.*

Asante, M. O., Liyanapathiranage, S. W. S., & Pinheiro, R. (2023). Public Service Resilience in a Post-COVID-19 World: Digital Transformation in Nordic Higher Education. In Pinheiro, R., Balbachevsky, E., Pillay, P., & Yonezawa, A. (Eds.), *The Impact of Covid-19 on the Institutional Fabric of Higher Education.* Palgrave Macmillan. 10.1007/978-3-031-26393-4_10

Bento, F., Giglio Bottino, A., Cerchiareto Pereira, F., Forastieri de Almeida, J., & Gomes Rodrigues, F. (2021). Resilience in Higher Education: A Complex Perspective to Lecturers' Adaptive Processes in Response to the COVID-19 Pandemic. In *Education Sciences (Vol. 11*, Issue 9, p. 492). MDPI AG. 10.3390/educsci11090492

Bozkurt, A. (2022). *Resilience, adaptability, and sustainability of higher education: A systematic mapping study on the impact of the corona virus (COVID-19) pandemic and the transition to the new normal.* Research Gate.

Bozkurt, A., Karakaya, K., Turk, M., Karakaya, Ö., & Castellanos-Reyes, D. (2022). The impact of COVID-19 on education: A meta-narrative review. *TechTrends,* 66(5), 883–896. 10.1007/s11528-022-00759-035813033

Di Pietro, G. (2023). The impact of Covid-19 on student achievement: Evidence from a recent meta-analysis. In *Educational Research Review* (Vol. 39, p. 100530). Elsevier BV. 10.1016/j.edurev.2023.100530

García-Morales, V. J., Garrido-Moreno, A., & Martín-Rojas, R. (2021). The transformation of higher education after the COVID disruption: Emerging challenges in an online learning scenario. *Frontiers in Psychology,* 12, 616059. 10.3389/fpsyg.2021.61605933643144

Jaume, D., & Willén, A. (2019). The Long-Run Effects of Teacher Strikes: Evidence from Argentina. *Journal of Labor Economics, 37*(4). University of Chicago Press, Chicago. 10.1086/703134

Joshi, D. R., Khanal, J., & Dhakal, R. H. (2023). From Resistance to Resilience: Teachers' Adaptation Process to Mediating Digital Devices in Pre-COVID-19, during COVID-19, and post-COVID-19 Classrooms in Nepal. *Education Sciences,* 13(5), 509. 10.3390/educsci13050509

Kaffenberger, M. (2020). *Modelling the Long-Run Learning Impact of the COVID-19 Learning Shock: Actions to (More Than) Mitigate Loss.* RISE. 10.35489/BSG-RISE-RI_2020/017

Naidu, S. (2021). Building resilience in education systems post-COVID-19. In *Distance Education* (*Vol. 42*, Issue 1, pp. 1–4). Informa UK Limited. 10.1080/01587919.2021.1885092

OCDE. (2020). *Education at a Glance 2020: OECD Indicators.* OCDE. 10.1787/69096873-

Pokhrel, S., & Chhetri, R. (2021). A literature review on the impact of the COVID-19 pandemic on teaching and learning. *Higher education for the future, 8*(1), 133-141.

Post-COVID-19 success in higher education marketing. (2023, October 2). Higher Level Education. https://higherleveleducation.com/post-covid-higher-education/

Purcell, W. M., & Lumbreras, J. (2021). Higher education and the COVID-19 pandemic: Navigating disruption using the sustainable development goals. *Discover Sustainability*, 2(1), 6. 10.1007/s43621-021-00013-235425919

Raghunathan, S., Darshan Singh, A., & Sharma, B. (2022, January). Study of resilience in Learning environments during the COVID-19 pandemic. In *Frontiers in Education* (*Vol. 6*). Frontiers Media SA. 10.3389/feduc.2021.677625

Rasli, A., Tee, M., Lai, Y. L., Tiu, Z. C., & Soon, E. H. (2022). Post-COVID-19 strategies for higher education institutions in dealing with unknowns and uncertainties. In *Frontiers in Education* (*Vol. 7*). Frontiers Media SA. 10.3389/feduc.2022.992063

Shaya, N., Abukhait, R., Madani, R., & Khattak, M. N. (2022). Organizational resilience of higher education institutions: An empirical study during COVID-19 pandemic. *Higher Education Policy*, 1–27.

Zhang, L., & Wang, Y. (2023). Reshaping the Resilience in Higher Education Based on Lower-Grade Undergraduate Students' Performance in Literature Course During Covid-19. In *Atlantis Highlights in Social Sciences, Education and Humanities* (pp. 597–608). Atlantis Press International BV. 10.2991/978-94-6463-192-0_78

Zubaidy, S. A., & Khan, W. (2022). Proposed resilience strategy for higher education institutions post-COVID-19. *International Journal of Learning and Change*, 14(5-6), 706–722. 10.1504/IJLC.2022.126448

Compilation of References

. Eskrootchi, R., Arjmandi, M. K., Langarizadeh, M., & Yuvaraj, M. (2020). Key factors influencing the adoption of Cloud Computing Technology in the Medical Sciences University libraries. *Library Philosophy and Practice*, 1-27.

. Plummer, D. C., Bittman, T. J., Austin, T., Cearley, D. W., & Smith, D. M. (2008). Cloud computing: Defining and describing an emerging phenomenon. *Gartner, 17*, 1-9.

. Uzoma, B. C., & Okhuoya, I. B.(2022) A research on cloud computing.

Aarts, E. (2020). Ambient Intelligence. J. Denning (ed.) *The Invisible Future*. McGraw Hill, New York.

Aarts, E., Harwig, H., & Schuurmans, M. Ambient Intelligence. In Denning, J. (Ed.), *The Invisible Future* (pp. 235–250). McGraw Hill.

Abbas, A. M. H., Ghauth, K. I., & Ting, C. Y. (2022). User Experience Design Using Machine Learning: A Systematic Review. *IEEE Access : Practical Innovations, Open Solutions*, 10, 51501–51514. 10.1109/ACCESS.2022.3173289

Abbas, Y., Zhang, Y., Taherkordi, A., & Skeie, T. (2018). Zhang, A. Taherkordi, and T. Skeie. Mobile edge computing: A survey. *IEEE Internet of Things Journal*, 5(1), 450–465. 10.1109/JIOT.2017.2750180

Abdallah, R., & Shen, X. S. (2018). A lightweight lattice-based homomorphic privacy-preserving data aggregation scheme for smart grid. *IEEE Transactions on Smart Grid*, 9(1), 396–405. 10.1109/TSG.2016.2553647

Aboodh, K. S. (2013). The New Integral Transform Aboodh Transform. *Global Journal of Pure and Applied Mathematics*, 9(1), 35–43.

Abu-Libdeh, H., Princehouse, L., & Weatherspoon, H. (2010). RACS: A case for cloud storage diversity. *Proceedings of the 1st ACM symposium on Cloud computing SoCC*. Research Gate. 10.1145/1807128.1807165

Compilation of References

Acar, A., Backes, M., Fahl, S., Garfinkel, S., Kim, D., Mazurek, M. L., Stransky, C., & Yamada, K. (2019). Exploring the Design Space of Graphical Passwords on Smartphones: (Or: How to Build a More Secure Pattern Lock). *Proceedings on Privacy Enhancing Technologies. Privacy Enhancing Technologies Symposium*, 2019(4), 402–422.

Adamopoulou, E., & Moussiades, L. (2020). Chatbots: History, technology, and applications. *Machine Learning with Applications*, 2, 100006. 10.1016/j.mlwa.2020.100006

Adams, R., Kewell, B., & Parry, G. (2018). Blockchain for good? Digital ledger technology and sustainable development goals. *Handbook of sustainability and social science research*, 127-140. Springer. 10.1007/978-3-319-67122-2_7

Addey, D., Ellis, J., Suh, P., & Thiemecke, D. (2003). *Content management systems (tools of the trade)*. Glasshaus.

Adele, G., Borah, A., Paranjothi, A., & Khan, M. S. (2024). A Survey and Comparative Analysis of Methods for Countering Sybil Attacks in VANETs. *2024 IEEE 14th Annual Computing and Communication Workshop and Conference (CCWC)*, (pp. 178–183). IEEE.

Agbo, C. C., Mahmoud, Q. H., & Eklund, J. M. (2019). Blockchain technology in healthcare: A systematic review. *Health Care*, 7(2), 56.30987333

Aggarwal, G., Bawa, M., Ganesan, P., Garcia-Molina, H., Kenthapadi, K., Motwani, R. (2005). Two Can Keep a Secret: A Distributed Architecture for Secure Database Services. *Proceedings of Innovative Data Systems Research Conference*. Research Gate.

Aggarwal, A., Agrawal, R., & Prakash, A. (2021). Hybrid Multi-Cloud Data Encryption Scheme Using Chaotic Logistic Map. *Journal of Information Security*, 12, 203–218.

Agrawal, K., & Bhatt, N. (2015). *Survey On Scalability In Cloud Environment*, 2(3), 18–22.

Ahmadi, S. A. P., Hosseinzadeh, H., & Cherati, A. Y. (2019). A New Integral Transform for Solving Higher Order Linear Ordinary Differential Equations. *International Journal of Applied and Computational Mathematics*, 19(2), 243–252. 10.1007/s40819-019-0712-1

Ahmed, M., & Litchfield, A. T. (2018). Taxonomy for identification of security issues in cloud computing environments. *Journal of Computer Information Systems*, 58(1), 79–88. 10.1080/08874417.2016.1192520

Ahmim, A., Maglaras, L., Ferrag, M. A., Derdour, M., & Janicke, H. (2019). A novel hierarchical intrusion detection system based on decision tree and rules-based models. *2019 15th International Conference on Distributed Computing in Sensor Systems (DCOSS)*. IEEE. 10.1109/DCOSS.2019.00059

Ainous, R. (2023). *The Political Integration of ICT in Higher Education: Evidence Case Study with Structural Equation Modelling*.

Ai, W., Li, K., Lan, S., Zhang, F., Mei, J., Li, K., & Buyya, R. (2016). *On Elasticity Measurement in Cloud Computing* (Vol. 2016). Sci. Program.

Al-Ansi, A. M., Jaboob, M., Garad, A., & Al-Ansi, A. (2023). Analyzing augmented reality (AR) and virtual reality (VR) recent development in education. *Social Sciences & Humanities Open*, 8(1), 100532. 10.1016/j.ssaho.2023.100532

Alavi, M., & Leidner, D. E. (2001). Knowledge management and knowledge management systems: Conceptual foundations and research issues. *Management Information Systems Quarterly*, 25(1), 107–136. 10.2307/3250961

Albasir, A. A., & Naik, K. (2014). SMOW: An energy-bandwidth aware web browsing technique for smartphones. *IEEE Access : Practical Innovations, Open Solutions*, 2, 1427–1441. 10.1109/ACCESS.2014.2365091

Ali-eldin, A., Tordsson, J., Elmroth, E., & Kihl, M. (2013). *Workload Classification for Efficient Auto-Scaling of Cloud Resources.*

Aljawarneh, S., Alshaikhli, I. F., Aldweesh, A., & Saeed, M. (2022). Blockchain-Based Secure Cloud Data Storage Model. *Journal of Cyber Security Technology*, 6(1), 1–18.

Aljedaani, W., Mkaouer, M. W., Ludi, S., & Javed, Y. (2022). Automatic Classification of Accessibility User Reviews in Android Apps. *Proceedings - 2022 7th International Conference on Data Science and Machine Learning Applications, CDMA 2022*. IEEE. 10.1109/CDMA54072.2022.00027

Alladi, T., Agrawal, A., Gera, B., Chamola, V., & Yu, R. (2023). Ambient Intelligence for Securing Intelligent Vehicular Networks: Edge-Enabled Intrusion and Anomaly Detection Strategies. *IEEE Internet of Things Magazine*. IEEE.

Alom, M. Z., Taha, T. M., Yakopcic, C., Westberg, S., Sidike, P., Nasrin, M. S., Hasan, M., Van Esesn, B., Awwal, A. A. S., & Asari, V. K. (2021). A Survey on Privacy-Preserving Deep Learning. *ACM Computing Surveys*, 54(4), 1–35.

Alshammari, N. O., Mylonas, A., Sedky, M., Champion, J., & Bauer, C. (2015). Exploring the adoption of physical security controls in smartphones. *Proceedings of the International Conference on Human Aspects of Information Security, Privacy, and Trust*, (pp. 287–298). Springer. 10.1007/978-3-319-20376-8_26

Alzheimer's Association. (2020). *Alzheimer's and Dementia disease facts and figures*. Wiley. https://alz-journals.onlinelibrary.wiley.com/doi/full/10.1002/alz.12068.

Amin, M. R. (2020). *51\% attacks on blockchain: a solution architecture for blockchain to secure iot with proof of work*. Research Gate.

Amin, A., Eldessouki, A., Magdy, M. T., Abdeen, N., Hindy, H., & Hegazy, I. (2019). AndroShield: Automated android applications vulnerability detection, a hybrid static and dynamicanalysis approach. *Information (Basel)*, 10(10), 326. 10.3390/info10100326

Amponsah, A. A., Adekoya, A. F., & Weyori, B. A. (2022). Improving the financial security of national health insurance using cloud-based blockchain technology application. *International Journal of Information Management Data Insights*, 2(1), e100081. 10.1016/j.jjimei.2022.100081

Compilation of References

Anand, V., Singh, A., Kumar, N., & Goyal, D. (2020). Secure Data Storage and Processing in Cloud Computing: A Survey. *Journal of King Saud University. Computer and Information Sciences*, 32(11), 1325–1344.

Anbalagan, B., Radhika, R., Jayanthi, R., & Rama Prabha, K. P. (2022). Leveraging Machine Learning Based Human Voice Emotion Recognition System from Audio Samples. *AIP Conference Proceedings*, 2455(1). 10.1063/5.0101448

Androutsellis-Theotokis, S., & Spinellis, D. (2004, December). A survey of peer-to-peer content distribution technologies. *ACM Computing Surveys*, 36(4), 335–371. 10.1145/1041680.1041681

Anitah, J. N. (2019). *Industry 4.0 Technologies and Operational Performance of Fast Moving Consumer Goods Manufacturers in Kenya: A Case Study of Unilever Kenya and L'oreal East Africa* [Doctoral dissertation, University of Nairobi].

Anjum, N., Karamshuk, D., Shikh-Bahaei, M., & Sastry, N. (2017). Survey on peer-assisted content delivery networks. *Computer Networks*, 116, 1339–1351. 10.1016/j.comnet.2017.02.008

Annarelli, A., & Palombi, G. (2021). Digitalization capabilities for sustainable cyber resilience: A conceptual framework. *Sustainability (Basel)*, 13(23), 13065. 10.3390/su132313065

Arif, Y. M., Putra, D. D., Wardani, D., Nugroho, S. M. S., & Hariadi, M. (2023). Decentralized recommender system for ambient intelligence of tourism destinations serious game using known and unknown rating approach. *Heliyon*, 9(3), e14267. 10.1016/j.heliyon.2023.e1426737101510

Armbrust, M., Fox, A., Griffith, R., Joseph, A. D., Katz, R. H., Konwinski, A., & Zaharia, M. (2009). *Above the clouds: A berkeley view of cloud computing (Vol. 17)*. Technical Report UCB/EECS-2009-28, EECS Department, University of California, Berkeley.

Arora, A., & Lata, P. (2021). Enhanced Security Mechanisms for Cloud Data Storage using Homomorphic Encryption. *International Journal of Advanced Computer Science and Applications*, 12(6), 495–502.

Asante, M. O., Liyanapathiranage, S. W. S., & Pinheiro, R. (2023). Public Service Resilience in a Post-COVID-19 World: Digital Transformation in Nordic Higher Education. In Pinheiro, R., Balbachevsky, E., Pillay, P., & Yonezawa, A. (Eds.), *The Impact of Covid-19 on the Institutional Fabric of Higher Education*. Palgrave Macmillan. 10.1007/978-3-031-26393-4_10

Aske, A., & Zhao, X. (2018). Supporting Multi-Provider Serverless Computing on the Edge. *Proceedings of the 47th International Conference on Parallel Processing Companion*. ACM. 10.1145/3229710.3229742

Ateniese, K., Fu, K., Green, M., & Hohenberger, S. (2006). Improved proxy re-encryption schemes with applications to secure distributed storage. *ACM Transactions on Information and System Security*, 9(1), 1–30. 10.1145/1127345.1127346

Avram, M. G. (2014). *Advantages and challenges of adopting cloud computing from an enterprise perspective*. Procedia Technology. 10.1016/j.protcy.2013.12.525

AWS. (2014a). *2U Case Study*. Amazon Web Services (AWS). https://aws.amazon.com/solutions/case-studies/2u/.

AWS. (2014b). *6waves Case Study*. Amazon Web Services (AWS). https://aws.amazon.com/solutions/case-studies/6waves/

AWS. (2016). *91App Case Study*. Amazon Web Services (AWS). https://aws.amazon.com/solutions/case-studies/91app/

AWS, . (2018). Pinterest Case Study. https://aws.amazon.com/solutions/case-studies/pinterest/

AWS. (n.d.-a). 9Splay Case Study. Amazon Web Services (AWS). https://aws.amazon.com/solutions/case-studies/9splay/.

AWS. (n.d.-b). *Abema TV Case Study*. Amazon Web Services (AWS). https://aws.amazon.com/solutions/case-studies/abema-tv/..

AWS. (n.d.-c). *abof Case Study*. Amazon Web Services (AWS). https://aws.amazon.com/solutions/case-studies/abof/.

AWS. (n.d.-d). *ABP News Case Study*. Amazon Web Services (AWS). https://aws.amazon.com/solutions/case-studies/abp_news/.

AWS. (n.d.-e). *ACTi Case Study*. Amazon Web Services. https://aws.amazon.com/solutions/case-studies/acti-case-study/.

AWS. (n.d.-f). *Adobe Systems Case Study*. Amazon Web Services (AWS). https://aws.amazon.com/solutions/case-studies/adobe/.

AWS. (n.d.-g). *Cloud Computing Services*. Amazon Web Services (AWS). https://aws.amazon.com/

AWS. (n.d.-h). Expedia Case Study. AWS. https://aws.amazon.com/solutions/case-studies/expedia/

Aydin, M. N., & Yilmaz, Y. S. (2020). Enhancing Privacy in Cloud Computing: A Survey. *Journal of Information Security*, 11, 77–87.

Aysan, A. F., Bergigui, F., & Disli, M. (2021). Blockchain-based solutions in achieving SDGs after COVID-19. *Journal of Open Innovation*, 7(2), 151. 10.3390/joitmc7020151

Ayyaswamy, K. (2024). Enhancing Digital Technology Planning, Leadership, and Management to Transform Education. In Bhatia, M., & Mushtaq, M. T. (Eds.), *Navigating Innovative Technologies and Intelligent Systems in Modern Education* (pp. 1–9). IGI Global. 10.4018/979-8-3693-5370-7.ch001

Azmat, F., Lim, W. M., Moyeen, A., Voola, R., & Gupta, G. (2023). Convergence of business, innovation, and sustainability at the tipping point of the sustainable development goals. *Journal of Business Research*, 167, 114170. 10.1016/j.jbusres.2023.114170

Compilation of References

Baarzi, A. F., Kesidis, G., Joe-Wong, C., & Shahrad, M. (2021). On Merits and Viability of Multi-Cloud Serverless. *Proceedings of the ACM Symposium on Cloud Computing. SoCC '21.* Association for Computing Machinery. 10.1145/3472883.3487002

Bach, T. A., Khan, A., Hallock, H., Beltrão, G., & Sousa, S. (2024). A Systematic Literature Review of User Trust in AI-Enabled Systems: An HCI Perspective. *International Journal of Human-Computer Interaction*, 40(5), 1251–1266. 10.1080/10447318.2022.2138826

Bag, S., Bhowmick, P., & Harit, G. (2011). Recognition of Bengali Handwritten Characters Using Skeletal Convexity and Dynamic Programming. *2011 Second International Conference on Emerging Applications of Information Technology.* IEEE. 10.1109/EAIT.2011.44

Bakari, K., Chaudhari, N. S., & Cokova, Z. (2019). Privacy-Preserving Machine Learning Techniques for Cloud-Based Data Analytics. *Procedia Computer Science*, 156, 378–385.

Balachandran, A., Sekar, V., Akella, A., & Seshan, S. (2013). Analyzing the potential benefits of CDN augmentation strategies for internet video workloads. *Proceedings of the 2013 conference on Internet measurement conference - IMC '13*, (pp. 43–56). ACM. 10.1145/2504730.2504743

Balcombe, L. & De Leo, D. (2022). Human-Computer Interaction in Digital Mental Health. *Informatics 2022, 9*(1). .10.3390/informatics9010014

Banker, G., & Jain, G. (2014). *A Literature Survey on Cloud AutoScaling Mechanisms. International Journal of Engineering Development and Research, 2*(4).

Barik, R. K., Gudey, S. K., Reddy, G. G., Pant, M., Dubey, H., Mankodiya, K., & Kumar, V. (2017). Foggrid: Leveraging fog computing for enhanced smart grid network. CoRR.

Basu, S., Bardhan, A., Gupta, K., Saha, P., Pal, M., Bose, M., & Sarkar, P. (2018, January). Cloud computing security challenges & solutions-A survey. In *2018 IEEE 8th Annual Computing and Communication Workshop and Conference (CCWC)* (pp. 347-356). IEEE. 10.1109/CCWC.2018.8301700

Beaumont, D. (2014). *How to explain vertical and horizontal scaling in the cloud - Cloud computing news.* IBM. https://www.ibm.com/blogs/cloud-computing/2014/04/09/explain-vertical-horizontal-scaling-cloud/

Benlian, A., Kettinger, W. J., Sunyaev, A., & Winkler, T. J. (2018). Special section: The transformative value of cloud computing: a decoupling, platformization, and recombination theoretical framework. *Journal of Management Information Systems*, 35(3), 719–739. 10.1080/07421222.2018.1481634

Bento, F., Giglio Bottino, A., Cerchiareto Pereira, F., Forastieri de Almeida, J., & Gomes Rodrigues, F. (2021). Resilience in Higher Education: A Complex Perspective to Lecturers' Adaptive Processes in Response to the COVID-19 Pandemic. In *Education Sciences (Vol. 11*, Issue 9, p. 492). MDPI AG. 10.3390/educsci11090492

Benz, K., & Bohnert, T. M. (2015). Elastic Scaling of Cloud Application Performance Based on Western Electric Rules by Injection of Aspect-oriented Code. *Procedia Computer Science*, 61, 198–205. 10.1016/j.procs.2015.09.193

Bhandary, A., & Maslach, D. (2018). *Organizational memory. The Palgrave Encyclopedia of Strategic Management*. Palgrave Macmillan.

Bhatia, J., Patni, S., Trivedi, H., & Bhavsar, M. (2018). *Infrastructure as a Code in Cloud Environment for Dynamic Auto Scaling*, 16(1), 159–164.

Bhupathi, J. (2023). MMF Clustering: A On-demand One-hop Cluster Management in MANET Services Executing Perspective. *International Journal of Novel Research and Development*, 8(4), 127-132.

Bhushan, S. (2012). *A Comprehensive Study on Cloud Computing*. Research Gate.

Bhuyar, P. (2012). Horizontal Fragmentation Techniques in Distributed Database. *International Journal of Scientific and Research Publications, 2*(5).

Bican, P. M., & Brem, A. (2020). Digital business model, digital transformation, digital entrepreneurship: Is there a sustainable "digital"? *Sustainability (Basel)*, 12(13), 5239. Advance online publication. 10.3390/su12135239

Billinghurst, M. (2010). *Hartmut Seichter*. Human-Centric Interfaces for Ambient Intelligence.

Biswas, A., Majumdar, S., Nandy, B., & El-Haraki, A. (2017). A hybrid auto-scaling technique for clouds processing applications with service level agreements. *Journal of Cloud Computing (Heidelberg, Germany)*, 6(1), 29. 10.1186/s13677-017-0100-5

Biswas, S., Paul, S., Bera, P., & Mandal, J. K. (2022). Secure Data Sharing and Storage in Multi-Cloud Using Homomorphic Encryption. *Journal of King Saud University. Computer and Information Sciences*, 34(1), 100938.

Bodemer, O. (2023). Decentralized Innovation: Exploring the Impact of Blockchain Technology in Software Development. *Authorea Preprints*.

Bonomi, R. A. (2012). Fog computing and its role in the internet of things. *Proc. MCC workshop on SIGCOMM*. Research Gate.

Bordonaro, A., De Paola, A., Lo Re, G., & Morana, M. (2020). Smart Auctions for Autonomic Ambient Intelligence Systems. *2020 IEEE International Conference on Smart Computing (SMARTCOMP)*. IEEE. 10.1109/SMARTCOMP50058.2020.00043

Bosri, R., Rahman, M. S., Bhuiyan, M. Z. A., & Al Omar, A. (2020). Integrating blockchain with artificial intelligence for privacy-preserving recommender systems. *IEEE Transactions on Network Science and Engineering*, 8(2), 1009–1018. 10.1109/TNSE.2020.3031179

Bowers, K. D., Juels, A., & Oprea, A. (2008). Hail: A high availability and integrity layer for cloud storage. IACR. https://eprint.iacr.org/

Compilation of References

Bozkurt, A. (2022). *Resilience, adaptability, and sustainability of higher education: A systematic mapping study on the impact of the corona virus (COVID-19) pandemic and the transition to the new normal.* Research Gate.

Bozkurt, A., Karakaya, K., Turk, M., Karakaya, Ö., & Castellanos-Reyes, D. (2022). The impact of COVID-19 on education: A meta-narrative review. *TechTrends*, 66(5), 883–896. 10.1007/s11528-022-00759-035813033

Broberg, J., Buyya, R., & Tari, Z. (2009). MetaCDN: Harnessing 'Storage Clouds' for high performance content delivery. *Journal of Network and Computer Applications*, 32(5), 1012–1022. 10.1016/j.jnca.2009.03.004

Browne, P. S. (1971). Data privacy and integrity: an overview. *Proceeding of SIGFIDET '71 Proceedings of the ACM SIGFIDET (now SIGMOD)*. ACM. 10.1145/1734714.1734733

Buchmann, J. A. (2009). *Introduction to Cryptography* (4th Indian reprint ed.). Springer.

Buhalis, D., Harwood, T., Bogicevic, V., Viglia, G., Beldona, S., & Hofacker, C. (2019). Technological disruptions in services: Lessons from tourism and hospitality. *Journal of Service Management*, 30(4), 484–506. 10.1108/JOSM-12-2018-0398

Butt, S. A. (2016). Study of agile methodology with the cloud. Pacific Science Review B. *Humanities and Social Sciences*, 2(1), 22–28.

Cai, Y., Cao, Y., Li, Y., Huang, T., & Zhou, B. (2016). Cascading failure analysis considering interaction between power grids and communication networks. *IEEE Transactions on Smart Grid*, 7(1), 530–538. 10.1109/TSG.2015.2478888

Çakmak, T., & Yılmaz, B. (2012). Overview of the Digitalization Policies in Cultural Memory Instutions, *International Symposium on Information Management in Changing World.* Research Gate.

Canetti, R., & Krawczyk, H. (2001). Analysis of key-exchange protocols and their use for building secure channels. *International Conference on the Theory and Applications of Cryptographic Techniques.* Springer. 10.1007/3-540-44987-6_28

Capgemini Consulting Chosnek, J. (2010). Maintaining the corporate memory. *Journal of Loss Prevention in the Process Industries*, 23(6), 796–798. 10.1016/j.jlp.2010.08.004

Capgemini. (2011). *Digital Transformation: A Roadmap for Billion-Dollar Organization (Report)*.

Carofiglio, G., Morabito, G., Muscariello, L., Solis, I., & Varvello, M. (2013). From content delivery today to information centric networking. *Computer Networks*, 57(16), 3116–3127. 10.1016/j.comnet.2013.07.002

Carroll, A., Barnes, J., & Scornavacca, E. (2005). *"Consumer perceptions and attitudes towards mobile marketing," in Selected Readings on Telecommunications and Networking.* IGI Global.

Chaabane, A., & Bouguila, N. (2021). Privacy-Preserving Data Mining in Cloud Computing: A Comprehensive Survey. *IEEE Access : Practical Innovations, Open Solutions*, 9, 38551–38571.

Chang, C.-W., Liu, P., & Wu, J.-J. (2012). Probability-Based Cloud Storage Providers Selection Algorithms with Maximum Availability. *2012 41st International Conference on Parallel Processing*, (pp. 199-208). IEEE. 10.1109/ICPP.2012.51

Chang, A., El-Rayes, N., & Shi, J. (2022). Blockchain technology for supply chain management: A comprehensive review. *FinTech*, 1(2), 191–205. 10.3390/fintech1020015

Chen, Y., Xu, W., Peng, L., & Zhang, H. (2019). Light-weight and privacy-preserving authentication protocol for mobile payments in the context of IoT. IEEE Access. 10.1109/ACCESS.2019.2894062

Cheng, H., Zhang, X., Shi, H., Yu, H., & Zhou, X. (2020). A Secure Multi-Party Computation Framework for Privacy-Preserving Data Sharing in Cloud Computing. *IEEE Transactions on Services Computing*, 13(2), 334–347.

Cheng, Y., Qin, Y., Lu, R., Jiang, T., & Takagi, T. (2019). Batten down the hatches: Securing neighborhood area networks of smart grid in the quantum era. *IEEE Transactions on Smart Grid*, 10(6), 6386–6395. 10.1109/TSG.2019.2903836

Chen, J., Yu, H., Guan, Q., Yang, G., & Liang, Y.-C. (2022). Spatial Modulation Based Multiple Access for Ambient Backscatter Networks. *IEEE Communications Letters*, 26(1), 197–201. 10.1109/LCOMM.2021.3124277

Chen, J., Zhang, Y., & Su, W. (2015). An anonymous authentication scheme for plug-in electric vehicles joining to charging/discharging station in vehicle-to-grid (v2g) networks. *China Communications*, 12(3), 9–19. 10.1109/CC.2015.7084359

Chen, L., Zhou, J., Li, Q., & Li, Y. (2023). Privacy-Preserving Data Sharing and Storage in Cloud Computing. *Journal of Computer Science and Technology*, 38(1), 78–92.

Chen, X., & Metawa, N. (2020). Enterprise Financial Management Information System based on cloud computing in a big data environment. *Journal of Intelligent & Fuzzy Systems*, 39(4), 5223–5232. 10.3233/JIFS-189007

Chin, T., Shi, Y., Singh, S. K., Agbanyo, G. K., & Ferraris, A. (2022). Leveraging blockchain technology for green innovation in ecosystem-based business models: A dynamic capability of values appropriation. *Technological Forecasting and Social Change*, 183, 121908. 10.1016/j.techfore.2022.121908

Chowdary, M. K., Nguyen, T. N., & Hemanth, D. J. (2021). Deep learning-based facial emotion recognition for human–computer interaction applications. *Neural Computing & Applications*, 35(32), 23311–23328. 10.1007/s00521-021-06012-8

Chowdhury, S. R., Mahmood, A. N., & Hong, C. S. (2020). A Survey on Privacy-Preserving Techniques in Cloud Computing: Taxonomy and Open Challenges. *Future Generation Computer Systems*, 112, 901–918.

Compilation of References

Cisco, "Cisco Global Cloud Index : Forecast and Methodology, 2014–2019. (2014). (pp. 1–41). White Pap.

Cleary, P., & Quinn, M. (2016). Intellectual capital and business performance: An exploratory study of the impact of cloud-based accounting and finance infrastructure. *Journal of Intellectual Capital*, 17(2), 255–278. 10.1108/JIC-06-2015-0058

Corno, F., De Russis, L., & Monge Roffarello, A. (2021). *Devices, Information, and People: Abstracting the Internet of Things for End-User Personalization.Lecture Notes in Computer Science (including subseries Lecture Notes in Artificial Intelligence and Lecture Notes in Bioinformatics).* Springer. 10.1007/978-3-030-79840-6_5

Curino, C., Jones, E. P. C., Popa, R. A., Malviya, N., Wu, E., & Madden, S. (2011). Relational Cloud: The Case for a Database Service. *Proceedings of 5th Biennial Conference on Innovative Data Systems Research*. Research Gate.

Dabić, M., Maley, J. F., Švarc, J., & Poček, J. (2023). Future of digital work: Challenges for sustainable human resources management. *Journal of Innovation & Knowledge*, 8(2), 100353. 10.1016/j.jik.2023.100353

Dahiya, P., & Tanwar, S. (2021). Privacy-Preserving Techniques in Cloud Computing: A Systematic Literature Review. *International Journal of Information Security*, 20, 151–176.

Dai, Y., Xu, D., Maharjan, S., Chen, Z., He, Q., & Zhang, Y. (2019). Blockchain and deep reinforcement learning empowered intelligent 5g beyond. *IEEE Network*, 33(99), 1. 10.1109/MNET.2019.1800376

Dang, H. T., Tran, N. H., & Vo, D. C. (2023). A Novel Privacy-Preserving Data Storage Scheme Using Homomorphic Encryption in Cloud Computing. *Journal of Ambient Intelligence and Humanized Computing*, 14(3), 2715–2726.

Das Odelu, A. K., Wazid, M., & Conti, M. (2016). Provably secure authenticated key agreement scheme for smart grid. *IEEE Transactions on Smart Grid*, 9(3), 1900–1910.

Das, A., & Pramanik, S. (2022). Enhancing Privacy in Cloud Data Storage using Attribute-Based Encryption. *Journal of Ambient Intelligence and Humanized Computing*, 13(9), 8707–8718.

Davis, A., Thomas, J. Parikh, S. Pichai, E. Ruvinsky, D. Stodolsky, M. Tsimelzon, W., & Weihl, E. (2003). Java application framework for use in a content delivery network (CDN). *Provisional Appl. Ser. No. 60/347,481.*

De Villiers, C., Kuruppu, S., & Dissanayake, D. (2021). A (new) role for business–Promoting the United Nations' Sustainable Development Goals through the internet-of-things and blockchain technology. *Journal of Business Research*, 131, 598–609. 10.1016/j.jbusres.2020.11.066

Delac, G., Silic, M., & Krolo, J. (2011). Emerging security threats for mobile platforms. *Proceedings of the 34th International Convention MIPRO*, (pp. 1468–1473). IEEE.

Deloitte. (2010). Executive Forum – *Cloud Computing: risks, mitigation strategies, and the role of Internal Audit.* Deloitte. http://www.deloitte.com

Derhab, A., Guerroumi, M., Gumaei, A., Maglaras, L., Ferrag, M. A., Mukherjee, M., & Khan, F. A. (2019). Blockchain and random subspace 13 learning-based ids for sdn-enabled industrial iot security. *Sensors (Basel)*, 19(14), 3119. 10.3390/s1914311931311136

Desai, K., & Patel, J. (2021). A Review on Privacy-Preserving Data Mining Techniques in Cloud Computing. *International Journal of Computer Applications*, 182, 1–6. 10.5120/ijca2021921737

Dev, H., Sen, T., Basak, M., & Ali, M. E. (2012). An Approach to Protect the Privacy of Cloud Data from Data Mining Based Attacks. *Proceedings of the Third International Workshop on Data Intensive Computing in the Clouds Data Cloud.* IEEE. 10.1109/SC.Companion.2012.133

Dewasiri, N. J., Baker, H. K., Banda, Y. W., & Rathnasiri, M. S. H. (2022). The Dividend Decision Model: A Possible Solution for the Dividend Puzzle. In *Exploring the Latest Trends in Management Literature.* Emerald Publishing Limited. 10.1108/S2754-586520220000001013

Dewasiri, N. J., Dharmarathna, D. G., & Choudhary, M. (2024). Leveraging Artificial Intelligence for Enhanced Risk Management in Banking: A Systematic Literature Review. Singh, R., Khan, S., Kumar, A., & Kumar, V. (Ed.) *Artificial Intelligence Enabled Management: An Emerging Economy Perspective.* De Gruyter. 10.1515/9783111172408-013

Dhandra, , B. (2010b). English character recognition. *International Journal of Computer Applications*, 146–150.

Dhandra, B. V. (2010a). Spatial features for handwritten Kannada and English character recognition. *International Journal of Computer Applications*, 146–150.

Dhingra, S., Savalgi, A. A., & Jain, S. (2016). Laplace Transformation based Cryptographic Technique in Network Security. *International Journal of Computer Applications*, 136(7), 6–10. 10.5120/ijca2016908482

Di Pietro, G. (2023). The impact of Covid-19 on student achievement: Evidence from a recent meta-analysis. In *Educational Research Review* (Vol. 39, p. 100530). Elsevier BV. 10.1016/j.edurev.2023.100530

Diao, F., Zhang, F., & Cheng, X. (2015). A privacy-preserving smart metering scheme using linkable anonymous credential. *IEEE Transactions on Smart Grid*, 6(1), 461–467. 10.1109/TSG.2014.2358225

Diaz, C. G., Perry, P., & Fiebrink, R. (2019). Interactive machine learning for more expressive game interactions. *IEEE Conference on Computatonal Intelligence and Games, CIG.* IEEE. 10.1109/CIG.2019.8848007

Díaz, M., Martín, C., & Rubio, B. (2016). State-of-the-art, challenges, and open issues in the integration of the Internet of things and cloud computing. *Journal of Network and Computer Applications*, 67, 99–117. 10.1016/j.jnca.2016.01.010

Dino, M. J. S., Davidson, P. M., Dion, K. W., Szanton, S. L., & Ong, I. L. (2022). Nursing and human-computer interaction in healthcare robots for older people: An integrative review. *International Journal of Nursing Studies Advances*, 4, 100072. 10.1016/j.ijnsa.2022.10007238745638

Disli, M., Abd Rabbo, F., Leneeuw, T., & Nagayev, R. (2022). Cryptocurrency comovements and crypto exchange movement: The relocation of Binance. *Finance Research Letters*, 48, 102989. 10.1016/j.frl.2022.102989

Djordjevic, I. B., & Djordjevic, I. B. (2019). Conventional Cryptography Fundamentals. *Physical-Layer Security and Quantum Key Distribution*, (pp. 65–91). Research Gate.

Dolezel, D., & McLeod, A. (2019). Managing security risk: Modelling the root causes of data breaches. *The Health Care Manager*, 38(4), 322–330. 10.1097/HCM.0000000000000028231663871

Dougherty, B., White, J., & Schmidt, D. C. (2012). Model-driven auto-scaling of green cloud computing infrastructure. *Future Generation Computer Systems*, 28(2), 371–378. 10.1016/j.future.2011.05.009

Ducatel, K., Bogdanowicz, M., Scapolo, F., Leijten, J., & Burgelman, J. (2003). *Ambient Intelligence: From Vision to Reality*. IST Advisory Group Draft Rep., Eur. Comm.

Durairaj, M., & Manimaran, A. (2015). A study on security issues in cloud-based e-learning. *Indian Journal of Science and Technology*, 8(8), 757–765. 10.17485/ijst/2015/v8i8/69307

Dutta, S., Gera, S., Verma, A., & Viswanathan, B. (2012). SmartScale: Automatic Application Scaling in Enterprise Clouds. *2012 IEEE Fifth International Conference on Cloud Computing*, , pp. 221–228. 10.1109/CLOUD.2012.12

Dutta, S., Saha, P., & Pal, S. (2022). A Survey on Privacy-Preserving Data Mining Techniques in Cloud Computing. *Journal of Information Privacy and Security*, 18(1), 1–26.

Du, X., Xiao, Y., Chen, H.-H., & Wu, Q. (2006, May). Secure Cell Relay Routing Protocol for Sensor Networks. *Wireless Communications and Mobile Computing*, 6(3), 375–391. 10.1002/wcm.402

Ebrahimpour, R., Esmkhani, A., & Faridi, S. (2010, July 25). Farsi handwritten digit recognition based on mixture of RBF experts. *IEICE Electronics Express*, 7(14), 1014–1019. 10.1587/elex.7.1014

Edeh, M. O., Ugorji, C. C., Nduanya, U. I., Onyewuchi, C., Ohwo, S. O., & Ikedilo, O. E. (2021). Prospects and Limitations of Machine Learning in Computer Science Education. *Benin Journal of Educational Studies*, 27(1), 48–62. http://beninjes.com/index.php/bjes/article/view/70

Efi Arazi School of Computer Science. (2016). *DDoS and Cloud Auto-Scaling Mechanism*. Efi Arazi School of Computer Science.

Elkotob, M., & Andersson, K. (2012). Challenges and opportunities in content distribution networks: A case study. In *GC'12 Work. 4th IEEE Int* (pp. 1021–1026). Work. Mobil. Manag. Networks Futur. World Challenges. 10.1109/GLOCOMW.2012.6477717

Elshafey, E. I., Ali, A. H., Hassanien, A. E., & Oliva, D. (2021). A Comprehensive Survey on Privacy-Preserving Data Mining in Cloud Computing. *Journal of Ambient Intelligence and Humanized Computing*, 12(11), 12955–12975.

Elzaki, T. M. (2011). The New Integral Transform Elzaki Transform. *Global Journal of Pure and Applied Mathematics*, 7(1), 57–64.

Er, G. S., & Pal, P. (2017). Cloud Computing Risks and Benefits. *International Journal of Advanced Research in Computer Science*, 8(4).

Evangelidis, A., Parker, D., & Bahsoon, R. (2017). Performance Modelling and Verification of Cloud-Based Auto-Scaling Policies. *Proc. - 2017 17th IEEE/ACM Int. Symp. Clust. Cloud Grid Comput. CCGRID 2017*, (pp. 355–364). IEEE. 10.1109/CCGRID.2017.39

Falaiye, T., Elufioye, O. A., Awonuga, K. F., Ibeh, C. V., Olatoye, F. O., & Mhlongo, N. Z. (2024). Financial Inclusion Through Technology: A Review Of Trends In Emerging Markets. *International Journal of Management \& Entrepreneurship Research, 6*(2), 368–379.

Famaey, J., Latré, S., van Brandenburg, R., van Deventer, M. O., & De Turck, F. (2013). *On the Impact of Redirection on HTTP Adaptive Streaming Services in Federated CDNs*. Springer. 10.1007/978-3-642-38998-6_2

Fan, C.-I., Huang, S.-Y., & Lai, Y.-L. (2013). Privacy-enhanced data aggregation scheme against internal attackers in smart grid. *IEEE Transactions on Industrial Informatics*, 10(1), 666–675. 10.1109/TII.2013.2277938

Fang, S., Misra, S., Xue, G., & Yang, D. (2012). Misra, G. Xue, and D. Yang, "Smart grid - the new and improved power grid: A survey,". *IEEE Communications Surveys and Tutorials*, 14(4), 944–980. 10.1109/SURV.2011.101911.00087

Fan, K., Wang, S., Ren, Y., & Li, H. (2019). Secure Data Sharing and Storage Scheme Based on Blockchain in Cloud Computing. *IEEE Access : Practical Innovations, Open Solutions*, 7, 167794–167803.

Fan, Q., Yin, H., Min, G., Yang, P., Luo, Y., Lyu, Y., Huang, H., & Jiao, L. (2018). Video delivery networks: Challenges, solutions and future directions. *Computers & Electrical Engineering*, 66, 332–341. 10.1016/j.compeleceng.2017.04.011

Fazli, A. & Shulman, J. (2017). *The Effects of Autoscaling in Cloud Computing on Product Launch.*

Ferdous, M. S., Chowdhury, F., & Alassafi, M. O. (2019). In search of self-sovereign identity leveraging blockchain technology. *IEEE Access : Practical Innovations, Open Solutions*, 7, 103059–103079. 10.1109/ACCESS.2019.2931173

Fernandez-Carames, T. M., & Fraga-Lamas, P. (2021). A Review on the Role of Edge Computing in the Internet of Things. *IEEE Access : Practical Innovations, Open Solutions*, 9, 1307–1354.

Compilation of References

Ferrag, M. A., Babaghayou, M., & Yazici, M. A. (2020). Cyber security for fog-based smart grid SCADA systems: Solutions and challenges. *Journal of Information Security and Applications*, 52, 102500. 10.1016/j.jisa.2020.102500

Ferrag, M. A., Derdour, M., Mukherjee, M., Derhab, A., Maglaras, L., & Janicke, H. (2019). Blockchain technologies for the internet of things: Research issues and challenges. *IEEE Internet of Things Journal*, 6(2), 2188–2204. 10.1109/JIOT.2018.2882794

Ferrag, M. A., Maglaras, L., & Janicke, H. (2019). *"Blockchain and its role in the internet of things," in Strategic Innovative Marketing and Tourism.* Springer.

Ferrag, M. A., Maglaras, L., Moschoyiannis, S., & Janicke, H. (2020). Deep learning for cyber security intrusion detection: Approaches, datasets, and comparative study. *Journal of Information Security and Applications*, 50, 102419. 10.1016/j.jisa.2019.102419

Figueres, N. B., Petrlic, R., Sebe, F., Sorge, C., & Valls, M. (2016). Efficient ´ smart metering based on homomorphic encryption. *Computer Communications*, 82, 95–101. 10.1016/j.comcom.2015.08.016

Filipinas, J. L. D. C., & Convicto, V. C. (2017). On another type of transform called Rangaig transform. *International Journal (Toronto, Ont.)*, 5(1), 42–48.

Foroughi, H., Corailo, D., Foster, W. M. (2020). Organizational Memory Studies. *Organization Studies, 41*(12), https://10.1177/0170840620974338

Fouda, M. M., Fadlullah, Z. M., Kato, N., Rongxing Lu, , & Xuemin Shen, . (2011). A Light-weight Message Authentication Scheme for Smart Grid Communications. *IEEE Transactions on Smart Grid*, 2(4), 675–685. 10.1109/TSG.2011.2160661

Fraga-Lamas, P., & Fernández-Caramés, T. M. (2019). A review on blockchain technologies for an advanced and cyber-resilient automotive industry. *IEEE Access : Practical Innovations, Open Solutions*, 7, 17578–17598. 10.1109/ACCESS.2019.2895302

Fraga-Lamas, P., & Fernández-Caramés, T. M. (2020). Leveraging blockchain for sustainability and open innovation: A cyber-resilient approach toward EU Green Deal and UN Sustainable Development Goals. In *Computer Security Threats*. IntechOpen. 10.5772/intechopen.92371

Frangoudis, P. A., Polyzos, G. C., & Rubino, G. (2016). Relay-based multipoint content delivery for wireless users in an information-centric network. *Computer Networks*, 105, 207–223. 10.1016/j.comnet.2016.06.004

Gaetani, E., Aniello, L., Baldoni, R., Lombardi, F., & Margheri, A. (2020). Blockchain-based database to ensure data integrity in cloud computing environments. *Proc. Int. Conf. on Mainstreaming Block Chain Implementation (ICOMBI),* (pp. 1–4). Research Gate.

Gai, K., Choo, K. K. R., Qiu, M., & Zhu, L. (2018). Privacy-preserving content-oriented wireless communication in internet-of-things. *IEEE Internet of Things Journal*, 5(4), 3059–3067. 10.1109/JIOT.2018.2830340

Gai, K., Qiu, M., Ming, Z., Zhao, H., & Qiu, L. (2017). Spoofing-jamming attack strategy using optimal power distributions in wireless smart grid networks. *IEEE Transactions on Smart Grid*, 8(5), 2431–2439. 10.1109/TSG.2017.2664043

Gandhi, A., Dube, P., & Karve, A. (2014). Adaptive, Model-driven Autoscaling for Cloud Applications. *11 th USENIX Conf. Auton. Comput.* Research Gate.

Gandhi, A., Dube, P., Karve, A., Kochut, A. P., & Zhang, L. (2017). Providing Performance Guarantees for Cloud-deployed Applications. *IEEE Transactions on Cloud Computing*, 7161(c), 1–14.

Gao, X., Alimoradi, S., Chen, J., Hu, Y., & Tang, S. (2023). Assistance from the Ambient Intelligence: Cyber-physical system applications in smart buildings for cognitively declined occupants. *Engineering Applications of Artificial Intelligence*, 123, 106431. 10.1016/j.engappai.2023.106431

García-Morales, V. J., Garrido-Moreno, A., & Martín-Rojas, R. (2021). The transformation of higher education after the COVID disruption: Emerging challenges in an online learning scenario. *Frontiers in Psychology*, 12, 616059. 10.3389/fpsyg.2021.61605933643144

Garmehi, M., & Analoui, M. (2016, October). Envy-Free Resource Allocation and Request Routing in Hybrid CDN–P2P Networks. *Journal of Network and Systems Management*, 24(4), 884–915. 10.1007/s10922-015-9359-3

Gatica-Perez, D., Lathoud, G., McCowan, I., Odobez, J.-M., & Moore, D. (2019). Audio-visual speaker tracking with importance particle filters. *Proceedings IEEE ICIP*. IEEE.

Gharpure, R. (2021). Effect of Cloud computing technology adoption on Reduction in Costs: A critical review from the business perspective. [TURCOMAT]. *Turkish Journal of Computer and Mathematics Education*, 12(10), 4391–4399.

Ghorashi, N. S., Rahimi, M., Sirous, R., & Javan, R. (2023). The Intersection of Radiology With Blockchain and Smart Contracts: A Perspective. *Cureus*, 15(10). 10.7759/cureus.4694138021752

Ghorbel, A., Ghorbel, M., & Jmaiel, M. (2017). Privacy in cloud computing environments: A survey and research challenges. *The Journal of Supercomputing*, 73(6), 2763–2800. 10.1007/s11227-016-1953-y

Ghosal, A., & Conti, M. (2019). Key management systems for smart grid advanced metering infrastructure: A survey. *IEEE Communications Surveys and Tutorials*, 21(3), 2831–2848. 10.1109/COMST.2019.2907650

Gkioulos, V., Wangen, G., Katsikas, S., Kavallieratos, G., & Kotzanikolaou, P. (2017). Security awareness of the digital natives. *Information (Basel)*, 8(2), 42. 10.3390/info8020042

Gobinath, V. M., Kathirvel, A., Rajesh Kanna, S. K., & Annamalai, K. (2024). Smart Technology in Management Industries: A Useful Perspective. *Artificial Intelligence Applied to Industry 4.0*. Wiley. 10.1002/9781394216147.ch5

Compilation of References

Gobinath, V., Ayyaswamy, K., & Kathirvel, N. (2024). Information Communication Technology and Intelligent Manufacturing Industries Perspective: An Insight. *Asian Science Bulletin*, 2(1), 36–45. 10.3923/asb.2024.36.45

Gochhait, S., Butt, S. A., Jamal, T., & Ali, A. (2022). Cloud Enhances Agile Software Development. In I. Management Association (Ed.), *Research Anthology on Agile Software, Software Development, and Testing* (pp. 491-507). IGI Global. 10.4018/978-1-6684-3702-5.ch025

Goel, P. K., Pandey, H., Singhal, A., & Agarwal, S. (Eds.). (2024). *Analyzing and Mitigating Security Risks in Cloud Computing*. IGI Global. 10.4018/979-8-3693-3249-8

Goel, P. K., Pandey, H., Singhal, A., & Agarwal, S. (Eds.). (2024). *Improving Security, Privacy, and Trust in Cloud Computing*. IGI Global. 10.4018/979-8-3693-1431-9

Gogniat, G., Wolf, T., Burleson, W., Diguet, J., Bossuet, L., & Vaslin, R. (2008). Reconfigurable hardware for high-security/highperformance embedded systems: The SAFES perspective. *IEEE Transactions on Very Large Scale Integration (VLSI)Systems*, 16(2), 144–155.

Goldenberg, N., & Wool, A. (2013). Accurate modeling of modbus/tcp for intrusion detection in scada systems. *International Journal of Critical Infrastructure Protection*, 6(2), 63–75. 10.1016/j.ijcip.2013.05.001

González-Martínez, J. A., Bote-Lorenzo, M. L., Gómez-Sánchez, E., & Cano-Parra, R. (2015). Cloud computing and education: A state-of-the-art survey. *Computers & Education*, 80, 132–151. 10.1016/j.compedu.2014.08.017

Gopal Dhaker, D. S. S. (2014). #1, Auto-Scaling, Load Balancing and Monitoring As service in public cloud\n,. *IOSR Journal of Computer Engineering*, 16(4), 39–46. 10.9790/0661-16413946

Goseva-Popstojanova, K., Anastasovski, G., Dimitrijevikj, A., Pantev, R., & Miller, B. (2014). Characterization and classification of malicious Web traffic. *Computers & Security*, 42, 92–115. 10.1016/j.cose.2014.01.006

Goyal, D., Gupta, N., & Kumar, V. (2022). Blockchain-Based Secure Data Sharing in Cloud Computing: A Systematic Review. *Journal of Cloud Computing (Heidelberg, Germany)*, 11(1), 1–25.

Grewal, B. S. (2005). *Higher Engineering Mathematics*. Khanna Publishing.

Grover, V., Tseng, S.-L., & Pu, W. (2022). A theoretical perspective on organizational culture and digitalization. *Information & Management*, 59(4), 103639. 10.1016/j.im.2022.103639

Gruschka, N., & Jensen, M. (2010). Attack surfaces: A taxonomy for attacks on cloud services. *Cloud Computing (CLOUD) 2010 IEEE 3rd International Conference*. IEEE. 10.1109/CLOUD.2010.23

Guan, J., Li, J., Wu, L., Zhang, Y., Wu, J., & Du, X. (2017). Achieving efficient and secure data acquisition for cloud-supported internet of things in smart grid. *IEEE Internet of Things Journal*, 4(6), 1934–1944. 10.1109/JIOT.2017.2690522

Guan, Y., Si, G., Zhang, X., Wu, L., Guizani, N., Du, X., & Ma, Y. (2018). Privacy-preserving and efficient aggregation based on blockchain for power grid communications in smart communities. *IEEE Communications Magazine*, 56(7), 82–88. 10.1109/MCOM.2018.1700401

Guan, Z., Zhang, Y., Zhu, L., Wu, L., & Yu, S. (2019). Effect: An efficient flexible privacy-preserving data aggregation scheme with authentication in smart grid. *Science China. Information Sciences*, 62(3), 32103. 10.1007/s11432-018-9451-y

Gunasekar, T., & Raghavendran, P. (2024). The Mohand transform approach to fractional integro-differential equations. *Journal of Computational Analysis and Applications*, 33, 358–371.

Gunasekar, T., Raghavendran, P., Santra, S. S., Majumder, D., Baleanu, D., & Balasundaram, H. (2024). Application of Laplace transform to solve fractional integro-differential equations. *Journal of Mathematics and Computer Science*, 33(3), 225–237. 10.22436/jmcs.033.03.02

Gunasekar, T., Raghavendran, P., Santra, Sh. S., & Sajid, M. (2024). Existence and controllability results for neutral fractional Volterra Fredholm integro-differential equations. *Journal of Mathematics and Computer Science*, 34(4), 361–380. 10.22436/jmcs.034.04.04

Gunasekar, Th., Raghavendran, P., Santra, Sh. S., & Sajid, M. (2024). Analyzing existence, uniqueness, and stability of neutral fractional Volterra-Fredholm integro-differential equations. *Journal of Mathematics and Computer Science-JM*, 33(4), 390–407. 10.22436/jmcs.033.04.06

Guo, B., Ouyang, Y., Guo, T., Cao, L., & Yu, Z. (2019). Enhancing mobile app user understanding and marketing with heterogeneous crowdsourced data: A review. *IEEE Access : Practical Innovations, Open Solutions*, 7, 68557–68571. 10.1109/ACCESS.2019.2918325

Gupta, M., Sharma, S., & Sharma, C. (2022). Security and Privacy Issues in Blockchained IoT: Principles, Challenges and Counteracting Actions. In *Blockchain Technology* (pp. 27–56). CRC Press.

Gupta, M., Boyd, L., & Kuzmits, F. (2011). The evaporating cloud: A tool for resolving workplace conflict. *International Journal of Conflict Management*, 22(4), 394–412. 10.1108/10444061111171387

Gupta, M., & Kumar, D. (2014). State-of-the-art of Content Delivery Network. *International Journal of Computer Science and Information Technologies*, 5(4), 5441–5446.

Gupta, R. K., Almuzaini, K. K., Pateriya, R., Shah, K., Shukla, P. K., & Akwafo, R. (2022). An improved secure key generation using enhanced identity-based encryption for cloud computing in large-scale 5G. *Wireless Communications and Mobile Computing*, 2022, 14. 10.1155/2022/7291250

Hackbarth, G., & Grover, V. (1999). The knowledge repository: Organizational memory information systems. *Information Systems Management*, 16(3), 21–30. 10.1201/1078/43197.16.3.1 9990601/31312.4

Hasimi, L., & Penzel, D. (2023). A Case Study on Cloud Computing: Challenges, Opportunities, and Potentials. In *Developments in Information and Knowledge Management Systems for Business Applications* (Vol. 6, pp. 1–25). Springer Nature Switzerland. 10.1007/978-3-031-27506-7_1

Compilation of References

Hatamian, M. (2020). Engineering privacy in smartphone apps: A technical guideline catalog for app developers. *IEEE Access : Practical Innovations, Open Solutions*, 8, 35429–35445. 10.1109/ACCESS.2020.2974911

Hayes, J., Aneiba, A., Gaber, M., Islam, M. S., & Abozariba, R. (2023). FBA-SDN: a federated byzantine approach for blockchain-based collaborative intrusion detection in edge SDN. *2023 IEEE International Conference on Communications Workshops (ICC Workshops)*, (pp. 427–433). IEEE. 10.1109/ICCWorkshops57953.2023.10283805

Haynie, M. (2009). Enterprise cloud services: Deriving business value from Cloud Computing. *Micro Focus*, 56-61.

He, D., Chan, S., & Guizani, M. (2015). Mobile application security: Malware threats and defenses. *IEEE Wireless Communications*, 22(1), 138–144. 10.1109/MWC.2015.7054729

Hekkala, J., Muurman, M., Halunen, K., & Vallivaara, V. (2023). Implementing post-quantum cryptography for developers. *SN Computer Science*, 4(4), 365. 10.1007/s42979-023-01724-1

Hellerstein, J., Faleiro, J., Gonzalez, J., Schleier-Smith, J., Screekanti, V., Tumanov, A., & Wu, C. (2019). Serverless Computing: One Step Forward, Two Steps Back. arXiv:1812.03651.

Hema, C., & Garcia Marquez, F. P. (2023). Emotional speech Recognition using CNN and Deep learning techniques. *Applied Acoustics*, 211, 109492. 10.1016/j.apacoust.2023.109492

Hirani, M., Halgamuge, M. N., & Hang, P. D. T. (2019). Data security models developed by blockchain technology for different business domains. *2019 11th International Conference on Knowledge and Systems Engineering (KSE)*, (p. 1–10). Research Gate.

Hirashima, Y., Yamasaki, K., & Nagura, M. (2016). Proactive-reactive auto-scaling mechanism for unpredictable load change. *Proc. - 2016 5th IIAI Int. Congr. Adv. Appl. Informatics, IIAI-AAI 2016*, pp. 861–866. IEEE. 10.1109/IIAI-AAI.2016.180

Hiwarekar, A. P. (2012). A new method of cryptography using Laplace transform. *International Journal of Mathematical Archive*, 3(3), 1193–1197.

Hlavacs, H., Haddad, M., Lafouge, C., Kaplan, D., & Ribeiro, J. (2005, May). The CODIS Content Delivery Network. *Computer Networks*, 48(1), 75–89. 10.1016/j.comnet.2004.10.004

Hochheiser, H., & Valdez, R. S. (2020). Human-Computer Interaction, Ethics, and Biomedical Informatics. *Yearbook of Medical Informatics*, 29(1), 93–98. 10.1055/s-0040-170199032823302

Hofmann, M., & Beaumont, L. R. (2005). *Content networking : architecture, protocols, and practice*. Morgan Kaufmann.

Ho, P.-H., Li, M., Yu, H.-F., Jiang, X., & Dán, G. (2017, February). Special Section on Mobile Content Delivery Networks. *Computer Communications*, 99, 62. 10.1016/j.comcom.2017.01.008

Hsu, C. L., & Lin, J. C. C. (2016). Factors affecting the adoption of cloud services in enterprises. *Information Systems and e-Business Management*, 14(4), 791–822. 10.1007/s10257-015-0300-9

Huang, C., Wang, A., Li, J., & Ross, K. W. (2008). Understanding hybrid CDN-P2P. *Proceedings of the 18th International Workshop on Network and Operating Systems Support for Digital Audio and Video - NOSSDAV '08*, (pp. 75). IEEE.

Huang, Y., & Li, M.. (2023, September). Performance Optimization for Energy-Efficient Industrial Internet of Things Based on Ambient Backscatter Communication: An A3C-FL Approach. *IEEE Transactions on Green Communications and Networking*, 7(3), 1121–1134. 10.1109/TGCN.2023.3260199

Hussain, A., Imad, M., Khan, A., & Ullah, B. (2022). Multi-class Classification for the Identification of COVID-19 in X-Ray Images Using Customized Efficient Neural Network. *AI and IoT for Sustainable Development in Emerging Countries*. Springer. 10.1007/978-3-030-90618-4_23

Hussain, A., Ahmad, B., Imad, M., & Cane, S. (2023). Obstacle Recognition for Visually Impaired People Based on Convolutional Neural Network. *Machine Intelligence for Internet of Medical Things: Applications and Future Trends Computational Intelligence for Data Analysis*, 2, 194–209. 10.2174/9789815080445123020015

Hwang, K., Bai, X., Shi, Y., Li, M., Chen, W. G., & Wu, Y. (2016). Cloud Performance Modeling with Benchmark Evaluation of Elastic Scaling Strategies. *IEEE Transactions on Parallel and Distributed Systems*, 27(1), 130–143. 10.1109/TPDS.2015.2398438

Hyunjoong, S. (2011). PcubeCast: A novel peer-assisted live streaming system. *2011 IEEE International Conference on Peer-to-Peer Computing*, (pp. 212–215). IEEE. 10.1109/P2P.2011.6038738

Imad, M. (2022). *A Comparative Analysis of Intrusion Detection in IoT Network Using Machine Learning* (pp. 149–163). Springer. 10.1007/978-3-031-05752-6_10

Imad, M., Hassan, M. A., & Bangash, S. H. (2023). Naimullah; Machine Learning Solution for Orthopedics: A Comprehensive Review. *Machine Intelligence for Internet of Medical Things: Applications and Future Trends Computational Intelligence for Data Analysis*, 2, 120–136. 10.2174/9789815080445123020011

Imad, M., Ullah, F., & Hassan, M. A. (2020). Pakistani Currency Recognition to Assist Blind Person Based on Convolutional Neural Network. *Journal of Computer Science and Technology Studies*, 2(2), 12–19.

Ionescu, S. A., & Diaconita, V. (2023). Transforming Financial Decision-Making: The Interplay of AI, Cloud Computing and Advanced Data Management Technologies. *International Journal of Computers Communications & Control, 18*(6), e5735, 1-19.

Islam, M. R., Rahman, M. M., Mahmud, M., Rahman, M. A., Mohamad, M. H. S., & Associates. (2021). A review on blockchain security issues and challenges. *2021 IEEE 12th Control and System Graduate Research Colloquium (ICSGRC)*. IEEE.

Islam, M. T., Nasir, M. K., Hasan, M. M., Faruque, M. G. G., Hossain, M. S., & Azad, M. M. (2021). Blockchain-based decentralized digital self-sovereign identity wallet for secure transaction. *Adv. Sci. Technol. Eng. Syst. J*, 6(2), 977–983. 10.25046/aj0602112

Compilation of References

Islam, S. N., Baig, Z., & Zeadally, S. (2019). Physical layer security for the smart grid: Vulnerabilities, threats, and countermeasures. *IEEE Transactions on Industrial Informatics*, 15(12), 6522–6530. 10.1109/TII.2019.2931436

Issa, T., & Isaias, P. (2022). *Usability and Human–Computer Interaction (HCI)*. Sustainable Design. 10.1007/978-1-4471-7513-1_2

Itani, W., Kayssi, A., & Chehab, A. (2009). Privacy as a Service: Privacy-Aware Data Storage and Processing in Cloud Computing Architectures. *Eighth IEEE International Conference on Dependable Autonomic and Secure Computing*. IEEE. 10.1109/DASC.2009.139

Jackson, P. (2010). *Web 2.0 Knowledge Technologies and the Enterprise, Smarter, Lighter and Cheaper*. Chandos Information Professional Series. Chandos.

Jain, V., Gupta, G., Gupta, M., Sharma, D. K., & Ghosh, U. (2023). Ambient intelligence-based multimodal human action recognition for autonomous systems. *ISA Transactions*, 132, 94–108. 10.1016/j.isatra.2022.10.03436404154

Jaiswal, A., Krishnama Raju, A., & Deb, S. (2020). Facial emotion detection using deep learning. *2020 International Conference for Emerging Technology, INCET 2020*. IEEE. 10.1109/INCET49848.2020.9154121

Jaume, D., & Willén, A. (2019). The Long-Run Effects of Teacher Strikes: Evidence from Argentina. *Journal of Labor Economics, 37*(4). University of Chicago Press, Chicago. 10.1086/703134

Jayapandian, N. (2021). Cloud dynamic scheduling for Multimedia Data encryption using Tabu Search Algorithm. *Wireless Personal Communications*, 120(3), 2427–2447. 10.1007/s11277-021-08562-5

Jayawardena, N. S., & Dewasiri, N. J. (2023). *Food Acquisition and Consumption Issues of South Asian Countries: A Systematic Literature Review and Future Research Agenda*. FIIB Business Review. 10.1177/23197145231194113

Jesus, P., Baquero, C., & Almeida, P. S. (2014). A survey of distributed data aggregation algorithms. *IEEE Communications Surveys and Tutorials*, 17(1), 381–404. 10.1109/COMST.2014.2354398

Jhurani, J. (2022). *Driving Economic Efficiency and Innovation: The Impact of Workday Financials in Cloud-Based ERP Adoption. International Journal of Computer Engineering and Technology*. IJCET.

Jiang, D., & Shi, G. (2021). Research on Data Security and Privacy Protection of Wearable Equipment in Healthcare. *Journal of Healthcare Engineering*, 2021, 1–7. 10.1155/2021/665620433628404

Jiang, H., Zhao, D., & Ren, W. (2023). Privacy-Preserving Data Sharing and Storage Techniques in Cloud-Based Healthcare Systems: A Review. *International Journal of Environmental Research and Public Health*, 20(4), 2161–2178.

Ji, Y. G., & Salvendy, G. (2002). Development and validation of user-adaptive navigation and information retrieval tools for an intranet portal organizational memory information system. *Behaviour & Information Technology*, 21(2), 145–154. 10.1080/01449290210136756

Jordan, M. (2015). Machine learning: Trends, perspectives, and prospects. *Science (1979)*, *349*(6245), 255–260. .10.1126/science.aaa8415

Joshi, D. R., Khanal, J., & Dhakal, R. H. (2023). From Resistance to Resilience: Teachers' Adaptation Process to Mediating Digital Devices in Pre-COVID-19, during COVID-19, and post-COVID-19 Classrooms in Nepal. *Education Sciences*, 13(5), 509. 10.3390/educsci13050509

Kaffenberger, M. (2020). *Modelling the Long-Run Learning Impact of the COVID-19 Learning Shock: Actions to (More Than) Mitigate Loss*. RISE. 10.35489/BSG-RISE-RI_2020/017

Kalech, M. (2019). Cyber-attack detection in scada systems using temporal pattern recognition techniques. *Computers & Security*, 84, 225–238. 10.1016/j.cose.2019.03.007

Kalyani, Y., & Collier, R. (2021). A systematic survey on the role of cloud, fog, and edge computing combination in smart agriculture. *Sensors (Basel)*, 21(17), 5922. 10.3390/s2117592234502813

Kamiya, Y. & Shimokawa, T. (2020). *A Study about Web Application Inter-Cloud.*

Kane, G. C., Palmer, D., Phillips, A. N., & Kiron, D. ve Buckley, N. (2015). *Strategy, not technology, drives digital transformation*. MIT Sloan Management Review and Deloitte University Press.

Kang, S., & Yin, H. (2010). A Hybrid CDN-P2P System for Video-on-Demand. *2010 Second International Conference on Future Networks*, (pp. 309–313). IEEE. 10.1109/ICFN.2010.83

Kant, R., Sharma, S., Vikas, V., Chaudhary, S., Jain, A. K., & Sharma, K. K. (2023, April). Blockchain–A Deployment Mechanism for IoT Based Security. In *2023 International Conference on Computational Intelligence, Communication Technology and Networking (CICTN)* (pp. 739-745). IEEE. 10.1109/CICTN57981.2023.10140715

Karunarathna, K. S. S. N., Dewasiri, N. J., Singh, R., & Rathnasiri, M. S. H. (2024). What Does Artificial Intelligence–Powered ChatGPT Bring to Academia? A Review. Singh, R., Khan, S., Kumar, A., & Kumar, V. (Ed.) *Artificial Intelligence Enabled Management: An Emerging Economy Perspective*. De Gruyter. 10.1515/9783111172408

Kathirvel, A. (2023). *Systematic Number Plate detection using improved YOLOv5 detector*. Institute of Electrical and Electronics Engineers. .10.1109/ViTECoN58111.2023.10157727

Kathirvel, A., & Gobinath, V. M. (2024). A Review on Additive Manufactuing in Industrial. *Modern Hybird Machince and Super Finishing Process: Technology and Application*. CRC Publiser/Chapman and Hall.

Compilation of References

Kathirvel, A., & Maheswaran, C. P. (2023). Chapter 8: Enhanced AI-Based Intrusion Detection and Response System for WSN. *Artificial Intelligence for Intrusion Detection Systems.* CRC Publiser/Chapman and Hall. https://www.taylorfrancis.com/chapters/edit/10.1201/9781003346340 -8/enhanced-ai-based-intrusion-detection-response-system-wsn-kathirvel-maheswaran10.1201/ 9781003346340-8

Kathirvel, A., & Pavani, A. (2023). *Machine Learning and Deep Learning Algorithms for Network Data Analytics Function in 5G Cellular Networks.* Institute of Electrical and Electronics Engineers Inc publisher. .10.1109/ICICT57646.2023.10134247

Kathirvel, A., & Shobitha, M. (2023). *Digital Assets Fair Estimation Using Artificial Intelligence.* Institute of Electrical and Electronics Engineers. .10.1109/ViTECoN58111.2023.10157310

Kathirvel, A., Maheswaran, C. P., Subramaniam, M., & Naren, A. K. (2023). Quantum Computers Based on Distributed Computing Systems for the Next Generation: Overview and Applications. *Handbook of Research on Quantum Computing for Smart Environments.* IGI Global.10.4018/978-1-6684-6697-1.ch025

Kathirvel, A., Rithik, G., & Naren, A. K. (2024). Automation of IOT Robotics. In *Predicting Natural Disasters With AI and Machine Learning.* IGI Global. 10.4018/979-8-3693-2280-2.ch011

Kathirvel, A., Subramaniam, M., Navaneethan, S., & Sabarinath, C. (2021). Improved IDR Response System for Sensor Network. *Journal of Web Engineering, 20*(1). 10.13052/jwe1540-9589.2013

Kathirvel, A., Sudha, D., Naveneethan, S., Subramaniam, M., Das, D. & Kirubakaran, S. (2022). AI Based Mobile Bill Payment System using Biometric Fingerprint. *American Journal of Engineering and Applied Sciences, 15*(1), 23-31. 10.3844/ajeassp.2022.23.31

Kathirvel, A. (2024a). Applications of Serverless Computing: Systematic Overview. In Aluvalu, R., & Maheswari, U. (Eds.), *Serverless Computing Concepts, Technology and Architecture* (Vol. 221-233). IGI Global. 10.4018/979-8-3693-1682-5.ch014

Kathirvel, A. (2024b). Innovation and Industry Application: IoT-Based Robotics Frontier of Automation in Industry Application. In Satishkumar, D., & Sivaraja, M. (Eds.), *Internet of Things and AI for Natural Disaster Management and Prediction* (pp. 83–105). IGI Global. 10.4018/979-8-3693-4284-8.ch004

Kathirvel, A., Gopinath, V. M., Naren, K., Nithyanand, D., & Nirmaladevi, K. (2024). Manufacturing Smart Industry Perspective an Overview. *American Journal of Engineering and Applied Sciences*, 17(1), 33–39. 10.3844/ajeassp.2024.33.39

Kathirvel, A., & Naren, A. K. (2024a). Critical Approaches to Data Engineering Systems Innovation and Industry Application Using IoT. In *Critical Approaches to Data Engineering Systems and Analysis.* IGI Global. 10.4018/979-8-3693-2260-4.ch005

Kathirvel, A., & Naren, A. K. (2024b). Diabetes and Pre-Diabetes Prediction by AI Using Tuned XGB Classifier. In Khang, A. (Ed.), *Medical Robotics and AI-Assisted Diagnostics for a High-Tech Healthcare Industry* (pp. 52–64). IGI Global. 10.4018/979-8-3693-2105-8.ch004

Kathirvel, A., Naren, K., Nithyanand, D., & Santhoshi, B. (2024). Overview of 5G Technology: Streamlined Virtual Event Experiences. *Advances of Robotic Technology*, 2(1), 1–8. 10.23880/art-16000109

Kaur, G., Habibi Lashkari, A., Sharafaldin, I., & Habibi Lashkari, Z. (2023). Blockchain Security. In *Understanding Cybersecurity Management in Decentralized Finance: Challenges, Strategies, and Trends* (pp. 71–89). Springer. 10.1007/978-3-031-23340-1_4

Kaur, I., Narula, G. S., Wason, R., Jain, V., & Baliyan, A. (2018). Neuro fuzzy—COCOMO II model for software cost estimation. *International Journal of Information Technology: an Official Journal of Bharati Vidyapeeth's Institute of Computer Applications and Management*, 10(2), 181–187. 10.1007/s41870-018-0083-6

Khalid, A., Butt, S. A., Jamal, T., & Gochhait, S. (2022). Agile Scrum Issues at Large-Scale Distributed Projects: Scrum Project Development At Large. In *Research Anthology on Agile Software, Software Development, and Testing, edited by Information Resources Management Association* (pp. 388–398). IGI Global. 10.4018/978-1-6684-3702-5.ch019

Khan, A. A. Z. (2019). Misuse intrusion detection using machine learning for gas pipeline scada networks. *Proceedings of the International Conference on Security and Management (SAM)*. The Steering Committee of The World Congress in Computer Science.

Khan, N. (2020). COVID-19 Classification based on Chest X-Ray Images Using Machine Learning Techniques. *Journal of Computer Science and Technology Studies*, 01-11.

Khanal, S. S., Prasad, P. W. C., Alsadoon, A., & Maag, A. (2020, July). A systematic review: Machine learning based recommendation systems for e-learning. *Education and Information Technologies*, 25(4), 2635–2664. 10.1007/s10639-019-10063-9

Kharde, U. D. (2017). An Application of the Elzaki Transform in Cryptography. *Journal for Advanced Research in Applied Sciences*, 4(5), 86–89.

Khashman, A. (2008, November). A Modified Backpropagation Learning Algorithm with Added Emotional Coefficients. *IEEE Transactions on Neural Networks*, 19(11), 1896–1909. 10.1109/TNN.2008.200291318990644

Khuat, T. T., Kedziora, D. J., & Gabrys, B. (2022). The Roles and Modes of Human Interactions with Automated Machine Learning Systems. https://arxiv.org/abs/2205.04139v1

Kim, D., Kim, J. H., Moon, C., Choi, J., & Yeom, I. (2016). Efficient content delivery in mobile ad-hoc networks using CCN. *Ad Hoc Networks*, 36, 81–99. 10.1016/j.adhoc.2015.06.007

Kim, J., Kim, D., & Lee, S. (2021). Federated Learning for Privacy-Preserving Machine Learning in Cloud Environments: A Comprehensive Survey. *Future Generation Computer Systems*, 125, 146–164.

Kim, R., Chitti, R., & Song, J. (2010). Chitti, and J. Song. Novel defense mechanism against data flooding attacks in wireless ad hoc networks. *IEEE Transactions on Consumer Electronics*, 56(2), 579–582. 10.1109/TCE.2010.5505973

Compilation of References

Kishore, K., & Sharma, S. (2016). Evolution of Wireless Sensor Networks as the framework of Internet of Things-A Review. *International Journal OfEmerging Research in Management &TechnologyI*, 5(12), 49–52.

Kobsa, A., & Schreck, J. (2003). Privacy through pseudonymity in user-adaptive systems. *ACM Transactions on Internet Technology*, 3(2), 149–183. 10.1145/767193.767196

Koh, S., Wi, H. J., Hyung Kim, B., & Jo, S. (2019). Personalizing the Prediction: Interactive and Interpretable machine learning. *2019 16th International Conference on Ubiquitous Robots, UR 2019*. IEEE. 10.1109/URAI.2019.8768705

Koppanati, R. K., & Kumar, K. (2020). P-MEC: Polynomial congruence-based Multimedia encryption technique over cloud. *IEEE Consumer Electronics Magazine*, 10(5), 41–46. 10.1109/MCE.2020.3003127

Korczak, J., Hernes, M., & Bac, M. (2017). Collective intelligence supporting trading decisions on FOREX market. *Proceedings of the International Conference on Computational Collective Intelligence*, (pp. 113–122). Springer. 10.1007/978-3-319-67074-4_12

Kounev, S., Herbst, N., Abad, C., Iosup, A., Foster, I., Shenoy, P., Rana, O., & Chien, A. (2023). Serverless Computing: What It Is, and What It Is Not? *Communications of the ACM*.

Kriushanth, M., Arockiam, L., & Mirobi, G. J. (2013). Auto Scaling in Cloud Computing : An Overview. *International Journal of Advanced Research in Computer and Communication Engineering*, 2(7), 2870–2875.

Kumar, R., & Ahmad Khan, R. (2024). Securing military computing with the blockchain. *Computer Fraud \& Security, 2024*(2).

Kumar, S., & Buyya, R. (2012). Green cloud computing and environmental sustainability. *Harnessing green IT: principles and practices*, 315-339.

Kumari, S., Tanwar, S., Tyagi, S., Kumar, N., Obaidat, M. S., & Rodrigues, J. J. P. C. (2019). Tanwar, S. Tyagi, N. Kumar, M. S. Obaidat, and J. J. Rodrigues, "Fog computing for smart grid systems in the 5g environment: Challenges and solutions,". *IEEE Wireless Communications*, 26(3), 47–53. 10.1109/MWC.2019.1800356

Kumar, K., & Lu, Y. H. (2010). Cloud computing for mobile users: Can offloading computation save energy? *Computer*, 43(4), 51–56. 10.1109/MC.2010.98

Kumar, N. M., & Chopra, S. S. (2022). Leveraging blockchain and smart contract technologies to overcome circular economy implementation challenges. *Sustainability (Basel)*, 14(15), 9492. 10.3390/su14159492

Kumar, N., Aujla, G. S., Das, A. K., & Conti, M. (2019). ECCAuth: Secure Authentication Protocol for Demand Reponse Management in Smart Grid Systems. *IEEE Transactions on Industrial Informatics*, 15(12), 6572–6582. 10.1109/TII.2019.2922697

Kumar, P. R., Raj, P. H., & Jelciana, P. (2018). Exploring data security issues and solutions in cloud computing. *Procedia Computer Science*, 125, 691–697. 10.1016/j.procs.2017.12.089

Kundra, V. (2010). *State of public sector cloud computing*. Federal Chief Information.

Kushare, S. R., Patil, D. P., & Takate, A. M. (2021). The new integral transform, Kushare transform. *International Journal of Advances in Engineering and Management*, 3(9), 1589–1592.

Lai, X., Zhang, Y., & Luo, H. (2024). A low-cost blockchain node deployment algorithm for the internet of things. *Peer-to-Peer Networking and Applications*, 17(2), 1–11. 10.1007/s12083-023-01615-5

Lakshmi, G. N., Kumar, B. R., & Sekhar, A. C. (2011). A cryptographic scheme of Laplace transforms. *International Journal of Mathematical Archive*, 2, 2515–2519.

Lankadasu, N. V. Y., Pesarlanka, D. B., Sharma, A., Sharma, S., & Gochhait, S. (2024). Skin Cancer Classification Using a Convolutional Neural Network: An Exploration into Deep Learning. *2024 ASU International Conference in Emerging Technologies for Sustainability and Intelligent Systems (ICETSIS)*, (pp. 1047–1052). IEEE. 10.1109/ICETSIS61505.2024.10459368

Lee, R., Assante, M., & Conway, T. (2016). *Analysis of the cyber attack on the Ukrainian power grid*. NERC. https://www.nerc.com/pa/CI/ESISAC/Documents/EISAC SANS Ukraine DUC 18Mar2016.pdf

Leitner, P., Wittern, E., Spillner, J., & Hummer, W. (2019). A mixed-method empirical study of Function-as-a-Service software development in industrial practice. *Journal of Systems and Software*, 149, 340–359. 10.1016/j.jss.2018.12.013

Leng, J., Ruan, G., Jiang, P., Xu, K., Liu, Q., Zhou, X., & Liu, C. (2020). Blockchain-empowered sustainable manufacturing and product lifecycle management in industry 4.0: A survey. *Renewable & Sustainable Energy Reviews*, 132, 110112. 10.1016/j.rser.2020.110112

Leng, J., Zhou, M., Zhao, J. L., Huang, Y., & Bian, Y. (2020). Blockchain security: A survey of techniques and research directions. *IEEE Transactions on Services Computing*, 15(4), 2490–2510. 10.1109/TSC.2020.3038641

Li, H. (2021). Big data and ambient intelligence in IoT-based wireless student health monitoring system. *Aggression and Violent Behavior*. Elsevier Ltd.

Liang, G., Weller, S. R., Luo, F., Zhao, J., & Dong, Z. Y. (2018). Distributed blockchain-based data protection framework for modern power systems against cyber attacks. *IEEE Transactions on Smart Grid*, 10(3), 3162–3173. 10.1109/TSG.2018.2819663

Liang, G., Zhao, J., Luo, F., Weller, S., & Dong, Z. (2017). A review of false data injection attacks against modern power systems. *IEEE Transactions on Smart Grid*, 8(4), 1630–1638. 10.1109/TSG.2015.2495133

Compilation of References

Liang, X., Li, X., Lu, R., Lin, X., & Shen, X. (2013). Li, R. Lu, X. Lin, and X. Shen, "UDP: Usage-based dynamic pricing with privacy preservation for smart grid,". *IEEE Transactions on Smart Grid*, 4(1), 141–150. 10.1109/TSG.2012.2228240

Li, B. L., & Liu, P. (2011). Secure and privacy-preserving information aggregation for smart grids. *IJSN*, 6(1), 28–39. 10.1504/IJSN.2011.039631

Li, B., Xiao, G., Lu, R., Deng, R., & Bao, H. (2019). On feasibility and limitations of detecting false data injection attacks on power grid state estimation using d-facts devices. *IEEE Transactions on Industrial Informatics*.

Li, D., Guo, H., Zhou, J., Zhou, L., & Wong, J. W. (2019). Scadawall: A cpi-enabled firewall model for scada security. *Computers & Security*, 80, 134–154. 10.1016/j.cose.2018.10.002

Li, H., Lin, X., Yang, H., Liang, X., Lu, R., & Shen, X. (2013). Eppdr: An efficient privacy-preserving demand response scheme with adaptive key evolution in smart grid. *IEEE Transactions on Parallel and Distributed Systems*, 25(8), 2053–2064. 10.1109/TPDS.2013.124

Li, Q., & Cao, G. (2011). Multicast authentication in the smart grid with onetime signature. *IEEE Transactions on Smart Grid*, 2(4), 686–696. 10.1109/TSG.2011.2138172

Liu, Y., Rameshan, N., Monte, E., Vlassov, V., & Navarro, L. (2015). ProRenaTa: Proactive and reactive tuning to scale a distributed storage system. *Proc. - 2015 IEEE/ACM 15th Int. Symp. Clust. Cloud, Grid Comput.* (pp. 453–464). IEEE. 10.1109/CCGrid.2015.26

Liu, N., Chen, J., Zhu, L., Zhang, J., & He, Y. (2012). A key management scheme for secure communications of advanced metering infrastructure in smart grid. *IEEE Transactions on Industrial Electronics*, 60(10), 4746–4756. 10.1109/TIE.2012.2216237

Liu, P., Zhu, G., Wang, S., & Jiang, W. (2023, January). Toward Ambient Intelligence: Federated Edge Learning With Task-Oriented Sensing, Computation, and Communication Integration. *IEEE Journal of Selected Topics in Signal Processing*, 17(1), 158–172. 10.1109/JSTSP.2022.3226836

Liu, S., Chan, F. T., Yang, J., & Niu, B. (2018). Understanding the effect of cloud computing on organisational agility: An empirical examination. *International Journal of Information Management*, 43, 98–111. 10.1016/j.ijinfomgt.2018.07.010

Liu, Y., & Yu, S.-Z. (2016, April). Network coding-based multisource content delivery in Content Centric Networking. *Journal of Network and Computer Applications*, 64, 167–175. 10.1016/j.jnca.2016.02.007

Liu, Y., Zhang, Z., & Wang, Q. (2022). Secure Query Processing Techniques for Privacy-Preserving Data Analytics in Cloud Computing: A Review. *Computers & Security*, 113, 102460.

Li, Y., Amelot, J., Zhou, X., Bengio, S., & Si, S. (2020). Auto Completion of User Interface Layout Design Using Transformer-Based Tree Decoders. arXiv. https://arxiv.org/abs/2001.05308v1

Li, Y., Kumar, R., Lasecki, W. S., & Hilliges, O. (2020). Artificial intelligence for HCI: A modern approach. *Conference on Human Factors in Computing Systems – Proceedings*. ACM. 10.1145/3334480.3375147

Li, Z., & Simon, G. (2013, September). In a Telco-CDN, Pushing Content Makes Sense. *IEEE Transactions on Network and Service Management*, 10(3), 300–311. 10.1109/TNSM.2013.043013.130474

Lone, A. H., & Naaz, R. (2021). Applicability of Blockchain smart contracts in securing Internet and IoT: A systematic literature review. *Computer Science Review*, 39, 100360. 10.1016/j.cosrev.2020.100360

Lorido-Botrán, T., Miguel-Alonso, J., & Lozano, J. (2013). Comparison of Auto-scaling Techniques for Cloud Environments. *Actas las XXIV Jornadas Paralelismo*.

Lorido-Botran, T., Miguel-Alonso, J., & Lozano, J. A. (2014). A Review of Auto-scaling Techniques for Elastic Applications in Cloud Environments. *Journal of Grid Computing*, 12(4), 559–592. 10.1007/s10723-014-9314-7

Lu, R. X., Heung, K., Lashkari, A. H., & Ghorbani, A. A. (2017). A Lightweight Privacy-Preserving Data Aggregation Scheme for Fog Computing-enhanced IoT. *IEEE Access: Practical Innovations, Open Solutions*, 5, 3302–3312. 10.1109/ACCESS.2017.2677520

Lu, R., Liang, X., Li, X., Lin, X., & Shen, X. (2012). Eppa: An efficient and privacy-preserving aggregation scheme for secure smart grid communications. *IEEE Transactions on Parallel and Distributed Systems*, 23(9), 1621–1631. 10.1109/TPDS.2012.86

Lv, Z. (2022). Deep Learning for Intelligent Human–Computer Interaction, *Applied Sciences,12*(22), 11457. .10.3390/app122211457

Ma, M., Wang, Z., Su, K., & Sun, L. (2016). *Understanding Content Placement Strategies in Smartrouter-based Peer CDN for Video Streaming*.

Maglaras, L. A., Kim, K.-H., Janicke, H., Ferrag, M. A., Rallis, S., Fragkou, P., Maglaras, A., & Cruz, T. J. (2018). Cyber security of critical infrastructures. *Ict Express*, 4(1), 42–45. 10.1016/j.icte.2018.02.001

Mahalle, A., Yong, J., & Tao, X. (2020). ITIL process management to mitigate operations risk in cloud architecture infrastructure for the banking and financial services industry. *Web Intelligence*, 18(3), 229–238. 10.3233/WEB-200444

Maharjan, Q., Zhu, Q., Zhang, Y., Gjessing, S., & Basar, T. (2013). Zhu, Y. Zhang, S. Gjessing, and T. Basar. Dependable demand response management in the smart grid: A stackelberg game approach. *IEEE Transactions on Smart Grid*, 4(1), 120–132. 10.1109/TSG.2012.2223766

Mahfuzur, R. (2016). *Improved Virtual Machine (VM) based Resource Provisioning in Cloud Computing*.

Compilation of References

Mahgoub, M. M. A. (2016). The New Integral Transform Mahgoub Transform. *Advances in Theoretical and Applied Mathematics*, 11(4), 391–398.

Mahmood, K., Chaudhry, S. A., Naqvi, H., Kumari, S., Li, X., & Sangaiah, A. K. (2018). An elliptic curve cryptography based lightweight authentication scheme for smart grid communication. *Future Generation Computer Systems*, 81, 557–565. 10.1016/j.future.2017.05.002

Ma, L., Gupta, R. K., & Onyema, E. M. (2022). Optimization of Intelligent Network Information Management System under Big Data and Cloud Computing. *Scalable Computing: Practice and Experience*, 23(3), 91–101. 10.12694/scpe.v23i3.2001

Malallah, H. S., Qashi, R., Abdulrahman, L. M., Omer, M. A., & Yazdeen, A. A. (2023). Performance analysis of enterprise cloud computing: A review. *Journal of Applied Science and Technology Trends*, 4(1), 1–12. 10.38094/jastt401139

Malik, U. M., & Javed, M. A. (2022). Ambient Intelligence assisted fog computing for industrial IoT applications. [Elsevier Ltd.]. *Computer Communications*, 196, 117–128. 10.1016/j.comcom.2022.09.024

Manzoor, A. (2019). Cloud Computing Applications in the Public Sector. In *Cloud Security: Concepts, Methodologies, Tools, and Applications* (pp. 1241-1272). IGI Global. 10.4018/978-1-5225-8176-5.ch063

Marston, S., Li, Z., Bandyopadhyay, S., Zhang, J., & Ghalsasi, A. (2011). Cloud computing—The business perspective. *Decision Support Systems*, 51(1), 176–189. 10.1016/j.dss.2010.12.006

Mathew, V., Sitaraman, R. K., & Shenoy, P. (2012). *Energy-aware load balancing in content delivery networks. 2012 Proceedings IEEE INFOCOM*. IEEE.

Mathew, V., Sitaraman, R. K., & Shenoy, P. (2015, June). Energy-efficient content delivery networks using cluster shutdown. *Sustainable Computing : Informatics and Systems*, 6, 58–68. 10.1016/j.suscom.2014.05.004

Mathis, F., Vaniea, K., & Khamis, M. (2022). Prototyping Usable Privacy and Security Systems: Insights from Experts. *International Journal of Human-Computer Interaction*, 38(5), 468–490. 10.1080/10447318.2021.1949134

Maurer, M., Breskovic, I., Emeakaroha, V. C., & Brandic, I. (2011). *Revealing the MAPE Loop for the Autonomic Management of Cloud Infrastructures*. IEEE. 10.1109/ISCC.2011.5984008

Mavoungou, S., Kaddoum, G., Taha, M., & Matar, G. (2016). Surveyon threats and attacks on mobile networks. *IEEE Access : Practical Innovations, Open Solutions*, 4, 4543–4572. 10.1109/ACCESS.2016.2601009

McDaniel, D., & McLaughlin, S. E. (2009). Security and privacy challenges in the smart grid. *IEEE Security and Privacy*, 7(3), 75–77. 10.1109/MSP.2009.76

McElwee, S. (2017). Active learning intrusion detection using k-means clustering selection. SoutheastCon 2017. IEEE.

Mekni, M., & Mekni, M. (2021). An Artificial Intelligence Based Virtual Assistant Using Conversational Agents. *Journal of Software Engineering and Applications*, 14(9), 455–473. 10.4236/jsea.2021.149027

Mell, P., & Grance, T. (2011). *The NIST definition of cloud computing*. NIST. https://nvlpubs .nist.gov/nistpubs/Legacy/SP/nistspecialpublication800-145.pdf

Mell, P., & Grance, T. (2011). *The NIST Definition of Cloud Computing. National Institute of Standards and Technology*. NIST.

Melton, A. W. (1963). Implications of short-term memory for a general theory of memory. *Journal of Verbal Learning and Verbal Behavior*, 2(1), 1–21. 10.1016/S0022-5371(63)80063-8

Merino, L.-H., & Cabrero-Holgueras, J. (2023). Secure Multi-Party Computation. *Trends in Data Protection and Encryption Technologies*, (pp. 89–92). IEEE.

Mikhaylov, D., Zhukov, I., Starikovskiy, A., Kharkov, S., Tolstaya, A., & Zuykov, A. (2013). Review of malicious mobile applications, phone bugs and other cyber threats to mobile devices. *Proceedings of the 5th IEEE International Conference on Broadband Network & Multimedia Technology*, (pp. 302–305). IEEE. 10.1109/ICBNMT.2013.6823962

Miklosik, A., & Evans, N. (2020). Impact of big data and machine learning on digital transformation in marketing: A literature review. *IEEE Access : Practical Innovations, Open Solutions*, 8, 101284–101292. 10.1109/ACCESS.2020.2998754

Miroslav, N. (2011). Image preprocessing for optical character recognition using neural networks. *Journal of Patter Recognition Research.*

Mohammed A. (2020). *Cloud computing security: From Single to Multi-clouds*. La Trobe University.

Moreno, L., Petrie, H., Martínez, P., & Alarcon, R. (2023). Designing user interfaces for content simplification aimed at people with cognitive impairments. *Universal Access in the Information Society*, 1, 1–19. 10.1007/S10209-023-00986-Z/FIGURES/1037361672

Mort, G. S., & Drennan, J. (2005). Marketing m-services: Establishing a usage benefit typology related to mobile user characteristics. *Journal of Database Marketing & Customer Strategy Management*, 12(4), 327–341. 10.1057/palgrave.dbm.3240269

Muda, J., Tumsa, S., Tuni, A., & Sharma, D. P. (2020). Cloud-enabled E-governance framework for citizen centric services. *Journal of Computer and Communications*, 8(7), 63–78. 10.4236/jcc.2020.87006

Mylonas, A., Kastania, A., & Gritzalis, D. (2013). Delegate the smartphone user? Security awareness in smartphone platforms. *Computers & Security*, 34, 47–66. 10.1016/j.cose.2012.11.004

Naidu, S. (2021). Building resilience in education systems post-COVID-19. In *Distance Education* (*Vol. 42*, Issue 1, pp. 1–4). Informa UK Limited. 10.1080/01587919.2021.1885092

Nakao, K., Inoue, D., Eto, M., & Yoshioka, K. (2009). Practical correlation analysis between scan and malware profiles against zero-day attacks based on darknet monitoring. *IEICE Transactions on Information and Systems*, E92-D(5), 787–798. 10.1587/transinf.E92.D.787

Nandgaonkar, S. V., & Raut, A. B. (2014). A comprehensive study on cloud computing. *International Journal of Computer Science and Mobile Computing*, 3(4), 733–738.

Nandi, M., & Chaki, R. (2020). Privacy-Preserving Techniques for Data Analytics in Cloud Computing: A Review. *International Journal of Cloud Applications and Computing*, 10(3), 23–41.

Naredla, N. R., & Adedoyin, F. F. (2022). Detection of hyperpartisan news articles using natural language processing technique. *International Journal of Information Management Data Insights*, 2(1), 100064. 10.1016/j.jjimei.2022.100064

Naseer, I. (2023). AWS Cloud Computing Solutions: Optimizing Implementation for Businesses. Statistics. *Computing and Interdisciplinary Research*, 5(2), 121–132. 10.52700/scir.v5i2.138

Naveneethan, S. (2022). Identifying and Eliminating the Misbehavior Nodes in the Wireless Sensor Network. In *Soft Computing and Signal Processing*. Springer International Publishing. 10.1007/978-981-16-7088-6_36

Nayak, S., Nagesh, B., Routray, A., & Sarma, M. (2021). A Human–Computer Interaction framework for emotion recognition through time-series thermal video sequences. *Computers & Electrical Engineering*, 93, 107280. 10.1016/j.compeleceng.2021.107280

Nazar, M., Alam, M. M., Yafi, E., & Su'ud, M. M. (2021). A Systematic Review of Human–Computer Interaction and Explainable Artificial Intelligence in Healthcare With Artificial Intelligence Techniques. *IEEE Access : Practical Innovations, Open Solutions*, 9, 153316–153348. 10.1109/ACCESS.2021.3127881

Netto, M. A. S., Cardonha, C., Cunha, R. L. F., & Assuncao, M. D. (2015). Evaluating auto-scaling strategies for cloud computing environments. *Proc. - IEEE Comput. Soc. Annu. Int. Symp. Model. Anal. Simul. Comput. Telecommun. Syst. MASCOTS*, (pp. 187–196). IEEE.

Ni, B., Zhang, K., Lin, X., & Shen, X. S. (2019). Balancing Security and Efficiency for Smart Metering against Misbehaving Collectors. *IEEE Transactions on Smart Grid*, 10(2), 1225–1236. 10.1109/TSG.2017.2761804

Nicanfar, H., Jokar, P., & Leung, V. C. (2011). Smart grid authentication and key management for unicast and multicast communications. 2011 IEEE PES Innovative Smart Grid Technologies. IEEE.

Nicanfar, H., Jokar, P., Beznosov, K., & Leung, V. C. (2013). Efficient authentication and key management mechanisms for smart grid communications. *IEEE Systems Journal*, 8(2), 629–640. 10.1109/JSYST.2013.2260942

Nicho, M., Fakhry, H., & Haiber, C. (2011). An integrated security governance framework for effective PCI DSS implementation. [IJISP]. *International Journal of Information Security and Privacy*, 5(3), 50–67. 10.4018/jisp.2011070104

Nikmehr, N., & Ravadanegh, S. (2015). Optimal power dispatch of multimicrogrids at future smart distribution grids. *IEEE Transactions on Smart Grid*, 6(4), 1648–1657. 10.1109/TSG.2015.2396992

Nikravesh, A. Y., Ajila, S. A., & Lung, C. H. (2015). Towards an Autonomic Auto-scaling Prediction System for Cloud Resource Provisioning, *Proc. - 10th Int. Symp. Softw. Eng. Adapt. Self-Managing Syst. SEAMS 2015*, (pp. 35–45). IEEE. 10.1109/SEAMS.2015.22

Nilabja Roy, A. (2011). Efficient Autoscaling in the Cloud using Predictive Models for Workload Forecasting. *IEEE 4th Int.Conf. Cloud Comput.* IEEE.

Nithila, E. E., Rosi, A., & others. (2024). A Survey about Post Quantum Cryptography Methods. *EAI Endorsed Transactions on Internet of Things, 10.*

Nygren, E., Sitaraman, R. K., & Sun, J. (2010, August). The Akamai network. *Operating Systems Review*, 44(3), 2–19. 10.1145/1842733.1842736

OCDE. (2020). *Education at a Glance 2020: OECD Indicators*. OCDE. 10.1787/69096873-

Ochoa, S. F., Herskovic, V., Pineda, E., & Pino, J. A. (2009). A transformational model for Organizational Memory Systems management with privacy concerns. *Information Sciences*, 179(15), 2643–2655. 10.1016/j.ins.2009.01.041

Okai, S., Uddin, M., Arshad, A., Alsaqour, R., & Shah, A. (2014). Cloud computing adoption model for universities to increase ICT proficiency. *SAGE Open*, 4(3), 1–10. 10.1177/2158244014546461

Okay, F. Y., & Ozdemir, S. (2016). A fog computing based smart grid model. *Proc. ISNCC*, (pp. 1–6). IEEE. 10.1109/ISNCC.2016.7746062

Oliveira, P. F., Lima, L., Vinhoza, T. T. V., Barros, J., & Médard, M. (2010). Trusted storage over untrusted networks. *IEEE Globecom Workshops.*

Olivera, F. (2000). Memory systems in organizations: An empirical investigation of mechanisms for knowledge collection, storage and access. *Journal of Management Studies*, 37(6), 811–832. 10.1111/1467-6486.00205

Onyema, E. M., Khan, R., Eucheria, N. C., & Kumar, T. (2023). Impact of Mobile Technology and Use of Big Data in Physics Education During Coronavirus Lockdown. *Big Data Mining and Analytic*, 6(3), 381–389. 10.26599/BDMA.2022.9020013

Ortiz, G., Garc'ıa-de-Prado, A., Berrocal, J., & Hernandez, J. (2019). Improving resource consumption in context- aware mobile applications through alternative architectural styles. *IEEE Access: Practical Innovations, Open Solutions*, 7, 65228–65250. 10.1109/ACCESS.2019.2918239

Özhan, E. (2017). Kurumsal hafızanın korunmasında sistemin önemi. *Arşiv dünyası*, (18-19), 1-10.

Padhy, R. P., Patra, M. R., & Satapathy, S. C. (2011). Cloud computing: Security issues and research challenges. [IJCSITS]. *International Journal of Computer Science and Information Technology & Security*, 1(2), 136–146.

Compilation of References

Pagani, A. (2022). QUIC Bitcoin: Fast and Secure Peer-to-Peer Payments and Payment Channels. *2022 IEEE Future Networks World Forum (FNWF)*, (pp. 578–584). IEEE.

Pallis, G., & Vakali, A. (2006, January). Insight and perspectives for content delivery networks. *Communications of the ACM, 49*(1), 101–106. 10.1145/1107458.1107462

Pamies-Juarez, L., García-López, P., Sánchez-Artigas, M., & Herrera, B. (2011). Pedro Garc__a-L_opez, Marc S_anchez-Artigas and Blas Herrera, "Towards the Design of Optimal Data Redundancy Schemes for Heterogeneous Cloud Storage Infrastructures". *Computer Networks, 55*(5), 1100–1113. 10.1016/j.comnet.2010.11.004

Papageorgiou, A., Strigkos, M., Politou, E., Alepis, E., Solanas, A., & Patsakis, C. (2018). Security and privacy analysis of mobile health applications: The alarming state of practice. *IEEE Access : Practical Innovations, Open Solutions, 6*, 9390–9403. 10.1109/ACCESS.2018.2799522

Patel, M., & Thakkar, S. P. (2015). Handwritten character recognition in english: A survey. *International Journal of Advanced Research in Computer and Communication Engineering, 4*(2), 345–350. 10.17148/IJARCCE.2015.4278

Pathan, A. K., & Buyya, R. (2006). A Taxonomy and Survey of Content Delivery Networks. *Grid Comput. Distrib. Syst. GRIDS Lab. Univ. Melb. Park. Aust., 148*, 1–44.

Penno, R., Chen, R., Labs, B., & Technologies, L. (2004). An Architecture for Open Pluggable Edge Services (OPES). *Status; Riksorgan för Sveriges Lungsjuka*, 1–17.

Perez, R. L., Adamsky, F., Soua, R., & Engel, T. (2018). Machine learning for reliable network attack detection in scada systems. *2018 17th IEEE International Conference On Trust, Security And Privacy In Computing And Communications/12th IEEE International Conference On Big Data Science And Engineering (TrustCom/BigDataSE)*. IEEE. 10.1109/TrustCom/BigDataSE.2018.00094

Pettcy, C., & Tudor, B. (2010). *Gartner says the worldwide cloud services market to surpass $68 billion in 2010.* Gartner Inc.

Petty, J. W., Titman, S., Keown, A. J., Martin, P., Martin, J. D., & Burrow, M. (2015). *Financial Management: Principles and Applications.* Pearson Higher Education.

Pimentel, H. M., Kopp, S., Simplicio, M. A.Jr, Silveira, R. M., & Bressan, G. (2015). OCP: A protocol for secure communication in federated content networks. *Computer Communications, 68*, 47–60. 10.1016/j.comcom.2015.07.026

Pise, A., Yoon, B., & Singh, S. (2023). Enabling Ambient Intelligence of Things (AIoT) healthcare system architectures. [Elsevier Ltd.]. *Computer Communications, 198*, 186–194. 10.1016/j.comcom.2022.10.029

Pokhrel, S., & Chhetri, R. (2021). A literature review on the impact of the COVID-19 pandemic on teaching and learning. *Higher education for the future, 8*(1), 133-141.

Post-COVID-19 success in higher education marketing. (2023, October 2). Higher Level Education. https://higherleveleducation.com/post-covid-higher-education/

Prince, M., Knapp, M., Guerchet, M., McCrone, P., & Prina, M. (2014). *Dementia UK: - Overview*.

Provost, F., & Fawcett, T. (2013). Data science and its relationship to big data and data-driven decision making. *Big Data*, 1(1), 51–59. 10.1089/big.2013.150827447038

Purcell, W. M., & Lumbreras, J. (2021). Higher education and the COVID-19 pandemic: Navigating disruption using the sustainable development goals. *Discover Sustainability*, 2(1), 6. 10.1007/s43621-021-00013-235425919

Quadar, N., Chehri, A., Jeon, G., Hassan, M., & Fortino, G. (2022). Cybersecurity Issues of IoT in Ambient Intelligence (AmI) Environment. *IEEE Internet of Things Magazine*. IEEE.

Qu, C., Calheiros, R. N., & Buyya, R. (2016). *Auto-scaling Web Applications in Clouds: A Taxonomy and Survey* (Vol. V).

Rachinger, M., Rauter, R., Müller, C., Vorraber, W., & Schirgi, E. (2019). Digitalization and its influence on business model innovation. *Journal of Manufacturing Technology Management*, 30(8), 1143–1160. 10.1108/JMTM-01-2018-0020

Raghavendran, P., Gunasekar, T., Balasundaram, H., Santra, S. S., Majumder, D., & Baleanu, D. (2023). Solving fractional integro-differential equations by Aboodh transform. *Journal of Mathematics and Computer Science*, 32, 229–240. 10.22436/jmcs.032.03.04

Raghunathan, S., Darshan Singh, A., & Sharma, B. (2022, January). Study of resilience in Learning environments during the COVID-19 pandemic. In *Frontiers in Education* (*Vol. 6*). Frontiers Media SA. 10.3389/feduc.2021.677625

Rajasekaran, R., Govinda, K., Masih, J., & Sruthi, M. (2020). Health Monitoring System for Individuals Using Internet of Things. In *Incorporating the Internet of Things in Healthcare Applications and Wearable Devices* (pp. 150–164). IGI Global. 10.4018/978-1-7998-1090-2.ch009

Ramachandran, N., Sivaprakasam, P., Thangamani, G., & Anand, G. (2014). Selecting a suitable cloud computing technology deployment model for an academic institute: A case study. *Campus-Wide Information Systems*, 31(5), 319–345. 10.1108/CWIS-09-2014-0018

Ramana, T. V., Thirunavukkarasan, M., Mohammed, A. S., Devarajan, G. G., & Nagarajan, S. M. (2022). Ambient intelligence approach: Internet of Things based decision performance analysis for intrusion detection. *Computer Communications*, 195, 315–322. 10.1016/j.comcom.2022.09.007

Ramkumar, M. O., Sarah Catharin, S., & Nivetha, D. (2019). Survey of Cognitive Assisted Living Ambient System Using Ambient Intelligence as a Companion. *IEEE Proceeding of International Conference on Systems Computation Automation and Networking*. IEEE. 10.1109/ICSCAN.2019.8878707

Ramzan, B., Bajwa, I. S., Jamil, N., Amin, R. U., Ramzan, S., Mirza, F., & Sarwar, N. (2019). An Intelligent Data Analysis for Recommendation Systems Using Machine Learning. *Scientific Programming*, 2019, 1–20. 10.1155/2019/5941096

Compilation of References

Rasli, A., Tee, M., Lai, Y. L., Tiu, Z. C., & Soon, E. H. (2022). Post-COVID-19 strategies for higher education institutions in dealing with unknowns and uncertainties. In *Frontiers in Education* (*Vol. 7*). Frontiers Media SA. 10.3389/feduc.2022.992063

Rathee, G., Kerrache, C. A., & Calafate, C. T. (2022). Ambient Intelligence for Secure and Trusted Pub/Sub Messaging in IoT Environments. [Elsevier Ltd.]. *Computer Networks*, 218, 109401. 10.1016/j.comnet.2022.109401

Rathnasiri, M. S. H., Dewasiri, N. J., & Kumar, A. A. (2024). Policy Framework and Implementation Strategies for Sri Lanka's Transition to a Net-Zero Economy. In *Net Zero Economy, Corporate Social Responsibility and Sustainable Value Creation: Exploring Strategies, Drivers, and Challenges* (pp. 43–60). Springer Nature Switzerland. 10.1007/978-3-031-55779-8_3

Rautaray, S. S., & Agrawal, A. (2018). Vision based hand gesture recognition for human computer interaction: A survey. Artificial Intelligence. *RE:view*, 43.

Rayappan, D., & Pandiyan, M. (2021). Lightweight Feistel structure based hybrid-crypto model for multimedia data security over uncertain cloud environment. *Wireless Networks*, 27(2), 981–999. 10.1007/s11276-020-02486-x

Reese, G. (2008). *On Why I Don't Like Auto-Scaling in the Cloud.* O'Reilly Broadcast. http://broadcast.oreilly.com/2008/12/why-i-dont-like-cloud-auto-scaling.html

Rehan, H. (2024). Revolutionizing America's Cloud Computing: The Pivotal Role of AI in Driving Innovation and Security. *Journal of Artificial Intelligence General Science, 2*(1), 239–240.

Rehmani, M. H., Davy, A., Jennings, B., & Assi, C. (2019). Software defined networks based smart grid communication: A comprehensive survey. *IEEE Communications Surveys and Tutorials*, 21(3), 2637–2670. 10.1109/COMST.2019.2908266

Reis, J., Amorim, M., Melão, N., Cohen, Y., & Rodrigues, M. (2020). Digitalization: A Literature Review and Research Agenda. In: Anisic, Z., Lalic, B., Gracanin, D. (eds) *Proceedings on 25th International Joint Conference on Industrial Engineering and Operations Management – IJCIEOM. IJCIEOM 2019.* Lecture Notes on Multidisciplinary Industrial Engineering. Springer, Cham. 10.1007/978-3-030-43616-2_47

Resmi, A. M., & Chezian, R. M. (2016). An extension of intrusion prevention, detection and response system for secure content delivery networks. *2016 IEEE Int. Conf. Adv. Comput. Appl.*, (pp. 144–149). IEEE. 10.1109/ICACA.2016.7887940

Reyzin, L., & Reyzin, N. (2002). Better than biba: Short one-time signatures with fast signing and verifying. *Australasian Conference on Information Security and Privacy*. Springer. 10.1007/3-540-45450-0_11

Ricci, F. (2022). Recommender Systems: Techniques, Applications, and Challenges, *Recommender Systems Handbook*. CSE. doi:.10.1007/978-1-0716-2197-4_1/COVER

Rogers, Y. (2012). *HCI Theory.* Springer. .10.1007/978-3-031-02197-8

Roman, L. F., Gondim, P. R., & Lloret, J. (2019). Pairing-based authentication protocol for v2g networks in smart grid. *Ad Hoc Networks*, 90, 101745. 10.1016/j.adhoc.2018.08.015

Rosan, K. H. (2012). *Discrete Mathematics and Its Applications*. McGraw Hill.

Rosenthal, A., Mork, P., Li, M. H., Stanford, J., Koester, D., & Reynolds, P. (2010). Cloud computing: A new business paradigm for biomedical information sharing. *Journal of Biomedical Informatics*, 43(2), 342–353. 10.1016/j.jbi.2009.08.01419715773

Sabie, D., Ekmekcioglu, C., & Ahmed, S. I. (2022). A Decade of International Migration Research in HCI: Overview, Challenges, Ethics, Impact, and Future Directions. *ACM Transactions on Computer-Human Interaction*, 29(4), 1–35. 10.1145/3490555

Sabit, H., Peter, H. J. C., & Kilby, J. (2019). Ambient Intelligence for Smart Home using The Internet of Things. *2019 29th International Telecommunication Networks and Applications Conference (ITNAC)*. IEEE. 10.1109/ITNAC46935.2019.9078001

Saffar, A. H., Mann, T. K., & Ofoghi, B. (2023). Textual emotion detection in health: Advances and applications. *Journal of Biomedical Informatics*, 137, 104258. 10.1016/j.jbi.2022.10425836528329

Sagar, S. (2016). *Auto Scaling Load Balancing Features in Cloud Richa Thakur*, 3(1), 21–25.

Saini, D., & Pandey, A. (2017). *Analysis of Scalability Factor in Cloud Computing*, 2(6), 675–678.

Salim, S. J., & Ashruji, M. G. (2016). Application of Elzaki Transform in Cryptography. *International Journal of Modern Sciences and Engineering Technology*, 3(3), 46–48.

Sangroya, D., Kabra, G., Joshi, Y., & Yadav, M. (2020). Green energy management in India for environmental benchmarking: From concept to practice. *Management of Environmental Quality*, 31(5), 1329–1349. 10.1108/MEQ-11-2019-0237

Sardar, S. K., Kumar, N., & Lee, S. C. (2022). A Systematic Literature Review on Machine Learning Algorithms for Human Status Detection. *IEEE Access : Practical Innovations, Open Solutions*, 10, 74366–74382. 10.1109/ACCESS.2022.3190967

Sari, R. A. T. N. A., & Kurniawan, Y. (2015). Cloud computing technology infrastructure to support the knowledge management process (a case study approach). *Journal of Theoretical and Applied Information Technology*, 73(3), 377–382.

Satti, S. R., Lankadasu, J. S. K., Sharma, A., Sharma, S., & Gochhait, S. (2024). Deep Learning in Medical Image Diagnosis for COVID-19. *2024 ASU International Conference in Emerging Technologies for Sustainability and Intelligent Systems (ICETSIS)*, (pp. 1858–1865). IEEE. 10.1109/ICETSIS61505.2024.10459430

Saxena, N., Choi, B. J., & Cho, S. (2015). Lightweight privacy-preserving authentication scheme for v2g networks in the smart grid. 2015 IEEE Trustcom/BigDataSE/ISPA (Vol. 1). IEEE.

Compilation of References

Saxena, N., Choi, B. J., & Lu, R. X. (2016). Authentication and Authorization Scheme for Various User-Roles and Devices in Smart Grid. *IEEE Transactions on Information Forensics and Security*, 11(5), 907–921. 10.1109/TIFS.2015.2512525

Schneider, S., & Sunyaev, A. (2016). Determinant factors of cloud-sourcing decisions: Reflecting on the IT outsourcing literature in the era of cloud computing. *Journal of Information Technology*, 31(1), 1–31. 10.1057/jit.2014.25

Schulz, K. A., Gstrein, O. J., & Zwitter, A. J. (2020). Exploring the governance and implementation of sustainable development initiatives through blockchain technology. *Futures*, 122, 102611. 10.1016/j.futures.2020.102611

Scott, J. E., & Vessey, I. (2000). Implementing enterprise resource planning systems: The role of learning from failure. *Information Systems Frontiers*, 2(2), 213–232. 10.1023/A:1026504325010

Sefidanoski, A. (2018). Deep learning and optimization of organizational memory. *SAR Journal-Science and Research*, 1(3), 115–118.

Selvon-Bruce, A. (2016). How Auto-Scaling Techniques Make Public Cloud Deployments. *Cogniz. 20-20 insights*. .

Senyo, P. K., Addae, E., & Boateng, R. (2018). Cloud computing research: A review of research themes, frameworks, methods and future research directions. *International Journal of Information Management*, 38(1), 128–139. 10.1016/j.ijinfomgt.2017.07.007

Sestino, A., Prete, M. I., Piper, L., & Guido, G. (2020). Internet of Things and Big Data as enablers for business digitalization strategies. *Technovation*, 98, 102173. Advance online publication. 10.1016/j.technovation.2020.102173

Seyyed Hashemi, S. N., & Bohlooli, A. (2018, July). Analytical modeling of multi-source content delivery in information-centric networks. *Computer Networks*, 140, 152–162. 10.1016/j.comnet.2018.05.007

Shah, S. K., & Nautiyal, A. (2022). Signal Quality Assessment for Speech Recognition using Deep Convolutional Neural Networks. *MysuruCon 2022 - 2022 IEEE 2nd Mysore Sub Section International Conference*. IEEE. 10.1109/MysuruCon55714.2022.9972718

Sharma, A., Guleria, V., & Jaiswal, V. (2022). The Future of Blockchain Technology, Recent Advancement and Challenges. In *Blockchain and Deep Learning: Future Trends and Enabling Technologies* (pp. 329–349). Springer.

Sharma, S., & Mishra, N. (2023). Horizoning recent trends in the security of smart cities: Exploratory analysis using latent semantic analysis. *Journal of Intelligent & Fuzzy Systems, Preprint*, 1–18. 10.3233/JIFS-235210

Sharma, A., Gupta, A., Bhargava, A., Rawat, A., Yadav, P., & Gupta, D. (2023). From Sci-Fi to Reality: The Evolution of Human-Computer Interaction with Artificial Intelligence, *Proceedings of the 2nd International Conference on Applied Artificial Intelligence and Computing, ICAAIC 2023*, (pp. 127–134). IEEE. 10.1109/ICAAIC56838.2023.10141431

Shaya, N., Abukhait, R., Madani, R., & Khattak, M. N. (2022). Organizational resilience of higher education institutions: An empirical study during COVID-19 pandemic. *Higher Education Policy*, 1–27.

Shen, H., Zhang, M., & Shen, J. (2017). Efficient privacy-preserving cube-data aggregation scheme for smart grids. *IEEE Transactions on Information Forensics and Security*, 12(6), 1369–1381. 10.1109/TIFS.2017.2656475

Shen, L., Zhu, L., Xu, C., Sharif, K., & Lu, R. (2020). Zhu, C. Xu, K. Sharif, and R. Lu, "A privacy-preserving data aggregation scheme for dynamic groups in fog computing,". *Information Sciences*, 514, 118–130. 10.1016/j.ins.2019.12.007

Shen, Z., Subbiah, S., Gu, X., & Wilkes, J. (2011). CloudScale: elastic resource scaling for multi-tenant cloud systems. *Proc. 2nd Symp. Cloud Comput.*, (pp. 1-14). 10.1145/2038916.2038921

Shishkova, T. (2021). IT threat evolution in Q3 2021. *Mobile statistics*. https://securelist.com/it-threatevolution-in-q3-2021-mobile-statistics/105020/

Shroff, S. J., Paliwal, U. L., & Dewasiri, N. J. (2024). Unravelling the impact of financial literacy on investment decisions in an emerging market. *Business Strategy & Development*, 7(1), e337. 10.1002/bsd2.337

Siano, P. (2014). Demand response and smart grids–a survey. *Renewable & Sustainable Energy Reviews*, 30, 461–478. 10.1016/j.rser.2013.10.022

Siddiq, M. (2023). Exploring the Role of Machine Learning in Contact Tracing for Public Health: Benefits, Challenges, and Ethical Considerations [AJEMB]. *American Journal of Economic and Management Business*, 2(3), 99–110. 10.58631/ajemb.v2i4.29

Silva, C. M., Silva, F. A., Sarubbi, J. F. M., Oliveira, T. R., Meira, W.Jr, & Nogueira, J. M. S. (2017, April). Designing mobile content delivery networks for the internet of vehicles. *Vehicular Communications*, 8, 45–55. 10.1016/j.vehcom.2016.11.003

Singh, A., & Chatterjee, K. (2017). Cloud security issues and challenges: A survey. *Journal of Network and Computer Applications*, 79, 88–115. 10.1016/j.jnca.2016.11.027

Singh, H. P., & Agarwal, A. (2014). Leveraging the Revolutionary Paradigm of Cloud Computing: The Case of Netflix. *MuMukshuJournal of HuManities Referred Journal*, 6(1), 177–185.

Singh, S., & Chana, I. (2016). A survey on resource scheduling in cloud computing: Issues and challenges. *Journal of Grid Computing*, 14(2), 217–264. 10.1007/s10723-015-9359-2

Singh, S., & Raj, P. (2023). Secure Multi-Party Computation for Privacy-Preserving Data Processing in Cloud Computing: A Survey. Journal of Cloud Computing: Advances. *Systems and Applications*, 12(1), 1–18.

Smits, M., Nacar, M., Ludden, G. D. S., & van Goor, H. (2021). *Stepwise Design and Evaluation of a Values-Oriented Ambient Intelligence Healthcare Monitoring Platform.Remote patient monitoring*. Elsevier Ltd.

Compilation of References

Sobhy, A. R., Khalil, A. T., Elfaham, M. M., & Hashad, A. (2018). Cloud Robotics: A Survey. *International Journal of Latest Research in Engineering and Technology*, 4(05), 46–52.

Solomon, D. D., & Sonia, M. (2024). Edge Computing empowered Cross-Platform Tool for Multifactorial Disorder Risk Assessment, *2024 11th International Conference on Computing for Sustainable Global Development (INDIACom)*, (pp. 1798–1803). IEEE. 10.23919/INDIACom61295.2024.10498639

Song, W., Tjondronegoro, D., & Docherty, M. (2010). Exploration and optimization of user experience in viewing videos on a mobile phone. *International Journal of Software Engineering and Knowledge Engineering*, 20(8), 1045–1075. 10.1142/S0218194010005067

Soundararajan, R., & Shenbagaraman, V. M. (2024). Enhancing financial decision-making through explainable AI and Blockchain integration: Improving transparency and trust in predictive models. *Educational Administration: Theory and Practice*, 30(4), 9341–9351.

Stallings, W. (2005). *Cryptography and network security* (4th ed.). Prentice Hall.

Stamos, K., Pallis, G., Vakali, A., & Dikaiakos, M. D. (2009). Evaluating the utility of content delivery networks. *Proceedings of the 4th edition of the UPGRADE-CN workshop on Use ofP2P, GRID and agents for the development of content networks - UPGRADE-CN '09*, (pp. 11). ACM. 10.1145/1552486.1552509

Stanoyevitch, A. (2002). *Introduction to cryptography with mathematical foundations and computer implementations*. CRC Press.

Stein, E. W. (1995). Organization memory: Review of concepts and recommendations for management. *International Journal of Information Management*, 15(1), 17–32. 10.1016/0268-4012(94)00003-C

Stephanidis, C., Salvendy, G., Antona, M., Chen, J. Y. C., Dong, J., Duffy, V. G., Fang, X., Fidopiastis, C., Fragomeni, G., Fu, L. P., Guo, Y., Harris, D., Ioannou, A., Jeong, K. K., Konomi, S., Krömker, H., Kurosu, M., Lewis, J. R., Marcus, A., & Zhou, J. (2019). Seven HCI Grand Challenges. *International Journal of Human-Computer Interaction*, 35(14), 1229–1269. 10.1080/10447318.2019.1619259

Stockburger, L., Kokosioulis, G., Mukkamala, A., Mukkamala, R. R., & Avital, M. (2021). Blockchain-enabled decentralized identity management: The case of self-sovereign identity in public transportation. *Blockchain: Research and Applications*, 2(2), 100014.

Streibelt, F., Böttger, J., Chatzis, N., Smaragdakis, G., & Feldmann, A. (2013). Exploring EDNS-client-subnet adopters in your free time. *Proceedings of the 2013 conference on Internet measurement conference - IMC '13*, (pp. 305–312). ACM. 10.1145/2504730.2504767

Subashini, S., & Kavitha, V. (2011). A Metadata Based Storage Model for Securing Data in Cloud Environment. *2011 International Conference on Cyber-Enabled Distributed Computing and Knowledge Discovery CyberC 2011.*

Subramaniam, M., Kathirvel, A., Sabitha, E., & Anwar Basha, H. (2021). Modified Firefly Algorithm and Fuzzy C-Mean Clustering Based Semantic Information Retrieval. *Journal of Web Engineering, 20*.10.13052/jwe1540-9589.2012

Sudha, D., & Kathirvel, A. (2022a). The effect of ETUS in various generic attacks in mobile ad hoc networks to improve the performance of Aodv protocol. *International Journal of humanities, law, and social sciences, Kanpur philosophers, 9*(1), 467-476.

Sudha, D., & Kathirvel, A. (2022b). An Intrusion Detection System to Detect and Mitigating Attacks Using Hidden Markov Model (HMM) Energy Monitoring Technique. *Stochastic Modeling an Applications, 26*(3), 467-476.

Sudha, D., & Kathirvel, A. (2023). The performance enhancement of Aodv protocol using GETUS. *International Journal of Early Childhood Special Education (INT-JECSE), 15*(2). 10.48047/INTJECSE/V15I2.11

Sultan, N. (2014). Making use of cloud computing for healthcare provision: Opportunities and challenges. *International Journal of Information Management, 34*(2), 177–184. 10.1016/j.ijinfomgt.2013.12.011

Sunyaev, A. (2020). *Cloud Computing, (in Internet Computing)*. Springer.

Suta, P., Lan, X., Wu, B., Mongkolnam, P., & Chan, J. H. (2020). An overview of machine learning in chatbots. *International Journal of Mechanical Engineering and Robotics Research, 9*(4), 502–510. 10.18178/ijmerr.9.4.502-510

Swan, M. (2015). *Blockchain: Blueprint for a new economy*. O'Reilly Media, Inc.

Tang, , Chen, Z., Hefferman, G., Pei, S., Wei, T., He, H., & Yang, Q. (2017). Incorporating Intelligence in Fog Computing for Big Data Analysis in Smart Cities. *IEEE Transactions on Industrial Informatics, 13*(5), 2140–2150. 10.1109/TII.2017.2679740

Tang, S., Li, X., Huang, X., Xiang, Y., & Xu, L. (2015). Achieving simple, secure and efficient hierarchical access control in cloud computing. *IEEE Transactions on Computers, 65*(7), 2325–2331. 10.1109/TC.2015.2479609

Tapia, D. I., Fraile, J. A., Rodríguez, S., Alonso, R. S., & Corchado, J. M. (2018). Integrating hardware agents into an enhanced multi-agent architecture for Ambient Intelligence systems. *Information Sciences, 222*, 47–65. 10.1016/j.ins.2011.05.002

Tapscott, D., & Tapscott, A. (2016). *Blockchain revolution: how the technology behind bitcoin is changing money, business, and the world*. Penguin.

Teixeira, M. S., Maran, V., Oliveira, J. P. M., Winter, M., & Machado, A. (2019). *Situation-aware model for multi-objective decision making in ambient intelligence. Applied Soft Computing*. Elsevier Ltd. 10.1016/j.asoc.2019.105532

Thakar, T., Saroj, R., & Bharde, V. (2021). Hand Gesture Controlled Gaming Application, *International Research Journal of Engineering and Technology*. www.irjet.net

Thanasis, G. (2012). *Storage and Analysis.* The International Conference for High Performance Computing Networking.

Thotadi, C., Debbala, M., Rao, S., Eeralla, A., Palaniswamy, B., Mookherji, S., Odelu, V., & Reddy, A. G. (2024). E-Brightpass: A Secure way to access social networks on smartphones. *Cyber Security and Applications*, 2, 100021. 10.1016/j.csa.2023.100021

Toala, R., Durães, D., & Novais, P. (2020). Human-computer interaction in intelligent tutoring systems. *Advances in Intelligent Systems and Computing*, 1003, 52–59. 10.1007/978-3-030-23887-2_7

Tozzi, C. (2021). What Is Serverless Computing? *ITPro Today*.

Tran, D., Tran, N., Nguyen, G., & Nguyen, B. M. (2017). A Proactive Cloud Scaling Model Based on Fuzzy Time Series and SLA Awareness. *Procedia Computer Science*, 108, 365–374. 10.1016/j.procs.2017.05.121

Tsai, J.-L., & Lo, N.-W. (2015). Secure anonymous key distribution scheme for smart grid. *IEEE Transactions on Smart Grid*, 7(2), 906–914. 10.1109/TSG.2015.2440658

Tseng, C., Tsai, M., Yang, Y., & Chou, L. (2018). A Rapid Auto-Scaling Mechanism in Cloud Computing Environment.

Tsolakis, N., Niedenzu, D., Simonetto, M., Dora, M., & Kumar, M. (2021). Supply network design to address United Nations Sustainable Development Goals: A case study of blockchain implementation in Thai fish industry. *Journal of Business Research*, 131, 495–519. 10.1016/j.jbusres.2020.08.003

Tumas, V., Rivera, S., Magoni, D., & State, R. (2023). Federated Byzantine Agreement Protocol Robustness to Targeted Network Attacks. *2023 IEEE Symposium on Computers and Communications (ISCC)*, (pp. 443–449). IEEE. 10.1109/ISCC58397.2023.10217935

Tutkunca, T. (2020). İşletmelerde Dijital Dönüşüm ve İlgili Bileşenlerinin Analiz Edilmesi Üzerine Kavramsal Bir Araştırma. Çağ Üniversitesi. *Sosyal Bilimler Dergisi*, 17(1), 65–75.

UCB. (2022). *Home.* UCB. https://www.ucb.com/

Vakali, A., & Pallis, G. (2003, November). Content delivery networks: Status and trends. *IEEE Internet Computing*, 7(6), 68–74. 10.1109/MIC.2003.1250586

Valcke, J. (2016). Best practices in mobile security. *Biometric Technology Today*, 2016(3), 9–11. 10.1016/S0969-4765(16)30051-0

Van Eyk, E., Iosup, A., Abad, C. L., Grohmann, J., & Eismann, S. (2018). A SPEC RG Cloud Group's Vision on the Performance Challenges of FaaS Cloud Architectures. *Companion of the 2018 ACM/SPEC International Conference on Performance Engineering*. ACM. 10.1145/3185768.3186308

Vaseei, M. (2024). A Conceptual Framework for Blockchain-Based, Intelligent, and Agile Supply Chain. In *Information Logistics for Organizational Empowerment and Effective Supply Chain Management* (pp. 150–162). IGI Global.

Vashishth, T. K., Sharma, V., Sharma, K. K., Kumar, B., Chaudhary, S., & Panwar, R. (2024). Intelligent Resource Allocation and Optimization for Industrial Robotics Using AI and Blockchain. In *AI and Blockchain Applications in Industrial Robotics* (pp. 82-110). IGI Global. DOI: 10.4018/979-8-3693-0659-8.ch004

Vashishth, T. K., Sharma, V., Sharma, K. K., Kumar, B., Chaudhary, S., & Panwar, R. (2024). Security and Privacy Challenges in Blockchain-Based Supply Chain Management: A Comprehensive Analysis. In *Achieving Secure and Transparent Supply Chains with Blockchain Technology* (pp. 70-91). IGI Global. 10.4018/979-8-3693-0482-2.ch005

Veljković, S. M., Raut, J., Melović, B., & Ćelić, Đ. (2020). Development of Digital Entrepreneurship and New Business Models as a Result of the Expansion of Information Systems. In: Anisic, Z., Lalic, B., Gracanin, D. (eds) *Proceedings on 25th International Joint Conference on Industrial Engineering and Operations Management.* Springer, Cham. 10.1007/978-3-030-43616-2_42

Venkatesan, K., & Rahayu, S. B. (2024). Blockchain security enhancement: An approach towards hybrid consensus algorithms and machine learning techniques. *Scientific Reports*, 14(1), 1149. 10.1038/s41598-024-51578-738212390

Verma, B. K. (1995). Handwritten Hindi Character Recognition Using Multilayer Perceptron and Radial Basis Function Neural Network. *IEEE International Conference on Neural Network.* IEEE. 10.1109/ICNN.1995.489003

Vihari, N. S., Yadav, M., & Panda, T. K. (2022). Impact of soft TQM practices on employee work role performance: Role of innovative work behaviour and initiative climate. *The TQM Journal*, 34(1), 160–177. 10.1108/TQM-03-2021-0092

Wang, L., Tao, J., Kunze, M., Castellanos, A. C., Kramer, D., & Karl, W. (2008). Scientific cloud computing: Early definition and experience. In *2008 10th IEEE international conference on high performance computing and communications* (pp. 825-830). IEEE.

Wang, P., Liu, S., Ye, F., & Chen, X. (2018). A fog-based architecture and programming model for iot applications in the smart grid. CoRR.

Wang, Y., Siau, K. L., & Wang, L. (2022). Metaverse and Human-Computer Interaction: A Technology Framework for 3D Virtual Worlds. *Lecture Notes in Computer Science (including subseries Lecture Notes in Artificial Intelligence and Lecture Notes in Bioinformatics)*, (pp. 213–221). 10.1007/978-3-031-21707-4_16

Wang, J., Wu, L., Choo, K.-K. R., & He, D. (2019). Blockchain based anonymous authentication with key management for smart grid edge computing infrastructure. *IEEE Transactions on Industrial Informatics.*

Wang, K., Wang, Y., Hu, X., Sun, Y., Deng, D., Vinel, A., & Zhang, Y. (2017). Wireless big data computing in smart grid. *IEEE Wireless Communications*, 24(2), 58–64. 10.1109/MWC.2017.1600256WC

Compilation of References

Wang, S., Zhang, X., Zhang, Y., Wang, L., Yang, J., & Wang, W. (2017). A survey on mobile edge networks: Convergence of computing, caching and communications. *IEEE Access: Practical Innovations, Open Solutions*, 5, 6757–6779. 10.1109/ACCESS.2017.2685434

Wang, Y., Shen, Y., Jiao, X., Zhang, T., Si, X., Salem, A., & Liu, J. (2017). Exploiting Content Delivery Networks for covert channel communications. *Computer Communications*, 99, 84–92. 10.1016/j.comcom.2016.07.011

Wang, Y., Zhang, L., & Yang, S. (2021). Homomorphic Encryption Techniques for Privacy-Preserving Data Processing in Cloud Computing: A Comprehensive Study. *Journal of Systems and Software*, 177, 110953.

Wang, Z. (2017). An identity-based data aggregation protocol for the smart grid. *IEEE Transactions on Industrial Informatics*, 13(5), 2428–2435. 10.1109/TII.2017.2705218

Wang, Z. (2019). Identity-based verifiable aggregator oblivious encryption and its applications in smart grids. *IEEE Transactions on Sustainable Computing*.

Wang, Z., Huang, J., & Rose, S. (2018). Evolution and challenges of DNS-Based CDNs. *Digital Communications and Networks*, 4(4), 235–243. 10.1016/j.dcan.2017.07.00534124418

Waycott, J. (2016). Ethical encounters in human-computer interaction, *Conference on Human Factors in Computing Systems – Proceedings*. ACM. 10.1145/2851581.2856498

Waycott, J. (2017). Ethical encounters in HCI: Implications for research in sensitive settings, *Conference on Human Factors in Computing Systems – Proceedings*. ACM. 10.1145/3027063.3027089

Wazid, M., Zeadally, S., & Das, A. K. (2019). Mobile banking: evolution and threats: malware threats and security solutions. *IEEE Consumer Electronics Magazine*, 8(2), 56–60. 10.1109/MCE.2018.2881291

Weichert, D., Link, P., Stoll, A., Rüping, S., Ihlenfeldt, S., & Wrobel, S. (2019). A review of machine learning for the optimization of production processes. *International Journal of Advanced Manufacturing Technology*, 104(5-8), 1889–1902. 10.1007/s00170-019-03988-5

Whig, P., Velu, A., & Ready, R. (2022). *Demystifying Federated Learning in Artificial Intelligence With Human-Computer Interaction*. IGI Global. 10.4018/978-1-6684-3733-9.ch006

William, J. (2014). *Networked Infomechanical Systems (NIMS) for Ambient Intelligence*. UCLA Center for Embedded Networked Sensing.

Williams, B., & Adamson, J. (2022). *PCI Compliance: Understand and implement adequate compliance with PCI data security standards*. CRC Press. 10.1201/9781003100300

Wind, S., Turowski, K., Repschläger, J., & Zarnekow, R. (2011). Target Dimensions of Cloud Computing. *Proceedings of IEEE Conference on Commerce and Enterprise Computing*. IEEE.

Wong, P. F., Chia, F. C., Kiu, M. S., & Lou, E. C. (2022). Potential integration of blockchain technology into smart sustainable city (SSC) developments: A systematic review. *Smart and Sustainable Built Environment*, 11(3), 559–574. 10.1108/SASBE-09-2020-0140

Xia, J., & Wang, Y. (2012). Secure key distribution for the smart grid. *IEEE Transactions on Smart Grid*, 3(3), 1437–1443. 10.1109/TSG.2012.2199141

Xiao, Z., Member, S., Chen, Q., & Luo, H. (2014). *Automatic Scaling of Internet Applications for Cloud Computing Services*, 63(5), 1111–1123.

Xia, P. (2021). Design of Personalized Intelligent Learning Assistant System Under Artificial Intelligence Background. *Advances in Intelligent Systems and Computing*, 1282, 194–200. 10.1007/978-3-030-62743-0_27

Xu, W., Dainoff, M. J., Ge, L., & Gao, Z. (2023). Transitioning to Human Interaction with AI Systems: New Challenges and Opportunities for HCI Professionals to Enable Human-Centered AI. *International Journal of Human-Computer Interaction*, 39(3), 494–518. 10.1080/10447318.2022.2041900

Xu, Y., Chen, Y., & Liu, Z. (2022). Privacy-Preserving Data Sharing Techniques in Cloud Computing: A Review of Recent Advances. *Future Internet*, 14(3), 58.

Yadav, A. (2021). *Virtual Assistant For Blind People*. doi: .10.51319/2456-0774.2021.5.0036

Yalamati, S. (2024). Data Privacy, Compliance, and Security in Cloud Computing for Finance. In Whig, W., Sharma, S., Sharma, S., Jain, A., & Yathiraju, N. *Practical Applications of Data Processing, Algorithms, and Modeling* (pp. 127–144). IGI Global.

Yang, C., Huang, Q., Li, Z., Liu, K., & Hu, F. (2017). Big Data and cloud computing: Innovation opportunities and challenges. *International Journal of Digital Earth*, 10(1), 13–53. 10.1080/17538947.2016.1239771

Yang, H., Cheng, L., & Chuah, M. C. (2019). Deep-learning-based network intrusion detection for scada systems. *2019 IEEE Conference on Communications and Network Security (CNS)*. IEEE. 10.1109/CNS.2019.8802785

Yang, J. (2018). Lightweight and privacy-preserving delegatable proofs of storage with data dynamics in cloud storage. *IEEE Transactions on Cloud Computing*. IEEE.

Yang, J., Liu, C., Shang, Y., Mao, Z., & Chen, J. (2013). Workload Predicting-Based Automatic Scaling in Service Clouds, *2013 IEEE Sixth Int. Conf. Cloud Comput.*, (pp. 810–815). IEEE. 10.1109/CLOUD.2013.146

Yan, Y., Qian, Y., Sharif, H., & Tipper, D. (2012). A survey on cyber security for smart grid communications. *IEEE Communications Surveys and Tutorials*, 14(4), 998–1010. 10.1109/SURV.2012.010912.00035

Youssef, A. E. (2012). Exploring cloud computing services and applications. *Journal of Emerging Trends in Computing and Information Sciences*, 3(6), 838–847.

Compilation of References

Yuniarto, D. (2023). Implementing cloud computing in companies to increase business efficiency. *Jurnal Info Sains: Informatika Dan Sains*, 13(02), 633–639.

Yu, R., Zhang, Y., Gjessing, S., Yuen, C., Xie, S., & Guizani, M. (2011). Cognitive Radio Based Hierarchical Communications Infrastructure for Smart Grid. *IEEE Network*, 25(5), 6–14. 10.1109/MNET.2011.6033030

Zantout, H., & Marir, F. (1999). Document management systems from current capabilities towards intelligent information retrieval: An overview. *International Journal of Information Management*, 19(6), 471–484. 10.1016/S0268-4012(99)00043-2

Zdanowska, S., & Taylor, A. S. (2022). A study of UX practitioners roles in designing real-world, enterprise ML systems. *Conference on Human Factors in Computing Systems – Proceedings*. ACM. 10.1145/3491102.3517607

Zhang, H., Zou, X., Xie, G., & Li, Z. (2022). Blockchain Multi-signature Wallet System Based on QR Code Communication. *CCF China Blockchain Conference*, (pp. 31–48). Research Gate. 10.1007/978-981-19-8877-6_3

Zhang, L., & Wang, Y. (2023). Reshaping the Resilience in Higher Education Based on Lower-Grade Undergraduate Students' Performance in Literature Course During Covid-19. In *Atlantis Highlights in Social Sciences, Education and Humanities* (pp. 597–608). Atlantis Press International BV. 10.2991/978-94-6463-192-0_78

Zhang, Z., Cao, W., Qin, Z., Zhu, L., Yu, Z., & Ren, K. (2017). When privacy meets economics: Enabling differentially-private batterysupported meter reporting in smart grid. In *IEEE/ACM 25th International Symposium on Quality of Service*. IEEE.

Zhang, A. (2022). Human Computer Interaction System for Teacher-Student Interaction Model Using Machine Learning. *International Journal of Human-Computer Interaction*, 1–12. 10.1080/10447318.2022.2115645

Zhang, H., Liu, X., & Wu, Q. (2023). Enhancing Data Privacy in Cloud Computing: A Systematic Literature Review on Privacy-Preserving Techniques. *Journal of Network and Computer Applications*, 214, 104043.

Zhang, J., Yin, Z., Chen, P., & Nichele, S. (2020). Emotion recognition using multi-modal data and machine learning techniques: A tutorial and review. *Information Fusion*, 59, 103–126. 10.1016/j.inffus.2020.01.011

Zhang, L., Zhao, L., Yin, S., Chi, C.-H., Liu, R., & Zhang, Y. (2019). A lightweight authentication scheme with privacy protection for smart grid communications. *Future Generation Computer Systems*, 100, 770–778. 10.1016/j.future.2019.05.069

Zhang, R. Yu., Xie, S., Yao, W., Xiao, Y., & Guizani, M. (2011). Home M2M networks: Architectures, standards, and QoS improvement. *IEEE Communications Magazine*, 49(4), 44–52. 10.1109/MCOM.2011.5741145

Zhang, Y., Yu, R., Nekovee, M., Liu, Y., Xie, S., & Gjessing, S. (2012). Cognitive machine-to-machine communications: Visions and potentials for the smart grid. *IEEE Network*, 26(3), 6–13. 10.1109/MNET.2012.6201210

Zhang, Z., Qin, Z., Zhu, L., Weng, J., & Ren, K. (2017). Cost-friendly differential privacy for smart meters: Exploiting the dual roles of the noise. *IEEE Transactions on Smart Grid*, 8(2), 619–626.

Zhao, H., Benomar, Z., Pfandzelter, T., & Georgantas, N. (2022). Supporting Multi-Cloud in Serverless Computing. *2022 IEEE/ACM 15th International Conference on Utility and Cloud Computing (UCC)*, (pp. 285–290). IEEE. 10.1109/UCC56403.2022.00051

Zheng, J., Huang, H., Li, C., Zheng, Z., & Guo, S. (2021). Revisiting double-spending attacks on the bitcoin blockchain: new findings. *2021 IEEE/ACM 29th International Symposium on Quality of Service (IWQOS)*. IEEE.

Zheng, Z., Xie, S., Dai, H.-N., Chen, X., & Wang, H. (2018). Blockchain challenges and opportunities: A survey. *International Journal of Web and Grid Services*, 14(4), 352–375. 10.1504/IJWGS.2018.095647

Zhu, L., Li, M., Zhang, Z., Xu, C., Zhang, R., Du, X., & Guizani, N. (2019). Privacy-preserving authentication and data aggregation for fog-based smart grid. *IEEE Communications Magazine*, 57(6), 80–85. 10.1109/MCOM.2019.1700859

Zubaidy, S. A., & Khan, W. (2022). Proposed resilience strategy for higher education institutions post-COVID-19. *International Journal of Learning and Change*, 14(5-6), 706–722. 10.1504/IJLC.2022.126448

Zubaydi, H. D., Varga, P., & Molnár, S. (2023). Leveraging Blockchain Technology for Ensuring Security and Privacy Aspects in Internet of Things: A Systematic Literature Review. *Sensors (Basel)*, 23(2), 788. 10.3390/s2302078836679582

About the Contributors

Saikat Gochhait teaches at Symbiosis Institute of Digital & Telecom Management, Symbiosis International Deemed University Pune, India. He is Ph.D and Post-Doctoral Fellow from the UEx, Spain. He was Awarded DITA and MOFA Fellowship in 2017 and 2018. His research publication with foreign authors indexed in Scopus, ABDC, and Web of Science. He is an IEEE member.

Redouan Ainous is an Assistant Professor at the University of Algiers3, Algeria. He obtained a doctorate degree in marketing. He has a group of academic research published on the local and international. He participated in a number of international Conference. He worked as an associate professor at the University of Tlemcen, University of Bel-abbes and the High School of Management. Ainous, R., Benhabib, A., Maliki, S. B. E., & Ayad, S. (2016). Research Paper Impact Of The Restaurant Atmosphere On Consumer Decision: Evidence From A Case Study Of Algerian Consumers. International Journal of Scientific Management and Development, 4(5), 159-166. Ayad, S., Ainous, R., & Maliki, S. B. E. (2016). The Role of Color in the Attainment of Customers' Intensive Buying Intention: An Exploratory Descriptive Case Study (SOR Model Application). International Journal of Innovation and Applied Studies, 16(1), 173. Redouan, A., Rahima, H., & Naima, O. (2017). Factors Affecting the Decision of Grant Bank Loans to Economic Institutions Ã¢ Â Â The Case of SMES Tlemcen. The Journal of Internet Banking and Commerce, 22(1), 1-18.

Rajiv Avacharmal is a leading expert in the field of AI/ML risk management, with a particular focus on generative AI. With a distinguished career spanning over 13 years, Rajiv has held leadership roles at several multinational banks and currently serves as the Corporate Vice President of AI and Model Risk at leading life Insurance Company. Rajiv's research interests lie at the intersection of AI/ML, risk management, and explainable AI.

Kathirvel Ayyaswamy, acquired, B.E.(CSE), M.E. (CSE) from Crescent Engineering College affiliated to University of Madras and Ph. D (CSE.) from Anna University. He is currently working as Professor, Dept of Computer Science and Engineering, Karunya Institute of Technology and Sciences, Coimbatore. He is a studious researcher by himself, completed 18 sponsored research projects worth of Rs 103 lakhs and published more than 110 articles in journals and conferences. 4 research scholars have completed Ph. D and 3 under progress under his guidance. He is working as scientific and editorial board member of many journals. He has reviewed dozens of papers in many journals. He has author of 13 books. His research interests are protocol development for wireless ad hoc networks, security in ad hoc network, data communication and networks, mobile computing, wireless networks, WSN and DTN. He is a Life member of the ISTE (India), IACSIT (Singapore), Life Member IAENG (Hong Kong), Member ICST (Europe), IAES, etc. He has given a number of guest lecturers/expert talks and seminars, workshops and symposiums.

Komal Bhardwaj is currently working at Maharishi Markandeshwar Institute of Management, Maharishi Markandeshwar Univeristy as Assistant Professor of Finance. She has a rich experience of more than 8 years of teaching in the field of Management. She has a research experience in the areas of Assets Pricing, Derivatives, Option Pricing and study on stock volatility. Her research interest includes consumer behavior, investments, corporate governance, and assets liability management. She also worked as a Thesis Supervisor for a program called upgrad-LJMU MBA at upgrade education private limited.

Narayanage Jayantha Dewasiri, Ph.D., is a Chartered Manager at the Chartered Management Institute, UK. He conducts research at the Open University of Sri Lanka and the Sri Lanka Institute of Marketing. He is the founding Editor-in-Chief of the South Asian Journal of Marketing. His research interests are in corporate social responsibility, corporate governance, marketing and sales, management, and finance. He is working as the Head of Field Force at the HMD Global Inc., Sri Lanka. He also serves as a senior lecturer at University of Sabaragamuwa, Sri Lanka.

Michael Onyema Edeh is currently the Deputy Dean, Faculty of Allied Health and Applied Sciences and also the Head of Department of Mathematics and Computer Science, Coal City University, Nigeria. He is also an Adjunct Professor at Shobhit University, India. He was listed among the Top Scientists in Nigeria by Elsevier (SciVal) 2021-2024. Michael is a Recipient of the prestigious Chancellor's Award for Best Staff of the Year 2020, and Vice Chancellor's Award for research Excellence 2023 both at Coal City University. He is also the current Chairman of Nigeria Computer Society (NCS), Enugu State Chapter, Nigeria. Michael has taught Computer Science courses to both postgraduate and undergraduate students in several tertiary education institutions, including Southwestern University; Coal City University; Spiritan University Nneochi; National Open University of Nigeria (NOUN); Alex Ekwueme Federal University Ebonyi State; Gregory University Uturu; Enugu State College of Education Technical affiliated to Nnamdi Azikiwe University Nigeria; Institute of Management and Technology (IMT) Enugu; African Thinkers Community of Inquiry College of Education (ATCOI-COE) Enugu; Pogil College of Health Technology Ogun State; and Federal Science and Technical College Ogun State. He is also an Adjunct Faculty, Saveetha School of Engineering, Saveetha Institute of Medical and Technical Sciences, Chennai, India. Dr. Michael has published over 100 scholarly papers in reputable journals, and also acted as an editor and Reviewer for many top journals. He has interest in Cybersecurity, Education, Machine Learning and cloud computing.

Ozlem Erdas Cicek is currently an Assistant Professor at Department of Computer Engneering, Necmettin Erbakan University in Turkey. She obtained her PhD in Computer Science from Middle East Technical University in Turkey. Her areas of interest include Data Science, Machine Learning and Deep Learning. She had interdisciplinary studies with Pharmaceutical Sciences, Energy Engineering, Architecture and Management.

Sangeetha Ganesan received her B.E degree in Computer Science and Engineering from Periyar University Salem, M.E degree in Computer Science and Engineering from Anna University, Chennai, and Ph.D., in Faculty of Information and Communication Engineering, Anna University, Chennai. She is currently working as an Associate Professor in R.M.K. Colllege of Engineering and Technology, Puduvoyal. Her research interests are Distributed Computing, Cloud Computing, Security, Data Science and Machine Learning.

Pawan Kr. Goel is a accomplished academician and researcher with 18 years of experience, is an Associate Professor at Raj Kumar Goel Institute of Technology, Ghaziabad. He holds a Ph.D. in Computer Science Engineering and is UGC NET qualified. His expertise spans various domains, including wireless sensor networks, cloud computing, and artificial intelligence. Dr. Goel has published extensively in prestigious journals and conferences, with notable papers on topics such as cybersecurity, IoT, and machine learning. He is an active member of numerous professional bodies, including the Computer Society of India and the International Association of Engineers. Recognized for his contributions, he has received several awards and certificates of appreciation. Dr. Goel is dedicated to fostering industry-academia collaborations and has organized numerous workshops and seminars. He is also involved in various training programs, MOOCs, and NPTEL certifications, contributing significantly to the advancement of education and research in his field.

About the Contributors

Tharmalingam Gunasekar, a distinguished expert in Artificial Intelligence and Data Science, serves as the Corresponding Author at the Indian Institute of Technology (IIT), India. With a research affiliation at Vel Tech Rangarajan Dr. Sagunthala R&D Institute of Science and Technology, his work contributes significantly to the advancement of AI. My passion for cutting-edge technologies is exemplified in his commitment to innovation and academic excellence.

Gaurav Gupta is an Associate Professor at the Yogananda School of Artificial Intelligence, Computers, and Data Science, Shoolini University, Solan, India. He specializes in machine learning with applications in healthcare and agriculture. Dr. Gupta holds a BE degree from Dr. B. R. Ambedkar University and a PG and Ph.D. in Computer Science Engineering from KSOU-VIT and Shoolini University, respectively. With 16+ years of teaching experience, he has published extensively, including 13+ books, with over 200 citations. Dr. Gupta has developed AI tools for healthcare and agriculture and received several IEEE awards. He also serves as a reviewer and editorial board member for several international journals and conferences. His research focuses on sustainable smart healthcare and agriculture disease prediction and diagnosis.

Rakesh Prasad Joshi is an assistant professor in computer science and application department in IIMT University, Meerut, U.P, India. His qualification is MCA, M.Tech. and pursuing Ph.D. from Motherhood University, Roorkee (U.K).

Prashant Kumar is an Assistant Professor in Computer Science and Application department in IIMT University, Meerut, U.P, India. His qualification is MCA. He has more than 5 years of experience.

Saigurudatta Pamulaparthyvenkata is a seasoned data engineer with over 8 years of experience in data architecture, data warehousing, and big data technologies. He has a strong track record of designing and implementing robust data solutions that enhance business intelligence and analytics across various industries, including finance, healthcare, and technology. He holds a Master of Science in Computer Science from the University of Illinois, where he built a solid foundation in computer science and data management. His professional journey has seen him consistently deliver high-quality data products that meet complex business needs. Currently, Saigurudatta is a Senior Data Engineer at VillageMD, where he leads a talented team of engineers. His responsibilities include developing scalable data pipelines and ensuring the integrity and accessibility of data across the organization. He leverages cutting-edge technologies such as Apache Spark and Hadoop and cloud platforms such as AWS and Azure to process and analyze large datasets. Known for his collaborative approach, Saigurudatta excels in communicating complex data concepts to non-technical stakeholders. He strongly advocates for data-driven decision-making and has a proven track record of mentoring junior engineers and fostering a culture of continuous learning within his teams. Beyond his technical skills, Saigurudatta is actively involved in the data engineering community. He contributes through speaking engagements, writing technical articles, and participating in open-source projects. His dedication to the field is evident in his commitment to staying updated with industry trends and advancements. In his personal time, Saigurudatta enjoys contributing to the data engineering community and staying abreast of the latest industry trends. His passion for data engineering is reflected in his continuous efforts to learn and grow within the field.

Prabakaran Raghavendran, an accomplished mathematician from Vel Tech Rangarajan Dr. Sagunthala R&D Institute of Science and Technology, brings a passion for numerical precision and problem-solving. As an esteemed author, his work reflects a deep commitment to advancing mathematical understanding. Mr. Raghavendran's contributions to the field exemplify his dedication to the pursuit of knowledge and excellence in mathematics.

Ajay Sharma is working as a Senior Technical Consultant (Data Science Faculty) at UpGrad and is currently deputed at Lovely Professional University Jalandhar Punjab India. Before joining UpGrad Ajay worked for a short duration of time as an Assistant Professor at the Apex Institute of Technology in Dept of Computer Science at Chandigarh University. Ajay has worked as a Junior Research Fellow for ~2.5 years in the Dept. of Biotechnology and Bioinformatics at the Jaypee University of Information Technology Solan Himachal Pradesh. He has obtained his master's degree in Computer Science Engineering, Specialization in Biomedical Image Processing and Deep Learning, and a bachelor's degree in Bioinformatics from Shoolini University. Mr. Ajay has earned his Diploma in Computer Science from Lovely Professional University Jalandhar Punjab. During his bachelor's, he has got the certificate or merit /Gold Medal.

Kewal Krishan Sharma is a professor in computer sc. in IIMT University, Meerut, U.P, India. He did his Ph.D. in computer network with this he has MCA, MBA and Law degree also. He did variously certification courses also. He has an overall experience of around 33 year in academic, business and industry. He wrote a number of research papers and books.

Shamneesh Sharma is an accomplished academic and IT professional with over 14 years of experience in the fields of Computer Science and Information Technology. Currently, he serves as Senior Manager- Programs in upGrad Education Private Limited, Bangalore, India and prior to this he was at iNurture Education Solution, Bangalore as Senior Faculty in Cloud Technology and Information Security and was deputed as the Head of the School of Computer Engineering at Poornima University, Jaipur. Previously, he was the IT-Head and Associate Professor at Alakh Prakash Goyal Shimla University, where he significantly contributed to the development and maintenance of the university's IT infrastructure, ERP system, and website. Sharma holds a B. Tech and M. Tech and is currently pursuing a Ph.D. in Computer Science and Engineering. He has authored more than 70 research papers and is actively involved in various international and national professional and academic organizations.

Vikas Sharma completed his Graduation and Post Graduation from Chaudhary Charan Singh University, Meerut, U.P. Currently Pursuing his Ph.D. in Computer Science and Engineering from Govt. Recognized University. Presently, he is working as an Assistant Professor in the Department of Computer Science and Applications, IIMT University, Meerut, U.P. He has been awarded as Excellence in teaching award 2019. He is the reviewer member of some reputed journals. He has published several book chapters and research papers of national and international reputed journals.

Tarun Kumar Vashishth is an active academician and researcher in the field of computer science with 22 years of experience. He earned Ph.D. Mathematics degree specialized in Operations Research; served several academic positions such as HoD, Dy. Director, Academic Coordinator, Member Secretary of Department Research Committee, Assistant Center superintendent and Head Examiner in university examinations. He is involved in academic development and scholarly activities. He is member of International Association of Engineers, The Society of Digital Information and Wireless Communications, Global Professors Welfare Association, International Association of Academic plus Corporate (IAAC), Computer Science Teachers Association and Internet Society. His research interest includes Cloud Computing, Artificial Intelligence, Machine Learning and Operations Research; published more than 35 research articles with 2 books and 40 book chapters in edited books. He is contributing as member of editorial and reviewers boards in conferences and various computer journals published by CRC Press, Taylor and Francis, Springer, IGI global and other universities.

About the Contributors

Mohit Yadav is an Associate Professor in the area of Human Resource Management at Jindal Global Business School (JGBS). He has a rich blend of work experience from both Academics as well as Industry. Prof. Mohit holds a Ph.D. from Department of Management Studies, Indian Institute of Technology Roorkee (IIT Roorkee) and has completed Master of Human Resource and Organizational Development (MHROD) from prestigious Delhi School of Economics, University of Delhi. He also holds a B.Com (Hons.) degree from University of Delhi and UGC-JRF scholarship. He has published various research papers and book chapters with reputed publishers like Springer, Sage, Emerald, Elsevier, Inderscience etc. and presented research papers in national and International conferences both in India and abroad. He has many best paper awards on his credit too. He is reviewer of various international journals like Computers in Human Behavior, Policing etc. His areas of interest are Organizational Behavior, HRM, Recruitment and Selection, Organizational Citizenship Behavior, Quality of work life and role.

Naga Venkata Yaswanth Lankadasu is a Computer Science and Engineering graduate from Lovely Professional University, where he specialized in AI-ML. Yaswanth's expertise lies in data science, with a focus on machine learning and data analysis. His notable projects include developing AyurBharat, a website utilizing symptom-based disease detection algorithms, and conducting exploratory data analysis on suicides in India. Yaswanth has also researched skin cancer classification using convolutional neural networks, where he fine-tuned CNN models for dermatoscopic image analysis. His strong foundation in programming languages, frameworks, and tools, combined with his research and project experience, highlights his proficiency and dedication to the field of data science.

Index

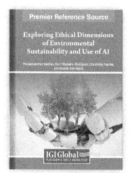

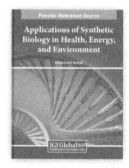

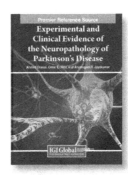
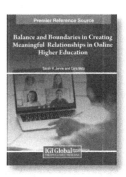

Individual Article & Chapter Downloads

US$ 37.50/each

- Browse Over *170,000+ Articles & Chapters*

- *Accurate & Advanced* Search

- Affordably Acquire *International Research*

- *Instantly Access* Your Content

- Benefit from the *InfoSci® Platform Features*

THE UNIVERSITY
of NORTH CAROLINA
at CHAPEL HILL

" It really provides *an excellent entry into the research literature* of the field. It presents a manageable number of *highly relevant sources* on topics of interest to a wide range of researchers. The sources are *scholarly, but also accessible* to 'practitioners'. "

- Ms. Lisa Stimatz, MLS, University of North Carolina at Chapel Hill, USA

Printed in the United States
by Baker & Taylor Publisher Services